CENTENNIAL
HISTORY OF DAVIDSON COUNTY

DAVIDSON COUNTY COURTHOUSE

CENTENNIAL HISTORY

OF

DAVIDSON COUNTY, NORTH CAROLINA

Rev. Jacob Calvin Leonard, D.D.

HERITAGE BOOKS
2020

HERITAGE BOOKS
AN IMPRINT OF HERITAGE BOOKS, INC.

Books, CDs, and more—Worldwide

For our listing of thousands of titles see our website
at
www.HeritageBooks.com

A Facsimile Reprint
Published 2020 by
HERITAGE BOOKS, INC.
Publishing Division
5810 Ruatan Street
Berwyn Heights, Md. 20740

Copyright © 1927 Dr. J. C. Leonard

Originally published Raleigh:
Edwards & Broughton Company
1927

— Publisher's Notice —
In reprints such as this, it is often not possible to remove blemishes from the original. We feel the contents of this book warrant its reissue despite these blemishes and hope you will agree and read it with pleasure.

International Standard Book Numbers
Paperbound: 978-0-7884-2642-1
Clothbound: 978-0-7884-5961-0

DEDICATION

TO THE MEMORY OF

THE CHOICE SPIRITS WHO BRAVED MANY
DIFFICULTIES IN THE PIONEER DAYS
OF FOUNDATION BUILDING

AND TO

THE SPLENDID MEN AND WOMEN, THEIR SUCCESSORS
DOWN TO THE PRESENT TIME, WHO HAVE
CONTRIBUTED VALUABLE SERVICE
TO THE MAKING OF DAVIDSON
COUNTY TRULY
GREAT

THIS CENTENNIAL HISTORY
IS GRATEFULLY DEDICATED

PREFACE

The material entering into this book has been gathered by the author through research covering a long period of years. The sketches of necessity in some instances overlap, and some important facts are therefore stated more than once. Davidson County has had an honorable history of one hundred years and more. It is eminently fitting that a record of the century should be made and kept in permanent form. Such a recital of the historical facts of a great county should serve as an inspiration to our young people of the present and future generations.

Readers will be aware that many valuable facts of Davidson County history are not recorded in this book, due to the fact that in many instances correct records have not been kept, making it impossible to give history in full. Many facts of supreme interest were never recorded at all. There are many vague traditions and legends but the true historian cannot record these as history. The author desires that this book may lead to a true appreciation of the value of recorded history.

Impetus to the publishing of these chapters was added through the "Centennial Luncheon" of the Lexington and Thomasville Rotary Clubs at Hotel March at noon, September 26, 1922, Mrs. Edith Vanderbilt (now Mrs. Gerry) and her daughter, Miss Cornelia Vanderbilt (now Mrs. Cecil), being guests of honor, when by invitation of these Clubs the author delivered the

"Centennial Address" on the history of Davidson County. The two Clubs gave hearty endorsement to the publication of this history.

The author is deeply indebted to many people and to many books and periodicals for assistance in gathering the facts of this work, and hereby expresses his sincere gratitude.

J. C. L.

LEXINGTON, NORTH CAROLINA.

CONTENTS

PAGE

Chapter I. Act Creating Davidson County 1

Chapter II. How and When the One Hundred Counties of North Carolina Originated 11

Chapter III. Building the Foundations of Davidson County 17
  1. General William Davidson 17
  2. Changes in a Century 21
  3. First Men to Serve the County 25

Chapter IV. Selection of a Capital for the New County 32

Chapter V. County Officers and Court Proceedings 44
  1. County Officials 44
  2. Courts of Justice and Court Proceedings 51
  3. Members of the Legislature of North Carolina from Davidson County 62
  4. Davidson County Members of Various State Conventions of North Carolina 71

Chapter VI. Farms, Farm Products, Grist Mills 72
  1. Livestock Improvement 72
  2. Farms and Farm Development 78
  3. Statistics of the Year 1920 86
  4. Grist Mills in Davidson County 95

Chapter VII. Banks of Davidson County 101
  1. Banks in Lexington 101
  2. Banks in Denton 110
  3. Banks in Thomasville 113

Chapter VIII. Davidson County Newspapers 116

Chapter IX. Junior Order United American Mechanics National Orphans' Home 119

Contents

	PAGE
Chapter X. Racial Types of Davidson County Citizenship	129
1. Racial Origin and Racial Characteristics	129
2. Life of the People, Manners and Customs	148
3. Representative Types	162
Chapter XI. Daniel Boone, Pioneer, Pathfinder	184
Chapter XII. General Nathaniel Green and Daniel Boone Tablet	202
1. Memorial Tablet Unveiled	202
2. Ghosts of Abbott's Creek	211
Chapter XIII. Public and Private Schools	218
1. Public Schools of Davidson County	218
2. Private Schools	222
(a) Bethany Academy	222
(b) Holly Grove Academy	223
(c) Pilgrim Academy	228
(d) Arnold Academy	229
(e) Hedrick's Grove Academy	230
(f) Other Academies	230
Chapter XIV. Davidson County in Military Service	232
1. The Revolutionary War	232
2. Davidson Men in the Spanish-American War	267
3. Confederate Soldiers of Davidson County	267
4. Davidson County in the World War	297
Chapter XV. Lexington, Capital of Davidson County	305
1. Facts and Figures	305
2. Some Lexington Factories	311
3. Lexington Schools	336
Chapter XVI. Thomasville a Thriving City	344
1. A Davidson County Asset	344
2. A Bird's-eye View	348
3. Thomasville in Its Beginning	352

Chapter XVI—Continued

PAGE

4. Some Thomasville Factories 362
5. Thomasville Graded School 368

Chapter XVII. Religious Forces of Davidson County.... 371

1. General Statement and Statistics 371
2. Lutheran Churches 376
3. Baptist Churches and Thomasville Baptist Orphanage 400
4. Methodist Protestant Churches, Methodist Protestant Children's Home, Yadkin College 420
5. Moravian Churches 432
6. Presbyterian Churches 433
7. Reformed Churches 446
8. Methodist Episcopal Churches 493
9. Grace Episcopal Church of Lexington 505

Chapter XVIII. A Unique County in the Heart of a Great State 508

1. A County of Extensive Area 508
2. A Free Yadkin River Bridge 508
3. Hydro-electrical Development 510
4. Superb North Carolina 516
5. Interesting Records in Two Old Books 518

ILLUSTRATIONS

SUBJECT	PAGE
Davidson County Courthouse	Frontispiece
Cicero F. Lowe	5
The State Capitol	9
Charles M. Hoover	13
G. Marshal Hoover	19
Lee V. Phillips	23
Charles M. Wall	27
Colonel Frank S. Lambeth	35
E. Odell Hinkle	39
P. James Leonard	45
William H. Moffitt	49
Samuel W. Wall	53
Emery E. Raper	59
John W. Finch	63
W. Lee Harbin	79
George Frank Hedrick	87
John D. Grimes	97
George W. Mountcastle	103
James Adderton	107
J. Tilden Hedrick	111
Jr. O. U. A. M. National Orphans' Home	121
John W. McCrary	135
Colonel G. Foster Hankins	141
Dr. R. Lee Reynolds	169
Daniel Boone	185
Boonesboro Fort	193
Tombstone at Grave of Squire Boone	197
Valentine Leonard	235
Captain Charles A. Hunt, Sr.	247
Colonel William E. Holt	271
The Conquered Banner	277

SUBJECT   PAGE

Monument at Grave of Wooldrich Fritz and Valentin
  Leonhardt 295
Holland E. Shoaf 309
Dr. J. Alex Smith and Davidson Hospital 313
Dacotah Cotton Mills 317
Irvin L. Sink 321
George L. Hackney 325
J. Clarence Grimes 329
John H. Cowles 333
Erlanger Cotton Mills 337
B. Cabell Philpott 341
Festus E. Sigman 345
William G. Hinkle 349
John W. Lambeth 353
T. A. Finch 359
A. H. Ragan 365
Auditorium of Thomasville Baptist Orphanage 413
Rev. Martin L. Kesler, D.D. 417
Dr. J. C. Leonard 487
Rev. William Arnold Lambeth, D.D. 499

CENTENNIAL HISTORY OF DAVIDSON COUNTY NORTH CAROLINA

CHAPTER I

ACT CREATING DAVIDSON COUNTY

The act creating the county of Davidson by dividing the territory of the county of Rowan was formally ratified by the General Assembly of North Carolina December 9, 1822. An exact copy of the act reads as follows:

(Private Laws 1822, Chapter 47)

AN ACT FOR THE DIVISION OF ROWAN COUNTY

Be it enacted by the General Assembly of the State of North Carolina, and it is hereby enacted by the authority of the same:

That all that part of the county of Rowan lying north of the following line, to wit: beginning on the east bank of the Yadkin River, where the same is crossed by the Surry line; thence down the said river to the ferry of Thomas P. Ives; thence a straight line to a point at the end of ten miles, in a line running north, forty-five degrees east from the Court House, in Salisbury, thence to the mouth of Abbott's Creek; and thence down the river, to the Montgomery line, be, and the same is hereby erected into a separate and distinct county, by the name of Davidson, with all the rights, privileges and immunites of the other counties in this State.

(Private Laws 1822, Chapter 48)

AN ACT SUPPLEMENTAL TO AN ACT, PASSED AT THE PRESENT GENERAL ASSEMBLY, ENTITLED "AN ACT FOR THE DIVISION OF ROWAN COUNTY"

Be it enacted by the General Assembly of the State of North Carolina, and it is hereby enacted by the authority of the same:

That four commissioners be and they are hereby appointed, to wit, John Andrews and James Smith, on the part of Rowan and Sebulon Hunt and George Smith, senior, on the part of Davidson, whose duty it shall be, as soon as practicable, after the first day of January next to run out and mark so much of the dividing line between the aforesaid counties as lies between the ferry of Thomas P. Ives, and the mouth of Abbott's Creek, according to the act of the present General Assembly, entitled "An act for dividing the county of Rowan," and that they cause to be made out two correct charts of said line, one for the use of each county, to be deposited in the office of their respective County Courts; and that the expense incurred in running said line shall be mutually paid by the two counties.

II. And be it further enacted, That Thomas Hampton, William Bodenhamer, Ranson Harris, Jacob Lopp and Joseph Spurgeon be, and they are hereby appointed commissioners; and it shall be the duty of said commissioners or a majority of them to ascertain, as near as practicable, the center of the county of Davidson; and that said commissioners, or a majority of them are hereby authorized to purchase, for the use of said county on the best terms possible twenty-five or more acres of land, situated at some healthy and advantageous spot, within two miles of the center; which land so purchased, or any part thereof, they shall lay off into lots of convenient size, and shall reserve one of the lots so laid off for the courthouse, and another for the jail of said county; and that the commissioners aforesaid, at such time, and on such terms as they may deem best, expose to public sale a part of the said lots in number not exceeding twelve; the proceeds of which they shall pay over into the hands of the county Trustee, for the use of the county; and that the lots and land remaining unsold shall be subject to the future disposition of the County Court. Further, that the deeds for said land shall be taken in the name of the Chairman of the County Court and his successors in office, for the use of the county; and the Chairman shall also execute conveyances for the lots that may be sold, either by the Commissioners or under any future order of the Court. Further, that the County Court of Davidson shall allow to the Commissioners a reasonable compensation for their services under this act.

III. And be it further enacted, That any one of the Justices of the Peace of the county of Rowan may administer the oaths prescribed by law to the Justices of the Peace appointed for the county of Davidson, at the first meeting for the purpose of organizing the County Court, on the fourth Monday in January next, as hereinafter appointed: *Provided,* That such of the appointed Justices of the Peace as may not be present at the said meeting may, after the organization of the Court, be qualified in the usual way.

IV. And be it further enacted, That the acting Magistrates for the county of Davidson shall, on the fourth Monday of January next, convene in Lexington; and they shall proceed, a majority being present, to lay a tax of not less than seventy-five cents on the white and black polls, and of not less than ten cents on every hundred dollars valuation of lands and lots, within said county, for the purpose of erecting a courthouse and jail in said county and for other public uses; which taxes shall be collected and accounted for by the Sheriff of said county, under the same rules and regulations as Sheriffs are subject to in collecting public taxes. Further, that the Magistrates aforesaid also proceed to the election of a Clerk of the Court of Pleas and Quarter Sessions, a Sheriff for said county, and all other officers usually elected by the several county courts in this State; which officers, so chosen, shall enter upon their duties under the same laws and restrictions as like officers in other counties are subject to. And the said Court, at the time and place aforesaid, shall appoint two or more Commissioners for the purpose of contracting for the erection of a court house and jail, and to superintend the building of the same; to be constructed of such materials and of such size and dimensions as the County Court may prescribe; *Provided,* That said jail shall be built in conformity to existing laws directing the manner of constructing jails in this State.

V. And be it further enacted, That the Court of Pleas and Quarter Sessions of said county, until the public buildings are completed, shall sit at such place as the Magistrates at their meeting on the fourth Monday of January next may agree upon and shall be held on the fourth week of January, April, July and October in each and every year, under the same rules and restrictions, and with the same powers, as other

CICERO F. LOWE, 1819-1892
Banker, Merchant, Clerk of the Court
Twenty-eight Years

county courts in the State. And an act, passed in the year one thousand eight hundred and eighteen, entitled "an act to establish a Court of Probate at Lexington, in the county of Rowan," be, and the same is hereby repealed.

VI. And be it further enacted, That all suits between the citizens of Davidson, in the Court of Pleas and Quarter Sessions of Rowan, remaining undetermined after the February term of said Court, shall be transmitted by the Clerk of Rowan to the Clerk of Davidson, in the same manner as suits are now sent from one county to another: *Provided,* That nothing contained in this act shall be so construed as to prevent the Sheriff of Rowan from collecting all arrears of taxes or all executions that have issued from any of the Courts of Rowan, or that may hereafter issue on any suits now pending in the Courts of said county, in the same manner as he could have done previous to the division of the county: *Provided,* nevertheless, That the Sheriff of Rowan shall not collect any taxes in the county of Davidson, or of the citizens of said county, imposed by the County Court of Rowan, and which are collectible in the year one thousand eight hundred and twenty-three; but that the same may be collected by the Sheriff of Davidson county, to the use of said county: *Provided* the County Court deem the collection essential to the interest of the county.

VII. And be it further enacted, That until the jail of Davidson county is completed, all offenders may be recognized or committed to the jail of Rowan in the same manner as if the offenses had been committed in Rowan: *Provided,* That the jail fees and expenses of keeping said offenders shall be paid by the county of Davidson.

VIII. And be it further enacted, That all militia officers within the bounds of the said county of Davidson shall continue to exercise the same authority as they have heretofore done in the county of Rowan, and shall be subject to the same penalties as like officers in other counties.

IX. And be it further enacted, That the County Court of Davidson, at its first meeting to be held under this act, shall appoint the time for holding an election for seven Wardens of the Poor for said county; who, when elected, shall forthwith enter upon the duties of their office as prescribed by the existing laws of the land: *Provided,* That such of the paupers of Davidson as are now in the poor house of Rowan shall continue there until the month of September next, when they shall be passed over to the Wardens of Davidson, who shall receive and take charge of them. Further, that an act passed in the year one thousand eight hundred and eighteen, entitled "an act to establish a poor house in the county of Rowan," be, and the same is hereby extended to the county of Davidson, and declared to be in full force in said county.

X. And be it further enacted, That all the militia heretofore belonging to the second regiment of Rowan, that may fall on the south side of the dividing line, be and they are hereby attached to the regiment heretofore called the first regiment of said county.

THE STATE CAPITOL, Raleigh

CHAPTER II

HOW AND WHEN THE ONE HUNDRED COUNTIES OF NORTH CAROLINA ORIGINATED

The late J. Bryan Grimes, who for over two score years was Secretary of State for North Carolina, enjoyed a reputation in the capital city as being an industrious scholar and a man who contributed much to the historical records of North Carolina. Among his historical contributions was an illustrative chart showing the dates of establishment and origins of the one hundred counties of the State.

The chart traces the growth of the counties by periods, the first period being between the years 1693 and 1722, during which time Albemarle, Bath and Clarendon counties were established.

During the second period, which covers the years 1722 to 1729, ten new counties were born, all of them in the eastern section of the State and most of them on the coast. These counties were: Pasquotank, Currituck, Perquimans, Chowan, Bertie, Tyrrell, Beaufort, Hyde, Carteret, Craven and New Hanover. Through the course of years these counties were subdivided.

Only one—Currituck—remained intact as long as a century. In 1870 this county gave birth to its first offspring, Dare County, which also is made up of parts of Tyrrell and Hyde counties.

Eight counties were formed between the years of 1729 and 1750, these being Edgecombe in 1738; Bladen, 1734; Anson, 1749; Onslow, 1734; Duplin, 1744; Johnston, 1746; Granville, 1746; and Northampton,

1741. Northampton was a subdivision of Bertie County. Edgecombe and Johnston counties were subdivisions of Craven County, while Granville was an early offspring of Edgecombe. Duplin, Onslow, Bladen and Anson were subdivisions of New Hanover County, an offspring of Clarendon, one of the three early counties.

New Hanover produced more counties through its subdivisions, which themselves were subdivided, than any of the ten counties in existence in 1729. From Duplin, a subdivision of 1744, came Sampson County in 1784. Onslow has remained intact. Pender County was a direct offspring of New Hanover County in 1875. A part of Bladen went to make up Orange County in 1751. A single subdivision in 1786 was the birth of Robeson. Cumberland, another Bladen offspring, was born in 1754, giving birth to Moore County in 1784; Harnett in 1855; and with Robeson, Hoke in 1911. From Anson County and its subdivisions sprang Richmond in 1779; Stanly in 1841; Union in 1842; Mecklenburg in 1762; Cabarrus in 1792; Tryon, which was abolished in 1763, giving birth to Lincoln and Rutherford counties; Gaston, 1846; Catawba, 1842; Cleveland, 1841; Polk, 1855; Davie, 1836; Rowan, 1753; part of which went to make up Guilford in 1770; Burke, 1777; Iredell, 1788; Buncombe, 1791; Haywood, 1808; Davidson, 1822; Macon, 1828; Cherokee, 1839; Clay, 1867; Graham, 1871; Swain, 1871; Jackson, 1850; Henderson, 1858; Transylvania, 1861; Madison, 1850; McDowell, 1842; Mitchell, 1861; Yancey, 1833; Surry, 1770; Wilkes, 1777; Ashe, 1787; Stokes, 1789; Alleghany, 1859; Watauga, 1849; Alexander, 1846;

CHARLES M. HOOVER, LEXINGTON AND THOMASVILLE
Secretary and Treasurer of the Hoover Chair Company

How and When Counties Originated

Caldwell, 1841; Avery, 1911; Yadkin, 1850; Forsyth, 1848.

In 1779 Gates County was formed from parts of Perquimans, Chowan and Hertford counties, the latter of which was an offspring of Bertie.

Martin County was founded in 1774; Washington in 1799; Pitt, 1761; Pamlico, 1872; Jones, 1779; Halifax, 1758; Bute, 1764 (later abolished); Franklin, 1779; Warren, 1779; Vance, 1881; Wilson, 1855; Durham, 1881; Lee, 1907; Alamance, 1848; Brunswick, 1764; Columbus, 1868; Orange, 1751; Chatham, 1770; Caswell, 1777; Person, 1791; Guilford, 1770; Wake, 1770; Rockingham, 1785; Randolph, 1779; Dobbs, 1758 (later abolished); Wayne, 1779; Glasgow, now Greene, 1799; and Lenoir, 1791.

The Dispatch, in the issue of September 14, 1922, has the following statement which is of general interest in this time when we are thinking in terms of time long gone by:

Davidson County, which begins the celebration of its Centennial on September 26, is the second North Carolina county of the same name. This information was called to the attention of *The Dispatch* in a letter from Major W. A. Graham, Commissioner of Agriculture, who recalled that one of the early sessions of the Legislature of North Carolina saw the creation of the county of Davidson, with Nashville as the capital.

Shortly after the creation of Davidson County the territory of the west seceded and formed the State of Franklin. In 1784 North Carolina ceded this territory to the Union as an independent state. The name was then changed to Tennessee, after the river that winds itself across that State several times and which got its name from the Indians that still roamed the country toward the Mississippi.

Davidson County, Tennessee, still remains and Nashville, its county seat, is the capital of the State. It was named after General William Lee Davidson, who fell at Cowan's Ford on May 1, 1780. Nashville was named for General Francis Nash, another distinguished North Carolinian, Major Graham notes.

From the time that Tennessee was created until 1822 there was no Davidson County in North Carolina, and the act of 1822 creating this county makes no mention of the earlier Davidson County. Major Graham thinks he has the act creating what is now Davidson County, Tennessee, among his records. A memorial of General Davidson was delivered by Major Graham at the celebration of the battle of Guilford Court House a few years ago, and one by Hon. A. M. Waddell on General Francis Nash was delivered at the same time.

CHAPTER III

BUILDING THE FOUNDATIONS OF DAVIDSON COUNTY

1. GENERAL WILLIAM DAVIDSON

From 1749 to 1822 Davidson County was included within the limits of Rowan County. There were no towns by the names of Lexington and Thomasville in those early years. Salisbury was the county seat, and it was an insignificant place through a long series of years. New Hanover County, originally covering a large section of the State, was formed in 1728. In 1734 Bladen County was cut off from New Hanover. In 1749 Rowan was constructed out of Bladen. Rowan at that time covered the whole of Western North Carolina and Tennessee, such distinction continuing until 1770, when Surry County was formed. Rowan was truly a great county. In the year 1822 Davidson County was erected from the portion of Rowan east of the Yadkin River. The name of the county was given in honor of General William Davidson, born in Lancaster County, Pennsylvania, in 1746. His father, George Davidson, emigrated to North Carolina in 1750, when his son, afterwards to be a distinguished general in the Revolutionary War, was a little lad only four years of age. His early years are shrouded in obscurity, though the records show that he went to school at the Charlotte Academy. When the Revolutionary War broke out he was a young man twenty-nine years of age. In 1776 he was a Major in the Fourth Regiment of North Carolina troops. In the battle of Colson's Mill, South Carolina, he was severely wounded, a ball passing entirely through his body. The wound was almost a fatal one and disabled him for two months. Prior to this he had been made Lieutenant Colonel. For conspicuous bravery he was again advanced to the rank of Brigadier General. General Davidson was with General Greene in his famous journey through North Carolina. At Cowan's Ford on the Catawba River it happened that he was stationed with 300 men at the very spot where Cornwallis tried to cross. This was the morning of February 1, 1781. When the British made the first attempt to cross the river, swollen by the recent rains, Davidson's men fired on them. This caused them to veer from the original point at which they expected to cross. General Davidson started to ride from the position he occupied to the point at which the British were now crossing the river. He was shot through the heart and fell from his horse dead. The death-dealing missile was a ball, and the natural inference was that he was shot by a Tory, because the British did not use rifles, but muskets. It is sad to chronicle the death of this strong, brave young officer at the hand of one who ought to have enlisted on his side but who to this day must bear the opprobrious name of Tory. Davidson County bears a worthy name, and in its name it honors a worthy man.

The name of the town of Lexington antedates the name of Davidson County, of which many years later it became the capital. In the year 1775 a store, a couple of houses and a "tavern" had been built on the road leading from Salisbury to Greensboro at the site of the present prosperous town. But the settlement

G. MARSHAL HOOVER, Lexington and Thomasville
President and General Manager, Hoover Chair Company

was too small to be given even the name of a village. The store occupied the site on which the residence of Mr. A. L. Clodfelter is now located, and the abandoned well at the edge of the street was the "public well" of those early days. April 19, 1775, the skirmish at Lexington, Massachusetts, was fought, one of the very first struggles of the Revolutionary War, in which seven Americans lost their lives. There were no telegraph lines in those days, and news of this incident did not reach this community until several weeks later. When the patriots heard of that battle, they at once gave the name of Lexington to the settlement in honor of the New England Lexington. Later when Davidson County was formed in 1822, Lexington was chosen as the shiretown, winning out over all other communities which bid for the honor.

Davidson is a great county. It embosoms valuable ores and precious metals. Its soil is fertile and richly rewards the labors of its numerous happy farmers. Its streams of water turn many factory wheels and also convert latent power into electrical energy. Its forests after ruthless denudation still cover thousands of acres. Davidson County is the home of numerous large cotton mills, furniture factories, flour mills, chair factories and numerous enterprises. It has strong banks and large mercantile establishments. There are fine public and private schools and academies, together with finely equipped orphans' homes.

2. Changes in a Century

The men and women who lived in Davidson County one hundred years ago never saw a railroad, an automobile, a harvesting machine, a photograph in its present perfection, a telegraph line, a wireless instrument, a daily paper, a printing machine, a sewing machine, a linotype machine, a phonograph, a typewriter, a telephone, an electric light, a railroad train, a trolley car, a kerosene lamp, an ocean steamer, a twine binder, a hospital, an anesthetic, a temperance society, a peace society, a Red Cross society, a Young Men's Christian Association, a Young Women's Christian Association, a Christian Endeavor society, a church organ or piano, a brick schoolhouse, a furniture factory, a department store, a roller mill, a paved street, a concrete sidewalk, an ice factory, a brick machine, a flying machine, a gasoline engine, an electric motor, a washing machine, a public laundry, a high school, a graded school, a real Sunday school, a garage, a fountain pen, a planing machine, a tractor, a concrete bridge, a radio outfit, a cotton mill, a steam shovel, a mowing machine, a steam thresher, a sky-scraper, a steel fork, a wire fence, a disk harrow, a grain drill, a steam piano, an ice factory, an electric fan, a fruit jar.

Not even a dreamer can imagine what great changes will come in the next century. It is asserted with all confidence that British scientists are on the eve of the greatest of all discoveries in physics in that they are about to break up the atom into its electrons and then reassemble them as they please. When that has been accomplished any substance can be changed into any other substance or element; clay into gold, soap into diamonds, iron into aluminum. Then new elements and new substances will be made with unsuspected and most desirable qualities. And beyond all this, the vast forces inherent in all substances will be released, making it possible for a pound of coal to generate sufficient energy

LEE V. PHILLIPS, Lexington
Secretary and Treasurer of the Linwood
Manufacturing Company

to haul a train of cars many miles. We stand on the edge of the greatest achievements of all time.

3. FIRST MEN TO SERVE THE COUNTY

Davidson County was formed from Rowan in 1822. Joseph Spurgeon was State Senator and George Smith and Charles Fisher were representatives in the House. Both Senator Spurgeon and Representative Smith were from that part of Rowan which soon became Davidson. This may throw light on the reasons for forming a new county at that time. In 1822 Henry Clay was Speaker of the House at Washington, while Nathaniel Macon and John Branch represented North Carolina in the United States Senate. Gabriel Holmes was Governor of North Carolina.

The territory out of which the new county was formed was not thickly populated. The lands for the most part were covered by dense forests. Probably less than fifteen hundred people lived in the new county. There were no villages except Lexington and Clemmonsville, neither of which contained more than fifty or a hundred people. Lexington was a small settlement prior to 1800. Randolph and Guilford formed part of the boundaries of the new county as they do now, while Stokes took the place of Forsyth in the north and Davie had not yet been created out of Rowan. Stage routes led through Davidson to Raleigh, to Danville, and to Fayetteville. The whistle of the locomotive was unknown and the use of the telegraph and telephone not yet dreamed of.

Pursuant to the Act of the General Assembly of North Carolina of 1822, the following Justices of the

Peace were commissioned with power to organize Davidson County. They were our "Conscript Fathers":

John Clemmons, Woodson Daniel, Jonathan Charles, Joseph Conrad, Alexander Shamwell, George Smith, James Burkhead, Solomon Davis, Amos Wright, Alexander Stephens, James Lowe, Alexander Caldcleugh, Henry Monroe, John Monroe, Peter Tice, Solomon Farrington, Absalom Williams, Isaac Kenny, David Mock, William W. Wiseman, Thomas Hampton, Zebulon Hunt, Ezekiel Teague, Joshua Lee, Andrew Swicegood, Joseph Spurgeon, Joshua Wilson, Ransom Harris, Benjamin Sherwood, William Piggott, Jonathan Manlove, Silas Peace, Ezekiel Brown, Jacob Brummel, John Ward, Jesse Hargrave.

These gentlemen constituted the first Court of Common Pleas and Quarter Sessions. John Giles kept the minutes of the first meeting. Charles Fisher, a prominent citizen of Rowan, was selected by the court to administer the oath of office to the justices.

John Monroe was unanimously elected chairman of the court. He served for three years. His resignation on March 23, 1826, was the occasion of the passage of resolutions both by the remaining members of the court and the bar of Davidson County, which resolutions "thanked the Worshipful Justice John Monroe for the able, impartial and dignified manner in which he had discharged the duties of his office." John Monroe was succeeded by Jesse Hargrave.

After reading the Act of the Legislature which created Davidson County, other county officers were elected by the county court as follows: County clerk, David Mock, who won out over Alexander Caldcleugh, James Lowe, Benjamin Rounsaville and Burgess Bell, contending

CHARLES M. WALL, Lexington
General Manager C. M. Wall & Son, Box Shooks and Lumber

candidates; to the office of high sheriff James Wiseman was elected; county attorney, James R. Dodge; public register, Ransom Harris; entry taker, Joshua Wilson; coroner, Samuel Farrington; county surveyor, Ezekiel Brown; county rangers, Andrew Swicegood, Alexander Stephens and Solomon Davis. David Mock, the first clerk of court, gave Alexander Gray, George Hoover, Sr., Joshua Lee and Peter Tice as securities, while Sheriff Wiseman gave as his bondsmen Jesse Hargrave, Alexander Ellis, James Smith, Isaac Wiseman and David Cox.

There being no public buildings in the new county, Jesse Hargrave, Alexander Caldcleugh and Peter Tice were appointed at the first meeting as commissioners to contract for and superintend building a courthouse and jail. To raise the necessary funds for this purpose, a tax of $1.00 was levied on each poll and 12½ cents on each $100 of property.

The office of constable was considered of great importance in early days. Candidates were elected by ballot if more than one applied for each place. The following were the first constables for Davidson County, elected by the County Court, and each gave bond in the sum of $4,000: David Manlove, John Bodenhamer, Godfrey Ratts, William Wiseman, Richard Ellis, David Huffman, Henderson Wilson, Jacob Wiseman, John Kennedy, Henry Shamwell, Daniel Sullivan, Jesse Holmes, George Smith, Philip Swicegood, Jacob Cook, James Tyer, Martin Owens, Robert Davis, John Gibbens, Joshua Wilson, Jr., William Lanning and Samuel F. Tomlinson.

The roads were of course maintained by the old labor system. Both the names of the overseers and the men who were to work under them were enrolled on the records of the County Court. Overseers were held to strict account for the condition of their part of the public roads. The following were appointed road overseers by the County Court at the organization meeting: William Bodenhamer, Daniel Huffman, John Davis, Thomas Baxter, Evans Davis, Robert Hampton, George Hege, Jacob Mikle, Christian Hege, Jacob Hege, William Hill, James Douthard, John Johnston, Samuel Green, Henry Ratts, Henry Shoaf, Andrew Darr, Adam Fritts, George Byerly, Daniel Leonard, Samuel Cecil, Meredith Pearce, Daniel Orel, Moses Teague, Joseph Rothrock, Jesse Swaim, Frederick Clayton, George Eller, George Stone, Benjamin Kendle, Jacob Mock, Benjamin Farabee, George Haines, John Welch.

Under the law, these jurors were selected to serve in Rowan County: Isaac Kenny, Peter Clemmons, Thomas Noah, Zebulon Hunt, Esq., Absalom Williams, Esq., Alexander Shamwell, Esq., Jacob Cook, John Clemmons, Esq., William Raper, Jr., Thomas Hampton, Esq., Peter Owens, Jr., William Cecil, Sr., and Joshua Parks.

The first jury for Davidson County Court of Pleas and Quarter Sessions consisted of Jacob Mock, Jr., John Walser, Daniel Myers, Isaac Teague, Richardson Wright, Joseph Sutlive, Butler Taylor, Daniel Evans, Jr., Aaron Morris, Daniel Bodenhamer, William Thompson, Jacob Lanier, Henry Wood, Richard Loflin, Matthew Skene, Richard Loflin, Jr., Jacob Koons, Jacob Summey, William Hesler, Isaiah Russell, William Ledford, John Holder, Thomas Cecil, John Shore, Henry Holliway, John Miller, Daniel Fishel, George Hedrick, John Fisher, Joshua Fisher.

The business of the court consisted among other things in binding out the orphans of the county. The following is a typical entry: "Alsa McKnight, an orphan girl aged eight years, is apprenticed to Thomas Gibbs until she arrives at eighteen years of age, to learn to read and write, to have at her freedom a cow and calf, a wheel and cards, and one bed and furniture." In case of orphan boys they were to be taught a trade and as far as the double rule of three, and on arriving at twenty-one years of age they were to be given a horse and saddle and either a suit of clothes or $25 in money as they chose.

The voting precincts in 1823 were: Haines, Hampton, Daniels, Lexington, Wards; the first two being in the upper part of the county, Daniels being in the lower part, and Wards in the Conrad Hill section. Clemmonsville was added in 1824.

The commissioners appointed by the General Assembly to run the dividing line between Davidson and Rowan were: George Smith, Zebulon Hunt and John Andrews. They were assisted by Ezekiel Brown and William Brown, surveyors, and David Smith and Joseph Clark, chain carriers.

There were no townships in the early days. In lieu thereof, the county was divided into military districts with a captain appointed over each. The first captains for the county, whose given names were omitted, were the following: Trantham, Miller, Hedrick, Harris, Kennedy, Frank, Orell, Owens, Gobble, Michael, Brown, Wires, Sullivan, Cecil, Fritts. The colonels for the county to whom the captains were responsible were: George Walk and Moses Welborn.

CHAPTER IV

SELECTION OF A CAPITAL FOR THE NEW COUNTY

Early in the history of Davidson County there arose a conflict over the location of the county site, the courthouse and public buildings. It was the custom in those days to locate the county capital in the exact center of the county or as near it as possible. Such was the law passed for Davidson. The General Assembly appointed Joseph Spurgeon (State Senator), Ransom Harris (public register), Thomas Hampton, Nathan Riley and William Bodenhamer as commissioners to ascertain the center of Davidson County, to purchase land, lay off lots for a town site and attend the sale of the same. Minas Ward and Ezekiel Brown were appointed surveyors to assist, while Isaiah Spurgeon, Charles Brown, Peter Barneycastle, Valentine Mikle, William Bell, William Newsom and William McCrary acted as chain carriers.

After severe labors this commission made report and located the center of the county on the lands of Martin Owens near the present County Home. Under the report John Monroe, Chairman of the county court, proceeded to buy 108 acres of land from said Martin Owens on the waters of Abbott's Creek, paying the sum of $300, also buying a small parcel from Christian Everhart for the same purpose for $22.50. Marion was to be the name of the county seat. A big sale was conducted at Marion, at which many lots were sold. William Kennedy cried the sale and some of the purchasers were: Martin Owens, Samuel E. Tomlinson, George Brown, Michael Brown, John Dow, James Hine, Abel Coffin, Thomas Holmes, Levy Barnet, Andrew Lindsay, Robert G. Murdock.

But the people at Marion were doomed to disappointment. None of the purchasers were ever to build on their lots. The people living in the village of Lexington not only got busy but they caused things to happen. The case was reopened. The papers of the survey for Davidson's capital were ordered delivered to Dr. William R. Holt and to be by him delivered to no less personage than the President of the University in order that he "may have the center of Davidson ascertained, then to be certified and delivered to the members of the Legislature, to be used by said Legislature and then returned to the County Court." When the Legislature met in 1823, Alexander Caldcleugh was State Senator for Davidson and Jesse Hargrave and William Bodenhamer members of the House. Then Lexington was put on the map. John Monroe, John Clemmons and David Cox were appointed by the Legislature as commissioners to settle the matter of Davidson's capital. They were ordered to sell as many as eighteen lots in Lexington, as they chose, sale to be the first Thursday in March, 1824, on credit of six, twelve and eighteen months. The record of deeds shows that on March 23, 1824, the founders and first-builders of Lexington, to wit, Alexander Caldcleugh, Benjamin D. Rousaville and Jesse Hargrave, deeded to John Monroe for the benefit of the county 25 acres of land in Lexington, the consideration being fifty cents to each. From the sale of this land, donated by these Lexington-loving citizens, a fund was to be raised to build a courthouse and jail without taxing the public. So far as the records show no protest was then made. Marion faded away, dying in its infancy. However, an election was also held later on the location of the courthouse, and Lexington won out again. People who had purchased lots at Marion were given their money back, and the lots were reconveyed to the original owners. In the meanwhile, a big sale was put on in Lexington, at which David Manlove was auctioneer, and as many as twenty-five to thirty lots were sold around the present courthouse, the sale aggregating $4,570.10. This money was ordered turned over to the commissioners of "public buildings." Shortly thereafter it was ordered that the courthouse be built in the center of the public square (then called Washington Square) not to cost over $5,000. The courthouse was completed, according to the best information, about the spring of 1825. William Nicholas, architect, was engaged to assist the building committee in planning the courthouse. Early in 1824 a wooden jail, whipping post and stocks were built near the courthouse in Lexington.

On June 22, 1825, Joseph Conrad, Henry Dusenberry and William R. Holt, Esq., were appointed commissioners to "contract and supervise the topping of the trees and to clear all the timber out of Washington Square." From this we judge that all Lexington at that time was much in the woods, and the clearing was not done except as necessary to give room for houses.

Captain Trantham's company had jurisdiction over Lexington, and the patrollers for 1824 were John Thomason, William McCrary, Levi Trantham, Gersham Hunt, John Hunt and Daniel Tussey.

COLONEL FRANK S. LAMBETH, THOMASVILLE
Secretary and Treasurer of the Standard Chair Company

Dr. William R. Holt, Benjamin D. Rounsaville and Joseph Conrad were appointed to make the first tax assessment of property in Lexington. Among those who in 1824 owned town lots in Lexington were: John Henly, Alexander R. Caldcleugh, Mack Crump, Benjamin Sherwood, Jonas Sneed, James Allison, Henry R. Dusenberry, Jesse Hargrave and G. Riley.

It was ordered at December court, 1825, that James Wiseman and William R. Holt purchase for the public use one-half acre of ground not less than half mile from the courthouse and not on any public road, and that they contract for the erection of a gallows thereon. In March, 1827, the County Court voted unanimously to build a poorhouse, to be constructed of brick, and John M. Smith, William R. Holt and Henry R. Dusenberry were appointed to attend to the building of the same. Only about 150 people resided in Lexington in 1824 and in 1859 the town had increased to only 300 or 400. The courthouse, a two-story brick building, occupied the center of the present square. Around the square were the stores of Henry R. Dusenberry, Jesse Hargrave and others. The jail, made of wood, was situated behind the present People's Drug store, and not far away were the whipping post and public pillory. The gallows was located close to the gate of the present cemetery.

The following is a transcript of the original deed for the county courthouse lands:

THIS INDENTURE Made the third day of March in the year of our Lord *Eighteen Hundred and Twenty-four*, between BENJAMIN D. ROUNSAVILLE, JESSE HARGRAVE and ALEXANDER R. CALDCLEUGH, Esquires, of the Town of Lexington in the County of Davidson, in the

State of North Carolina, of the first part, and JOHN MONROE, Esquire, Chairman of the County Court of Davidson and State aforesaid, of the second part:

WITNESSETH, That the said Benjamin, Jesse and Alexander, for and in consideration of the sum of *fifty cents* each to them in hand paid by the said Chairman, the receipt whereof the said Benjamin, Jesse and Alexander do hereby acknowledge, have bargained, sold, aliened, conveyed and forever quit-claimed and by these presents do bargain, sell, alien, convey and forever quit-claim unto the said Chairman and his successors forever, all that tract and parcel of land, situate, lying and being in the County of Davidson, adjoining the Town of Lexington and State of North Carolina, and bounded as follows:

BEGINNING—at a stake on the North West of Lexington in the orchard of the said Benjamin; running thence North 40 degrees East along his line seventeen chains and six and a half links to a stake on said Alexander's field; thence along this line South 50 degrees East fourteen chains and sixty links to a stake in said Alexander's wood land; thence South 40 degrees West along his line until it intersects the land of the said Jesse, seventeen chains and six and a half links to a stake in said Jesse's wood land; thence North 50 degrees West along his line, the extreme lots of Lexington and said Benjamin's line fourteen chains and sixty-five links to the beginning, containing twenty-five acres;

Together with all and singular the hereditaments and appurtenances to the above described land and premises belonging (except the trees, woods and timber now on said land to be removed presently) and side of the ground laid off to be enclosed round the courthouse or in any wise appertaining; and the remainders and reversions, and all the estate, right, title, interest and claim of them the said Benjamin, Jesse and Alexander, in and to the above described land and premises unto him the said Chairman and his successors.

E. ODELL HINKLE, Lexington
Junior Member Conrad & Hinkle, Wholesale and Retail Grocers

TO HAVE AND TO HOLD the same to him the said Chairman and his successors forever; and the said Benjamin D. Rounsaville, Jesse Hargrave, and Alexander R. Caldcleugh, for themselves and their heirs, shall and will forever quit-claim the right and title to the said above described land and premises, except the trees, woods and timber above excepted, to him, the said John Monroe, Chairman, against the claim or claims of all persons claiming under them or their heirs and his successors forever.

IN WITNESS WHEREOF the said Benjamin, Jesse and Alexander, have hereunto set their hands and seals the day and year first above written.

B. D. ROUNSAVILLE (Seal)
JESSE HARGRAVE (Seal)
ALEX. R. CALDCLEUGH (Seal)

Acknowledged in the presence of
E. BROWN
MACK CRUMP
ROBERT FOSTER
N. R. DUSENBERRY

STATE OF NORTH CAROLINA }
DAVIDSON COUNTY } MARCH SESSION 1824

The execution of the within deed was duly proven in open court by Ezekiel Brown, the subscribing witness. Recorded and ordered to be registered.

D. MOCK, C. C. C.

The original court square, reserved in the middle of the twenty-five acres which were bought for county purposes in 1824, remained intact and no one thought of ever disturbing same. The first courthouse, built of brick, occupied the exact center of the public square. A little later, in 1825 or 1826, a public well was dug and a market house (sometimes referred to as the belfry) was erected on the plot in front of the present

Development Building. At the meeting of the Legislature in 1873 an effort was made to pass a bill authorizing the Davidson County Commissioners to sell the three plots on the public square, but the bill failed to pass. But in spite of this failure to get the General Assembly to pass such law, at their meeting the first Monday in March, 1873, the county commissioners, W. L. Cecil, Abram Cross, James L. Smith, D. C. Kimel and T. W. Hartley, took the following action: "It is ordered that in consideration of the indebtedness of the county of Davidson and in consideration of the below described real estate belonging to the county of Davidson affording no income to said county, and it being to the interest of said county that said real estate be sold: It is therefore ordered that David W. Pickett be appointed to expose to public sale after advertising in six public places in Davidson County and also in the 'Salem Free Press Newspaper,' published in Salem, and the 'Era Newspaper,' published in the city of Raleigh, for thirty days, the following Town Lots situated in the town of Lexington to wit: the vacant lot on the northeast corner of the public square adjacent to the lots of Henderson Adams and Dr. James L. Dusenberry, the said commissioner to divide said lot into three equal lots and to sell each one thereof separately; also to divide and sell into three equal and separate lots the lot of ground opposite the before described lot and known as the southeast corner lot, adjoining the lots of Bennett Nooe, Henry Hix and General J. M. Leach; also to divide and sell into three equal and separate lots the lot known as the Public Well lot opposite to the Court House and adjacent to the lot of C. F. Lowe."

Mr. Pickett advertised the lots on the 4th of March, 1873, for sale on the Tuesday of next Superior Court, April 29, 1873.

The owners of adjacent property at once sought from the court an injunction restraining the county commissioners from selling these said lots. A temporary restraining order was granted by John M. Cloud, Judge of the Eighth Judicial District of North Carolina, April 22, 1873. The case finally reached the Supreme Court of North Carolina, and by ruling of this court the injunction against the selling of the lots was made to stand, the judgment of the lower court being affirmed.

The author has understood that this ruling of the courts had something to do with the location of the government post office in Lexington. It may be recalled that an effort was made by some citizens to have this building located in part upon the southeast plot of the square above named.

By the old plot of the courthouse square, four streets are shown leading out from the center, where the courthouse stood. North Main Street was called Davis Street; South Main, Steele; East Center, Stanly; West Center, Cameron. In this plot of the town East First was called Murphy and West First was Franklin; East First Avenue was Mebane and West First was Rounsaville. The names of the other streets are not given in the plot.

CHAPTER V

COUNTY OFFICERS AND COURT PROCEEDINGS

1. COUNTY OFFICIALS

Sheriffs of Davidson County from 1823:

James Wiseman	1823 to 1826
William Kennedy	1826 to 1836
John M. Smith	1836 to 1840
William Kennedy	1840 to 1842
B. B. Roberts	1842 to 1846
Jeremiah Adderton	1846 to 1850
J. P. Stimpson	1850 to 1854
E. D. Hampton	1854 to 1860
David Loftin	1860 to 1868
Jacob A. Sowers	1868 to 1874
David Loftin	1874 to 1880
John Michael	1880 to 1884
P. D. Leonard	1884 to 1890
C. M. Griffith	1890 to 1894
P. J. Leonard	1894 to 1898
T. S. F. Dorsett	1898 to 1906
A. T. Delap	1906 to 1912
C. C. Shaw	1912 to 1916
A. T. Delap	1916 to 1918
J. A. Tussey	1918 to 1920
F. C. Sink	1920 to 1922
R. B. Talbert	1922 to 1926
Fred C. Sink	1926 to ......

P. JAMES LEONARD, Lexington
Pioneer Teacher of Vocal Music. Served Davidson County as Sheriff Two Terms and Also as County Commissioner

County Officers and Court Proceedings

The following men have filled the office of Probate Judge, or Clerk of Superior Court for Davidson County:

David Mock, from the formation of the
county in..1823 to 1833
Sam Gaither ....1833 to 1837
Charles Mock ....1837 to 1845
C. F. Lowe ....1845 to 1861
J. K. Perryman ....1861 to 1867
John Haines ....1867 to 1868
L. E. Johnson ....1868 to 1874
C. F. Lowe ....1874 to 1886
H. T. Phillips ....1886 to 1894
G. E. Hunt ....1894 to 1898
H. T. Phillips ....1898 to 1906
C. E. Godwin ....1906 to 1918
S J. Smith ....1918 to 1922
E. C. Byerly ....1922 to ....

Registers of Deeds of Davidson County:

April	1829	R. Harris
January	1831	Jno. Haines
August	1853	Jno. Haines
December	1867	Robert Foster
August	1868	A. E. Hough
August	1870	A. E. Hough
September	1872	W. H. Moffitt
August	1874	J. W. Finch
November	1876	J. W. Finch
November	1878	J. W. Finch
November	1880	J. W. Finch
November	1882	J. W. Finch

November 1884 ....Fletcher R. Loftin
November 1886 ....Fletcher R. Loftin
November 1888 ....Fletcher R. Loftin
November 1890 ....S. W. Finch
November 1892 ....S. W. Finch
November 1894 ....Wm. C. Harris
November 1896 ....Wm. C. Harris
November 1898 ....S. L. Owen
November 1900 ....S. L. Owen
November 1902 ....S. L. Owen
November 1904 ....S. L. Owen
November 1906 ....S. L. Owen
November 1908 ....Geo. W. Miller
November 1910 ....Geo. W. Miller
November 1912 ....Walter S. Anderson
November 1914 ....Walter S. Anderson
November 1916 ....F. E. Sigman
November 1918 ....F. E. Sigman
November 1920 ....F. E. Sigman
May 1922 ....Hubert J. Swaim
November 1922............Wm. J. Parker
November 1924 ....Wm. J. Parker
March 1926 ....R. B. Robbins
November 1926 ....Jesse W. Dickens, Jr.

From 1822, the beginning of the county, until April, 1829, David Mock was both the Register of Deeds and the County Clerk of Court.

Treasurers of Davidson County:

August 1, 1868 ....W. L. Cecil
August 6, 1870 ....W. H. Hunt
August 3, 1872 ....W. H. Moffitt

WILLIAM H. MOFFITT, 1847-1917
Pioneer Lexington Grocery Merchant. County Register of Deeds

COUNTY OFFICERS AND COURT PROCEEDINGS 51

September 7,	1874	Wm. H. Hunt
December 4,	1876	W. H. Hunt
December 2,	1878	W. H. Hunt
December 6,	1880	J. W. McCrary
December 7,	1882	J. W. McCrary
December 1,	1884	J. W. McCrary
December 6,	1886	J. W. McCrary
December 3,	1888	J. W. McCrary
December 2,	1890	J. W. McCrary
December 3,	1892	J. W. McCrary
December 3,	1894	J. W. McCrary
December 7,	1896	W. N. Kinney
December 5,	1898	David T. Fritts
December 3,	1900	David T. Fritts
December 1,	1902	David T. Fritts
December 5,	1904	David T. Fritts
December 6,	1906	E. A. Rothrock
December 7,	1908	W. G. Fitzgerald
December 5,	1910	E. A. Rothrock
December 2,	1912	E. A. Rothrock
December	1914	Geo. McCarn

The office of Treasurer was abolished after 1916, and one of the local banks acts in that capacity.

2. COURTS OF JUSTICE AND COURT PROCEEDINGS

E. E. Raper, Esq., well known able lawyer of Lexington, examined the first court records for the author. It seems that there were no resident lawyers in those early years, and that the attorneys in the several first cases came to the county seat from other towns. This is as we might expect. Later on lawyers took up their residence here, and many of these men are known at home and abroad as among the strongest advocates at the bar.

The first record is for the April term, 1824. The first suit appearing is that of *William Brown against Step Wade* for debt. Attorney Dick appeared for the plaintiff. There were five cases on the docket. Such a small number would be the despair of the court attorneys in our time. No. 4 is *Peter W. Smith against Jesse Hargrave* for detinue. Attorneys appearing in these suits are Murphy (probably living in Salisbury), H. C. Jones (likely of Charlotte), Dodge, Martin, Cartee.

There were twelve cases brought to the October term in 1824. Lawyers marked as appearing for the parties in these cases are Settle, Shepperd, Cartee, Shober, Martin, Dodge, Murphy, Dick, Morehead (afterwards Governor of the State), Paschal, Jones, Mangum (afterwards United States Senator). At the October term, 1826, Attorney Hogan is marked as one of the lawyers. He probably resided at Lexington, and it seems quite likely that he is the first lawyer at the bar here. At that time it was the custom of the lawyers in a judicial district to attend all the courts of that district, going with the Judge and remaining until he left.

At the April term, 1829, among the attorneys are Pearson, Boyden, Nash. Pearson was the eminent Chief Justice. Richmond Pearson at the time lived in Mocksville. At the October term of the same year we find the name Giles among the lawyers. In the spring term of 1836 we find the names of Clemmons and Long. Clemmons was Junius Clemmons, who is generally reputed to have been the actual inventor of the electric

SAMUEL W. WALL, WALLBURG, 1834-1925
Manufacturer, Farmer. Member State Legislature
Four Terms

telegraph and Morse code. Long was the lawyer who lived out at what is now the crossing of the highway and the Southbound Railroad at the Michael place. At the fall term of 1847 we find the name of James Madison Leach marked as attorney for Valentine Crotts in his suit against Adam Rider.

This State derived its system of courts from England, which government established courts in its colonies similar to the ones at home. After the Revolutionary War, when independent government was set up, the states, for the most part, continued the system that had prevailed in the colonies. North Carolina adopted the former system with slight changes, only such changes as were made necessary by the new order. The system has been called the Common Law system, and the common law as a body was by statute made the law of the State. The courts under this system and under our State Constitution were as follows:

1. Courts of Justice of the Peace.
2. Courts of Common Pleas and Quarter Sessions.
3. Superior Courts.

There was a State Supreme Court to which appeals from the Superior Court could be taken, upon questions of law.

The courts of the Justice of the Peace had jurisdiction of petty criminal offenses and civil actions for small amounts, and to bind to peace. The jurisdiction of this court has remained about the same through all the years.

The Court of Common Pleas and Quarter Sessions was presided over by the Justices of the Peace of the county, and at least three were required to be present at each term, and were called "Worshipful Justices," and were at first paid per diem, receiving not less than $1.00 per day and not more than $3.00 per day. There were held four terms at designated times, each term to continue for one week. This court had jurisdiction in all suits for dower, partition of lands, legacies, distributive shares of estates, and all things relating to orphans, idiots, lunatics, and the management of their estates. The criminal jurisdiction was to try, hear and determine all petty larcenies, assaults and batteries, trespasses, breaches of the peace and other misdemeanors of an inferior nature, except such as are given to Justices of the Peace. This court was a court of record, and the records of all proceedings were kept by the Clerk and may be found in the Office of Clerk of Superior Court. A casual inspection of the records of the court show that many of the citizens of the county served as Worshipful Justices. Perhaps the one who served the longest was James Wiseman. Others whose names appear are J. H. Hargrave, George Riley, Samuel Hargrave, Meshack Pinxton, Alexander Owen, Samuel Gaither, W. R. Holt, Eli Penry, Joseph Spurgeon, Henry R. Dusenberry, Valentine Hoover, Alfred Smith, William Raper and Henry Walser.

The Superior Court had general jurisdiction of all matters not given to the Justices of the Peace and to the Court of Common Pleas and Quarter Sessions. Its terms were fixed by statute and were two in each year, and it was presided over by a Judge of the Superior Court. Judges were elected by the Legislature to serve for life or during good behavior, and they presided over the courts of a district. This court also

County Officers and Court Proceedings 57

was a court of Equity, and had a Clerk and Master in Equity in each county. Equity cases were tried without a jury.

So far as the writer can learn there has never been any lawyer, resident of this county, who has served as Judge of the Supreme Court or Superior Court. It may be noted that few active lawyers in this section of the State have ever aspired to hold judicial positions. They are either too modest or their practice is such that judicial positions have not appealed to them.

In the year 1868 the Legislature of the State adopted what is called a Code System, and materially changed the judicial system. The court of Common Pleas and Quarter Sessions was abolished, and its jurisdiction given to the Clerk of Superior Court and to the County Commissioners. The distinctions between law and equity were abolished, and both law and equity were enforced by the same court in one action. The procedure in the courts was simplified, and made less technical, and was intended to aid in the securing of just decisions and judgments. Judges were made elective by the popular vote and for a term of eight years, and this system has been followed ever since. In 1876 the judges were required to rotate and to be elected not by districts but by vote of the whole State.

The writer has not been able to obtain an accurate list of the lawyers who lived in the county before 1860. Before that time, and for some years thereafter, it was the custom for the lawyers to ride the circuits with the judges, attending the entire term, whether having any cases to try or not. The courts of this county were attended by the lawyers of this section of the State, from Hillsboro to Charlotte, and the best remembered lawyers of the State frequently appeared in cases tried here. The court records do not show the residence of the attorneys, but give the names of the attorneys appearing in civil actions. A Mr. Hogan appears to be the first resident lawyer in this county, and after that there were Mr. Long, Mr. Bradsher, Ben Kittrell and others. Junius L. Clemmons practiced law here and lived here for some years, going to Louisville, Ky., where he practiced many years. James Madison Leach came to Lexington from Randolph County and lived here and practiced law for nearly fifty years. He came about 1845 and at once became a leader at the bar and in the politics of the county. He was a man of great ability, of commanding appearance and manner, a gentleman of the old style. He was an orator, and his power on the hustings as well as at the bar was well known throughout the State. His intellect was keen and strong, and he was ever ready as a debater, quick, resourceful, powerful. When he spoke he could gesture with his hands, body and face, and he could modulate his voice, which was very powerful, at will. His power of sarcasm and invective was unsurpassed. He had wit and humor, and made free use of hyperbole in his speeches. Thus it appears he was adorned with all the natural gifts that make an orator, and he cultivated his gifts, and was a most accomplished debater and platform speaker. However, he was not a student of law as written in the books, and had no aptitude for business affairs. He was much in politics, serving in the State Legislature at different times, the last time in the Senate, and serving several terms in the United

EMERY E. RAPER, Esq., LEXINGTON
Prominent Attorney at Law. Former County Superintendent of Public Instruction

States Congress, serving both before the War Between the States and after the war, and serving in the Congress of the Confederate States.

Marshall Henry Pinnix came to Lexington from Caswell County about the year 1868 and practiced law here from that time till his death in 1897. He was a graduate of the State University, read law under Judge Pearson, and came well equipped. He enjoyed during the years he engaged in his profession a large and general practice, and had a devoted clientage. He was a large man of imposing appearance and manner. He was a student of the law, sincere, upright, forceful, with lofty ideals. He was interested in building up his town and county, and gave his time freely to all things that he considered conducive to progress and betterment and served several terms as Mayor of Lexington, probably without any pay. He took a great interest in politics and served in the State Legislature.

Captain Frank C. Robbins, who died in 1926, is entitled to be mentioned here. He came to Lexington from Randolph County about 1868 and began the practice of law, and continued to follow his profession up till a few years ago, when advancing age admonished him to retire. He was a graduate of the State University and was a school teacher prior to the War Between the States, in which war he served with distinction, surrendering at Appomattox, bringing home the title of Captain. His learning, ability and high ideals are still remembered by all, and he enjoyed the esteem of the entire people of the county. He also engaged in politics and served two terms in the State Senate, being a member of the Senate which tried Governor Holden and impeached him and removed him from office. He was also a member of the Constitutional Convention of 1876, in which body he was a member of the Committee on Elections, which is reported to "have held Robeson and saved the State." He gave much time to building up his community, standing for progress and betterment.

John H. Welborn also began the practice of the law here about 1870 and was a successful lawyer for some years, till failing health compelled his retirement. J. Ruffin Bulla came here from Greensboro and practiced for a few years, till declining health caused his retirement. Others to be mentioned are Charles L. Heitman, George M. Bulla, J. M. Leach, Jr., L. S. Benbow. Colonel W. F. Henderson was a lawyer, but had never studied law before being admitted, which was at a time no examinations were held and the only requirement to obtain license was to pay a fee of $20. He never took the trouble to acquire any knowledge of the law. Others perhaps might be named. No mention is made of the gentlemen who are now living and engaged in their profession. That is left to some future writer.

3. MEMBERS OF THE LEGISLATURE OF NORTH CAROLINA FROM DAVIDSON COUNTY

Joseph Spurgeon was the Senator and George Smith and Charles Fisher were the representatives from Rowan County in 1822, the year in which Davidson County was formed. Both Senator Spurgeon and Representative Smith were from that section of Rowan County east of the Yadkin River, the territory detached

JOHN W. FINCH, Lexington, 1841-1907
Merchant, Register of Deeds of Davidson County
Ten Years

that year by the Legislature from Rowan County and erected into the new county of Davidson. An interesting fact in connection with the formation of Davidson County is cited in the *History of North Carolina,* published by the Lewis Publishing Company, Volume II, pages 147 and 148. In the early years of the history of the State the center of population was far towards the eastern part of the commonwealth; but the census figures show that at each decade the increase of population in the western section was greater than that in the east. In fact between 1820 and 1830 there was an actual decline in the figures of population for three eastern counties. In 1833 there were sixty-four counties, the large counties being in the west and the small in the east. And yet in 1820 from twelve small counties thirty-six members were sent to the Legislature, while from Orange and Rowan, two large western counties with a population equal to that of the twelve small eastern counties, only six members of the Legislature were elected. This was a plain inequality needing correction. This same authority says: "In 1833 thirty-three counties, with little more than one-third of the total population, sent ninety-nine members, but on the basis of white population they had larger representation than thirty-one counties with more than two-thirds of the white population." One remedy for this inequality naturally suggesting itself was a division of the large western counties, but that would mean to the east a reduction of its political power. But whenever new counties were proposed in the west, the east came forward with a proposition for new counties in that section also. From 1776, the year of independence, to 1833, eleven years after the organization of Davidson County in the west, the western section of the State had gained three new counties over the new counties formed in the east. Such a small gain could not overthrow the sectional majority held by the east over the west. Plainly the west would want more and more counties formed. Each section east and west wanted to keep pace with the other in addition of new counties, but the west was very desirous of securing enough new counties to give it representation in the General Assembly equal to that of the east. Under the circumstances that was a very difficult matter. The west had the large counties as time passed out of which new counties ought to be made, while such territory in the east was exhausted. Accordingly fine diplomacy had to be resorted to in order to secure new western counties, as for instance the naming of new western counties for eastern leaders. In this way Burke, Caswell, Iredell, Ashe, Moore, Buncombe, Stanly and Davie in the west were secured each of them bearing the name of a prominent eastern man. The authority quoted above says further: "How acute was the sectional hostility to new counties is illustrated by events in 1822 and 1823. A bill was introduced and passed to create the new county of Davidson during the session of 1822; the next year every eastern man who voted for it failed to be reëlected. Among these was Ex-Governor Miller, of Warren, who was defeated by General M. T. Hawkins, on the ground that a new western county endangered the interests of the east and placed the Constitution in jeopardy." Sectionalism in the great commonwealth of North Carolina!

The author is indebted to Zeb V. Walser, Esq., Ex-Speaker of the House of Representatives, Ex-Attorney General of the State of North Carolina, prominent

COUNTY OFFICERS AND COURT PROCEEDINGS 67

lawyer of Lexington, for a correct list of the several members of the General Assembly from Davidson County from the year 1822 down to the present time.

1823—Senator, Alexander R. Caldcleugh; Representatives, Jesse Hargrave, William Bodenhamer.

1824—Senator, Jesse Hargrave; Representatives, William Bodenhamer and John Clemmons.

1825—Senator, Jesse Hargrave; Representatives, John M. Smith and Joseph Spurgeon.

1826—Senator, John M. Smith; Representatives, Thomas Hampton and John Ward.

1827—Senator, John M. Smith; Representatives, Thomas Hampton and Absalom Williams.

1828—Senator, John M. Smith; Representatives, Thomas Hampton and Absalom Williams.

1829—Senator, Ransom Harris; Representatives, Wm. W. Wiseman and Lewis Snyder.

1830—Senator, Ransom Harris; Representatives, Joseph Spurgeon and William W. Wiseman.

1831—Senator, Charles Hoover; Representatives, John A. Hogan and John W. Thomas.

1832—Senator, John A. Hogan; Representatives, William W. Wiseman and Henry Ledford.

1833—Senator, John A. Hogan; Representatives, William W. Wiseman and Henry Ledford.

1834—Senator, John A. Hogan; Representatives, George Smith and Charles Brummell.

1835—Senator, John A. Hogan; Representatives, George Smith and Charles Brummell.

1836—Senator, John L. Hargrave; Representatives, Charles Brummell and Meshack Pinckston.

1838—Senator, William R. Holt; Representatives, Burgess S. Beall and Charles Brummell.

1840—Senator, Alfred Hargrave; Representatives, Burgess S. Beall and Charles Brummell.

1842—Senator, John W. Thomas; Representatives, Charles Brummell and Henry Walser.

1844—Senator, Alfred Hargrave; Representatives, Benton C. Douthitt and Charles L. Payne.

1846—Senator, Samuel Hargrave; Representatives, Charles Hoover and Henry Walser.

1848—Senator, John W. Thomas; Representatives, James M. Leach and Henry Walser.

1850—Senator, Samuel Hargrave; Representatives, James M. Leach and Alfred G. Foster.

1852—Senator, Samuel Hargrave; Representatives, James M. Leach and William Harris.

1854—Senator, John W. Thomas; Representatives, James M. Leach and Henry Walser.

1856—Senator, John W. Thomas; Representatives, John P. Mabry and James M. Leach.

1858—Senator, Benton C. Douthitt; Representatives, Henry Walser and Hiram W. Brummell.

1860—Senator, John W. Thomas; Representatives, Lewis Hanes and Edmund B. Clark.

1862—Senator, Henderson Adams; Representatives, Robert L. Beall and Henry Walser.

1864—Senator, Henderson Adams; Representatives, C. F. Lowe and Lewis Hanes.

1865—Senator, James M. Leach; Representatives, S. S. Jones and Isaac Kinney.

1866—Senator, James M. Leach; Representatives, C. F. Lowe and J. H. Shelton.

1868—Senator, P. A. Long; Representatives, Jabez Mendenhall and George Kinney.

County Officers and Court Proceedings

1870—Senator, F. C. Robbins; Representatives, Jacob Clinard and J. T. Brown.

1872—Senator, John T. Cramer; Representatives, J. T. Brown and John Michael.

1874—Senator, Alfred Hargrave; Representatives, M. H. Pinnix and T. A. Mock.

1876—Senator, B. B. Roberts; Representatives, James M. Leach and M. H. Pinnix.

1879—Senator, James M. Leach; Representatives, J. C. Miller and G. F. Smith.

1881—Senator, Lewis Hanes; Representatives, P. C. Thomas and S. W. Wall.

1883—Senator, M. H. Pinnix; Representatives, J. F. Beall and H. J. Harris.

1885—Senator, P. C. Thomas; Representatives, George M. Bulla and S. W. Wall.

1887—Senator, S. E. Williams; Representatives, N. W. Beeson and J. G. Surratt.

1889—Senator, P. C. Thomas; Representatives, Zeb V. Walser and S. W. Wall.

1891—Senator, Zeb V. Walser; Representatives, W. A. Beck and J. A. Hedrick.

1893—Senator, W. S. Owen; Representative, John C. Thomas.

1895—Senators, S. W. Wall and J. F. Westmoreland; Representative, Zeb V. Walser.

1897—Representative, J. R. McCrary.

1899—Senator, John C. Thomas; Representative, C. M. Thompson.

1901—Senator, John C. Thomas; Representative, H. H. Hartley.

1903—Representative, Harllee McCall.

1905—Senator, S. E. Williams; Representative, G. F. Hankins.
1907—Representative, G. Foster Hankins.
1909—Senator, G. Foster Hankins; Representative, T. Earle McCrary and Benjamin W. Parham.
1911—Representative, B. W. Parham.
1913—Senator, W. H. Phillips; Representative, Ivey G. Thomas.
1915—Representative, C. H. B. Leonard.
1917—Senator, C. M. Thompson; Representative, J. R. McCrary.
1919—Representative, A. Mack Hiatt.
1921—Senator, J. Walter Lambeth; Representative, Benjamin F. Lee.
1923—Representative, H. D. Townsend.
1925—Senator, H. D. Townsend; Representative, Paul R. Raper.
1927—Representative, L. A. Martin.

The General Assembly met annually until the Constitution of 1835 changed the sessions into biennial ones. Davidson County had one senator and two representatives from the foundation of the county until 1891. Since that time, the county has constituted a district with other counties. Zeb V. Walser was the last senator who represented the county and W. A. Beck and J. A. Hedrick were the last two representatives. W. A. Beck was a Democrat and J. A. Hedrick was a Republican—something unusual. General James M. Leach served eight terms in the General Assembly, the longest service in the history of the county. Charles Brummell, John W. Thomas and Henry Walser each served six terms. John A. Hogan served five terms, four times in the Senate and once in the House. P. C.

Thomas served two terms in the Senate and two in the House. He and his father, John W. Thomas, served ten terms in the Senate and House. S. W. Wall served four terms. Alfred, Samuel and Jesse Hargrave served three terms each.

M. H. Pinnix, many years prominent, served one term in the Senate and two terms in the House. John A. Hogan served four terms in the Senate and one in the House. Captain F. C. Robbins sat in the Senate in 1870, more than half century ago; he died in 1926 at the age of ninety-three years. J. R. McCrary has served two terms in the House. Colonel G. Foster Hankins served two terms in the House and one in the Senate. Zeb V. Walser served as Senator and in the House twice. He was Speaker of the House in 1895. Among the Senators still in the flesh may be mentioned W. S. Owen, Major W. H. Phillips, C. M. Thompson and J. Walter Lambeth. Among the members of the House still living may be mentioned Zeb V. Walser, J. R. McCrary, C. M. Thompson, Harllee McCall, G. F. Hankins, T. E. McCrary, B. W. Parham, Ivey G. Thomas, C. H. B. Leonard, A. M. Hiatt, B. F. Lee, L. A. Martin.

4. Davidson County Members of Various State Conventions of North Carolina

1835—John A. Hogan, John L. Hargrave.
1861—B. C. Douthitt, B. A. Kittrell.
1865—Henderson Adams, S. S. Jones.
1868—Isaac Kinney,* S. Mullican.
1875—F. C. Robbins, B. B. Roberts.

---

* Isaac Kinney called the convention to order and presided until a permanent organization was perfected.

CHAPTER VI

FARMS, FARM PRODUCTS, GRIST MILLS

1. Livestock Improvement

The first permanent settlement of Davidson County farmers was made by people from Pennsylvania and New Jersey and old world countries, honest, hardworking, frugal and industrious people, as their descendants are today, and key to the arch of prosperity in this county. These people were of Dutch, German and English descent. They left home to find a good soil, a good climate, and a well-wooded and well-watered country, suitable for diversified farming and the raising of livestock. This they found when they reached this country. There is on file in Washington, D. C., the survey of a road from Lancaster, Pa., to the "Trading Ford" in Davidson County on the Yadkin River. This was called Trading Ford, from the fact that in the earliest history of this section, when the Indians were practically in possession of Western North Carolina, the inhabitants of the country just across the Blue Ridge Mountains met the Indians living in this section annually to trade, mostly for shad that were then caught here and at the fords below in quantity. In a rush they came up-stream each spring from the ocean to find clear waters higher up, where they could lay their eggs, and where the eggs would be hatched out in safety. Shad were caught at these fords as late as 1862 in small numbers. Having to run the gauntlet of nets, traps of every device, and seines of all kinds on the borders of South Carolina, the annual visits of shad ceased.

From one to two hundred years ago when settlers moved into a new country, they carried all their belongings, drawn by horses, mules or oxen. Their cows and sheep were driven. You can see what time-entailing hardship for man and beast was taken to travel over a comparatively unknown country, fording turbulent streams, over rough trails and bad roads and camping in the open, meeting bravely and fearlessly all kinds of weather and adverse conditions. Of such were the brave people from Pennsylvania, New Jersey and elsewhere who settled Davidson County. All these people were farmers. There were only villages in our section then, except Salem in Forsyth County. These early settlers were not only agriculturists, but they manufactured and made in their own homes all that they wore; they made their own harness and farm tools, and the wives and daughters hackled the flax for their linen and wove the wool and knitted and fashioned warm comfortable apparel for all the home. These immigrants when they reached Davidson County went no farther. They found an Eldorado. There were many prayers of thankfulness for all they found, the soil, the climate, the woods and streams. Here all the cereals, most of the grasses, all fruits and berries and vegetables and melons reach perfection with good cultivation. How splendid, how wonderful, what a country to abide in, for man and beast and fowl! There have always been raised in Davidson County during the past one hundred and fifty years or more good horses, mules, hogs, sheep and some good cows. Forty years ago Jersey cows were introduced into this section;

five years later they were bought in small numbers and introduced into this county. This was the beginning of a slow improvement in the milk-giving of our so-called "dairy cows" and in the richer milk given by the pure bred and half-pure Jerseys. The first marked impetus given to increased milk and butter fat production came when the Davidson County Creamery was established at Lexington as this made a cash market for cream. The wonderful growth of Lexington and the growth of other towns in this immediate section, the increased knowledge amongst people in general of the absolute necessity of milk in diet, there being nothing that will take its place as a tissue builder in sickness and in health, have increased interest in better types of dairy cows with a larger milk production. Much money is made from cream and milk through increased sales of "ice cream" in Lexington and in the county and near-by towns. There has been within the past five years and there is today a strong inquiry for good grade Guernsey cows. Belmont Farm and the meetings and sales conducted by the Guernsey Cattle Club there have advanced this breed of the "Channel Island" cattle to the front in popularity and in worth in the county and elsewhere in the South. Twenty years ago they were as a breed unknown; now they appear to be the dominant milk and butter and cream cattle of Davidson County, with their size, vigor, and constitution, and their known habit of converting food into rich milk, as the Jersey does. There are now 150 pure-bred bulls in this county of 4,000 farms. A few pure-bred Holsteins have been brought to Davidson County and used to cross with our native and grade stock. Unlike most of the Guernsey and Jersey pure-bred stock brought here, these Holsteins have not all been of dominant milk producing sires and dams. While the Erlanger Mill has a herd of Jerseys and the Thomasville Baptist Orphanage a herd of Holsteins, and while there are some good cows of each breed scattered over the county, the owners of these two breeds have done little to carry them forward in the county as have the owners of the Guernseys. Seventy-five years ago Dr. William R. Holt, then the owner of Linwood Farm, had a handsome herd of pure-bred Devon Cattle. Governor Thomas M. Holt, who bought this farm at the sale, also bought this herd of Devons, a breed that were blood-red, with straight, long horns. Numbers of farmers owned a few of this breed twenty-five to seventy-five years ago. However, it can be said that though this breed were "hustlers" and their milk was of good flavor and fairly rich in butter fat, these cattle were not heavy milkers and did little towards advancing the milk production or heavier beef cattle in this county. Penry and Hargrave, who bought the Linwood Farm from heirs of Governor Holt, bought and kept on their farm a good herd of pure-bred Aberdeen Angus cattle, the best breed of beef cattle for this county and for this section. This breed was not distributed widely. Mr. W. B. Meares, Sr., bought a herd of Red Polled cattle from Ohio and bred and kept them for several years. They were said to be "Dual Purpose"—they were registered and of good breeding. There was a good demand for their calves at good prices in the South for a time. Mr. Meares found that they were not uniform in their milk qualities; they were light milkers and not to be compared to the true beef type as beef cattle. A part of them were sold at a loss for beef. The best advancement made in this county in the cattle industry is the enforced tuberculin test and the inspection of cattle. This inspection ought to be required and demanded every six months, and the test every twelve months. The farmer ought not to have to pay for this. Cattle brought to our county and State for dairy purposes, not rigidly tested and inspected by the State Veterinarians in the states where they were bought, have not advanced our cattle industry. Within the past twenty years many good stock hogs have been brought into this county to cross with our native stock. Most of these have been Poland China, Berkshire and the Ohio Improved Chester White, the Duroc, the Hampshire and a few Yorkshires. The Berkshire and Poland China have given way to some extent to the Duroc. There is more demand for the true bacon type, though good pure-bred stock of all the breeds named are still liked. Within the past five years, and especially at this time, on account of the very low price of colts (both mules and horses) and the very low prices of ordinary work horses, there is no interest, as there had been for the past 150 years, in the breeding of horses and mules for our own use and for sale to near-by counties.

There is little interest in the sheep industry, though wool is higher than it ever has been. Our sheep industry has gone backward, taking into consideration the increased number of farms and farmers. There are many more dogs in this county than sheep. These dogs produce nothing; there are at least 4,000 dogs that cost their owners and others at least two dollars a month each in food. Nearly $100,000 a year is fed to worthless, non-supporting, marauding dogs. They should be taxed five dollars each instead of one dollar. These dogs produce fleas, mange and sometimes madness and death to good livestock and to man.

The fairs in Lexington and elsewhere (where there are livestock exhibits) have done much lately for this county and State. This county needs to be awakened: men, women, boys and girls should get all the information that they can secure from farm and livestock journals and from study of animals individually. By close observation and close attention to the right types they should learn more about the livestock of America and Europe and above all else keep their eyes on the dairy cow and make her better.

John W. Lambeth is proving on his farm near Thomasville that Herefords, fine for beef cattle, are successfully raised on good pastures in Davidson County.

Wheat, grown on the Linwood Farm, when owned by Governor Thomas M. Holt, won a first prize in the soft (winter wheat) class at the Chicago Exposition. Yellow corn is grown and matures in Davidson County when planted as late as July the first, provided that the land is deeply plowed and kept clean and is frequently and well cultivated, with a good sun exposure; the land must be good. Forty bushels of wheat, 75 bushels of oats (winter), and 100 bushels of corn are grown to the acre some years in this county by some of our farmers. Cotton, tobacco, corn, wheat and oats are grown side by side in Davidson County. Corn has been hung out, exposed to all winter weather in the shuck on the stalk from November to May and when the ears were taken from the shuck all grains were sound.

It has been proven by our farmers that the mutton and the combination wool and mutton sheep, the Southdown and the Shropshire, when pure bred thrive in this county on what we grow. Mule and horse colts, at six months old in the fall of the year, can remain out of doors all through our coldest winters, with an open shed or trees for a wind break, when they are well fed and housed at night in stables. Beef cattle, if well fed on grain and meadow hay, come out of our coldest winters in fine condition, after living out of doors day and night with only the trees for shelter. If stabled, of course, less feed is needed. As an all the year round climate to work in and to thrive in, Davidson County and the great Piedmont Section are unsurpassed for man and for beast.

2. Farms and Farm Development

Not until recent years have we had agricultural statistics, showing the development and progress of farm lands, with increased yields per acre by counties. The State and United States Department of Agriculture have in the past several years done a great work in experimenting, issuing bulletins, collecting data as to crop acreage and yields, and in numerous other ways through their agents secured valuable information. All this data is available to the farmer of Davidson County for the mere asking. And from the appearance of our farms, along with the great growth of our county seat, Lexington, one can readily see that our farmers are taking advantage of this free information, which is enabling them to build soil fertility and increase production, along with the growth of livestock in the county.

W. LEE HARBIN, Lexington
Builder and Contractor, Dealer in Builders' Supplies

The farmers should wake up to the fact that agricultural education with business methods is necessary if we expect to hold Davidson in first rank. The time has come when the farmer should realize that some form of organization is his only salvation. This is being worked out through the Farm Block in Congress, the Farm Bureau, and coöperative buying and selling, with the help of county agents. However, this is going to take time, and thorough coöperation on the part of the farmers.

General farming seems to predominate in the county; but in recent years the improvement and growing of livestock has received much attention, as there are a number of herds in the county of the different dairy breeds that are a credit to the South. This means a cash income every day and greater and more rapidly increased production of the soil. Farm crops marketed through livestock remove less phosphorus, potash, and nitrogen from the soil than any other known line of farming, especially when the manure is returned to the soil. With the almost prohibitive price the farmers are receiving for grain, and the appearance of the boll weevil, there will certainly be an increased interest taken in the county's livestock industry, which will bring about a richer and more productive soil especially if dairying is adopted. Our near-by markets and the county creamery will consume our products in the form of milk, butter and cream. Davidson's system of good roads and shipping facilities enable the dairyman to have easy access to our markets.

Corn is our staple crop which always holds its own and varies less than any other crop that we grow. In

1910 Davidson's acreage was 32,507; production 507,377 bushels; value $938,647.45. Davidson holds sixth place in the State in corn production, with an average of twenty-seven bushels per acre. The 1919 acreage was 33,500; yield 21 bushels; production 703,500 bushels; value at $1.85 per bushel, $1,301,475.00. Record yields of corn by club boys prove that natural conditions are here if we develop them.

Wheat is a very important crop in Davidson County, especially a section known as the "Jersey Settlement" of which Linwood is the center. Yields have been made there as high as forty and forty-five bushels per acre. A sample of wheat gathered from one of these Jersey farms took the first prize at the Chicago World's Fair in 1893, a fact that Davidson County should be proud of. Davidson stands second in the State in total yield of wheat, with 329,600 bushels, which demanded a price of $2.50 per bushel in 1920. At the present time, it is only $1.20 per bushel. In 1920 land in the Jersey Settlement was as high as $115 per acre, while the average for the county is only $78. Twenty years ago land was selling around $40 to $50 per acre, which shows an unusual advance in land values.

This county can produce all the hay needed, but considerable is imported every year, a practice which should be stopped. The county is adapted to the growing of clover, alfalfa, pea, soybean, vetch, and all the different grasses. Any of these hays properly cured demand a price from $20 to $30 per ton. Hay should be more extensively grown as it can be handled with improved machinery, a factor which greatly concerns the farmer with the high cost and scarcity of labor.

FARMS, FARM PRODUCTS, GRIST MILLS

Davidson's total hay acreage is 21,650, an average yield of 1.6 tons. The State average for alfalfa is 2.5 tons per acre.

Cotton, about the best money crop of the Davidson farmer, covered an acreage of 3,620 for 1922, with a yield of 259 pounds of lint cotton, which required an actual cost of 20 cents per pound to produce. This cost does not include overhead, supervision, or buildings. Much land in Davidson will produce a bale or over to the acre, bringing 13 cents in 1910 and up to 36 cents in 1919, when a short crop was reported.

Davidson County produces splendid yields of Irish and sweet potatoes, the Irish yielding 115 bushels and the sweet 130 bushels per acre.

Certain sections of the county produce very fine tobacco, which is the main cash money crop where the lighter soils exist. This county ranks thirty-sixth in the State with an acreage of 5,200; yield 565 pounds to the acre; production 2,938,000 pounds. The 1910 acreage 2,019; production 1,066,331 pounds shows a wonderful increase in acreage as well as in production. Tobacco from this county took first prize at the Vienna (Austria) Exposition and its money value goes a long way towards giving to North Carolina fourth place in value of crops.

Oats should be more extensively grown, as it is a very nutritious and valuable feed, especially for young stock. The average county yield is 18 bushels per acre. The 1920 acreage was 7,300; production 116,800 bushels, giving Davidson County sixth place in the State.

Davidson's cultivated area in 1922 was 97,180 acres, of which corn covered 29 per cent, wheat 30 per cent, tobacco 4 per cent, cotton 4 per cent, oats 8 per cent. There were 5,926 horses and mules worked.

Davidson's livestock enumerations are as follows:

	1920	1921	1922
Horses	4,249	4,121	3,826
Mules	2,608	2,749	2,766
Cattle	8,524	9,784	9,906
Hogs	9,839	10,668	9,313
Sheep	585	556	589

There has been a general exodus from farms to the towns, but we need not be alarmed at that. With modern methods and improved machinery one man can do the work of several in the old way. The country will produce a surplus; and with a poor export trade prices will continue to be low for farm products. The passing of the tenant, the farmer owning his own land, modern machinery, diversified farming, and business methods will bring a safer and more stable agriculture to the county.

Statistics have become absolutely essential in all organized industries, but the farmer has been the last to take advantage of this modern method of safeguarding his plans for production. This information means much to the farmer and the county. Farming for the last three years has been a losing proposition, but those who stick should be rewarded in the near future. The salvation of the farmer depends on coöperative buying and selling, improvement of the soil, increased yield and the adoption of business methods for the farm. A farm is like a bank account; if you keep drawing out and make no deposits, your account will soon be overdrawn.

FARMS, FARM PRODUCTS, GRIST MILLS 85

Why not make a deposit to the soil occasionally, and watch the returns grow with interest added?

In 1923 there were 4,093 farms in Davidson. The area cultivated by owners of land, 67,063 acres; by tenants, 30,117; horses and mules worked, 6,774. In 1921 3,954 tons of fertilizer were used in the county. But if we grow legumes properly, all that we will have to buy in commercial fertilizer is acid phosphate, the cheapest of all ingredients. Farm labor without board in 1922 was $39 per month. The number of cows milked this year compared with last year is 100 per cent increase. Supplies remaining on the farms in 1922 were: corn 43 per cent, wheat 24 per cent, and hay 34 per cent of the total yield. Shipments out of the county were: corn 8 per cent, wheat 17 per cent, hay 5 per cent.

The farmers' affairs greatly affect others, and until recently the bankers of the State had a limited knowledge of economic agriculture or of many problems experienced by farmers. They now welcome the idea that there is a state service which can supply fairly reliable basic agricultural information. They realize that possession of economic farm data would help them in facilitating credit to agricultural interests, and that the basis of all property begins on the farm. Our county and State is made up of 70 per cent farmers, being the largest industry in the State. Annually $11,000,000 is expended on agricultural features in the United States. This covers investigations, experiments, supervision and all features of plant and livestock of our eighty billion dollar industry. Agricultural interests amount to more than all other interests of the entire United States. In 1920 agricultural production amounted to twenty-five billion dollars. North Carolina stands fourth in crop value in the United States and Davidson County takes no small part when it comes to making this showing in the Old North State. In 1919 North Carolina farmers produced half as much as their farms and buildings were worth. That year Davidson County had a bumper wheat crop, for which the farmers received around three dollars per bushel at threshing time.

Farmers must get together and coöperate with bankers and manufacturers and all pull together, making Davidson County stand first in all branches of agriculture.

3. Statistics of the Year 1920

A study of the last government census brings to light exceedingly interesting facts. A comparison with figures of former years would be quite valuable; but we content ourselves for the present purpose in giving figures of the last reports without any comment.

Davidson County embraces an area of 569 square miles. This is nearly half the size of the state of Rhode Island, which has an area of 1,250 square miles. There are in the county 364,160 acres. There are 130,689 acres still covered with timber in spite of the fact that the woodman's axe has been plied most vigorously through many years past. Within the county are 3,770 farms of various sizes. The total population of the county is 35,201; urban population 10,930 and rural 24,271. There are only two counties in the State that have within their borders two cities, and Davidson is one of these, Thomasville having a population of 5,676 and Lexington 5,254.

The value of all domestic animals in the county is given as $1,338,909. Horses on the farms 4,010, valued

GEORGE FRANK HEDRICK, Lexington
Confederate Soldier. Owner and Manager Mount Carmel Farm

at $465,318; mules 2,546, value $301,568; donkeys 8, value $875; cattle 9,666, value $411,630; dairy cattle 61,213, value $350,417; sheep 614, value $4,055; goats 164, value $1,148; hogs 12,068, value $154,315; chickens, 164,763 and eggs 423,550 dozen, value of both chickens and eggs, $281,147; bees 3,052 stands, value $10,088; honey 27,649 pounds, value $7,337; dairy products— milk 1,856,113 gallons; butter, 416,264 pounds; value of both $308,408.

The following figures give the number of animals not on farms, but figures of values seem to be lacking: horses 266, mules 61, cattle 683, sheep 10, goats 13, hogs 2,007.

In the county are men farmers 3,601, and women farmers 169; there are 3,538 white farmers and 323 colored farmers. On the 3,770 farms the farm machinery is valued at $918,069. There are two farms listed with less than three acres and two with over 1,000 acres. The average value per acre is $36.72, and the average value per farm is $4,326. The value of all farm property is $16,310,246.

Davidson County stands second in the State in the per capita ownership of automobiles, the total number licensed up to June 30 being 3,327, which means one machine to every 10.6 people. Among the counties Davidson stands tenth in the total number of automobiles owned.

The total value of all crops is as follows: cereals, $1,696,736; hay and forage, $486,903; other grains and seeds, $25,781; fruits and nuts, $41,968; vegetables, $513,137; all other crops, $1,572,025. Total, $4,336,550. The figures by items are as follows: corn, 27,979 acres,

494,597 bushels; oats, 3,819 acres, 42,505 bushels; wheat, 31,157 acres, 264,673 bushels; rye, 990 acres, 5,739 bushels; buckwheat, 9 acres, 61 bushels; other grains, 45 acres, 124 bushels; dry peas, 470 acres, 2,229 bushels; peanuts, 20 acres, 425 bushels; hay and forage, 19,953 acres, 18,043 tons; cultivated grasses, 9,751 acres, 9,378 tons; timothy, 9 acres, 11 tons; timothy and clover mixed, 199 acres, 234 tons; clover, 4,663 acres, 4,388 tons; alfalfa, 27 acres, 35 tons; other grasses, 4,873 acres, 4,710 tons; wild grasses, 4,050 acres, 5,777 tons; small grains cut for hay, 74 acres, 82 tons; legumes, 508 acres, 497 tons; silage crops, 57 acres, 245 tons; cut corn, 5,489 acres, 2,039 tons; kaffir, 20 acres, 22 tons; root crops, 4 acres, 3 tons; Irish potatoes, 488 acres, 39,204 bushels; sweet potatoes, 1,020 acres, 125,446 bushels; other vegetables, 281 acres; tobacco, 3,912 acres, 2,320,331 pounds; cotton, 2,850 acres, 1,398 bales; sorghum, 491 acres, 1,857 tons; syrup, 27,824 gallons; strawberries, 21 acres, 19,626 quarts; blackberries and dewberries, 24 acres, 12,716 quarts; apple trees, 50,666; pear trees 9,271; peach trees, 50,-125. Total value of all crops $4,336,550.

The first manufacturing enterprise in Davidson County of a pretentious nature was "The Lexington Manufacturing Company." This is also the first corporation having in its title the name of the county seat. The records show that three distinct purchases of land were made for the use of this company: January 16, 1839, sixty-one and a quarter acres were bought of William Owens, executor of Joel Owens, on Abbott's Creek. On July 2, 1839, eighteen acres were bought of Samuel Hargrave for $350. The price of the first

Farms, Farm Products, Grist Mills 91

purchase was $105.50. February 12, 1840, five and a half acres were bought of Joseph B. Dobson for $15. On a part of this property the Lexington Manufacturing Company erected the first cotton mill in Davidson County in the year 1839. This was one of twenty-five cotton mills in the whole State of North Carolina reported in 1840. Alfred Hargrave was president of the company. The location of this cotton mill was near the present intersection of the Southern Railway and East Center Street. I have often heard my father, the late Valentine Leonard, born in 1824, died 1895, tell about this mill. He said there was a big well dug on the premises for the use of all the "hands" living in the tenant houses built on the grounds around the mill. He said the building of this mill created great interest in the community and the whole county. It promised to be the beginning of a great industrial development. But unfortunately this mill was destined to have a very brief career of service to the county. It was destroyed by fire in the winter of 1844-45 and was never rebuilt. The records show that the land was sold off to various parties during the next two years.

But this cotton mill was the harbinger of many great enterprises yet to follow. The North Carolina Railroad, extending from Charlotte to Goldsboro, a distance of 223 miles, was chartered in 1849 and opened in 1856. It passes through the middle of the county a distance of nearly thirty miles. The Southbound Railroad, opened 1910, crosses the Southern (originally the North Carolina) at right angles in Lexington, the county seat. The latter traverses the whole length of the county, and of the ninety odd miles of the entire length of this line, the county of Davidson has about fifty-five miles. The county has another railroad extending from High Point in Guilford County to High Rock in Davidson, where it connects with the Southbound—the High Point, Thomasville and Denton railroad.

The great Civil War came on in 1861 and put a stop to all industrial development for many years. Several decades rolled by before Davidson County saw another cotton mill within its boundaries. However, her people were of a stock who could not be daunted. Through many years past we have experienced a great revival of industry, and the county is now right up in the front ranks. The outlook for the future is roseate with promise.

DAVIDSON COUNTY, NORTH CAROLINA, SUMMARY OF MANUFACTURES FOR 1919 AND 1899

	1919	1899	Per cent of Increase
Number of establishments	133	99	734.3
Wage earners (average No.)	3,742	879	325.7
Capital	$ 10,128,017	$ 609,277	1,562.3
Wages	2,890,558	158,779	1,720.5
Cost of material	9,272,962	624,278	1,385.4
Value of products	16,719,602	1,046,589	1,497.5
Value added by manufacture	7,436,640	422,311	1,660.9

This table shows the striking growth of Davidson County in manufactures. In the comparatively short space of two decades the capital invested in manufactures has increased from $609,000 to more than $10,000,000, an increase of nearly 1,600 per cent. Corresponding increases are also shown in the amounts paid in wages, cost of materials, and value of products.

The figures showing the growth of the county would be even more striking if statistics for the hand-trades and neighborhood and house industries were eliminated from the 1899 census. In connection with this census statistics were obtained for these industries but this practice was not followed in 1919. In this census year the statistics of manufactures were confined to those establishments which were conducted under the factory system.

VALUE OF PRODUCTS AND WAGE EARNERS RANKED FOR TWENTY LEADING COUNTIES

Counties	Wage Earners		Value of Products	
	Average Number	Rank	Amount	Rank
Forsyth	14,229	1	$ 208,981,632	1
Durham	7,847	4	83,180,547	2
Guilford	11,074	2	62,571,982	3
Mecklenburg	6,242	5	48,496,831	4
Gaston	9,906	3	44,230,478	5
Rockingham	6,132	6	32,319,737	6
Cabarrus	5,913	7	28,129,586	7
Alamance	4,455	8	19,300,028	8
Rowan	4,012	9	18,242,697	9
Davidson	3,742	11	16,719,602	10
New Hanover	2,477	16	15,932,426	11
Stanly	3,475	12	15,290,314	12
Iredell	2,593	15	14,552,672	13
Wake	2,690	14	14,370,049	14
Catawba	3,781	10	14,171,859	15
Vance	1,978	19	12,924,977	16
Buncombe	2,256	18	11,925,208	17
Cleveland	2,361	17	11,814,379	18
Rutherford	3,042	13	10,262,201	19
Johnston	1,596	20	10,159,313	20
Total	99,801		$ 693,576,518	

This table shows the rank of the twenty leading manufacturing counties of the State with respect to value of products and average number of wage earners. Davidson County ranks tenth in value of products and eleventh with respect to the number of persons employed, a very good showing among the 100 counties of the State. The ten leading counties, including Davidson, reported 60 per cent of the value of all manufactured products for the State of North Carolina at the 1919 census. These counties also reported nearly 47 per cent of all earners employed in manufactures.

In 1899, the only other year for which manufactures data are available, the State ranked twenty-sixth with respect to the value of products and twenty-second in number of wage earners employed.

STATISTICS FOR DAVIDSON COUNTY, NORTH CAROLINA, CENSUS MANUFACTURES 1919

Industry	Number Establishments	Capital	Average Number of Wage Earners	Value of Products
Total for the county	133	$ 10,128,017	3,742	$ 16,719,602
Cotton goods	6	6,283,970	1,637	8,541,174
Furniture	11	2,280,919	1,420	4,523,317
Lumber and timber products	69	608,564	318	1,196,041
Flour and grist mill products	15	197,218	26	767,188
Planing-mill products	5	136,477	40	225,942
Mineral and soda waters	3	62,564	16	96,905
Printing and publishing newspapers, periodicals	4	69,205	10	27,640
All other industries	20	489,100	275	1,341,305

All other industries embrace:

Artificial stone products, 1; boxes, wooden packing, except cigar boxes, 1; bakery products other than biscuits and crackers, 3; building brick, fancy, ornamental, vitrified, glazed, and enameled, 2; brooms from broom corn, 1; butter, 1; carriage and wagon materials, 1; men's clothing, 1; confectionery, 2; ice, manufactured, 1; power-machine knit goods, 2; dyeing and finishing textiles, exclusive of that done in textile mills, 1; monuments and tombstones, 1; mattresses and spring beds, not elsewhere specified, 1; job printing, 1.

This table presents detailed statistics for Davidson County, showing the importance of industries for which data can be shown without disclosing the operation of individual establishments; cotton goods, furniture and lumber and timber products, ranking among the more important industries.

4. Grist Mills in Davidson County

In this day of modern inventions and changed customs the average citizen of Davidson County does not realize the important part these old mills played in the earlier history of this county. At the present time there are numerous manufacturing industries in the county which far outstrip that of flour making, but the time has not been so long since the grist mill was considered a necessity for each community. In fact, for a long period of years these mills contained all the power-driven machinery in this county as well as many others. Gradually other enterprises have been developed until now grain milling comprises only a small portion of our total manufacturing.

The grist mill of the early and even late part of the nineteenth century was entirely different from that in operation now. Until about 1880 every mill in Davidson county, except one, was located on the banks of some stream in order that power might be obtained with which to turn the crude machinery which ground all the flour consumed by the generations of those days. These old mill houses and the machinery in them excite great interest when the nature of their construction is known. The buildings, comparatively large for the time, were put up of enormous timbers hewed out by hand. Another noticeable feature was the distance they were elevated above the ground; but this was in order that the floor might not be reached by the high waters of freshets. Until late in the nineteenth century the common grist mill contained only three distinct pieces of machinery: a "smutter" for cleaning the wheat, buhrstones made from large pieces of stone, and a long reel for separating the flour from the bran.

When wheat was brought to the mill the miller carried it on his shoulder to the second or perhaps third floor where the "smutter" was located. Here the wheat was cleaned and spouted back to the first floor where it was ground by the buhrstones. From the buhrs the ground product was carried by elevators back to the upper floor where it went through the long bolting machine which sifted the flour from the bran. In the early history of the county some mills did not even have the power-driven bolting machines and the flour was sifted from the bran by hand. This was a slow and tiresome process of making flour.

In those days "going to mill" was considered an important event. This was especially true during the summer months when many of these mills were forced to

JOHN D. GRIMES, 1852-1918
Built in Lexington the First Roller Process Mill in the State

Farms, Farm Products, Grist Mills

suspend operations for lack of sufficient water to furnish the power. Then it often happened that many farmers were compelled to go long distances to get their flour and meal made. But this was not considered such an irksome task for they often went expecting to have to spend the night, and so went prepared. Even under more favorable circumstances "going to mill" often meant one's waiting at the mill for hours, or perhaps leaving his grain in the mill till the next day before it could be ground, for each man received the flour and bran from his own wheat; and besides the miller served his customers after the order in which they came. But each man had his name on his bags, and so it was comparatively easy to keep the different lots in order.

Abbott's Creek and its tributaries furnished more power to run these mills than any other stream in the county. It is impossible to state the exact number of mill sites located on this stream and the smaller ones running into it, but there have been at least twenty-five or thirty. Howard, Hoover, Wagoner, Berrier, Fritts, Green, Finch, Young, Holmes, and others have operated mills on Abbott's Creek; while Siceloff, Haynes, Kennedy, Kennell, Ward, Leonard, and several others have operated mills on creeks flowing into Abbott's. The Ward mill was built over a hundred years ago and the building is still being used though now equipped with modern machinery.

Likewise the Yadkin River, which borders the county on the south and west, furnished power for several mills. In the lower section of the county the Addertons once operated a mill. A little farther up the stream was located the Holmes, later called the Stafford mill. Joseph Clouse built a mill on the Yadkin in 1820; but it, as well as many others, was burned by raiding parties of the Federal army during the Civil War. Other mills on the river were once owned by Swicegood, Walser, Hartley, Grimes, and possibly others. Peter Hairston, a very wealthy slaveholder, built a mill near the river in the upper part of the county about 1820. Other sections of the county had mills at very early dates. A mill was built on the recent Kennedy site, north of Thomasville, very soon after the Revolutionary War. Other mills were likely in existence before this war. The Thomas mill, in Thomasville, was built during the Civil War, and used steam instead of water to furnish power. This was the first mill ever operated by steam in Davidson County. After some years of more or less successful operation this mill burned down and chair factories now occupy its site. All these were once the old-fashioned buhr mills, most of which have been torn away.

The second steam driven mill was built by Grimes Brothers in Lexington. Being very progressive, they installed rolls soon after its erection. This marked the beginning of a new epoch in the milling industry, not only in the county but in the entire State, for this was the first roller mill in North Carolina. The flour from this process was so much better that in a few years other roller mills were established in the county. Among the first of those to put in rolls was the Granger mill at Arcadia, which is still in operation under a different name. This changing of the process of milling continued until all the old buhr mills were forced to suspend operations. Now all our flour is ground on rolls. In recent years the number of mills has been steadily decreasing until at present there are probably not half as many mills running in the county as there were thirty years ago.

CHAPTER VII

BANKS OF DAVIDSON COUNTY

1. BANKS IN LEXINGTON

The year 1859 saw the first activity towards establishing a bank in Davidson County. An act was passed in the General Assembly February 16, 1859, which gave a charter to the Bank of Lexington at Lexington, Davidson County, with permission to open the books for subscription to the stock and to accept such subscriptions for a period of sixty days. Andrew Hunt, George Riley, Henderson Adams, Samuel L. Hargrave, Alfred Hargrave and W. D. Lindsay were appointed in the charter to have charge of the affairs of the bank. This first bank was granted wide privileges with reference to subscriptions to stock, permission being given for the opening of books at Salisbury, N. C., with B. B. Roberts, Joel Jenkins and William Murphy in charge; at Thomasville with J. W. Thomas, D. C. Johnson and Jesse Shelby in charge; at Greensboro with Ralph Gorrell, C. P. Mendenhall and R. P. Dick in charge; at Salem with Thomas J. Wilson, Nathan Chaffin and John Vogler in charge; at Asheboro with Jonathan Worth, B. F. Hoover and H. B. Elliott in charge; at Mocksville with Braxton Bailey, J. M. Clement and Ephriam Gaither in charge; at Clemmonsville with A. C. Wharton, H. Eccles and A. W. Cooper in charge; at High Point with William Sheek, John Carter and William Boman in charge; and at such other places and under the charge of such other persons as might be designated by the commissioners appointed to receive subscriptions at Lexington.

A section near the end of the charter provides that books may be opened at Graham in charge of Edwin M. Holt, Thomas Ruffin, Jr., Jesse Gant and John Trolinger. It was also provided that if one thousand shares should be subscribed at Graham, a branch bank should be established in that town. However, as far as can be ascertained the only place at which the Bank of Lexington opened for business was at the parent location of Lexington, and it was active in the business life of the town with such men as Cicero F. Lowe, B. F. Kittrell and others in active control of the bank, Mr. Kittrell being president and Mr. Lowe cashier. The War Between the States in 1861 brought to a close the business career of the first bank chartered in Davidson County and located in Lexington, tradition stating that the entire assets of the bank were carried away during the night and buried on some isolated spot in Hampton Township, in order that the gold should not come into the hands of the Federal troops who were being at that time stationed in Lexington.

The next movement looking toward banking facilities for Lexington came in the year 1887 when the Bank of Lexington was opened as a private banking institution at Lexington with W. L. Ketchum as president and G. Homer Jones as cashier. These gentlemen were residents of Michigan, but moved to Lexington for the purpose of engaging in the banking business. The capital stock of this private bank was $10,000 and the offices used for the purpose were nearly upon the same site as the first bank operated in the county, this location being just north of the courthouse.

GEORGE W. MOUNTCASTLE, Lexington
Manufacturer, Banker, President Bank of Lexington

facing the square. In 1889, two years after the private bank was organized, during the month of September, John W. Boring and George W. Mountcastle of Johnson City, Tenn., came to Lexington and negotiated with the owners, Messrs. Ketchum and Jones, for the purchase of the bank. The transaction was carried through and the new owners associated with themselves local men, John D. Grimes, Thomas J. Grimes and W. G. Penry, as stockholders in the bank and with John W. Boring as president and George W. Mountcastle as cashier, having raised the capitalization to $15,000, conducted the business successfully. A building was erected for the bank on the Stimpson property just below the March Hotel on South Main Street, where the business was conducted for some time with the officers remaining the same until the interest of John W. Boring was purchased by the other stockholders, and H. T. Phillips was then elected president.

After having been operated for seven years as a private bank, in the year 1894 a charter was secured under the laws of North Carolina, incorporating the bank with a capital stock of $30,000. At that time John D. Grimes assumed the presidency. The year 1896 brought about a wider distribution of the stock and removal from the inadequate quarters then occupied to a more modern and better equipped banking room on the corner of First Avenue and Main Street, in the March Hotel building, at which time George W. Mountcastle was elected president and W. D. Biggers, who had been with the bank for quite a number of years, was elected cashier. Ten years of financial and industrial growth in Lexington and Davidson County required additional capital for the bank; so in 1906 the amount was raised to $50,000 and the officers serving at that time were George W. Mountcastle, president, and W. H. Mendenhall, cashier. In the year 1919 another increase in capitalization was made, bringing the amount up to $100,000. In 1922 the Bank of Lexington took over and liquidated the Lexington Bank and Trust Company, which had succeeded the First National Bank, and moved into the building which it now occupies.

For forty years the Bank of Lexington's service and assistance have been used by the people of Lexington and Davidson County and the bank has been identified with Davidson County's growth and development, and for the major portion of that time George W. Mountcastle has been with the institution as an officer and is at the time of writing this history serving as president. W. H. Mendenhall has been in the service of the bank for thirty-one years and is now vice president. Charles D. Hunt has been with the bank for seventeen years and is filling the office of cashier. Charles A. Mountcastle and James E. Williams are the assistant cashiers. The total assets of the Bank of Lexington are over two million dollars.

The Commercial and Savings Bank was organized March 4, 1907, with $25,000 capital stock, by J. W. McCrary, J. T. Hedrick, E. B. Craven, D. L. Brinkley, D. H. Hinkle, B. H. Finch, E. J. Buchanan and W. H. Walker. The officers elected were J. W. McCrary, president; Dr. E. J. Buchanan, vice president; J. F. Deaderick, cashier, and E. B. Craven, manager of the Insurance Department. The $25,000 capital stock remained unchanged until February, 1921, when it was doubled. At the annual meeting of the stockholders

JAMES ADDERTON, Lexington
Banker, Cashier Commercial and Savings Bank

in January, 1922, it was voted to increase the capital stock from $50,000 to $100,000. The bank has paid to its stockholders in cash and stock dividends since 1907 the sum of $165,031 and earned a surplus of $85,000. The bank's resources are now over $1,000,000. The bank occupied quarters from its organization until December, 1923, in the Hinkle & Grimes building on North Main Street. It then moved to new and larger quarters in the Hege-Harmon building on the Court House Square.

John W. McCrary, prominent county official, and for years a successful funeral director and furniture dealer in Lexington, was president of the Commercial and Savings Bank until his death September 28, 1924. The directors chose J. H. Greer, a leading business man of Lexington and the county, long at the head of the Lexington Hardware Corporation, with branches in several other towns and cities, as the successor of Mr. McCrary as president of this strong financial institution. The continued prosperity of the bank under his administration demonstrates the wisdom of their choice. Dr. E. J. Buchanan has been vice president since the first. J. F. Deaderick was cashier until his death in March, 1918. James Adderton was elected to succeed Mr. Deaderick, and has continued in that position to the present, giving his fine business ability to the large interests of this financial institution. E. B. Craven has been manager of the insurance department of the bank since its organization.

The Bank of Davidson was organized February 18, 1909, with $10,000 capital stock. The officers elected were: J. B. Smith, president; J. W. Noell and C. L. Leonard, vice presidents; and James Adderton, cashier. The directors elected were: L. F. Barr, W. L.

Harbin, C. L. Leonard, J. A. Lindsay, J. W. Noell, L. J. Peacock, J. B. Smith, Z. I. Walser and Z. V. Walser. The bank continued in business until August 25, 1911, when it was consolidated with the Commercial and Savings Bank.

The National Bank of Lexington was organized October 18, 1900, with capital stock $25,000. It started business January 31, 1901. Zeb V. Walser, president; J. B. Smith, vice president; R. L. Burkhead, cashier. Directors: J. B. Smith, Z. V. Walser, R. L. Burkhead, James Adderton, J. L. Peacock, W. A. Beck, C. U. G. Biesecker, D. F. Conrad, E. M. Ward, Z. I. Walser. It was located in the building now occupied by L. T. Fry, until 1905; then moved into the newly built Development building on the corner; stayed there until December 8, 1908, and controlling interest sold to Foy & Shemwell, who organized the First National Bank, which was succeeded by the Lexington Bank and Trust Company.

2. BANKS IN DENTON

The first bank at Denton bears date of November 24, 1906. It was chartered with an authorized capital of $25,000, beginning business with $5,000 paid in. The stockholders were J. W. Noell, S. W. Finch, Wade H. Phillips. It was called the Bank of Denton.

A second bank bearing the title the Bank of Denton was organized April 19, 1910, with an authorized capital of $7,500 and $5,000 paid in. The stockholders were C. C. Shaw, A. A. Hill, J. M. Daniels, B. A. Peacock, B. I. Harrison, L. E. Workman.

Both of the above named banks went out of business several years ago.

J. TILDEN HEDRICK, Lexington
Manufacturer, Banker, President Elk Furniture Company
Former Mayor of Lexington

BANKS OF DAVIDSON COUNTY   113

The Carolina Bank and Trust Company of Denton was organized February 11, 1924, with an authorized capital of $100,000 and $15,000 paid in. The incorporators named were: T. J. Finch, Arthur Ross, R. L. Pope, W. W. Rapp, R. C. Rapp, J. F. Garner, Charles F. Phillips, George D. Finch. The officers are: T. J. Finch, president; Arthur Ross, vice president; J. F. Garner, cashier; Baxter Carter, assistant cashier.

3. BANKS IN THOMASVILLE

The first bank to do business in the town of Thomasville was chartered by the State February 25, 1861. The official title was "The Thomasville Bank." The charter carried with it blanket privileges. The capital stock was limited to three hundred thousand dollars. The par value of the shares was fifty dollars. Within twenty days after ratification books were to be opened in Thomasville under the superintendence of Jesse Shelly, David Loftin, D. W. C. Johnson and David Hepler; at Lexington under Samuel Hargrave, Ben. Kittrell, Alfred Hargrave, E. D. Hampton and J. Adderton; in Greensboro under C. P. Mendenhall, Ralph Gorrell, J. M. Morehead; at Asheboro under Jonathan Worth, B. F. Hoover, J. M. Worth; at Gold Hill under Moses Holmes, Brantly Harris, Reuben Holmes; at Clemonsville under A. C. Wharton, Lewis Hanes and B. C. Douthitt. The bank could open for business under seven directors when the sum of twenty-five thousand dollars should be paid in. A further provision was that when fifty thousand dollars should be subscribed in Concord, Cabarrus County, a branch bank should be established in that town. A similar provision was made for Beaufort or Morehead

8

City in Carteret County. The Thomasville Bank was opened in due time in harmony with the provisions of the charter, in charge of Romulus Shelly. It was located on a part of the lot now occupied by the United States postoffice. It prospered greatly until the war caused depression in all lines of business, sometimes bringing on complete paralysis. Finally under such exigencies Mr. Shelly and his associates decided to close the bank.

August 1, 1899, the Bank of Thomasville was chartered with a capital stock of $25,000.

The People's Bank of Thomasville bears date of July 18, 1916. The authorized capital was $100,000.

Both of the above named banks went out of business in 1921.

The Thomasville Loan and Trust Company was chartered June 24, 1904. The stockholders named were: R. L. Burkhead, G. F. Hankins, C. M. Hoover, J. A. Green, G. M. Hoover, with $10,000 subscribed. April 18, 1907, the Thomasville Loan and Trust Company was converted into the First National Bank of Thomasville. This bank has a capital of $100,000 and a surplus of the same sum. Its resources amount to about one and a half million dollars. Its board of directors consists of the following: T. J. Finch, A. H. Ragan, Dr. C. A. Julian, C. L. Harris, J. A. Green, Dr. C. H. Phillips, T. A. Finch, W. G. Hinkle, M. B. Hite, J. W. Boyles, J. W. Lambeth, Jr., A. S. Miller, W. H. Tudor, J. W. Lambeth, C. F. Finch. The officers are: T. J. Finch, president; J. W. Lambeth, Jr., vice president; R. L. Pope, cashier; W. W. Rapp, assistant cashier.

The Page Trust Company of Thomasville began business November 1, 1923. This bank is a branch of the Page Trust Company of Aberdeen, which has assets of nearly six million dollars. J. R. Page is president and H. A. Page, Jr., is treasurer. E. H. Mahone is cashier of the Thomasville branch of the corporation.

CHAPTER VIII

DAVIDSON COUNTY NEWSPAPERS

During the long years of a century there have been various newspaper enterprises launched in the county. Many of the papers established with the best of intentions and the fondest hopes survived only a short while. Others have been more fortunate. Each has contributed its influence for the upbuilding of the great interests of the county.

The first county paper was established in Lexington in the year 1855, *The Lexington and Yadkin Flag,* owned and edited by James A. Long, Esq. He built the house on North Main Street later owned by Mr. G. W. Harris, and this house was his printing shop. From the same office a few years later he issued for a short time *The Little Adder,* a free suffrage paper. In those days one could not vote unless he was a freeholder. This paper advocated free suffrage for all men. That was not yet the day of woman suffrage. In 1875 Colonel William F. Henderson established *The Central.*

The next paper to be established in Lexington was *The Banner,* by Charles Bruner, of Salisbury, in 1878. This venture had but a short career. In 1880 Captain L. C. Hanes founded *The Lexington Exchange.* This weekly continued less than two years. It was suspended temporarily, but its publication was never resumed.

In 1882 T. B. Eldridge established *The Davidson Dispatch.* He was an energetic newspaper man and he made *The Dispatch* a success from the first. The paper came into the possession of Colonel H. B. Varner in

1896, and, with the exception of a short interval, continued under his proprietorship until his death in 1925. For several years past the paper has gone under the name of *The Lexington Dispatch*. It has exerted a strong moulding influence in the county during the whole of its long and useful life. Starting in a small rented house at the corner now occupied by the Development Building, it has grown and reached out until it now occupies its own home, the Varner Building, in the block between First and Second avenues. Formerly the paper came out weekly, but for several years past it has been issued as a semiweekly. *Southern Good Roads* was a monthly.

Other papers in Lexington have been: *The Herald, The Davidsonian, The Ledger, The Record, The Daily Star, The Southern Normal, The High School Magazine, The Lexhipep*. At Denton *The Herald* was issued for a while. During a short period a paper called *Sunshine* was issued out from Denton in the country.

The year 1887 saw two weekly papers established in Thomasville; one in the spring, *Charity and Children,* as the mouthpiece of the Thomasville Baptist Orphanage, the other on September 26, *The Times,* a town paper. *Charity and Children* was established by John H. Mills, "the father of Orphanage work in North Carolina." Mr. Mills was a brilliant writer, though the pressure of his duties as General Manager of the Baptist Orphanage prevented him from giving as much time to the paper as its importance demanded. In 1895 the paper changed hands, Archibald Johnson, of Scotland County, being elected editor by the Board of Trustees of the Orphanage.

The Thomasville Times was established by J. F. Westmoreland, who edited it until his death in 1913. The paper then fell into the hands of his son, David, who edited it until 1918. It was then sold to D. F. Crinkley, of Raleigh, who sold it in April, 1920, to J. T. Westmoreland, another son of the founder.

In 1910 a second local, weekly paper was established in Thomasville, *The Davidsonian*. L. A. Martin and Archibald Johnson were the first editors. It was then sold to T. J. Finch and edited by P. S. Vann. In 1915 it ceased to appear. *The Chairtown News* was established July 29, 1920, by C. F. Finch with H. G. West as editor. On June 1, 1921, Charles M. Sturkey became associated with the paper as managing editor. In 1926 *The Chairtown News* and *The Times* were consolidated.

CHAPTER IX

THE JUNIOR ORDER UNITED AMERICAN MECHANICS NATIONAL ORPHANS' HOME

Davidson County won out over all other competitors in a state-wide rivalry for the branch home of the Jr. O. U. A. M. The North Carolina State Council of this large fraternity for many years worked on a proposition to have the National Council establish in North Carolina a branch of the National Junior Order Home at Tiffin, Ohio. This was finally accomplished. Word went out in 1922 that this home would be located at some point in North Carolina. At once Lexington Council No. 21 appointed the following Central Committee: J. T. Hedrick, Dr. J. C. Leonard, F. O. Sink, J. A. Lindsay, E. A. Timberlake.

This committee worked assiduously until success richly crowned their labors. The National Committee, with National Councilor J. D. Tunison, of New York, as chairman, made several tours of inspection over the several valuable sites offered by different communities in the State. Final word as to definite decision in favor of the Davidson County offer came in a telegram at Christmas. The construction of this great institution is now under way, and it will not be long until hundreds of orphan children will be cared for in this home.

A thousand children; a million dollar institution—these are things reasonably expected from the building at South Lexington of the branch Junior National Orphans' Home. This is what is in the minds of the distinguished gentlemen from Nation and State.

There is expected to be available for early construction at least a half million dollars. The home will be designed first for 500 children, but the plans will be laid out on such comprehensive scope that the future additions will fit in exactly with all that has gone before. Just what buildings will now be erected will be determined by the trustees who will have charge of the planning and execution of the work. There will be an administration building, dormitories, or rather group homes, a school building, central heating plant, laundry, workshop where boys may learn valuable crafts, and special facilities for instructing girls in domestic arts. It is the stated purpose of the Junior Order to make this an institution second to none of its nature in the entire United States. Its graduates are expected to be well equipped young men and women, capable of coping with the task of life with a better chance than their average fellows.

Besides the large number of children who will come from many states, there will be a staff of matrons, teachers, instructors, superintendent and others that will eventually number more than a hundred. These trained and consecrated workers will be a decided asset to the community. There will be a railroad station in front of the property and a fifty-foot street will lead from the grounds to the station. President Fries of the Southbound has given assurance that the station will be an attractive one and in keeping with its surroundings.

Streets will be laid out throughout the grounds, which will be very extensive. Where now is a fine body of woods back of the green wheat field coming nearly to the road near the Taylor residence, buildings

JR. O. U. A. M. NATIONAL ORPHANS' HOME, SOUTH LEXINGTON
Eventually to Cost a Million Dollars and House a Thousand Children

will be located. The front group of buildings will stand well back from the highway and railroad. A large amount of landscape work will be done to make the grounds attractive and it is expected that many flowers, shrubs, and ornamental trees will be employed in giving the buildings beautiful settings.

The location of the home at this place is expected to result in several other developments. One of these is the construction of a hard surface highway from Lexington to that point if not beyond. Coupled with this will be an arrangement for eliminating the grade crossing in the southern part of the city. An overhead bridge will be built. Much building will also follow in the territory between the city proper and the home, especially after the proposed hard surface road is located.

This institution will be an additional attraction for tourists, especially those who are members of the Junior Order, and it is expected that many hundreds will take the side trip while passing through here to and from Florida and the mountains. This tourist traffic is increasing and will increase the year round. Contracts have already been asked for much of the stretch of bad road between Roanoke and Rocky Mount, in Virginia, which will eliminate the chief barrier to free passage of motor traffic through the Shenandoah Valley into North Carolina. When it is stated that from Staunton, Virginia, to New York City there is practically an unbroken stretch of hard surface road—and mostly surfaced road between Staunton and Roanoke—it is seen how important this road is and how much traffic will flow over it.

The State Highway Commission has already been asked to take over the stretch of highway passing the Orphans' Home site, which would fill in a link in a direct north and south highway from New York to Florida, crossing Central Highway here. This would bring thousands of tourists by the home each year.

A great meeting was held in Lexington, attended by hundreds of people from many states, when the formalities of presentation and acceptance of the location were conducted. Prayer was offered by Dr. J. C. Leonard. National Councilor J. D. Tunison was the principal speaker. Among other things of great interest he stated that over the Orphans' Home at Tiffin, Ohio, there are 330,000 fathers sponsoring the little folks who are being cared for there. Everything possible is being done for the children. The institution idea about the orphanage is rapidly being abolished and a home-like atmosphere established.

Mr. Tunison said that at the Junior Home at Tiffin there is one building that always impresses more than the others. This is the nursery where thirty-four little tots are cared for, and those in charge of this feature of the home are endeavoring to supply that which is missing—the parents' love—and right well are they succeeding. He told of many visits by various men, and the incidents that served to bring tears to their cheeks, as they learned of the work being done with the children.

In commending Lexington upon the branch here, the speaker told of the home at Tiffin, giving an idea of what Lexington may expect to have some day. The National Councilor expressed thanks to each city in the State that offered a site for the home, and to the chairmen of the various committees. He paid a compliment to J. T. Hedrick, of Lexington, chairman of the local central committee, declaring that Lexington had the best chairman in the State. He also expressed thanks to W. A. Cooper, of Raleigh, chairman of the State site committee, for his untiring efforts in aiding the committee in the selection of a site for the home.

The deed for the land upon which the new orphanage is to be located was presented to National Councilor Tunison by J. T. Hedrick, the following brief address being delivered:

Honorable Trustees of the National Council, Junior Order United American Mechanics, members of the committee on the selection of location for the orphans' home, ladies and gentlemen:

The act which in the name of Lexington Council No. 21, Junior Order United American Mechanics, the citizens of Lexington, of Davidson County and of the State of North Carolina, I am about to perform gives me very keen pleasure. The care of the orphan is a holy exercise of the finest religious sentiment of the human heart. The only specific definition of religion given to us in Heaven's inspired Book embodies care of these little ones left without the protection of earthly father or mother or both, dependent upon the sympathetic support of those whose hearts cheerfully respond to such call. The Holy Bible tells us that the man who does not respond to this noble appeal does not have in his soul the element of pure and undefiled religion.

With pride and joy we claim that North Carolina is one of the really great and progressive states of the Union. We delight to herald abroad to other North Carolinians that Davidson County stands in the front line of the forward-facing and upward-looking counties of the State. We have no hesitancy in proclaiming abroad our unfailing belief in Lexington as one of the most desirable cities in the whole State in which to live.

Through the years it has been our privilege to see many new enterprises established in and around Lexington. We have had the erection of splendid churches on our thoroughfares, and we have been gladdened to witness the prosperity in the growth of strong and influential congregations. We have seen the development of fine schools and school buildings. Our stores, banks, mills, factories, various industrial enterprises, have come among us with wonderful outpouring of blessings upon our people. In all this prosperity we have greatly rejoiced. We are ready always to encourage the coming of many more such enterprises, and all who desire to find locations for business of such type and character will find Lexington hospitable. Our gates are wide open to such people.

When it was made known that the National Council, Junior Order United American Mechanics, had decided to establish an orphans' home in North Carolina, our people at once became deeply interested in the location to be decided by the committee appointed on the selection of a site. The local Junior Order council immediately began to set up an organization whose supreme purpose would be to convince the committee that Lexington is the one city in the State for the location of the proposed home. The local council had the hearty and unanimous support of the other fraternities and clubs of the city and our citizens entered whole-heartedly into the campaign thus launched. We were conscious from the first that the friendly rivalry of numerous other communities in the State made it necessary for Lexington to put forth her best efforts. Nothing short of a long pull, a strong pull, and a pull together would amount to anything. Other worthy competitors would offer most attractive propositions. If Lexington would win, we must do ourselves credit in the offer we would make.

The most cheering news reaching Lexington in many a day came Sunday evening, December 23, 1923, in a telegram from Honorable Joseph D. Tunison, National Councilor, saying that by unanimous decision of the committee the proposition made by Lexington for the new orphans' home had been accepted.

Dear friends, trustees and other representatives of the National Council, it gives me supreme, unalloyed pleasure, in the name and in behalf of the people of Lexington and Davidson County, to present to you here and now this deed conveying as a donation three hundred acres of land, together with other considerations, to the National Council, Junior Order United American Mechanics.

Mr. Tunison received the deed, in the name of the Board of Trustees, as Chairman of the National Council, and expressed the thanks of every member of the order in the donation made by Lexington and community.

C. H. Kernan, superintendent of the Junior Orphans' Home at Tiffin, Ohio, was presented, and in a few words he paid tribute to the spirit of the Old North State, which he declared is exceeded nowhere. He said that Lexington would have a better home than Tiffin, for the new home will profit by the mistakes of the old.

Rev. W. L. Hutchins then bade adieu to the visitors, and expressed the wish that they might soon return. Rev. Mr. Hutchins and Dr. C. A. Owens led the assembly in singing the "Doxology," and the benediction was pronounced by Dr. Owens, bringing to a close a day that will be a most memorable one in the history of Lexington, of Davidson County, of North Carolina, of the Junior Order, and above all in the hearts of every man, woman and child in the United States.

As the successful bidder for the new orphanage of the Junior Order, Lexington and surrounding community are indeed fortunate, for the new project will mean much in the future of the city, county and, indeed, the whole State. The need for additional orphanage facilities is well established, and the new home will serve in a great measure to supply this need. As a branch of the home at Tiffin, Ohio, the new orphanage is an earnest of the future of the institution, which is steadily progressing toward a reality.

Plans for the home call for a million dollar project, with accommodations for one thousand children, and all arrangements and preparations are being made with that plan in view. It was stated that immediate construction will care for five hundred children, and will entail expenditure totaling $500,000. Approximately three hundred acres are included in the tract donated to the order, a number of acres being covered with forests of pine, poplar, cedar, forest pines and hardwoods, and it is interesting to note that the timber on some of the land is such that its value is estimated to equal the amount paid for the land.

The site for the orphanage cost $30,000, all of the money for purchase being received from Lexington and Davidson County; Lexington Council No. 21, of the Junior Order, with 724 members, contributed $8,000 toward securing the site. The location is an ideal one, easily accessible to the city of Lexington and also reached in short time from all parts of the Piedmont section. To reach the site from the center of Lexington one travels south on Main Street to Tenth Avenue, turning to the left.

CHAPTER X

RACIAL TYPES OF DAVIDSON COUNTY CITIZENSHIP

1. RACIAL ORIGIN AND RACIAL CHARACTERISTICS

The people of the whole South are 98 per cent pure American stock. North Carolina has almost no foreigners. Davidson County has a people of pure strain of blood. Our people, however, are the product of a mingling of the best blood of Europe. Our ancestors came from overseas to find a new home in a land of religion, of schools and of freedom. When they came here they at once set about attaining these several ends. We citizens of Davidson County, now celebrating the centennial of this great political division of North Carolina, owe an everlasting debt of gratitude to those fine men and women who in the early years laid the foundations of such a fine civilization. Subsequent generations have builded thereupon. Our country is great today largely because of right beginnings. Our people today are a composite of the English, the German, the French, the Scotch-Irish, the Swiss, the Dutch. Each of these nationalities has contributed to the making of the character of the people now composing the citizenship of Davidson County. Some one should write up in full the contribution made by each, and the author hopes that the future will bring out historians who will take an interest in this subject, and give to us records for permanent information. We herewith give an outline study of the Germans, Swiss, and French in the early years of their coming to Piedmont North Carolina, particularly as the subject relates to Davidson County.

Two great historic events in Old World history are to be credited with the emigration of thousands to the New World:

1. The "Thirty Years War" in Germany.
2. The "Revocation of the Edict of Nantes" in France.

The Thirty Years War came finally to a close in the year 1648 with the peace of Westphalia. From this time forward Holland and Switzerland were to be independent; religious freedom was to be granted to the Protestant states of Germany; Alsace was to go to France; and a good share of Pomerania was to come into possession of Sweden.

But while peace came to Germany in 1648 after thirty long years of bloody strife and conflict and warfare, peace came too late to save Germany that which was her rightful heritage—a united and loyal population. As Carlyle says: "The whole land had been tortured, torn to pieces, wrecked and brayed as in a mortar." Two-thirds and more of the population had disappeared through the ravages of a bloody war, and through famine and pestilence as a consequence of war, and through emigration because of the devastation wrought by long continued war. It is said that whole villages were depopulated of all inhabitants except dogs that prowled around deserted homes.

When Henry of Navarre came to the throne of France in 1589 a new era dawned upon that sad and unfortunate country. Under his predecessors the Protestants had been given no privileges, and had been ignominously persecuted. His administration of public affairs brought to the whole land a benign calm after these long wars which had continued through so many years. Under the Edict of Nantes he granted toleration to the Huguenots. This edict became for many years the "Magna Charta" of the French Protestants to which they always appealed for protection. If Henry of Navarre had lived indefinitely the Protestants would have fared well. But he was murdered, and his successors set about to take away from the Huguenots the protection guaranteed by the Edict of Nantes. Cardinal Richelieu, the adviser of Louis XIII, turned his unlimited powers against the Protestants. Finally in 1685 the Edict of Nantes was revoked.

Between the two significant dates 1648 (which marks the close of the Thirty Years War) and 1685 (when the Edict of Nantes was revoked) preparation for the great tide of emigration from France and Germany was being unconsciously made in those two countries. The French Huguenots, on the taking away of their religious liberties by the revocation of the Edict of Nantes, fled to Germany, thinking that they would find an asylum there. France lost much of her best blood through this, but the Huguenots were destined to disappointment in Germany, for religious freedom was in fact a thing unknown there.

England saw in the sad state of these French Huguenots and German Palatines a desirable people with which to settle her great American colonies. Hence liberal inducements were held out to them to come to England and find an asylum. This offer was cheerfully accepted and thousands went over into England, whence they afterwards came to America. Many of these French and German people fled to Holland and afterward to England on the special invitation of the English people. Holland was an independent country at that time, and took a deep interest in her sadly persecuted neighbors, the Palatine Germans and the French. They afterwards went to England at the invitation of Queen Anne.

It happens that the Protestants of these several countries, viz.: France, the Palatinate in Germany and Holland, were nearly all members of the Reformed Church. The Huguenots formed the only Protestant church in France at that time, and that was the Reformed Church. The Electorate in Germany, called the Palatinate, was the German Reformed stronghold. And the Holland people (called the Dutch) were almost exclusively Reformed. But among the German emigrants, especially from outside of the Palatinate, were many Lutherans and Moravians as well as Reformed. There were of course other sects represented, but these three denominations predominated.

England encouraged emigration to America for the purpose of settling her provinces in the New World. This explains England's great interest in her persecuted neighbors. I hope there was also a higher element of goodness in English interest. England wanted colonists for her American provinces, but at the same time she wanted to keep her own population at home. Hence England held out strong inducements to other peoples and nationalities to go to the English colonies in America and become British subjects. There was English selfishness in it; but the hand of God was also in it. "Behind the dim unknown standeth God within the shadow keeping watch above his own."

England intended that these first emigrants should go to her own possessions in America, especially New York and Carolina. Pennsylvania and Delaware were at that time in possession of a private individual, William Penn, by grant of the British government in payment of a debt. But it happened that many of these early emigrants went to Pennsylvania instead of New York or Carolina. The reason of this was that William Penn was very anxious to have his possessions in America also settled, and he offered full religious liberty to all colonists settling in Pennsylvania. The Germans felt that Penn was a near kinsman of theirs, both by blood and religion, because his mother was a Dutch lady of Rotterdam and a member of the Reformed Church. Afterwards Pennsylvania came into possession of the British, and they naturally continued to encourage immigration into that province.

The "Colonial Records" of Pennsylvania record the names of more than 30,000 male immigrants from 1727 to 1776. Counting the women and children there must have been fully 125,000 Germans and Huguenots who landed at the port of Philadelphia within that period. All the men above the age of sixteen years had to take an oath of allegiance to the British crown by signing their names or making their marks to the following declaration:

We subscribers, natives and late inhabitants of the Palatinate upon the Rhine and places adjacent, having transported ourselves and families into this province of Pennsylvania, a colony subject to the crown of Great Britain, in hopes and expectation of finding a retreat and peaceable settlement therein, do solemnly promise and engage that we will be faithful and bear true allegiance to his present Majesty, King George the Second, and his successors, Kings of Great Britain, and will be faithful to the proprietor of this Province; and that we will demean ourselves peaceably to all his said Majesty's subjects, and strictly observe and conform to the laws of England and this Province, to the utmost of our power and the best of our understanding.

It is from these immigrants who came to Pennsylvania that our German ancestors came to North Carolina. Some of them settled for a while in that State and later came south. Others came directly to this State without having taken up a residence in the former State at all. Still others were the sons and daughters of those who settled in Pennsylvania. The records show that our German ancestors affixed their names to the above declaration on coming to the port of Philadelphia. One of my own personal possessions that I prize most highly is a copy of the signature of my paternal great-great-grandfather in German script to the above paper.

The German immigration into North Carolina was most pronounced from 1745 to 1755. The old deeds and grants to individuals and churches recorded in the archives at Raleigh and Columbia and in the old county courthouses form an interesting study. Our German ancestors settled in the most fertile sections, usually the rich creek and river bottoms, of North and South Carolina. They were not slow to gather their people into religious congregations and their children into day schools.

These old deeds and grants give the names of our German ancestors; and these same names are still found

JOHN W. McCRARY

Pioneer Undertaker. Cabinet Maker and Furniture Dealer of Lexington. Eighteen Years Treasurer of Davidson County.

in the counties covering the original territory settled by this nationality. The German settlements do not cover a large section of the State. They are embraced within the present counties of Alamance, Guilford, Randolph, Davidson, Forsyth, Davie, Stokes, Rowan, Stanly, Cabarrus, Lincoln, Catawba, Cleveland, Caldwell and Burke. Of course German settlers went to other sections of the State, but not in large numbers. However, descendants of the original German settlers are now found in nearly all the counties of the State and nearly all the states of the Union.

The names of these Germans are themselves an interesting study. The German name is distinctive, and always reveals the origin of its possessor. Some of them have been changed, translated, or anglicized in such a way as almost to take away all resemblance to the original. As a consequence some families do not know their ancestral history and are utterly ignorant of the fact that they are of German descent. They think they are English, when in fact they are as Dutch as sauerkraut itself. Take the common name Carpenter; that looks quite English, when in fact in this section of North Carolina it is not English at all, but pure German. How does that come about? Through translation of the original name of Zimmerman, which means a carpenter. So also Little and Small are translations of the German name Klein, which means small or little. The name Taylor looks so English that its possessors turn up their noses when it is suggested that they are German. But if the Taylors will just stop to see that the name Taylor is a translation of the German Schneider they will acknowledge themselves of German descent. In German a Schneider is a man who makes garments, hence a tailor. In this State it is commonly corrupted into Snider.

A list of names culled from the Pennsylvania archives will be interesting. These are names of early settlers of German descent in North Carolina, and the names are common in the several original German settlements to this day. Some of them are French rather than German for the reason that there were many French Huguenots among the German immigrants. The name Delap, for instance, is French, and is properly written De Lap. So also Levan (Le Van), often pronounced Lev-an. Some of the more common German names found at the present are Frey, Fritz, Meyer, (Myers), Zimmerman, Kuntz (Coonts), Kuhn (Coon), Diehl (Deal), Hartman, Hoffman (Huffman), Klopp (Clapp), Miller, Syegrist (Sechriest), Jung (Young), Arndt, Hage (Hege), Thar (Darr, Derr), Sauer (Sowers), Kratz (Crotts), Everhart, Lohr, Kress, Christman, Byerly, Wehrle (Whirlow), Weidner (Whitener), Friedle, Michael, Frank, Boger, Suther, Ramsauer, Hedrick, Beck (Peck), Lopp, Rothrock, Leibegood (Livengood), Wildfang (Wilfong), Kern, Zysloop (Siceloff), Schaaf (Shoaf), Conradt (Conrad), Lingle, Berger (Barrier, Berrier, Barger), Wagner, Grubb, Schneider, Huyet (Hyatt), Lantz, Zinck (Sink), Huntsicker, Creim (Grimes), Haffner, Rauch (Rowe), Leonhardt (Leonard), Reinhardt, Fischer, Schaeffer (Shaver), Wentz (Vance), Lutz, Waltzer (Walser), Wahrlick, Jantz (Younts), Weber (Weaver), Hoch (Hoke), Hinkle, Krauss (Crouse), Brinkley.

This list might be multiplied indefinitely. Many of the names of early settlers have entirely disappeared, as is proved by the Raleigh Records, by tombstones in numerous graveyards, and by streams, localities, etc., still bearing these names. For example, in Davidson County is a stream now called "Swearing Creek." There are several traditions of later date as to the origin of this name, none of which is correct. It received its name from a family once living near its head-waters, viz., Swearingen, a name now lost in that community. The name of the stream would still properly be "Swearingen Creek." In the same way another stream is called "Tinker's Creek" from the original family name Tinker, though the Tinkers have all disappeared long ago.

The Germans have given to this section of North Carolina distinctive characteristics. They have been a sturdy, religious, liberty-loving people. They have not made themselves felt in the public affairs of the State as have their English and Scotch-Irish neighbors, but they have given a dignity to their counties which is lacking in some other counties.

There are reasons for their modesty in pushing to the front in public affairs, chief among them being their use of the German language. The Germans have always loved their native tongue. It was spoken in all the homes of the first German settlers in North Carolina, and even to this day there are still living those who can speak the German which they learned from the lips of their mothers. The German is a beautiful language, capable of expressing shades of meaning that no other language can begin to express. It is preeminently the language of theology, poetry and science.

Our German ancestors were slow to give up the tongue of the fatherland. But North Carolina was preeminently an English state. The business of all public offices was conducted in the English language, and hence they were debarred from public office by language. The Germans who came to North Carolina were an agricultural people. Their poetic nature led them to love close communion with Nature and with Nature's God. They were by choice and by nature tillers of the soil. They loved the country and their large farms of hundreds and thousands of acres of land. But they were also a patriotic and liberty-loving people. They always stood ready to heed whatever call their country might make in defense of their adopted land. They even went from the Yadkin and Catawba valleys to assist the mountain people in their conflicts with the Indians. The Germans took a conspicuous part in the Revolutionary War, most of them fighting bravely as private soldiers. But there were prominent leaders and generals among them; in our own State, Barringer, Forney and Cortner. Baron Steuben, of Washington's army, was an elder in the German Reformed Church. In the Civil War the names of General Ramsaur and General Hoke stand out prominently.

It would have been, for one good reason, natural to expect the Germans to be loyal to the British in the Revolution; they had been given homes in a free country by the British, and they had taken oath of allegiance to that country. But they knew by bitter experience what oppression was; and under the eloquence of the German ministers (who for the most part were patriots) they rose up in arms against the British. One of the most thrilling chapters in North Carolina history centers in Rev. Samuel Suther, a German Reformed minister, who was pastor of many

COLONEL G. FOSTER HANKINS, Lexington
Owner and Manager of the Foster Pottery Company

Reformed and Lutheran congregations at the time of the Revolution. He was an ardent patriot and under his fiery eloquence his people enlisted in the American army. He was the pastor of my own great-great-grandfather, Valentine Leonard, who was in General Greene's army. The last battle in which my ancestor was engaged was that of Guilford Court House in March, 1781. Soon afterwards he returned to his home, where in November following he was treacherously and cruelly murdered by Tories in his own home. At the same time another German, Wooldrich Fritz, met a like fate. Their bodies lie side by side in the old Leonard's Church graveyard; the spot is marked by soapstone slabs placed there one hundred and fifty years ago, and also by a tall marble shaft placed there thirty-two years ago by loyal citizens in grateful remembrance.

Perhaps the most marked characteristic of the Germans was their devotion to religion and education. Well nigh all of these Germans were members of the Lutheran, Reformed or Moravian church. The Moravians established a colony at Salem, Forsyth County, took up many thousands of acres of valuable land, established church and school and lived in a common fraternity. In this they had an advantage over their German brethren of the Reformed and Lutheran faith. The latter did not colonize the members of their churches, but individuals selected their own places of residence. Being accustomed to good schools and regular church services at home, they were naturally zealous to enjoy the same privileges in this country. Most of the communities had professional school-teachers among them, but ministers were very scarce. The

Germans brought with them their Bibles, catechisms and hymn-books. They always held religious services, whether they had ministers or not. In the absence of a minister the school-teacher was pressed into service to make an address or read a printed sermon. Often the elders of the church conducted the services. But there were some German ministers in those early years who made visits more or less regularly to all the German settlements. The earliest of the German preachers to make his appearance was Rev. Christian Theus. He preached to the German Reformed and Lutherans in the Carolinas from 1739 to 1775. The Rev. Mr. Martin came in 1759, and the Rev. Mr. Dupert in 1764. Following these came Rev. Samuel Suther in 1768. This is the gentleman of whom Governor Tryon spoke in his journal, saying he heard him preach. The governor appointed him chaplain of the Rowan and Mecklenburg battalion for the reason that these soldiers were nearly all Germans. All the above named ministers were of the Reformed Church, the Reformed being more fortunate in this respect than their Lutheran brethren. The first Lutheran minister who came to the German settlements in North Carolina was Rev. Adolph Nussman, who arrived in 1773. Following him came Rev. C. E. Bernhardt in 1787.

These Reformed and Lutheran Christians lived in delightful fellowship. Many of their churches were union, and to this day a few union churches remain. Theus, Martin, Dupert and Suther (Reformed ministers) dispensed the means of grace also to their Lutheran brethren who had no ministers at that time. The Rev. Mr. Storch (a Lutheran minister) taught theology to George Boger, a Reformed student. It is also known that he indoctrinated a class of catechumens in the Heidelberg catechism and confirmed them as members of the Reformed Church.

With these German settlers religion and education went hand in hand. The schoolhouse always stood hard by the church, and in some cases the same building answered the purposes of both church and schoolhouse. This is natural with a people who believe in and teach educational religion as do the Reformed, Lutheran, and Moravian churches. The three leading German denominations in the State at an early day established their own institutions of higher education: the Moravians at Salem, the Reformed at Newton and Hickory, and the Lutherans at Mount Pleasant, Hickory and Charlotte.

The Germans have always been a music-loving people. To this day the Germans lead the world in the field of sacred composition and musical rendition. One who has never heard the rendition of Christian hymns by a large German congregation has never heard real music.

Just think how many of the world's great musicians have been Germans: Handel, Hayden, Mozart, Beethoven, Wagner, Bach, Gluck, Spohr, Mendelssohn. These are names that stand out bold like stars of the first magnitude, far outshining all others in their magnificent brilliance. The Germans in North Carolina have always been devoted to music. Sweet music always appeals to the German heart.

Everybody's Magazine relates a story like the following: Many years ago, in a town of Salzburg, two little children lived in a cottage surrounded by vines, near a pleasant river. They both loved music, and when only six years old Frederica could play on the harpsichord. But from her little brother such strains of melody would resound through the humble cottage as were never heard before from so young a child. Their father was a teacher of music, and his own children were his best pupils. There came times so hard these children had scarcely enough to eat, but they loved each other and were happy in the simple enjoyment that fell to their lot. One pleasant day they said: "Let us take a walk in the woods. How sweetly the birds sing, and the sound of the river as it flows is like music." So they went. As they were sitting in the shadow of a tree, the boy said thoughtfully: "Sister, what a beautiful place this would be to pray." Frederica asked wonderingly: "What shall we pray for?" "Why, for father and mother," said her brother. "You see how sad they look. Poor mother hardly ever smiles now, and I know it must be because she has not always bread enough for us. Let us pray to God to help us." "Yes," said Frederica, "we will." So these two sweet children knelt down and prayed, asking the Heavenly Father to bless their parents and make themselves a blessing to them. "But how can we help father and mother?" asked the sister. "Why, don't you know?" replied Wolfgang. "My soul is full of music, and by and by I shall play before great people, and they will give me plenty of money, and we will live in a fine house and be happy." At this a loud laugh astonished the boy, who did not know that any one was near them. Turning, he saw a fine gentleman who had just come from the woods.

The stranger made inquiries, which the little girl answered, telling him: "Wolfgang means to be a great musician; he thinks he can earn money, so that we shall no longer be poor." "He may do that when he has learned to play well enough," replied the stranger. Frederica answered: "He is only six years old, but plays beautifully, and can compose pieces." "That can not be," replied the gentleman. "Come to see us," said the boy, "and I will play for you." "I will go this evening," answered the stranger. The children went home and told their story, and the parents seemed much pleased and astonished. Soon a loud knock was heard at the door, and on opening it the little family were surprised to see men bringing in baskets of richly cooked food in variety and abundance. They had an ample feast that evening. Thus God answered the children's prayer. Soon after, while Wolfgang was playing a cantata which he had composed, the stranger entered and stood astonished at the wondrous melody. The father recognized in his guest Francis I, the Emperor of Austria. Not long afterward the family were invited by the Emperor to Vienna, where Wolfgang astonished the royal family by his wonderful powers. At the age of fifteen years Wolfgang was acknowledged by all eminent composers as a master. This was the great German composer, Wolfgang Mozart. He was a good Christian as well as a great musician. The simple trust in God which he had learned in childhood never forsook him. In a letter to his father he says: "I never lose sight of God; I acknowledge His power and dread His wrath; but at the same time I love to admire His goodness and mercy to His creatures. He will never abandon His servant. By the fulfillment of His will mine is satisfied." The simple trusting faith of the young musician was remarkable, and it teaches old and young a lesson.

Of such a race of people—liberty-loving, patriotic, devoted to religion and education, lovers of music and poetry—of such descent as this are the Germans of North Carolina. Blood is thicker than water; blood will tell. The North Carolina Germans have taken their rightful place in these later years in the social, business, educational, political and religious interests of this great State. The Germans of this State love North Carolina. The people of no race, of no nationality, surpass the Germans in their love and devotion to the State of their birth and their choice. Every one of them will heartily give this toast:

> Here's to the land of the long-leaf pine,
> The summer land where the sun doth shine,
> Where the weak grow strong and the strong grow great,
> Here's to down home, the Old North State.

2. Life of the People, Manners and Customs

The general means of transportation in those days was by wagon or on horseback. "To ride in a buggy," to quote J. W. McCrary, "was to be considered an aristocrat." The stage passed, however, each day between Salisbury and Greensboro and was the means of passenger travel for long distances. The arrival of the stage was the leading daily event in Lexington. As its four horses trotted up with the sumptuous appearing vehicle, the village turned out to see the sight. Often the driver got down from his high seat, while the crowd followed him to hear the news from the neighboring towns, perhaps to read the Greensboro *Patriot* or Raleigh *Register,* weekly papers in those days; or if the crowd was lucky the driver might have a Washington or New York paper ten days old from which one could get the very latest news.

At the same time our antecedents of 1825 and 1830 did not lack other amusements. In 1831, William Kennedy, High Sheriff, reported to the County Court, the amount of special taxes collected on: "Stage players, sleight of hand performers, rope dancers, tumblers, wire dancers, company of circus riders, equestrian performers and exhibitions of natural or artificial curiosities." First Mondays, being the days when the County Court met, were always big days. But the largest festival of the year perhaps was the general muster. There were no townships. The county was divided into a dozen or more military districts with a captain over each. In these districts two petit musters were held each year by company. The county was divided into two sections, each commanded by a colonel. The general muster for the upper part of the county was held near Midway Church, while in southern Davidson it was held in Cotton Grove Township near the old Palmer place. Everybody attended; old friends met again, the young people socially, while the militia drilled and the venerable colonels commanded with due dignity. The young men of school age organized a game of "high ball," and some of our elders report that on occasion a horse race or two was staged with a few wagers on the side to lend interest.

Considering them as a whole, the people of a hundred years ago in Davidson were industrious. While the slave-owning class did not as a general rule find time to do much manual labor themselves, they saw to it that every one about them was kept busy. There was of course obviously one danger in the social system—the creation of an aristocratic caste which was no more popular among the non-slaveowning population of the South than it was in the North. Early in the history of Davidson County, there was a division of sentiment among our people as to the slavery question, and as a result between 1840 and 1860, many of the best of our people went west seeking new homes on government lands rather than live where men were "half slave and half free." However, many of the slave-owners were noble people, dealing with a just and gentle hand over those whose lives and bodies belonged to them. In many cases it was not so much what the master did to his slaves that set back the march of human progress; it was rather what the ownership and use of slaves did for the master. Only a small portion of the county was cultivated in those days and that rather badly. The principal market for surplus crops of cotton, corn and wheat was at Fayetteville which was reached by a plank road. The needs of our people were small; they were for the most part self-sustaining. Homespun clothes were the rule and the women generally knew no finery other than they were able to create with their own needles from the flax and cotton grown by the men. This self-reliance in material things made our forefathers free and independent in all things. But they were law-abiding and religious. Honesty was the

RACIAL TYPES OF DAVIDSON CITIZENSHIP 151

rule in dealings with each other. Shame and disgrace were coupled with crime and this had a greater effect than the fear of punishment. It was not the physical pain of the pillory that the offender dreaded half so much as becoming the object of ridicule and disgrace in the eyes of his county people.

The records of the Superior Court of Law are replete with strange matters and things that interest us, which at the same time show a step in our evolution.

Beginning in March, 1824, only two sessions of the Superior Court of Law were held each year. At the first term, Judge John R. Donnell presided, while Edward Jones prosecuted as Solicitor.

James Wiseman was appointed Sheriff and Benjamin D. Rounsaville, Clerk. Edwin Paschal was Clerk and Master in Equity. The following was the Superior Court jury: Benjamin Sherwood, Jacob Brummell, Amos Wright, William Peggott, William Douthet, Matthew Macy, Jacob Black, Beverly Surratt, George Myers son of Peter, John Bowers, Robert Wilson, George Sours, Robert Green, John Spurgeon, Isaac Wiseman, John Lopp, Benjamin Billings, Michael Smith, Samuel Green, William Kennedy, Ezekial Teague, George Hardman, John Darner, Stephen Gisford, George Kanoy, Mington Pickett, Frederick Young, George Myers son of Jacob, John Michael, Jr., Gotlieb Grimes and George Cross.

The County Court was a combination of our present Board of County Commissioners and Superior Court. The County Court also tried petty misdemeanors like our recorder's court system. The Superior Court of Law tried appeals from the County Court and had jurisdiction in grave crimes and felonies, and certain civil cases. For the first quarter of a century in our county history, from the records of this court, it would seem our ancient kinsmen were law-abiding to a great degree. The court rarely lasted more than three or four days, or on an average only eight days in the year. There were not so many laws but they seem to have been well enforced. Largely they were the old laws of England.

The defendant in one case was convicted of grand larceny, punishable then by death. Being asked why the death sentence should not be pronounced, he prayed the benefit of clergy, which was granted. Judgment by Judge Nash was that the prisoner "be taken to the public whipping post between the hours of 12 and 2 p.m. and there receive thirty lashes on his bare back and then go to jail until he paid the costs of the prosecution." Benefit of clergy came to us from the English law. In olden times the church intervened to save the criminal, claiming he was a clerk or in orders subject to the church courts, which if true freed him from the civil courts. The ancient church then took the prisoner away behind closed doors, put all his fellow clerks on the jury, took the testimony of the defendant's witnesses only and turned the defendant loose. However, if the crime was of an infamous sort, heinous in the eyes of the law, then the benefit of clergy was not allowed, it being a privilege in the discretion of the court. And only once in his life could a man obtain it.

Before Judge Norwood in 1826 a defendant was convicted of forgery, an offense also punishable by death. The guilty man was sentenced to receive thirty-nine lashes on his bare back that day and thereafter on June 20 he was to stand in the public pillory between the hours of ten and twelve, was then to pay a fine of ten cents and be imprisoned six months and until the costs were paid. The whipping was always administered by the sheriff or his deputy on the culprit's bare back with stout lashes. The prisoner's hands were tied behind his head to the post. Often the man receiving punishment could be heard to scream for a long distance. At pillory or stocks the culprit was placed with his head fastened between two boards which closed around his neck, his hands being likewise passed through holes in the board and his feet tied. The pillory and whipping post were always placed where the crowd could witness the punishment. After receiving his beating at the hands of the law, on being liberated it is said that the suffering man would flee from this place of pain not unlike a beaten dog. Such were the stern methods of our forefathers in their efforts to make men obey the law. To us it seems barbarous perhaps and brutal, but does ten years in the penitentiary serve any better purpose? I dare say fewer men were twice whipped then than are now serving a plurality of terms.

The case of Jesse Upton, convicted of murdering his wife, at September term 1826 before Judge Joseph Daniel, shows that less than a hundred years ago learned lawyers allowed superstition of the rankest kind to creep into the law courts. Upton's case came from Randolph, where he could not get a fair trial. Frederick Nash was counsel for the accused. Upton was promptly convicted and prayed for a new trial on these grounds:

154 CENTENNIAL HISTORY OF DAVIDSON COUNTY

Thirdly. The defendant's counsel offered the Almanack to show what time the moon fulled and changed. The court stated to counsel in the hearing of the jury that it was laid down by modern authors that the moon had no influence upon the system in producing or increasing mental derangement and that the ancient doctrine was deemed a superstition. But the court let the counsel introduce the Almanack and examined two physicians as to their opinion what effect the moon had on the human system in increasing or affecting a derangement of the mind. The counsel remarked fully on this testimony to the jury. The court when it came to charge the jury gave no opinion upon the effect of this evidence.

The Supreme Court gave Upton a new trial and his case was removed to Guilford. From Hon. W. C. Hammer we learned that Upton was convicted and hanged in Guilford County. So it was that neither the moon nor removal to three counties saved this guilty man, though many people believed him insane at the time.

Except for the more frequent use of capital punishment, the penalty for offenses was lighter than now. Fighting was frequently indulged in, but such personal battles were fairly fought, deadly weapons being only used to kill. Under the old English law, an affray was punished with the fine of a six pence. Many cases appear on our old records where the venerable justices in trying such cases imposed the rather unusual fine of "six cents," following, it seems, the old English custom. The sentence for manslaughter and grand larceny was generally by burning the letter "M" or "L" in the hand and sometimes also on the brawn of the left thumb. Slaves were generally punished less severely than free men. In 1831, for example, Judge Swain sentenced Washington Taburn for larceny to thirty lashes on his bare back thrice to be repeated on three separate days, while Daniel, a slave, for manslaughter was awarded only thirty-nine lashes and then discharged.

Referring to the early laws and lawyers, we are indebted to T. B. Eldridge, former citizen of Lexington and former owner of *The Dispatch,* for the following interesting item. Mr. Eldridge says:

James R. Dodge, mentioned as the county attorney, was somewhat of a celebrity. He was a nephew of Washington Irving. Subsequent to his official career in Davidson he was appointed clerk of the Supreme Court of North Carolina. In the days of Dodge the lawyers used to make the rounds of the far-extended circuit with the judge. On one occasion, as related in the *History of Western North Carolina,* when Judge Swain was holding court in one of the western counties, there were present besides Dodge, Samuel Hillman and Thomas Dews. While Dodge was addressing the jury, Judge Swain was reminded of a punning epitaph which he had read. Copying it on a scrap of paper, he passed it around among the lawyers, provoking much merriment. When Dodge had taken his seat the paper was handed to him. This is what met his eye:

EPITAPH ON JAMES R. DODGE

Here lies one Dodge, who dodged all good,
And dodged a lot of evil;
But after dodging all he could
He could not dodge the devil.

Recognizing the writing of the judge, and connecting the lawyers present with the joke, Dodge tried his hand at rhyming, with this result:

EPITAPH ON THREE LAWYERS

Here lie a Hillman and a Swain—
Their lot let no man choose.
They lived in sin and died in pain,
And the devil got his Dews.

If it be true that he laughs best who laughs last, the county attorney for Davidson had the best of this joke.

There was no trouble in getting the best men to hold county office. The small places even were frequently held by leading citizens. Neither the job of tax lister nor election judge went begging.

The following were inspectors of elections in 1833: Clemmonsville—Henry Eakel, John Johnson, Abraham Brindle; Haines—John Swicegood, Barney Idol, John Beckerdite; Hampton—Henry Grubb, Daniel Weisner, Richard Ellis; Lexington—Henderson Wilson, Isaac Kinney, Alfred Hargrave; Wards—Joseph Goss, Ransom Harris, Philip Frank; Daniels—James Adderton, William Burkhead, Tarvis Daniels; Lees—Frederick Goss, Valentine Hoover, John Lee.

The tax assessors for 1833 were: Alfred Hargrave, William Adderton, William Raper, Andrew Swicegood, Abraham Brindle, Valentine Hoover, Joseph Waggoner, Philip Hedrick, Jesse Holmes, John Wade, Peter Owens, Henry Grubb, John W. Lindsay, Levin Gordy, Jesse Hill, Daniel Weisner.

In early days our county had three coroners appointed each year by the County Court. Those for 1832 were: Gesham Tussey, William Adderton, Samuel Cecil.

In addition to the two colonels who commanded in the county, Davidson County had a Brigadier General of Militia who was in charge of the two regiments. General Gaither held this office for a long time.

Constitutional Convention of 1835

On November 9, 10, and 11, 1835, an election was held in Lexington on the question of calling a Constitutional Convention. John A. Hogan and John L. Hargrave were elected members of this Convention from Davidson. Davidson cast 1,014 votes for the Convention and only 47 against it, and later by almost the same vote this county ratified the amendments submitted by the Convention. The amendments were of no great importance. The two political parties in those days were the Whig and Democratic. The county was generally carried by the Whigs. For example, in 1836 the county gave 583 votes for Hugh L. White (Whig) against 109 for Martin Van Buren (Democrat) for President; in 1840 there were 1,441 votes for William H. Harrison (Whig) and 390 for Van Buren, while in 1844 Henry Clay (Whig) received 1,091 votes in Davidson County and James K. Polk (Democrat) 610.

Growth and Progress

At the end of the first ten years, the new county of Davidson had made progress along material lines. Industries began to spring up. Mining operations were engaged in at the Conrad Hill gold mine, and Silver Hill was being prospected. About 1839 Lexington had its first cotton factory, called the Lexington Manufacturing Company. The factory was located near the site of the present colored Baptist Church, was made of brick with a number of tenement houses for the operatives. One of these houses is still standing. After running for some time the first cotton factory was burned down and was never rebuilt.

In 1827 Lexington obtained a charter from the Legislature for the organization of a town. It provided for the annual election of five commissioners who had to be landowners. Other town officers were: a magistrate of police, a treasurer, and a constable. The city taxes were limited to twenty-five cents on the poll and ten cents on the $100 property valuation, which money could be used for streets or for whatever purpose the city fathers considered for "the prosperity and advancement" of the town. The commissioners were also empowered to appoint a patrol consisting of all white males between ages twenty-one and fifty, to be divided into companies which by turns were ordered to patrol the town.

Sheriff William Kennedy's report for 1833 shows something of the financial condition of the county. There were 310,939 acres of land valued at $794,904. This gave the average value of land per acre at $2.56. New land was entered between 1815 and 1833 amounting to 3,310 acres. There were 1,267 free polls and 681 black polls in the county. The free males from twenty-one to forty-five years of age numbered 1,444, the slaves from twelve to fifty years of age were 979, and the total poll tax for the county was $455.53. The total State revenue from the county was: land tax, $433.76; town property tax, $15.25; poll tax, $361.15; store tax, $90.24; peddler tax, $56.40; shows, $28.30; gate tax, $4.70. Thus the total amount paid by the Sheriff to the State for that year was only $1,022.13.

The cheapness of our early government is due to many things, mainly that they had neither public schools nor improvements. Road taxes were unknown and the State spent little or nothing on internal improvement. In spite of these handicaps, Davidson made progress, increased in population and industry. There were influences at work in the county for the betterment of living conditions, for improvement in methods of agriculture. A hundred years ago Davidson had quite a number of leading men, prominent abroad as well as at home, who were working in season and out for the upbuilding of the county and its people.

A Real Christmas in Dixie

With the flying years, new faces come and go and customs change. The manner of observing Christmas in the South is not the same today that it once was, though there still lingers in many hearts a recollection of Christmas festivities as observed in the days before the great War Between the States. The emancipation proclamation had a wondrous effect in changing all customs of domestic life in the old-fashioned homes of Dixie. Before the war the colored people were a different folk from what they are now. The social life of every plantation was very greatly influenced by the institution of slavery. People not acquainted with the customs of those days will never have a just appreciation of the relation between master and slave. The writer of this book was born after that awful conflict; my eyes saw the light of day after peace in name at least had come to our distracted land. But those whose lives looked back into the days of slavery brought down to all of us younger people a correct knowledge of conditions as they prevailed in the former days. Indeed on many plantations freedom for the negroes did not bring about much change. The cabins formerly their homes remained the places of their habitation. Thousands of slaves refused to leave kind masters and mistresses, and the work went on just about as in former days. Slavery, in a sense such a curse to the South, has been greatly misunderstood and consequently to this day in words is greatly abused by those not acquainted with its bright side. It developed many great characters in both races, but this type of greatness is rapidly passing away because the conditions which gave rise to it are rapidly passing away. The old men of the South who were slave-owners are growing fewer as the years rapidly pass. Likewise it is only occasionally that we meet an old-time colored man who politely takes off his hat in the presence of a white person and assures you with evident great pride: "Yes, suh, Boss; I's a ole-time slav-ry nigger." Those who know the "ole-time slav-ry nigger" are the ones who honor him most, and they are also the ones who desire that the rising generations of both races shall preserve the memory of his great virtues.

The highest and most important holiday and festival of those days throughout the South was Christmas. It was a day and season of supreme joy and festivity not only in the "big house," but also in the humblest cabin of the plantation. It was a day looked forward to by every one, little and big, black and white, for weeks and weeks before its arrival. Great preparations were made on all hands for its proper celebration. It was the one time in the year for everybody of both races to be happy. Good cheer and merry-making prevailed everywhere, and all hearts were light and gay. It was the prevailing custom to allow all the colored people a holiday of absolute freedom from work not only for the twenty-fifth of December, but also for as many days thereafter as the "yule-log" should remain unconsumed in the fireplace of the great mansion. To prolong the life of the yule-log the colored people were allowed license to resort to innocent trickery; accordingly sometimes for days preceding Christmas eve, this particular piece of wood having been selected with great care with reference to its fire resisting qualities, it was left immersed in the creek flowing through the plantation. And then on the eventful day with great ceremony the log was carried by some of the strong "young bucks" and carefully deposited in the back of the fireplace of the "big house." There it simmered and sang and steamed, but burned very slowly for many a day, thus giving prolonged life to the merry holiday season. This was the old-fashioned South; this was Dixie in its high tide of glory. Those were the good old days when master and slave thoroughly understood each other and entered the one into the other's sympathies.

It must not be inferred that the religious significance was forgotten by the white and colored people of those days. Christmas meant then the birthday of Christ in a splendid sense, sense of which I very greatly fear we have lost the spirit in these days. There was the hour of worship in the great house when all met to read the story of the Christ-child's birth made known by the angels to the shepherds on the plains of Bethlehem; to offer prayers in thanksgiving for the new-born Saviour; to sing the glad Christmas carols; to receive presents from the beautiful Christmas tree; to extend mutual greetings of gladness and good cheer. The people exhorted each other in song:

Come and worship, come and worship;
Worship Christ, the new-born King.

The curtain has long since fallen upon the customs and manners of the old South. The present generation is living in a new South. The big plantations have been broken up into many smaller farms. Towns and cities, rich with great cotton mills and other manufacturing enterprises, have sprung up as by magic all over Dixie. Steam and electric lines thread the whole South, and every section is a busy hive of activity. Only the memory of the old past survives. But especially at the Christmas-tide memory calls back the beautiful customs of former years, and dwells with delight upon the manner in which the men and women, boys and girls, of those happy times observed the birthday of our Saviour.

3. Representative Types

From the forming of the county until his death in 1868, Dr. William R. Holt was identified with every forward movement of Davidson County and its people. He helped fix the present county boundaries. He took a prominent part in locating the first courthouse and in the location of the county seat at Lexington. In 1827 he became a member of the County Court, and was at once elected chairman of the court. He continued a member of the County Court for many years, serving as chairman time and time again. He was a member of the County Finance Committee. He was State Senator for Davidson in 1838. He helped plan and supervise the building of the first county home. His home in Lexington was the same as the residence of the late Mr. and Mrs. C. A. Hunt, Sr., on Main Street.

But he spent only part of his time in town, for he had large farms about Linwood. Most of the facts as to Dr. Holt are taken from *Biographical History of North Carolina*, by Ashe and Weeks.

William Rainey Holt was born October 30, 1798, in Alamance County, the son of Michael Holt and Rachel Rainey. He graduated at the University of North Carolina before he was nineteen years old. He attended Jefferson Medical College in Philadelphia where he graduated. He located at Lexington and was a leading physician of the county until his death.

Dr. Holt was a student and a great scholar all his life. He often returned to Philadelphia for special courses in order to keep abreast of his profession. He became eminent as a physician, and his advice was often sought throughout North Carolina. Dr. Holt was married in 1822 to Mary Gizeal Allen, who lived ten years and bore him five children. One of his daughters married Joseph Erwin, of Morganton, and another married Colonel Ellis, a brother of Governor Ellis.

Two years after the death of his first wife, Dr. Holt married Louisa Allen Hogan, daughter of Colonel William Hogan, whose father, John Hogan, was a Revolutionary officer. Nine children were born of the second marriage. Of these William Michael Holt died in 1863 at Richmond, an officer of the Confederate army; Eugene Randolph, being taken prisoner, died on Johnson's Island in 1865 when just twenty-one years of age; Claudia E. Holt married D. C. Pearson, Esq., Frances married C. A. Hunt, Sr., of Lexington, and Amelia Holt married William E. Holt, whose son is W. E. Holt, Jr., of Lexington.

Though deeply occupied with his practice as a physician, Dr. Holt purchased a plantation in the Jersey settlement near the Yadkin River, adjoining the lands of Governor Ellis and Anderson Ellis. He named the plantation Linwood. Dr. Holt was a great student of farming. He believed the South would supply the world with cotton, and he entered with zeal into cotton growing. He fertilized his fields, using the most improved methods, thorough ditching, deep plowing, turning under clover and peas until neighboring farmers thought him somewhat demented, not realizing the science of his method. He studied the new farm implements and introduced them into Davidson County. He was a highly successful farmer. He had improved cattle and sheep. Dr. Holt owned a large number of slaves, but he was careful of their comfort and saw to their good treatment.

After seven years of unceasing labors, Dr. Holt's Jersey farm was one of the agricultural wonders of the county; his meadows leveled and well drained, yielding fine crops of hay, clover, and grass, and the wheat and cotton fields were the talk of the State. "Not a stone was to be found in the fields, nor a bramble nor a brush or weed, scientific culture had eliminated everything in the way of a nuisance—everything useless had given way to the useful." Agriculturists from Baltimore and Richmond visited the Linwood farm and urged him to write his experiences for publication. Among the famous men who visited Dr. Holt was the historian Bancroft, who went to witness the conquest of nature and the scientific art of compelling her to yield up her resources.

Dr. Holt became so interested in his farm that he had almost given up his practice when in 1857 and 1858 an epidemic of typhoid fever broke out in the State, spreading over Davidson County. He gave himself back to his profession with all his powers, insisting on strict hygiene, clean wells, and almost modern sanitation. By putting squads of men to work cleaning up and whitewashing all buildings on his farm, the scourge passed over his laborers. However, despite all his precautions, he lost two of his own sons by the dread disease, one being at home and the other at Chapel Hill.

Dr. Holt's fame as a farmer was more than statewide. He helped promote the North Carolina Agricultural Society and, succeeding Chief Justice Ruffin, he was president of this Society continuously until his death.

He was likewise interested in railroad development in the State. When the North Carolina Railroad Company was chartered he joined hands with Governor John M. Morehead, W. S. Ashe, and others in putting the project through. He had much to do with the course of this railroad through Davidson County and two stations were named for him, Linwood and Holtsburg.

His boundless energies reached out and included an interest in the cotton factories of his brother, Edwin M. Holt; also the Fries at Winston. He stood for the erection of a hospital for the insane and took the lead for a State public school system. His farseeing mind reached out much ahead of his time, and he assisted in laying the foundation of many good works which have since borne fruit for humanity.

In politics, Dr. Holt belonged to the Democratic household, and when the war came on he was a strong secessionist. His brother, Edwin M. Holt, and his friend, Governor John M. Morehead, were both just as strong against the cause of the South, being ardent Whigs. But Dr. Holt continued strong in his friendship for them and attended Governor Morehead at Greensboro during his last illness.

Dr. Holt's home in Lexington, on the highway between Greensboro and Salisbury, was a stopping place for many of the distinguished people of the old South. He was of commanding personality, of unconquerable will, but at the same time kindly and courteous. He was much broken by the stress of war, but continued to supervise his farming until his death from rheumatism in 1868. Davidson County owes much to this great spirit, whose forceful mind and sympathetic heart were occupied for forty-six years in laying broad and deep the foundation of our county government, our county health and industrial progress, agricultural advance, and general welfare.

John W. McCrary was a man characterized by the highest integrity. And there is nothing higher than that to be said of a good man. Having been born in 1839, he lived through the long period of four and a quarter score years. What a long life for service to one's fellow-men and to the Kingdom of God! His father died when he was four years of age, and his mother when he was ten. The orphan boy was industrious and devoted to his work. He made the best possible use of the meager educational advantages afforded by those trying years. Mr. McCrary learned the cabinet-maker's trade. Later in life he located in Thomasville, where for four years he conducted his cabinet and undertaker's business. He made all his furniture and coffins by hand in the early years. In 1865 Mr. McCrary located in Lexington to conduct the same line of business he had followed in Thomasville. He was in business here practically for half a century. His line of business brought him into many homes and into touch with many people. He conducted funerals all over this county, and in Randolph, Guilford, Montgomery, Forsyth, Davie, Rowan, and even beyond the limits of these counties. Mr. McCrary was one of the first men whom this writer learned to know. I recall his coming into our home at the death of my grandmother. He was a man of unfailing sympathy. During my public life I have been with him in many funerals. I never knew him to show more consideration to one family than another. He treated rich and poor alike.

Mr. McCrary's business necessarily imposed upon him many hardships. There were no good roads in the early years. There were no automobiles. There were no protecting comforts in travel, such as we have now. Many of his funerals took him from home whole days, and some of them two whole days. It was common for him to be out late into the night. He was exposed to cold and heat. I have ridden with him on the high seat of the old-fashioned horse-drawn hearse when both of us were well-nigh numb with the extreme cold. On more than one occasion Mr. McCrary drove through freezing rain until his clothes became stiff with ice and were frozen to the seat. He endured hardships like the old preachers who traveled over the same country he did. His life was fraught with blessing to those whom he served. Mr. McCrary always stood for the highest and best in the Christian life. His creed embraced honesty, virtue, nobility, cleanness, purity of thought and act, faith in Jesus Christ, devotion to the Kingdom of God. To some people his piety seemed stern, and indeed it was of a puritanical type. His religion was rugged and strong.

This strong man served his county eighteen years as a public official, showing that its citizens loved and trusted him. His name indicates the family name as Scotch, or Scotch-Irish. But blood from other sources coursed through his veins. He had many characteristics of the Palatine Germans and the French Huguenots, inherited through the maternal side of his ancestors. He lived to see Lexington grow from a small village to its present proportions as a respectable city. The citizens of today need to be reminded that it is to men such as he, of rugged Christian character and true loyalty to the community interests, we owe a good county in which to live.

The Early Years of County History as Seen by J. W. McCrary

I came to Lexington in 1865, right after the close of the war. I was raised about two miles from here, just above Lexington. General Leach was here when I came. John Welborn came a few years after. B. A. Kittrell was here. There was a young lawyer here who raised a valuable army, who was killed, but I cannot think of his name. Kittrell and Leach were the only two lawyers. Leach lived in the old house in the section called "tater row" (right about where A. L. Sink's store now is). Rev. William Hamner sold

DR. R. LEE REYNOLDS, Lexington
Dental Surgery, Director Shoaf-Sink Hosiery Mill Company,
Member firm of Reynolds & Raper Automobile Dealers

the property where R. L. McCrary now lives and took in payment thereof Confederate money: a man by the name of Hillyard bought it; and then Colonel Henderson bought it from Hillyard.

Dr. R. L. Payne, Sr., and his father lived here, Dr. Dusenberry lived here, was raised here and practiced. Dr. A. A. Hill came from Statesville, located here, raised his army. Dr. Charlie Payne practiced here a little while and later went to Washington as a minister of the Gospel.

The Methodist Church was around the corner, and the Presbyterian Church was just where it is now. The Episcopal Church was where Webster Koonts's house is. Old man J. P. Stimpson was the leading man here at the time. Rev. R. J. Barrett was the first Methodist preacher, this was some time later. A Mr. Johnson was the first Presbyterian preacher; he stayed here a long, long time, and went from here to Winston.

I was born the 3d of August, 1839, on the farm up the Salem road. I had three brothers: Levi, Alexander, and William. I had five sisters: Eva married Henry Heitman; Elizabeth married Andrew Stewart; Isabella married Jacob Stewart; Emmaline married a Mr. Clark, a Union soldier, and lived in Indianapolis after the Civil War. My father's name was John McCrary; my grandfather's name also was John McCrary. My great grandfather lived in Pennsylvania, came from Ireland. My mother was named Sarah Raker. My grandmother and grandfather lived on the farm up on the left-hand side of the Winston-Salem road, still farther back from the road. My grandfather came from Ireland to Pennsylvania and then came out here. My father died in 1843, and my mother died in 1849.

I joined the church when I was nineteen years old. I was married the 27th of September, 1860, to Drusilla Leonard, daughter of Daniel Leonard. We were married at the old Daniel Leonard house. R. K. Perryman was Clerk of the Court, and I saw him at a sale the day before and he asked me about when we were going to be married and said he wanted to marry us, and I told him when and he came over. We had a big dinner. Old Mrs. Leonard was living; she was a Wagoner. Mrs. McCrary's mother once saw Daniel Boone. She was a strong, wonderful woman. The old man's name was Daniel; he died in 1852. We lived in Thomasville when we were first married. When we were first married my wife stayed at home and I worked up here with Rev. Henry Heitman. I moved to Thomasville in March 1861, bought a home over there, down in this end of town where the Thomasville Chair Company now is. The railroad was built in 1854. The biggest rain I ever saw was the day the first train ran. Governor Graham delivered the address at the depot. It cleared off about ten o'clock and he spoke then. The trains had probably been running before this, but this was the celebration, the 4th day of July. There was a public dinner.

I lived in Thomasville four years and was in the cabinet business. I made all the furniture I sold, all the coffins, etc. Alfred Myers worked for me in Thomasville and worked with me here two or three years. I had a hearse while in Thomasville, just a home-made thing. The old Day family lived on the Dave Fritts place. I knew old lady Katie Day. They sold out and moved to Illinois. Nathan Parks was another undertaker here; he died just after I came and I buried him. Then his son, Albert, took up the business and sold it out to me. He then married and moved to Texas. My first home was right across the street from where I now live on North Main Street. I bought the lot from A. C. Hege, who had the power of attorney to sell the Caldcleugh property. The old Hunt store was the first store here, right where Jule Smith's place is. Old man Andrew Hunt also had a store; then King & Hege's store came next. King & Hege built their store. And Bob Foster's store was where Bob Leonard's property is; then there were several little offices along there. Old man Lowe's store was where Fred Thompson's store is now. Eli Penry's store was where the Lexington Drug Store is now. The Nooe store was where T. J. Grimes's property is now; the firm was Earnhardt & Nooe. The old hotel was down about where Dr. Vestal's office is. David Loftin was elected Sheriff in 1856.

The first convention I remember—the Whigs had a convention here and nominated J. U. Stone for Sheriff. Old man Henry Walser was elected to the Senate. Loftin was defeated by Stone for Sheriff. Stone got out of the way and they put up Tom Daniels, and Thomas announced himself an independent candidate. And then Loftin was elected Sheriff and he held the office for a long time, even after the war. Loftin was a Whig. After the war he was run as a Democrat and elected. I. K. Perryman was County Clerk. Mr. Heitman was Clerk Superior Court. Heitman stayed in until after the Civil War and Johnson defeated him. Johnson and his wife taught school in the old brick academy, which was right in front of the M. E. parsonage. About four hundred or five hundred people lived here and there were about ten or twelve thousand people in the county.

I remember the courthouse right in the middle of the street. It was a brick building, two stories, with courtroom up-stairs and offices below. The main entrance was from the upper end, with a hall straight through, two doors at each end. This was torn away in 1854 and the other one built. The brick for second courthouse were made just off the Salem road, just below the cemetery. I remember when the present courthouse was built. They used to say it was the best courthouse in the State. It was burned down in 1866. Some tried to leave the impression that the Yankees burned it. Several of the Yankees stayed in the courthouse and had offices there. I suppose they just took possession of them. Burk and Estes, two Yankee officers, did not stay there. They had a store in the Penry house. In the dust and ashes they found some gold. The Yankee camp at that time was all around here, and tents stood everywhere. They kept their horses about where Sam Cecil lived. The horses were branded with "U. S." They sold them at auction right about where Jule Smith's building now is. The first jail was right where Cindy Davis (colored) used to live. There was a whipping-post. I attended the general muster. The petty muster was out at the Michael place. The general muster was right about the Long place at Midway Church. I remember they had a cannon. In 1862 we had a draft. That was the first draft, and I was drafted. They put the names into a hat and some one drew them out, and I was one of the six drafted. The old militia was controlling things then. A man who had already volunteered came and asked me if I wanted a substitute and said he would go for $50; and I went over and got the money from Mr. Hege.

Judge Pearson, Chief Justice of North Carolina, began an investigation and he decided if a man hired a substitute that he had complied with the law. I went up there and had myself arrested and T. C. Ford was an officer and went with me; he turned to Mr. Ford and said: "Now, the Supreme Court meets next week in Raleigh and I shall hold you responsible until the case is decided. I don't know how the other two will decide." They met and one of the justices agreed with him and the other disagreed. They had Congress to meet and the Confederate Congress passed an act to take in all these men. Vance was Governor. I had the exemption paper I got from Raleigh. Captain Berrier came in as a private; he was a militia captain and was made a private of the Home Guards. We were called out by the Governor. I was in the Home Guards then. Some went to Wilmington, I went to Goldsboro. When we got to Kinston there were not enough to make two full companies and they sent half of the commissioned officers back, and I was sent back. We went down there right after the Yankees burned the bridge; that was in 1864. Joe Sowers and Jake Sowers were in Charleston in the navy. Hugh Clodfelter, Hugh Smith, John Leonard, brother of Joe A. Leonard, and Reuben McCrary were killed.

When I was a boy we would go to John P. Hedrick's mill; sometimes to Freedle's mill.

The first paper published was *The Lexington and Yadkin Flag*. It was printed right where the old Harris house now is. James A. Long built it to print the paper in. In about 1850 he ran another paper also, *The Little Adder*—free suffrage. This was the time when a man could not vote unless he owned fifty acres of land or was a freeholder.

The postoffice was in A. C. Hege's place. He was postmaster. I was in the undertaker's business from 1861 to 1914. Dr. J. C. Leonard preached about half of the funerals I conducted after he was old enough to preach. Henry Heitman preached several. Joseph Miller preached many funerals in his time. Old Rev. Thomas Long preached a number.

Who were considered the rich men around here? The Hargraves. Jake Lopp had many negroes. The Caldcleughs were wealthy at one time, but that was before I came. I was elected Treasurer of Davidson County in 1880, and was in office for eighteen years.

I remember going to Winston one time when I was a boy. I never went to Greensboro or Salisbury when I was a boy. I worked hard as a boy on the farm, plowed, etc. My first recollection is with a hoe. I never could milk a cow. We played marbles, bull-pen, base-ball, townball, etc. Phil Everhart had a still at his house and I would go there and get a pint of brandy for ten cents and put paint in it and stain the coffins. I went to Sunday school when I was a boy. When they did not have it at Ebenezer I would come down to Lexington. Jim Long taught the Young Men's Bible Class. He married a Caldcleugh and lived up here in the old Lowe house. The first bank was down where Conrad & Hinkle's store is now. B. A. Kittrell was president and C. F. Lowe was cashier. This was in 1850. The bank was there during the Civil War, and failed during the war. The Bank of Lexington was the name of it. They issued money. Jones and Ketchum came in about 1880 from Michigan and that was the beginning of the Bank of Lexington as we have it now. R. S. Dobson was agent of the Southern Railway; then followed Holt, and then Captain Trice.

Racial Types of Davidson Citizenship 177

S. S. Bailey, of Chandler, was one of the most interesting and remarkable men of Davidson County. For ten successive years after the overthrow of the carpetbag rule in North Carolina, he was a member of the Board of County Commissioners and sat through various terms with such men as B. B. Roberts, Alfred Hargrave, Samuel Jones, H. C. Hedrick, Daniel Ware, A. R. Craver and M. B. Orrell. When he was made commissioner the county debt was $18,000 and the Treasury was bankrupt. Such a thing as county credit was unknown. The members of the board had to stand for supplies furnished the inmates for the county home. Within ten years the county debt was paid and $5,000 was in the treasury. Mr. Bailey rendered the county good service and we today should feel a sense of gratitude for same. Although his education was limited to the ability to sign his name, having never attended a school in his life for a single day, he was a successful business man, worth perhaps $25,000. In all his dealings he never lost a cent, kept books in his head and was hale and hearty in spite of his years.

That the man who made the first circular saw was one of the early settlers in Lexington and lived here for many years, surprising as it may seem, is nevertheless vouched for by one of our esteemed older citizens, who had the information from the man himself. It was in this wise: Joseph Conrad, a cabinet maker, the father-in-law of W. B. Hamner, prior to his coming to Lexington about 1820 lived in Philadelphia, and while there, following his trade as cabinet maker, he received a very large order for veneering for picture frames. In order to handle the business with dispatch he put his wits to work and made a circular saw. One day he was sawing away, making much more progress than he could possibly have done with a hand saw, when an old Quaker passed his shop. Hearing the buzzing he stopped and investigated. Then seeing the saw he turned to Conrad and said: "Conrad, there is a fortune in that for you." But before Mr. Conrad could take any steps toward securing a patent, some other man got ahead of him, secured the patent and made the fortune. The saw itself is to be seen at the home of Mr. Ernest C. Conrad some distance from town, and is now one hundred years old.

You could hardly conceive of a dense forest covering that portion of Lexington lying below the courthouse, along Main Street, yet the timbers in the shop occupied by W. B. Hamner, opposite the postoffice, were cut from the stump between Mr. Hamner's shop and the courthouse. The house was built many years ago by this same Joseph Conrad, who came here from Philadelphia in 1820.

Davidson has the honor of having been the native county of Governor John W. Ellis. He was born on the old Ellis plantation in the Jersey settlement in 1820, and his body rests in the old Ellis burying ground at that place. Our old men talk of the matter with considerable feeling and are proud of the fact that Davidson gave birth to this noble man. His education was conducted under Robert Allison, Esq., at Beattie's Ford, and was afterwards continued at Randolph Macon College, in Virginia, and finished at our own University in 1841. His law studies were with Judge Pearson. In 1844 his public life began when he was elected to the

House of Commons. In 1848 he was elected Judge of the Superior Court of law and equity, and later became Governor.

Junius L. Clemmons, Esq., is remembered here as the man who invented telegraphy, although perhaps only the older citizens of our county know that Mr. Clemmons was the true discoverer of the value of electrcity in transmitting messages. He lived to be nearly one hundred years old, but to the last his writing was very legible and one would not think it came from the pen of a man nearly a century old. He was a student in college at the age of seventeen when he made his discovery and placed an application for a patent in the hands of a friend. Professor Morse has been recorded as the inventor of the telegraph. This friend after a time reported that he was unable to secure a patent and Mr. Clemmons seems to have dropped the matter. Inside of three years Morse had a line from Washington to Baltimore and had secured a patent as well as fame for himself, and money arising from same. Mr. Clemmons was one of the first lawyers in Lexington. It is said of this gentleman that he would not take a case for a client that he thought would be in vain without telling his client exactly how it stood. In fact he would discourage useless and doubtful litigation. He did not cultivate trouble.

The family of the late A. C. Hege, of Lexington, have in their possession a very valuable collection of silver ores taken from the old Silver Hill mine years ago by R. A. King, Mrs. Hege's father. There are no two specimens exactly alike, either as to color or formation. Some are very beautiful, being highly colored, incrusted with crystals; others show plainly the solid silver, one specimen having a large piece. Three cabinets are filled with the ores and the whole collection excites the interest of even one not acquainted with mineralogy. The Hege family also have a silver cup made of silver mined in the Silver Hill mine by Mr. King. Upon it is this inscription: "A birthday present to George Alexander Hege from his grandfather, Roswell A. King, made of silver mined by him in 1838, being the first obtained in the United States. 1855." While there may be no positive proof that this was the first silver mined, it is evident that Mr. King believed it to be the first. Mr. King came to this county from Dublin, Ireland, many years ago, and built up a considerable fortune by mining operations. He owned and worked the Silver Hill mine.

Soon after the war in a campaign in which Governor Caldwell and Judge Furches were speaking, General J. M. Leach went to Mocksville one day, at which place the above gentlemen were billed to speak. There was a large number of people out, and the Republicans were there in full force. General Leach asked for a division of time. He was told that they would let him speak on one condition, namely, that he speak between them, and have no reply. The general hummed and hawed, and declared it was an outrage and growled and grunted, and finally very grudgingly consented to speak after one and before the other. Caldwell spoke first. He "laid all the bars down," expecting Furches to follow Leach and put them up, incidentally smashing the general. But they didn't know what they were up against. General Leach got up and went after them. He spoke on and on and on. The sun went down behind the trees and still he spoke. Some fellow pulled his coat tails and told him to sit down. The general roared: "They thought they would act the dog with me, but they don't know the first principle of dog!" Finally he literally spoke the crowd away, and Furches never got to put in a word edgewise. That was General Leach. He was of the quickest perception, shrewd, and you could not down him.

Before the war the town had no special municipal government, a board of commissioners having general oversight of the place. Citizens, in the absence of police, by turns looked after the "protection of life and property." Their chief duty was to see that the slaves behaved and stayed at home. Each month a certain number of men was detailed to act for the month, and then each night three or four men made the rounds, patrolled the town, and were called "paterollers," hence that ancient ditty, "Run nigger run, the paterollers 'll get you." If a slave was caught away from his quarters without a pass, he was whipped. Curiously enough he had the right to select the man he wanted to whip him. It is needless to say that one caught would try to pick a man to chastise him who he thought would be easy. Once when the "paterollers" were in flower one Ike McCrary gave them no end of trouble. They could never catch him. He would show himself to them and then outrun them. On one occasion the captain of a squad took after him and ran him to his home. Now in the road near Ike's house was a good sized mud-hole and Ike sprang across it. The pursuing patrol never noticed it and fell in head foremost, whereupon Ike danced gleefully and made the welkin roar with his African "Wah! wah! wah!" But they were never able to catch Ike without a pass.

In the center of the square there formerly stood a house devoted to the sale of fresh meats, a market house in fact, but one quite different from those we have now. It had a belfry in which was a bell that sent the tidings out whenever a farmer brought meat to town. A man would kill a beef, bring the carcass to the market house and cut it up. He would then ring the bell and the folks would know something was doing. This was a custom followed all over the State, it is true, but young folks know nothing of it. Then, too, the house was used as a calaboose.

One of the most remarkable men of the early days in Davidson was Henry Walser. Men who remember him say that his was a very wonderful mind, although he had little book education. He was several times representative from this county. Illustrative of his ability and shrewdness as a politician the following episode is related: In one campaign Colonel Charles H. Fisher, Democrat, and Mr. Barringer, Whig, were billed to speak at Mocksville. Barringer and Fisher were both pretty smart men and were evenly matched, so that the campaign was rather warm and interesting. But the day before the speaking was to take place, Barringer fell ill, and it was seen that he would not be able to meet Fisher. Now the Whigs knew it would never do to allow Fisher to address the voters without opposition for it spelled disaster. After a good deal of anxiety it was finally agreed that Mr. Walser should be sent for. He lived ten miles away. Early on the day of the speaking a man named Nail went after him and found him in the field at work. Mr. Walser said he couldn't go, he wasn't prepared and wasn't fixed up, being clad in his working garments. Being strenuously importuned, he consented at length and went. Fisher was informed that Mr. Walser would take Barringer's place. Fisher looked at him, saw the old gentleman in his soil-stained clothes and was agreeable. "All right," said he, "all right," thinking to have an easy time with his opponent. Having finished he gave way to Mr. Walser, who wound him up to suit the queen's taste. He was a sharp speaker, and gave Fisher all he wanted. Surprised and chagrined, Fisher could only ask, "Where did that old clodhopper spring from?"

The following excerpt is taken from Volume II, *North Carolina Regimental History,* page 146, written by James F. Beall, Major of the regiment. Major Beall was afterwards better known as Doctor Beall, of Linwood, Davidson County. At the battle of Strassburg, Virginia, Major W. J. Pfohl, commander of the regiment, was killed. After the battle Major Beall assumed command of the regiment and held it until March 24, 1865. "I wish to recall another incident worthy of the observation of all ages. The night before we engaged the enemy in the battles around Richmond, private H. C. Walser (afterwards Major) who was then less than eighteen years of age had his ankle badly scalded. He was left in camp, excused by the surgeon, but soon after the firing commenced Walser made his appearance bare-footed and went through the whole battle in bamboo-briars and mud and water up to his knees."

CHAPTER XI

DANIEL BOONE, PIONEER, PATHFINDER

Daniel Boone, the great pioneer and trail-maker, once lived within the present territory of Davidson County. This truly great man is nationally known, and his fame extends far beyond the bounds of America. We owe much to J. R. McCrary, Esq., of Lexington, for his researches and for the records he has put into permanent form. To him we owe the existence and valuable work of the "Daniel Boone Memorial Association." This Association was incorporated by the General Assembly of the year 1909. The act of incorporation may be found in Chapter 496, Public Laws of North Carolina, and is as follows:

The General Assembly of North Carolina do enact:

Section 1. That the Daniel Boone Association be and is hereby created and made a corporation, with power to purchase and hold lands and other property, to erect suitable memorials, to solicit and collect funds, together with historical materials, and to do all and such things as are necessary to perpetuate the memory of the life of Daniel Boone in North Carolina.

Section 2. That the powers heretofore enumerated be and are hereby vested in a board of trustees, viz.: Philip Sowers, G. F. Cochran, J. R. McCrary, John S. Henderson, A. H. Boyden and F. A. Olds, and associates to the number of five additional trustees, to be selected by a majority of themselves. Said board shall have the power from time to time to fill vacancies by a vote of a majority of their number, and this power shall continue in and be exercised by their successors, so as to make said board a self-perpetuating one.

DANIEL BOONE, 1734-1820
He Resided at Boone's Cave on the Yadkin River

DANIEL BOONE, PIONEER, PATHFINDER 187

A pamphlet under the title, "The Daniel Boone Memorial Booklet," contains much valuable information concerning the great pioneer. It was written by J. R. McCrary, Esq., official historian of the association. From this booklet the following extracts are taken:

Since the passage of this act the association has accomplished much to perpetuate the memory of Boone. Philip Sowers, of Spencer, N. C., has generously donated to it by deed about five acres of land embracing several points of historical interest around the old Boone homestead in Boone Township, Davidson County, N. C. Citizens of Davidson County have given funds with which a replica of the Boone home has been constructed. This is a double-room log cabin in which the association has stored a permanent museum of relics of the olden times which are very interesting. Citizens of Rowan County (from which Davidson was cut off in the year 1822), the original home of the Boone family on its removal to North Carolina, have erected a unique native granite monument about fifteen feet high with its upper half in the shape of an immense Indian arrow-head. The society of the Daughters of the Revolution of Salisbury, N. C., have given a bronze tablet with a suitable inscription to the memory of the great hunter. The grounds have been put in fine shape for the reception of visitors who will always find some one to gladly show them Boone's Cave or Devil's Den on the banks of the Yadkin River and the other points of interest.

On the 30th of April, 1909, the association gave a big celebration on its grounds to honor the memory of the famous pioneer at which men prominent in the State and Nation delivered patriotic addresses. Among the speakers were Judge Jeter C. Pritchard and Congressman Robert N. Page.

The association has only begun its work. It intends to make of this beautiful and picturesque spot a Mecca for pilgrims from everywhere. It is about twelve miles from Lexington in one direction and an equal distance from Salisbury in the other. Although some distance from the railway any one who visits the historic spot will be amply repaid, for the very spirit of the mighty hunter and hero seems to hover in the air itself and echoes from the distant past can be heard in the rippling waters of the Yadkin and in the sighing of the winds in the trees which surround the old homestead. One may linger here until he can renew his youth and his imagination again run riot with visions of stealthy painted Indians being slain by the unerring rifle of the great Long Knife, as Daniel Boone was known to them. Visitors are always welcome.

Daniel Boone, the great hunter and hero, was born August 22, 1734, in Berks County, Pennsylvania, and was one of a family of nine children. His father was Squire Boone, the term Squire being his real name and not a title. His mother was Mary Morgan, a daughter of Edward Morgan. Boone's father was of English descent, and his mother a Quakeress. It is interesting to note that the grandmother of Abraham Lincoln was Anne Boone, a cousin of Daniel Boone, and that the Boones and Lincolns were closely interlinked by marriages in Kentucky.

The entire Boone family moved from Pennsylvania to North Carolina, May 1, 1750, and settled on the banks of the Yadkin River, in what was then Rowan, but now Davidson County. This is established both by history and local tradition. See Roosevelt's *Winning the West*, Sheets's *History of Liberty Baptist Association*, and Jethro Rumple's *History of Rowan*. A map in the year 1908, issued by the Department of Interior of the United States government, shows the travels of the principal explorers with Boone's route covering the traditional site in Boone Township, Davidson County.

At this early time Rowan County was a frontier country, the hills being covered with a great stretch of forest and teeming with deer, bear and other game. Squire Boone and his other sons settled down to the solid work of the farm, but Daniel loved his rifle and the woods, and from his youth to old age spent the larger part of his time in adventure.

The place where the Boone family lived is on a high hill overlooking the Yadkin River. Portions of their double log-house including about one-half of the rock chimney were standing until within the last twenty-five years. All these have been carried away by relic hunters, except a few of the large flat hearth rock, which were found in the cellars under the house by the Boone Association in rebuilding the cabin. The association also found several broken cups and dishes of the old-time flowered ware. Columbus Sowers, who lives on the old plantation, some years ago discovered a stone in one of the cellars with the name "D. Boone" inscribed on it. He sent this stone to the Chicago Exposition and has never been able to get it back.

About one hundred yards from the home site is the Boone spring, and a hundred yards in the opposite direction, on the river bank, is what has been known for generations as Boone's Cave or Devil's Den. This is an opening about two feet square, leading back into the solid rock, eighty feet in one direction and forty-five feet in another, and from three to five feet high. This is a beautiful and picturesque spot and all the surroundings are almost as primitive and wild as they were in olden times. Philip Sowers, the owner of the land which lies in Boone Township, and the owner of Boone's bottoms, has deeded to the association the old home site of about five acres of land. Close by is Boone's Ford, and across the river a short distance in Davie County once stood what was known as Boone's Ford Baptist Church. The records of the old church show that Boone's family were members, although Daniel himself never joined any church. An entry of July 1, 1774, shows that Rev. John McGlammery had an appointment to preach at Jonathan Boone's (Sheets's *History of Liberty Association,* p. 124). Jonathan Boone was an elder brother and was born in Pennsylvania, October 26, 1730.

Deed books 3, 4, and 5 in Rowan County contain various records of the Boone family title deeds. In the Clerk's office there is a marriage certificate on which Daniel Boone is a witness with his genuine signature attached. This is the same signature which appears beneath Boone's photo as the frontispiece to the second volume of Roosevelt's *Winning the West.* It is the same signature to a deed donated to the association by Miss Sallie Turner of Lexington, N. C. This deed was found in a secret drawer of an old chest, an heirloom descended from one David Byerly. This drawer also contained tax receipts and other papers running back to the colonial period of our history. The small boy who accidentally found the secret drawer badly mutilated the deed, which covers land owned by Philip Sowers not far from Boone's cabin. The grantee is one Joseph Hughes, who probably ran the Slaughter Hotel in Salisbury during the Revolution.

Soon after coming of age Boone married Rebecca Bryan, a daughter of Colonel Bryan who lived about four miles below the Boone home at the forks of the Yadkin River at what has long been known as the Point. She was a faithful wife and shared with him in his many toils and dangers and mourned with him the loss of two sons killed by the Indians during their life in Kentucky.

A short time after his marriage he is said to have pushed farther up the Yadkin River to what is now Wilkes County, and built him a cabin. Here he lived for a few years, constantly hunting and going farther west, making trips through the mountains of North Carolina and East Tennessee into the Watauga country where, till recent years, near Jonesboro, Tenn., an old beech tree was still standing with the inscription on it: "D. Boone cilled a bar on this tree in the year 1760."

In 1765 Boone went to Florida and purchased property, but his wife declined to go there to live. On May 1, 1769, he set out with five companions for Kentucky, meeting with numerous adventures and encounters with the Indians. One of his companions, John Stewart, was killed, being the first white man slain on Kentucky soil. Boone himself was captured but escaped. After a stay of several months he was joined by his brother, Squire Boone, Jr. The remainder of the party returned to the settlements, leaving the two brothers alone on their hunting grounds throughout the winter living in a little cabin. In May, 1770, Squire Boone went to the settlements to procure horses and ammunition and returned late the next July. For three months the hardy hunter lived alone in the wilderness without salt, sugar or flour and without the companionship of a person, horse or dog. (Roosevelt's *Winning the West*.) Yet history says that he was not lonely. This shows the wonderful courage of the man and his intense love of the out-door life which does not exist in this day and generation unless it might be in the hearts of a few choice spirits like Theodore Roosevelt, Dr. Grenfell or Lieutenant Peary. Would that there was more of the pioneer spirit!

In 1775 Judge Richard Henderson, one of the leading men in the Colony of North Carolina, formed a company to deal in the vast tract of Kentucky land which had been ceded to them by the Cherokee Indians. Judge Henderson was an ancestor of many prominent men by that name who have honored the name of this State. Among his descendants in the State are Colonel John S. Henderson and Colonel A. H. Boyden, of Salisbury, his great-grandsons, original members of the Boone Memorial Association. In 1776 Boone started out with several families from North Carolina, among whom was John Gray Blount, an ancestor of Colonel W. B. Rodman, of Charlotte, and whose sister, Miss Lida T. Rodman, of Washington, N. C., has several mementoes of this trip now in her possession. In Powell's Valley in East Tennessee the party was joined by forty or fifty other adventurers who went with them into Kentucky. They reached there after many desperate encounters with Indians. In one of these Boone's son was killed. Boone's wife and daughter, born in North Carolina, were the first white women

Kentucky's First Fort, Boonesborough, Kentucky. Erected in 1775 by Daniel Boone.

Boonesborough Fort, the First Fort Erected in Kentucky by Daniel Boone and the Early Settlers

that ever stood on the banks of the Kentucky River. They established a fort at Boonesboro and made frequent visits and excursions into the forest surrounding. On July 14, 1776, his daughter and two daughters of Colonel Calloway were captured by the Indians while strolling in the woods near the Fort, but the girls kept their wits about them and broke off twigs from the trees and tore off strips of their clothing and left them along the way by which their trail might be followed. On the next day Boone came back to the Fort and organized a pursuing party who took an oath not to return unless they brought back the girls. At last they came in sight of the Indians, killing several of them, and recaptured the girls whose names were Jemima Boone, Betsy and Fannie Calloway. Betsy Calloway later married Samuel Henderson, a brother of Judge Richard Henderson. Fannie Calloway married John Holder and Jemima Boone married Flanders Calloway. All three of these young men were in the party of nine who rescued the girls from the Indians. This incident has been used in Cooper's story, *The Last of the Mohicans*. The Calloway boys went from North Carolina with Boone to Kentucky. Flanders Calloway is one of the subscribing witnesses to the mutilated deed found in the old papers of David Byerly, referred to above.

In 1778 Boone with a party of others was captured by the Indians and carried to Detroit, where eleven of the prisoners were turned over to the British commander who attempted to ransom Boone. The Indians would not give him up but took him back to Old Chillicothe, where he was adopted into the family of Black Fish, the chief. He was treated kindly, but in about twelve months, learning of an intention to attack Boonesboro, he escaped and reached home, 160 miles away, in four days with only one solid meal during that time. The Indians attacked the fort, but were repulsed. In 1782 under General Clark he fought in the battle of Blue Licks, where his son, Israel, was killed at his side. In 1781, 1787, and 1791 Boone was in the Legislature of Kentucky. In 1786 he moved to Maysville, where he was tavern keeper, town trustee, trapper, hunter and trader. Boone failed to register his lands and subsequent settlers entered them and he lost vast tracts in litigation. Declaring that he would not live in Kentucky, he moved in 1798 to what is now West Virginia, but thinking that the country was becoming too thickly settled removed in 1799 to Missouri, then a Spanish possession. Here he was given 800 acres of land, but again failed to register the entry, and when the territory passed into the hands of the United States his title was declared invalid. He appealed to Congress and it confirmed his Spanish grant. When eighty years of age he went on a hunting trip to the Yellowstone Valley and still talked of moving westward. In 1813 his brave and loyal wife passed away. In 1820 he died at the home of his son, Major Nathan Boone, at Charette, Missouri. He was buried in a coffin made with his own hands and kept under his bed for some years before his death. In 1845, by request of the Legislature of Kentucky, the remains of both Daniel Boone and his wife, Rebecca Boone, were removed to the cemetery at Frankfort, where the State that once served him so ill has erected a handsome monument to "The Father of Kentucky."

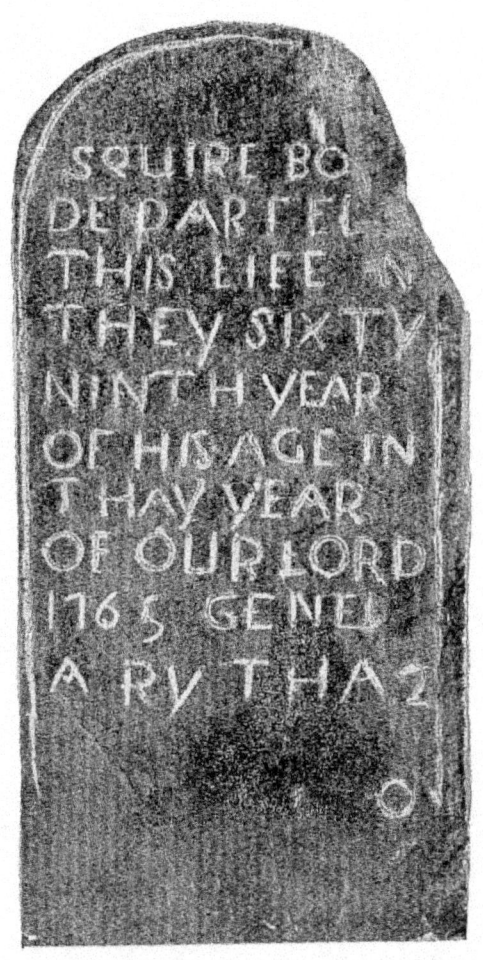

Tombstone at the Grave of Squire Boone, Father of Daniel Boone, Across the Yadkin River Opposite the Boone Home at Boone's Cave, Davidson County

Mr. Roosevelt in the sixth volume of his *Winning the West* states that his religion was as follows: "All the religion I have is to love and fear God, believe in Jesus Christ, do all the good to my neighbor and myself that I can, and do as little harm as I can help, and trust God's mercy for the rest." This was written by Boone in his old age to a relative. Daniel Boone's name became famous in this country and in Europe in his own day. The great poet Byron in his Don Juan, Canto VII, LXI, refers to the great name of Daniel Boone, backwoodsman of Kentucky and to the simplicity and nobleness of his life.

Squire Boone, the father of Daniel Boone, and other members of his family are buried in what is known as the old Joppa Cemetery near Mocksville, in Davie County, North Carolina. In fact the tombstone of Squire Boone is still in existence and the place of his burial has been visited by thousands of people. A short time ago some vandals broke off the letters "ne" from the end of the name. To protect the stone from further sacrilege, W. L. Sanford, of Mocksville, one of the Boone descendants, removed the stone from its resting place only some two or three months ago and placed it in a bank vault. He is now having made for it a steel cage, which when completed will be placed over the grave at the Joppa Cemetery and within it, set in cement, will be placed the old stone on which appears the following inscription and spelling: "Squire Boone departed this life they sixty-ninth year of his age in thay year of our Lord 1765 Genelary tha 2."

Lord Byron's Eulogy

Who passes for in life and death most lucky,
Of the great names which in our faces stare,
Is Daniel Boone, the backwoodsman of Kentucky.
Crime came not near him—she is not the child
Of solitude. Health shrank not from him, for
Her home is in the rarely trodden wild.
He was not all alone; around him grew
A sylvan tribe of children of the chase,
And tall and strong and swift on foot were they,
Beyond the dwarfing city's pale abortions,
Because their thoughts had never been the prey
Of care of gain; the green woods were their portions;
No sinking spirits told them they grew gray,
No fashion made them apes of her distortions;
Simple they were, not savage; and their rifles,
Though very true, were not yet used for trifles.
Motion was in their days, rest in their slumbers,
And cheerfulness the handmaid of their toils;
Corruption could not make their hearts her soil:
The lust which stings, the splendor which encumbers,
With the free foresters divide no spoil;
Serene, not sullen, were the solitudes
Of this unsighing people of the woods.

Mrs. Drusilla McCrary, wife of John W. McCrary, and mother of John Raymond McCrary, Esq., was the daughter of Catherine Leonard, nee Wagner, and her mother was eighty-three years of age when she died, July 12, 1875, having been born January 27, 1793, and is buried in Leonard's or Pilgrim Reformed churchyard, and her tombstone bears the above dates. She says that her mother often told her that she, Catherine Wagner Leonard, when a little girl, and her father, Jacob Wagner, many years ago started on a visit to another Jacob Wagner, a cousin living in Tennessee, and that somewhere in the mountains of the State of North

Carolina they met in the road a man dressed in a hunter's costume with a rifle, etc., who was accompanied by a male companion, and that on meeting in the road this hunter and the said Jacob Wagner threw their hats into the air and sprang into each other's arms and made much to do over each other and that the hunter was Daniel Boone, coming back to North Carolina on a visit from Kentucky, and that he and the old man Wagner were great friends. She further said that the said Jacob Wagner lived about three miles west of Lexington on Swearing Creek on a farm now owned by W. A. Watson, about twelve miles from the Boone home in Davidson County.

The author of this history, Dr. J. C. Leonard, visited the original home of Daniel Boone in Berks County, Pennsylvania, a few years ago. The old stone house is still in a fair state of preservation, though it seems strange that some historical society of that great commonwealth has not improved the property. It should be preserved for the future. The old mansion is two stories high and is constructed of stone, the walls being very thick and strong. It is built over a strong flowing spring of water as a matter of precaution in case the inmates should ever be besieged by Indians. One fireplace is over eight feet wide.

CHAPTER XII

GENERAL NATHANIEL GREENE AND DANIEL BOONE TABLET

1. MEMORIAL TABLET UNVEILED

[At the unveiling of the Greene-Boone tablet on the public square in Lexington on Sunday afternoon, December 1, 1919, the following address was delivered by Rev. J. C. Leonard, D.D. It has been suggested that it be published on account of the history it contains. The author wishes it explained that the legends are not to be taken too seriously. They were related because of their connection with a great historic fact.]

One of the men of historic fame whom today we delight to honor is General Nathaniel Greene, a native of the little state of Rhode Island. He was born in 1741. General Greene was one of the most successful officers of the Revolutionary War. He was a very brave and sagacious man. North Carolina owes more to him than to any other of the many heroes of those great times. His wise generalship saved North Carolina from the fate that had befallen Georgia and South Carolina, in which states the American armies had been defeated by the British. General Greene was a prominent officer in the battle of Trenton in 1776, and also in those that followed at Princeton and at Germantown up north. And then when later General Gates was so disastrously defeated by Lord Cornwallis at Camden, South Carolina, General Washington sent General Greene to take command of the American armies in the South. He reached Charlotte, North Carolina, December 2, 1780.

In times like the present there is a tendency to minimize the battles of Revolutionary times. During the progress of the World War we have been reading such large figures that we are disposed to discredit the importance of the numbers of men and guns during the Revolutionary War. For instance, the American Army at King's Mountain numbered only about a thousand men. But of these men history says: "They yelled like Indians and fought like demons." This was on October 7, 1780. When night came on, it was found that the officer of the British forces, Colonel Ferguson, together with 119 of his men lay dead on the field of battle. The wounded numbered 123, and 664 were taken prisoners. The American losses consisted of 28 killed and 62 wounded. How small these figures in comparison with the figures to which we have become accustomed. It is said that the killed in the World War numbered ten millions.

When General Greene arrived at Charlotte, he found a nondescript army. It was what he called "only the shadow of an army." He found some of the cavalry armed with swords that had been hammered out in country blacksmith shops. Some of the men even had no arms at all. Other military equipment was entirely lacking. Clothes worn by many of the soldiers were in shreds, so ragged that in many instances garments were held together by thorns broken from locust trees by the wayside. The militia had received almost no military training. They were farmers whose patriotism had prompted them to enlist for several months service.

But under the skillful generalship of the new commander a miracle was worked in a short time. General

Greene was a most patient man, and he went at his new task in an orderly and sympathetic way, and he soon had the confidence of all the troops.

On January 17, 1781, the important battle of the Cowpens in South Carolina, a few miles below the North Carolina border, was fought between the British under Colonel Tarleton and the Americans under General Morgan. The decided victory was in favor of the Americans, losing only 12 killed and 60 wounded or captured, while the British lost 784 killed and wounded and captured. The Americans secured as booty of war 100 horses, 35 wagons, 2 cannon and 800 muskets.

I mention the battle of the Cowpens because the defeat of the British there led to the famous pursuit of General Greene by Lord Cornwallis through North Carolina and finally the surrender of the British at Yorktown.

After his success at the Cowpens General Morgan lost no time in getting away to a place of safety out of reach of Cornwallis. He wanted to save his prisoners and his rich stores, and there was no doubt in his mind that Cornwallis would try to rescue these. With all haste Morgan sped to Cowan's Ford on the Catawba River. Here he was joined by General Greene who was very anxious to confer with him and make plans for future movements. To accomplish this feat the General had to ride a hundred miles, while the trusted General Huger took the army on towards Salisbury. Lord Cornwallis arrived at the west bank of the Catawba River January 31, the very day on which General Morgan was leaving the east bank for Salisbury. General William Davidson had remained with picked officers and men on this side of the Catawba to delay the crossing of the British. He had with him Colonel Polk and Captain Graham. There was a sharp battle here, and Cornwallis finally forced a crossing. General Davidson's 300 men could not hold back the trained British troops. When the British made the first attempt to cross the river, swollen by the recent rains, General Davidson's men fired on them. This caused them to veer from the original point at which they expected to cross. General Davidson started to ride from the position he occupied to the point at which the British were crossing the river. He was shot through the heart and fell from his horse dead. The death-dealing missile was a ball, and the natural inference is that he was shot by a Tory, because the British did not use rifles but muskets. It is sad to chronicle the death of this strong, young, brave officer at the hand of one who ought to have enlisted on his side, but who to this day must bear the opprobrious epithet, Tory. This is a word as hateful to most of us Americans as the word Slacker in our times. I regret to relate that there were a great many Tories, even in a great colony like North Carolina. As many as 1,300 Tories gathered at Ramsour's Mill in Lincoln County about this time. Colonel Francis Locke, of Rowan County, was dispatched to attack these Tories with such forces as he could muster along the way. It was a battle between Tories and Patriots, and in the battle people who had been neighbors and friends fought against each other. So close were the battle lines that the combatants could recognize each other. Many a man who fell there was shot by his former companion or even kinsman. No man on either side wore a uniform. The Tory was distinguished by a sprig of green pine pinned to his cap, while the Patriot was known by a piece of white paper fastened to his head-gear. The Tories were defeated.

The brilliant General Davidson was shot down by a Tory. But his bravery and his name have been perpetuated through the name of the great county of Davidson, North Carolina. When he was a mere boy four years of age, his father moved from Pennsylvania to North Carolina, and the future General received his education and his training in this hospitable climate. When the Revolutionary War broke out, he was a young man twenty-nine years of age. In the year 1776 he was a Major in the Fourth Regiment of North Carolina troops. In one of the South Carolina battles he was severely wounded, a ball passing entirely through his body. The wound was almost a fatal one and disabled him for two months. Prior to this he had been made Lieutenant Colonel. For conspicious bravery he was again advanced to the rank of Brigadier General.

General Davidson was with General Greene in his famous march through North Carolina until he lost his life on the banks of the Catawba River.

General Greene arrived at Salisbury the night of February 1, 1781. After riding all day in the rain he arrived at the home of Mrs. Elizabeth Steele, a woman whose attachment to the cause of America has marked her as a distinguished woman in the history of her country for all time. It is recorded that General Greene came to her house that night fatigued, hungry, alone and penniless. When Mrs. Steele heard this, the fire of her patriotism was greatly augmented. It was too much for her great soul to be conscious that the fortunes of her country's cause might be lost because this great general lacked the necessary comforts of life. Her womanly heart prompted her to a deed that will go down through all time. She will ever be remembered by the deed which she did through the promptings of her good and noble heart. When General Greene had been seated at the well-spread table before a cheerful fire, Mrs. Steele came in. She confessed that she had overheard the General's despondent remark to Dr. Read. She took from beneath her apron two small bags of gold, and she said earnestly: "Take these, for you will want them: I can do without them." This kind and thoughtful act enabled General Greene to resume his journey that night with a great load lifted from his heart. It was at this same time and in this same house that General Greene took from the wall of the room a picture of George III, and wrote on the back of the same: "O George, hide thy face and mourn." He then replaced the portrait with the face to the wall.

But General Greene did not tarry long in the hospitable home of Mrs. Steele. After a hasty supper he marched his troops to the Yadkin River in order to keep ahead of Cornwallis who was pursuing him. He would not allow his army to halt until all were safe over the Yadkin River. At the Catawba River Divine Providence had intervened through the swollen river to save the American army. The same was witnessed at the Yadkin. General Greene and his army were saved by a direct interposition of Providence. The cavalry forded the river and the infantry and baggage were transferred by flatboats. After all were safe over, the British army under Cornwallis came to the banks of the river at midnight. The position was a very dangerous one for the American army. But there was a great downpour of rain all night and the river was greatly swollen. And when dawn appeared the next morning, Cornwallis was greatly chagrined to see his prey again beyond his grasp. He ordered his gunners to fire across the river upon the Americans, and following the order there was furious cannonading. Dr. Read, a surgeon of the American army, has graphically described the scene: "At a little distance from the river was a small cabin, in which General Greene had taken up his quarters. At this the enemy directed their fire, and the balls rebounded from the rocks in the rear of it. But little of the roof was visible to the enemy. The General was preparing his orders for the army, and his dispatches to the congress. In a short time the balls began to strike the roof, and clapboards were flying in all directions. But the General's pen never stopped only when a new visitor arrived, or some officer for orders: and then the answer was given with calmness and precision, and Greene resumed his pen."

General Greene was determined not to give battle until he was sure of his strength and his ability to meet the larger forces of the British. When Cornwallis found that through the aid of Providence in the swollen Yadkin River at Trading Ford the Americans had eluded him, he at once determined to overtake them before they should be able to reach the Dan River and cross it. Accordingly he turned up the Yadkin and effected a crossing at Shallow Ford, a place pointed out to him by some Tory of the neighborhood. General Greene was apprised of this move, and to deceive Cornwallis he directed a part of his forces to move northward as if actually falling into Cornwallis' trap, and these men moved as far up as the town of Salem. But after crossing the Yadkin River Cornwallis, though puzzled by the movements of Greene in the division of his forces, was not entirely deceived. Tories who came into his confidence along the way kept him pretty well informed as to the general purposes of his enemy. Accordingly a part of the British under trusted officers followed the detachment of Americans under Colonel Otho H. Williams, who had been sent ahead by Greene in the hope that Cornwallis would think that the whole American army was moving in that direction. But Cornwallis, knowing that the main body of Greene's army was marching by a more southerly direction from Trading Ford on the Yadkin River towards Irwin's Ferry on the Dan River, kept the main part of his forces on the track of Greene's main forces. This fact accounts for the marching of these two great generals of Revolutionary times directly through this community. We can not assert positively that General Greene led his forces right over the ground now occupied by the town of Lexington; but it is a reasonable conclusion that he did, for a day later his forces were again united at Guilford Court House. He had hoped to give battle to the British when he could unite his forces, but he decided that he was not yet strong enough, and so he gave orders for the final dash across the Dan River, which he accomplished two days later to the chagrin of Cornwallis.

During Greene's march through North Carolina his forces were steadily increasing. The militia came in all along the line. On the 14th of March he found that he had in all 5,668 men in his army, of whom 1,700 were North Carolinians who formed his front line on March 15 when he joined battle with Lord Cornwallis at Guilford Court House. They had no dugouts and trenches such as we have been reading about over in France. Their only defense was a line of rail fence, over and through which the North Carolinia militia made it hot for the British.

We have several times referred to the Tories of North Carolina. But it must not for a moment be thought that a large per cent of our people were Tories, no more than it would be conceded that any large per cent of our people were slackers during the World War. The great majority of North Carolinians were Patriots who fought valiantly for American freedom and gained it. Many of the North Carolina militia under General Greene at Guilford Court House were farmers who had joined him on the way. They had not had a great deal of military training, but they knew well how to use a gun. They had been trained from boyhood to shoot the wild turkey and the deer. And sometimes they had to shoot the mean Indian to protect their homes. Such men made brave and sturdy soldiers. Among these men in the army of General Greene at Guilford Court House were my own great-great-grandfather, Valentine Leonard, and my great-grandfather, Jacob Leonard. Among them also was the ancestor of all the Fritts generation in this section, the old hero Wooldrich Fritts. Both Valentine Leonard and Wooldrich Fritts were later murdered by Tories in their own homes in the month of November in the same year. Their bodies lie buried under a handsome monument erected by a grateful citizenship in the year 1896, one hundred and fifteen years after their martyrdom.

General Greene with the larger part of his army passed over the very spot where we now stand, or very near it. Lord Cornwallis's men also marched two days later close in the rear.

2. Ghosts of Abbott's Creek

Many strange stories have been told of things seen and heard in the vicinity of Abbott's Creek at the Crotts Bridge crossing.

All these supernatural phenomena which have been reported as occurring at or near Crotts Bridge on Abbott's Creek are connected with a great historical fact. Cornwallis, the great head of the English army in the Revolutionary War, in his famous march through North Carolina, crossed Abbott's Creek a few hundred yards above the site of the present bridge at the sharp bend of the stream. This was in the last months of the year 1780 and the first months of the year 1781. One day in February Cornwallis crossed Abbott's Creek at the point stated. And from that day down through the years there has been trouble for many people in that vicinity.

It is said that when the British arrived at this point they still had in their possession very much money in gold and silver. Money was a commodity very difficult to carry along under the circumstances of continued forced marches. Cornwallis is quoted as having said it was much easier to carry food than money. Besides the Tories were very eager to furnish his army with supplies. And so for the present he must get rid of that sordid heavy load of coin. Under cover of the night he ordered certain of his men to lower the barrel full of gold and silver into the waters of Abbott's Creek. This order was carried out according to instructions, and from that day to this that stream has been the proud possessor of more wealth than any warm blooded citizen of the county. Think of that barrel of rich coins lying to this day at the bottom of Abbott's Creek. It is enough to cause the midnight ghosts to come out from their hiding places and prowl about in the entire neighborhood. And this very thing they are said to have been doing from that day to this. That barrel has been heard by reputable citizens, at all hours of the day and night, doing strange things. And the ghosts of the creek have gone out in the vicinity and have done strange things. The ghosts of Abbott's Creek at this point have been known to show themselves at night as lights moving along over the waters of the stream where the money was concealed, up its steep banks, through the forests on either side. But they would not allow a man who might be able to summon nerve and courage sufficient to come near and make an investigation. Indeed no man was ever found brave enough to try to form the acquaintance of the ghosts when they were prowling about with their lanterns in the night time. Many citizens were eye witnesses to the reality of these strange appearances of fire. And it is said that the supernatural lights always disappeared in Abbott's Creek at the point where Cornwallis crossed.

The ghosts had the habit of making excursions through the entire neighborhood. Many strange phenomena were witnessed by reputable citizens. Opossum hunters have perhaps had richer experiences in ghost lore in that section than any other class of people. This is perhaps due to the fact that night is the time to hunt this marsupial animal most successfully and that night is also the favorite time with ghosts to disport themselves. In the years long gone by there was a piece of timber in whose depths every hunter ignominiously and irretrievably lost his way. Try as he would he could not find his way out, and the only thing was to wait until Aurora began to paint the east with her rosy fingers. Hunters rarely went a second time into this forest, and never a third time, because the ghosts were always there. In the same piece of timber the best trained 'possum dogs would tree the object of search fair and square, but the most diligent search failed to reveal any sort of 'possum. He was not there. Time and again men would climb trees up which the dogs had chased the game, but the most careful scrutiny always failed to disclose the 'possum. It was only the phantom ghost that deceived the dogs. How these playful spirits must have laughed at the chagrin of men and dogs. On various occasions trees were cut down, after the usual manner of capturing the 'possum treed by faithful hunting dogs. But when the expected capture was not made, the dogs would trail off again and stop at a more accessible tree where the hunters would be sure the game would be found. But not a single 'possum could be taken. Of course not when the ghosts of Cornwallis were there deceiving dogs and men for their own sport and delectation.

A reputable citizen of the township was one evening going on horseback to his father's home a few miles away, accompanied by his faithful hunting dogs called by the names of Cash and Mean. True to their keen instincts these faithful dogs were ready for business. In a ridiculously short time they had treed a big fat 'possum on a medium sized persimmon tree. The man on his horse could see his outline in the moonlight. Tying his horse to a tree, he climbed up the other tree on which the 'possum sat grimly grinning, and shook him down. No sooner did the 'possum leave the limb than Cash and Mean tucked their tails between their legs and cowered in abject fear. Nor would they leave their master any more that night. Why? Because it was not an opossum at all that they had treed, but one of the ghosts of Abbott's Creek which chose that night to deceive both hunter and dogs.

During the Civil War a colored man was one night walking along the road near Crotts Bridge when suddenly he came face to face with another negro. The second negro blocked the way of the first and would not let him pass. He walked back and forth from side to side in the road, and the stranger did the same thing, ever keeping himself in front of the traveler. At last in desperation the first man said: "See here, nigger, ef you doan low me pass, Ise a gwinto knock you down wid dis hammer." No move was made by the other indicating compliance with his wishes, so he let drive with his hammer. The hammer went with a mighty dash not only against the other man, but right straight through him. The stranger glared and grinned into the face of the hammer-thrower, and then vanished into thin air. And so also did the other colored man disappear from the spot, literally outstripping the wind in his tremendous haste. And that was one time when it was correct to say that a black man's hair stood straight on his head. The apparition was one of the ghosts of the gold of Cornwallis who came out on that fateful night to frighten the colored man.

At another time a white man was riding horseback along by the same spot, when suddenly something jumped up on his horse behind him. The ghostly apparition scared the man half to death, as well as the horse which galloped every step of the way home at the height of his speed. In the meantime the thing left him as mysteriously as it had come. Here was evidently another one of the ghosts which had come up from the bottom of Abbott's Creek to take a respite from his vigils as watcher over the gold and silver deposited there years ago by the great English general, Lord Cornwallis.

At a certain house, the key to the front door generally hung on a nail above the mantel. A cat was observed many times to be looking straight at that key. Often the key was found lying in the front yard. It had not been touched by any human hand. Sometimes the door would open and sometimes it would refuse to open. One day the old lady said to some neighbor who had dropped in: "Bring me the axe and I will break it open." At that threat the door flew wide open of its own accord. The explanation is that one of Lord Cornwallis's ghosts of Abbott's Creek had possession of the cat and made it do strange things with the door and key.

That same barrel of gold has been heard by reputable citizens, at all hours of the day and night, especially in the night time, rolling down the hill and finally splashing into the waters of Abbott's Creek. No less a character than a well known justice of the peace who lived to be a very old man, departing this life thirty-eight years ago at the age of eighty-nine years, gave it upon his word of honor that he heard that barrel of money in one of its excursions go bumping down over rocks and roots and stumps through the forest, and at length plunge with a mighty splash into the creek. He could discern exactly the starting point, the course the barrel took on its way down the hillside, the point on the bank where it jumped into the stream. He looked to see the splash of the waves on the surface caused by the impact of the barrel. But not a wave did he see. No wonder the old gentleman's hair stood on end in its snowy whiteness, for was he not standing in the very presence of the ghosts of Abbott's Creek—ghosts too who were standing guard over the great treasure of gold and silver deposited there by the renowned Lord Cornwallis of the British army? Might it not be that the spirit of the great General himself had come back from the realms of the dead? Who could feel perfectly at home in company with such invisible visitors? Who would not leave such a spot with an accelerated pace?

Some men who were not acquainted with the fact that this portion of Abbott's Creek was the rendezvous of ghosts, or perhaps made light of it if they had heard it, went to this secluded spot to indulge in the delightful sport of swimming to their heart's content, clad only in the bathing suits provided by Nature, the mother of us all. The ghosts of peaceful Abbott's Creek thought this an opportune time to begin their favorite sport of rolling barrels of gold down the hillside and into the stream—invisible barrels of gold they were, and yet real barrels of gold placed there in the keeping of the ghosts by Lord Cornwallis—a sport enjoyed evidently by the ghosts as much as the bath by the men. The barrels came one after another from way up the hill with a rumbling like thunder and plunged over into the stream. But not a barrel did the swimmers see; not a wave did the barrels make on the surface of the waters. Each barrel took its place at the bottom in the silent sands which had accumulated there through the ages of geological time. So frightened were the bathers that they went out in great haste, nor did they tarry on the banks long enough to even adjust their neckties. And from that day to this they have never returned to that spot to delight themselves in the refreshing waters of Abbott's Creek, all because the guardians of the British gold left there by Lord Cornwallis came out to play at the very time these gentlemen came in to play. Who had the better right to the creek? Evidently the men conceded it to the ghosts.

CHAPTER XIII

PUBLIC AND PRIVATE SCHOOLS

1. Public Schools of Davidson County

The development of the school system of the county is an interesting story. The State of North Carolina, along with many other states of the Union, was rather backward in the establishment of a public school system. There were many fine private schools through a long period of years prior to the year 1839 when the State school law was adopted by the General Assembly (January 7, 1839). The University of North Carolina, center of the educational system of the State, was chartered in 1793, and actually founded October 12, 1793. The various religious denominations established academies, seminaries and colleges early in the history of the State. The first public school law, adopted in 1839, gained as advocates almost the whole body of the Legislature. It provided for an election in each county for the inauguration of public schools. In any county in which the election should be favorable for the establishment of schools under the law it became the duty of the county court to appoint a board of county superintendents; these were empowered to lay off school districts and appoint school commissioners for each district. The law required the court in the county voting in favor of schools to make a tax levy of $20 for each district, and this sum would be supplemented by $40 from the State Literary Fund. Following the enactment of this law there was a lively campaign in each of the counties. The arguments used against schools are even yet sometimes heard: 1. The local tax would be a burden to the poor. 2. It would be unjust to him who had no children to educate. 3. It would be unfair to the taxpayers who educated their children in private schools or under governesses. 4. The school districts would be too large and the salaries too small. 5. The proposed term of three months would be too short. 6. In addition to all this, some argued the uselessness of education because there were many selfmade, prosperous citizens who had never gone to school. But in general the stronger newspapers, the more progressive citizens and the outstanding citizens favored schools. Most of the counties voted to establish schools under the new State law. But there were seven counties that did not so vote, and the author regrets to record the fact that Davidson County was one of the exceptions. This fact in the history of our great county is mentioned mainly to show what strides forward in educational sentiment have been made since that date. Davidson County today stands right up in the front ranks of the progressive counties in education.

For the school year ending last spring there were in the county 93 rural and city schools. In these schools there were 112 primary teachers, 119 grammar grade teachers, and 30 high school teachers; a total of 261 teachers in the county schools. In all these schools there were 4,788 primary pupils, 3,978 grammar grade pupils, and 754 high school pupils; a total of 9,520 pupils in our county public schools. The reader understands that these are the figures solely of the city and rural public schools. No account is taken of the many private schools in the county, nor of the numerous young people of public school age who are elsewhere in school. School budget for 1921: $258,984.72.

Professor S. G. Hasty, County Superintendent of Schools, a man very diligent in his position, has prepared the following article for the Centennial sketch:

On August 17, 1843, the Board of Superintendents of Common Schools, consisting of the following members: John W. Thomas, Ira Fitzgerald, William Hanes, Ensley Harris, William R. Holt, William Raper, Meshack Pinkston, John Hassey, Jeremiah Adderton and Levi R. Cordy, met and organized for the purpose of establishing a common school system for Davidson County. On September 5 of the same year, the Board of Superintendents ordered that school districts be laid off by natural boundaries and in size not less than three nor more than four miles square, with 75 children as the ratio in each district, and $50 as an appropriation for each school.

In 1845 there were 43 school districts, 4,871 children, and an appropriation of $2,449.25 to the schools.

The schools were under the control of the Board of Superintendents for 22 years—until 1865. The number of school districts increased to 85 during the administration of said board. The length of school term was from two to three months each year.

Elisha Raper was County Examiner 1870-1875; Captain F. C. Robbins from 1876 to 1881.

H. T. Phillips was the first County Superintendent. He visited the schools, served from 1881 to 1884, and was succeeded by Captain S. E. Williams.

E. E. Raper was Superintendent from 1885 to 1888; R. H. Biesecker from 1888 to 1890; P. L. Ledford from 1890 to 1895. The Board of Education being abolished in 1895, the County Commissioners took charge of the schools and retained control until 1897, when the Board of Education met, organized and elected Robert L.

Green as Superintendent. In 1889 P. L. Ledford was reëlected as Superintendent and served to 1907.

Superintendent P. S. Vann was elected in 1907 and served until 1913, succeeded by Superintendent J. E. Hill, who served for one year. Prof. P. L. Feezor was elected as Superintendent and served until May, 1918, resigning to enter the World War. Prof. S. G. Hasty, the present Superintendent, was elected to fill this vacancy.

The first local tax district for rural schools was established in 1909, for Lexington No. 4, known as Happy Hill district. During the next four years twelve local tax districts were established. The school year 1921-1922 marked the greatest educational progress for the rural schools in the history of the county. The number of schools was reduced from 108 to 76, and seven consolidated schools voted by the people were established by the Board of Education.

Five modern school buildings were erected, thirteen trucks were purchased and put into operation, transporting about eleven hundred school children daily to larger type schools where efficient instruction is offered in high school as well as elementary school subjects. A new modern brick building has been erected in Thomasville consolidated district to accommodate three hundred pupils. Plans are being perfected for the erection of a modern school building for Denton that will accommodate about 400 pupils. These consolidated schools will offer high school instruction to at least one-third of the boys and girls in the county, conforming to the policy of the Board of Education in its efforts to give every boy and girl in the county an opportunity for a high school education. Following are statistics of rural schools in the county.

Property	$400,000
Number school children	12,386
Number rural children	8,389
Number city children	4,007
Number teachers	337
Rural teachers	280
City teachers	57
Number schools (rural)	76
1-Teacher	24
2-Teacher	36
3-Teacher	5
4-Teacher	2
Consolidated	9

2. Private Schools

(a) *Bethany Academy*

Bethany Academy was built in 1858. It was called Union Academy until the new church was built, and then it was called Bethany Academy. The building was put up by the community, and for that reason it was called Union Academy. The principal leaders were: John D. Bodenhamer, Joe Guyer, Israel Long, Charles Hoover, Andrew Lindsay, John Elliot, Philip and Alex. Siceloff, Daniel and Philip Sink. The building was a one-story wood building, painted white with green desks. The building had three rooms, one large room and two small ones, with a fireplace at each end. This building was burned in 1878.

The second academy was a two-story building with four rooms, but only three were ever finished. In 1896 this building was torn down and a public school building was erected just opposite from the old academy. The following persons are some that taught in these buildings: Adam Marsh was the first. Mr. Lane and Frank Blair, the second year, but Mr. Lane died before the close of the school and Mr. Blair finished; Mr. Britle from Yadkin College; Adam Blair, Jacob Clinard, Thomas Yewens, Bascum Palmer. It was while the latter was teaching that the first building was burned. J. D. Bundy next taught.

There was a period from 1878 until 1887 that there was only what they called a free school taught, among the teachers being Elijah Burton, Jacob and William Long, Preston Ledford. In 1887 Prof. R. H. Biesecker opened up a High School. Then came Prof. English, Professors Joe, Ed, and Will Regan, and Paul Welborn. Then the school went back again to free school with the following as some of the teachers: Alpheus Lindsay, P. E. Wicker, Effie Morris. In 1895 Prof. R. H. Biesecker came back again and opened a High School and taught two years. Miss Sue Siceloff ran a High School two years. Since then there has been only seventh grade rural work taught by the following teachers: Edd Teague, P. E. Wicker, Hoyle Sink, Mittie Long, C. M. Rothrock, J. M. Nifong, Hattie Teague and Maud Michael.

(b) *Holly Grove Academy*

This institution was established under the leadership of the Rev. Prof. W. P. Cline, D.D., at Holly Grove on the Raleigh road five miles east of Lexington, N. C., in the fall of 1884. Dr. Cline had just come to Davidson County as pastor of Pilgrim, Emmanuel, Beck's and New Jerusalem Lutheran congregations, and seeing the great need of education, he opened a school of academy grade and taught the first year (1884-85) in the old Quinn schoolhouse. In the early summer of 1885 Dr. Cline started the movement to erect the academy building. He canvassed two days—result, $30! This apparent failure did not discourage him. He hired hands and began to build. First they went to Jacob Lopp's woods where they cut the logs for the framing, donated by Mr. Lopp. Soon there was a "raising" with a picnic dinner prepared by Mrs. Cline, always so ready and willing; on that day the men of the neighborhood put up the frame of the building.

Lafayette Conrad, Sr., was employed as foreman, and he with a group of hands—some paid and some working free of charge—completed the building by December. Prof. Cline had the confidence of all the people. They admired his great energy and determination. Some stuck to him and helped to the end because they believed in him and in the work he was doing. Others helped because they "liked Mr. Cline," though they were sure the undertaking was foolish and hopeless. One "leading member" prophesied that the building would not be completed in seven years! Another who hauled logs free of charge asked Prof. Cline whether he should haul them to Holly Grove to rot or let them rot in the woods! "Haul them to Holly Grove," was the reply! But there were some right-hand men. Eli Younts (always calm and good) gave the beautiful site for the parsonage and academy building, and did much free work. Haley Myers paid the first dollar and said, "As others back out, I back in," and furnished weatherboarding, ceiling, doors, windows, hauling, work—above $500. Jacob Byerly did much carpenter work and furnished lumber from his own sawmill. Peter Younts worked on the building all the fall free of charge. William Beck paid to Stokes Adderton the last $100 due on the academy for borrowed money. Professor and Mrs. Cline furnished the shingles from their farm near Hickory, N. C. Prof. Cline worked much of the summer and fall on and for the building, and paid the foreman and other bills—$350. Henry Conrad, William Fritz, Lindsay Grimes and Peter Kepley were also among the chief helpers. Others helped in smaller amounts. The building was two-story with a large auditorium above and one small and two large recitation rooms below. Holly Grove Academy was an answer to the question, "What can a community that does not know itself do under wise, vigorous leadership?" The actual cost was never known—just as the actual value of Holly Grove Academy can never be measured in dollars and cents. No one cared how much it had cost; each was proud to have had some part in its erection. When the school moved into the completed building in December, 1885, there was great rejoicing and hopefulness in the entire county.

To understand what this academy meant to its community and section it is necessary to recall the conditions of the time. This was before the "Educational Awakening" led and heralded by Alderman and McIver. Interest in education was at a low ebb. The public schools averaged about three months with teachers of only meagre training, with "shacks" for schoolhouses and practically no equipment. Some of the parishioners, aware of these conditions, had made it known that they wanted a preacher who could teach school. They were most fortunate in securing Prof.

Cline. He was a graduate of our State University and had taught in Catawba College at Newton. He had vision, great energy, and good ideas about practical affairs. He at once stirred up much interest, won the confidence of his own and other people, and became a recognized leader.

After the erection of the parsonage and the academy building Prof. Cline and Mr. B. A. Whitener erected a large two-story building near to serve as a boarding house. For eight years Prof. Cline conducted the Academy with marked success. In 1887 Miss Ida Hedrick (Mrs. H. J. Conrad) was secured as teacher of music, and Robert Fritz became Prof. Cline's assistant. The students came from all parts of Davidson County and from neighboring towns and counties. Some boarded in the Whitener home, some in the parsonage, some in other homes near, some did light housekeeping, and some "batched." There was a remarkably large number of ambitious, mature young people ready and longing for educational opportunity, and Prof. Cline and the Academy came just at the psychological moment for them. Life around the school and the boarding houses was characterized by seriousness, industry and overflowing youthful joy and happiness. If ever there was a group of students who worked and played, and grew and developed, and had "a glorious time" with each other and their teachers it was the group that gathered at Holly Grove in the early years of the academy!

The establishing of Holly Grove Academy was a pioneer work. There was no school of the kind in this part of the State. It was not only a great force and influence in the educational, social and moral uplift and development of its community and section, but it was an example and inspiration for the entire State. Soon a similar Pilgrim Academy was built north of it, and Hedrick's Grove Academy south of it. The history of Holly Grove Academy is a worthy part of the history of our State, as is the history of other schools of similar kind, and should not be lost from the records. The good work done by Prof. and Mrs. Cline and their co-laborers in Holly Grove Academy in the lives and work of their students exerts a greater influence for good today than ever; and this influence will continue as the years pass. A bare list of these would be interesting reading—especially to those who were students at old Holly Grove in days long past. Only a few can be mentioned: Rev. John R. Miller, a prominent Baptist divine; Rev. A. R. Beck, D.D. and Rev. R. L. Fritz, Ph.D., able Lutheran ministers; Charles Finch, noted manufacturer; David F. Conrad, William Grimes, Alfred S. Miller, Tillett Gordon, Frank Dickens, John Prim, Charles Dickens, Luther Grimes, Robert Beck, Rev. Samuel W. Beck, Thomas Cauble, M.D.; Rebecca, Loula, Mary, Bud Kindley; Belle, Loula, Fannie, Alice, Luther, Arthur, Jacob, Rev. Everett Fritz; Mary, Ivy, Curtis, Roy, Ora, Chestie Lohr; Ellen, Alice, Julia Younts; Stella and Edgar Younts; George W. A. Beck; Washington Beck; Ella, Luther, Jack Curry; Jo Carter; John W. Bowers, Esq.; Charles and Lee Conrad; Jacob F. Bowers; Mary Quinn; Hargrave Robbins, a prominent cotton mill man, and many others!

Dr. Cline says that Holly Grove Academy was the beginning of Lenoir College in that it made him see that we could do even greater things in the education of our boys and girls. In 1891, answering the call to a greater work, Prof. Cline joined Dr. R. A. Yoder,

Dr. J. C. Moser and Rev. A. L. Crouse in the founding of Lenoir College, Hickory, N. C. His work and experience in the academy had prepared him admirably for this new, larger task. Also with him in this new work labored the first graduate of the academy, Prof. R. L. Fritz, who later was president of the college for eighteen and a half years, and under whose administration the college attained A-grade rating with an endowment of $350,000. Today Dr. R. L. Fritz is Head Professor of Mathematics in Lenoir-Rhyne, and Rev. Alfred R. Beck, D.D., another graduate of Holly Grove Academy, is a prominent member of the Board of Trustees of Lenoir-Rhyne College and secretary of same. Thus goes on, enlarges and expands the wholesome influence of Holly Grove Academy in the social, industrial, educational and religious life of our country.

After being Professor of Latin and History in Lenoir-Rhyne College for ten years, Dr. Cline was President of the Board of Trustees of the same for some years and then for ten years he was Superintendent of the Lowman Home for the Aged and Helpless at White Rock, S. C. On account of impaired health he has retired, and now lives in Columbia, S. C.

(c) *Pilgrim Academy*

Before the State high schools were established in Davidson County private academies were necessary in the life of young men and women who desired to prepare for college. The common schools were too short in duration to give the training necessary, even if the teachers had been trained for high school work. In general the public school teachers of those days had not received the necessary training for this kind of school work. As a consequence public-spirited citizens organized schools of high school grade and erected suitable buildings in which to conduct them.

Pilgrim Academy, four miles north of Lexington on the Central Highway, was founded in 1890, Rev. J. C. Leonard, then the young pastor of Pilgrim Reformed church, leading the people in this worthy enterprise. The building and grounds were the property of this congregation. In addition to the minister named, other teachers were Prof. R. H. Herman and Prof. Jesse B. Leonard. The public district school was conducted in connection with the academy. And when the necessity for high shool work ceased through the coming of the State schools, the owners of the building continued to donate its use to the county free of charge.

Among the numerous pupils trained in this academy may be mentioned Rev. William H. Causey, Rev. Joshua L. Bowers, Rev. David E. Bowers, Dr. Marvin A. Bowers, Rev. Edward P. Conrad.

(d) *Arnold Academy*

In 1891 L. Everhart, D. H. Hinkle and Riley Everhart built Arnold Academy in the village of that name five miles northwest of Lexington. Their purpose primarily was to provide school accommodations for their own sons and daughters; but it was also their desire to give to all the boys and girls of the neighborhood high school advantages. The young pastor at Pilgrim, Rev. J. C. Leonard, was also pastor of Beulah Reformed Church at Arnold. The above named citizens were members of this congregation, and they were encouraged by their pastor in this splendid enterprise. The school served its purpose through several years, only giving way after the State high schools came in to do the work which it had conducted successfully under private management. Among the teachers were Profs. J. B. Leonard, Allen Jones and Peeler Nifong.

(e) *Hedrick's Grove Academy*

Hedrick's Grove Academy was located six miles southeast of Lexington, near the Conrad Hill Gold Mine. It occupied the site of the present-day Hedrick's Grove Reformed Church, a handsome house of worship on Highway 75. The building was a combined schoolhouse and church, erected under the direction of Dr. Allen R. Holshouser, pastor of the congregation. It did work similar to that of the other academies of the county in those years and prepared numerous boys and girls for college. Among its principals were Dr. A. R. Holshouser, Robert E. Leonard, Crawford Clapp and Rev. William H. McNairy.

(f) *Other Academies*

Davidson County was well provided for by the academies whose histories have been written briefly for this story and by other academies of similar grade scattered throughout the county, which did the same grade of work and rendered similar excellent service to the youth. Among these were Tyro Academy, in the village of Tyro; Churchland Academy, in the community of the same name; Arcadia Academy, at

Arcadia village; Reeds Academy, at Reeds Crossroads; Shiloh Academy, at Shiloh Methodist Protestant Church; Denton Academy, at Denton; Davidson Academy, in the southern section of the county; Glen Anna Academy, a few miles south of Thomasville; Midway Academy, at Ellers; Wallburg Academy at Wallburg. Thomasville Female College had a successful career of several years, educating many young women.

CHAPTER XIV

DAVIDSON COUNTY IN MILITARY SERVICE

1. THE REVOLUTIONARY WAR

[There was no Davidson County by name in that period, this territory being still within the bounds of Rowan County. But there were brave patriots in the section. It is greatly to be regretted that permanent records were not more generally kept. In January, 1910, there was published in *The Pennsylvania German*, a monthly magazine issued at Lititz, Pennsylvania, an article under the title, "Valentin Leonhardt, the Revolutionary War Patriot," by the author of this historical sketch. It is published here as a part of the history of Davidson County because this man was an influential citizen of the county and a brave soldier in the great war fought for the independence of the American colonies. It is known that nearly every man mentioned in this sketch as a contemporary of Valentin Leonhardt was an American soldier in the same struggle, though in some instances documentary evidence to establish the fact is lacking. A further reason for publishing this story in connection with "The Centennial of Davidson County" is that it brings out the history of the oldest church in the whole county, and also of some other very old churches, and in connection with the same some biographical sketches of prominent men of those times. It is not now possible to secure a complete roster of the men of Davidson County who fought in the Revolutionary War; but there were many loyal patriots who fought through the whole or a part of this great struggle for American Independence. In addition to Valentin Leonhardt may be mentioned Wooldrich Fritts, Philip Leonard, Peter Hedrick, Jacob Leonard, Frederick Goss, Azariah Merrill, Benjamin Merrill, Philip Sauer, John Hogan.]

Among the German settlers who located in North Carolina during the high tide of the immigration of that nationality from 1745 onward was Valentin Leonhardt (Valentine Leonard, as the name would now be spelled). He took passage from Rotterdam on the ship *Neptune,* Captain Thomas Wilkinson. This vessel reached the port of Philadelphia, October 25, 1746. Here the subject of this sketch took the oath of allegiance to the Province and State of Pennsylvania. Just how long he stayed in Pennsylvania there are no records at hand to show. Most of the German settlers in North Carolina came from the German settlements in Pennsylvania. They took up their residence in that part of the State now covered by the counties of Alamance, Guilford, Davidson, Forsyth, Rowan, Stanly, Cabarrus, Lincoln, Catawba and parts of adjacent counties. Many of these men and women were born in the latter province as is attested by inscriptions in old Bibles and hymn books, on tombstones, etc. There is in the old "Leonhardt's Church" graveyard, a stone bearing the inscription, "Abraham Reichard was born in Pennsylvania in July, 1764. Died September 2, 1828." Another reads as follows: "Adam Hetrich war geboren in Penselvani in Lencaster Caunty im Jahre 1741, den 12 Ocdober." But some of the settlers came from the old world, especially those who came in the earlier years. Some of these came by way of the port of Charleston; but most of them made their way first to Pennsylvania, thence to North Carolina and other provinces. Valentin Leonhardt was among the latter class. The inscription on his tombstone is as follows: "Valentin Leonhardt, geboren in der Kuhr Pfaltz in Katzenbach den 13 Ocdober 1718, und ist in dem Herrn entschlafen den 13 November, 1781. Nun hier ligt eine Handvoll Aschen mit Christi Blut gewashen." A free translation is as follows: "Valentin Leonhardt was born at Katzenbach, in the Electorate of Palatinate, October 13, 1718, and died November 13, 1781. Here now lies a handful of ashes washed in the blood of Christ."

Valentin Leonhardt came to America in 1746, and the probability is that if he tarried at all in Pennsylvania it was only for a few days. The records show that he was in North Carolina a few years later. The church, "Leonhardt's Church," bearing his name, was established as early as 1754, more likely a year earlier. This is a Reformed (German) Church now known by the name of Pilgrim, or the Church of the Pilgrims. The selection of the site of this church forms an interesting incident in the life of Valentin Leonhardt. One of his nearest neighbors was Jacob Berrier (Berger). One day in 1753 or 1754 the old man Berrier and two or three companions were riding through the country between the Yadkin River and Abbott's Creek. The Indians then still roved through this section of North Carolina. Mr. Berrier and his companions had visited several settlers on the lands between and on the waters of these two streams. These men were neighbors though they lived in some cases many miles apart. About three-quarters of a mile west of Abbott's Creek these gentlemen came to a beautiful spot in a grove of oak, hickory and sugar-maple trees, where was also a spring of sparkling water bubbling up. Here they paused, and Jacob Berrier said to his companions: "Got hat diese Stelle zur verehrung sines Namens geschaffen; hier mussen wir ein Versammlungshaus haben." (God fashioned this place for a house of worship; here we must have a meeting-

VALENTINE LEONARD, 1824-1894

Confederate Soldier, Fourth Generation Descendant of the Revolutionary War Patriot, Valentin Leonhardt

house.) This spot was near the Leonhardt homestead on the Henry McCulloh lands. McCulloh was the agent appointed by Lord Granville to collect rents in Carolina and, when land was sold to settlers, to make the proper deeds. Lord Granville also deeded several large tracts of land to McCulloh himself, and the latter disposed of his own holdings to settlers. It will be remembered that Lord Granville was one of the eight Lords Proprietors who held this part of Carolina when the other seven surrendered their interests back to the King. Many of the early settlers were in a sense "squatters," and this church may also be so classed. It was established on a tract of the Lord Granville lands lying between the lands of Valentin Leonhardt on the south and Philip Sauer on the north. Leonhardt's first deed bears date of April 17, 1762, and his second August 27, 1762. Sauer's first deed was made in 1763. Of course these men lived on their lands several years before securing titles. No title of the church is on record at the date of its occupation. After North Carolina was properly organized as a State, and the government had confiscated the Granville and McCulloh lands, three elders of the church legally entered the lands in the name of the congregation. The date is October 8, 1783.

The records of the Reformed Church at Katzenbach, Germany, do not chronicle the marriage of Valentin Leonhardt; hence there is uncertainty as to whether he married before leaving for America in 1746. He had then reached the age of twenty-eight years, and the probability is that he was married. The marriage records just after 1740 are very defective at Katzenbach and Rockenhausen in Germany. In the year 1745 only four marriages are recorded; in 1746 only five, and these stop with April. Under date of February 13, 1748, is recorded the marriage of Philip Leonhardt, brother of Valentin, to Anna Elizabeth Neuss. There is no positive record giving the maiden name of his wife. The church register gives her first name as Elizabeth. At the baptism of Elizabeth Sauer, daughter of Philip Sauer (mentioned above), born October 13, 1758, the sponsors were Valentin Leonhardt and his wife Elizabeth. It will be noticed that the little girl was born on the birthday of Mr. Leonhardt. Leonhardt and Sauer were neighbors, close friends and members of the same church.

The church register of the original Katzenbach, of the Rhine-Palatinate, Germany, gives in detail the records of the Leonhardt family. Valentin Leonhardt's parents were Martin and Anna Barbara Leonhardt (nee Spohn). They were married November 11, 1704, by Rev. Carl Gervinus, pastor of the Reformed Church at Katzenbach from 1691 to 1710. Valentin, born October 13, 1718, was the youngest of four sons. The older brothers were the following: Sebastian, baptized February 14, 1706; Henry, baptized July 24, 1713; Philip, baptized March 18, 1717. Valentin was baptized October 23, 1718, in the Reformed Church at Katzenbach by Rev. Gotthard Steitz, pastor. The sponsors were John Paul Neuss and his wife Anna Ottilia. He was confirmed a full member of the same church at Easter, 1733, by Rev. Henry Julius Wagner, pastor from 1719 to 1763. The father, Martin Leonhardt, had also a brother named Michael.

Valentin Leonhardt and wife came to North Carolina in 1746 and settled in Bladen (afterwards Anson, then Rowan and now Davidson) County on a large tract of land between Abbott's Creek and one of its tributaries since called Leonhardt's Creek after his name. To this couple were born eight children: Barbara, Valentin(e), Michael, Peter, Catharine, Elizabeth, Philip and Jacob. Each of these is mentioned in the last will and testament of the father, made August 22, 1779, two years prior to his tragic and cruel death. In his will he bequeathed to his wife Elizabeth the "Manor Plantation that I now live on, during her bearing the name Leonhardt, and in case she does not change her name she is to keep it to have full rule over it during her lifetime; and likewise I leave to my wife all my horses, cattle, and my personal estate wholly." This plantation was to go to his sons Philip and Jacob after the death of his wife. To his other three sons he bequeathed his other plantations, and to the three daughters each fifty pounds in gold and silver, as well as household property. After the death of his wife, the remainder of his estate was to be converted into money and divided equally among the eight children. It will be noticed that the will was made during the Revolutionary War. Valentin Leonhardt was a soldier at this time in the service of his country, fighting for American independence. He had seen many brave and strong men cut down in battle. Conscious that this might soon be his fate, he wisely made his will. The piety of the man is also seen in the wording of the will, which he wrote himself. It begins: "In the name of God, Amen. I, Valentin Leonhardt, of the county of Rowan and Province of North Carolina, being in perfect health of body, and of perfect mind and memory, thanks be given unto God, calling to mind the mortality of my body, do make and ordain this my last will and testament in manner following: I recommend my soul into the hand of Almighty God who gave it; and my body to the earth to be buried in decent Christian burial, . . . And as touching such worldly estate wherewith it has pleased God to bless me in this life, I give, devise and dispose of the same in the following manner and form." He named as executors Jacob Hamm and Philip Sauer. The name Hamm has entirely disappeared from the community in which Leonhardt lived, but the name Sauer (now written Sowers) is still very common in this section.

The Rockenhausen records, near the original Katzenbach in Germany, show that Martin Leonhardt was a farmer. His son Valentin learned the tailor's trade, but after he came to America he too became a farmer on a large scale. His estate covered many hundreds of acres of land, and he had many horses, cattle, sheep, hogs, etc. It is not postively known whether he was a slaveholder or not. None are named in his will along with other bequests. However, he may have owned slaves, as they would have been included in the clause, "my personal estate wholly." His sons, as is shown by their several wills, were large slaveholders. Until a few years ago there still lived a very aged colored woman who belonged to Philip Leonhardt, one of the sons of Valentin, who came into a large property from his father's estate. Her name was Lucy, and she was a remarkable and interesting character. Aunt Lucy did not know her exact age, but facts go to prove her considerably over one hundred years old. Her master Philip died about 1828, and Lucy was a grown woman at the time of his death, which she remembered and described with clear vividness. He was taken ill on Saturday night at the home of his brother, Jacob, whither he had gone to spend the night, expecting to attend church on Sunday. Jacob lived

DAVIDSON COUNTY IN MILITARY SERVICE 241

at the old home place quite near "Leonhardt's Church." Philip was not able to return home until Monday, and then he lived only a few hours after reaching his house. Lucy testified to the excellent character of her master. She said he was a good Christian man, an officer in the "Dutch Congregation" (Leonhardt's Church), and that he often entertained the preachers in his home. She said she and the other colored people on his plantation had to go to church whenever there was preaching, and that the singing and preaching were in "Dutch" (German). Lucy learned to speak German while in this German family and she could speak and understand that tongue as she heard it spoken then. By the last will and testament of her master Philip, Lucy came into the possession of his daughter Leah. By a strange oversight the date when this will was made is not written in the instrument itself, which was probated in 1830, of course after his death. The will was probably made about 1820. Subsequently Lucy was sold by Leah to an English lady whom she spoke of as "Granny Lowe." It is a fact worthy of note that Aunt Lucy in speaking of the several families of her acquaintance in those distant years always spoke of them as "Dutch" or "English." She invariably made that distinction. This is a distinction that no one in this section now thinks of making; in fact, a very small percentage of the people can even make a distinction in the German and English names. However, there are a few very old people of the white race still living who can speak the German which they learned at their mothers' knees. When freedom came to Aunt Lucy in President Lincoln's time, she was in the fourth generation of the Lowe family, having first belonged to "Granny Lowe," then to her son James, then to her grandson James, then finally to her great-grandson Cicero Lowe. The last named man died in 1892 at the age of 73 years. It is easy to see that the age of Lucy was far more than a hundred years. Lucy said that her master Philip was very kind to his colored people, as were also his children, especially his daughters. She said that some "speculators" came to his house one day, wanting to buy all the "niggers." She declared they had more money than she had ever seen in all her life. They poured it out on the table in a great heap. But the family would not hear to selling them, and the girls told the speculators to leave.

The name Leonard (Leonhardt) evidently is French. A celebrated French painter named Leonard died in 1580. There is a French town of that name southwest of Paris. All that can be found in regard to the name of this family points towards the flight of the Huguenots from France to Germany through Switzerland, some of whom tarried in the latter country. Katzenbach is only about twenty-five miles east of the Rhine and fifteen miles northeast of Heidelberg. It is a small village near the northern boundary of Baden at the present time, which is a Grand Duchy extending from Basel, Switzerland, along the Rhine to a short distance north of Heidelberg. The Kuhr Pfaltz (the Electorate or Palatinate) originally formed a part of Unter Pfaltz, of which Heidelberg was the capital.

Valentin Leonhardt took the side of the Patriots in the Revolutionary War. Some of the Germans in North Carolina were Tories. This was in a sense natural, since the English had offered to the persecuted Germans an asylum in the new world. Rev. Samuel Suther was the pastor of "Leonhardt's Church" from 1768 until after the close of the Revolutionary War. He was himself an intense Patriot and preached the doctrine of American independence from his pulpits. He was a brilliant man and an eloquent preacher, and his influence over those to whom he ministered was very great. Under his fiery eloquence the men of his congregations enlisted in the American army to fight against "taxation without representation." Leonhardt was himself past fifty-five years of age at the outbreak of the Revolution, but he did not hesitate to enlist in the American army. Before the close of the war all of his sons had also seen service in the army. The last battle in which they fought was that of Guilford Court House between Cornwallis and General Greene, March 15, 1781, thirty miles distant from the Leonhardt farm. After this battle General Greene's army was partly disbanded, and Leonhardt and his sons returned home.

The elder Leonhardt had considerable money in gold coin when the war broke out. There were no banks in which to deposit it for safekeeping. How should he dispose of it during those perilous times when property and money were frequently exposed to the depredations of conscienceless British soldiers? He took a piece of walnut timber about three inches square and twenty inches in length, bored a hole into it, put the gold in, stopped it up and concealed it in the cellar wall under his house. He told no one about the place of concealment except his youngest son Jacob, who was also in the Patriot army during the latter part of the war. He did not even tell his wife, fearing the cruel British soldiers might force her to reveal the place of concealment if she really knew. Much cruelty of this kind was practiced by the British. Peter Hetrich lived ten miles south of the Leonhardt estate. He was also a Patriot and enlisted in the army. While he was away from home one day a band of British and Tories came to his house, and, holding a pistol in the face of his wife, cursed her and told her to give up all she had or die. She answered that she was helpless, and begged them to spare her and her children and her property. They only abused her for her pitiful entreaties, and again told her to give up all she had or die. They took all of the provisions except a little salt, drove off the choice horses and cattle and shot the others, and then burned all the buildings. When Peter Hetrich returned a few weeks later and found his desolated home, he took his wife and children to Virginia until after the war, when he returned. The old soldier Leonhardt had in mind the possibility of just such torture as this when he concealed his money. If he and his son had both been killed, the probability is that the money would still be in the cellar wall. But the son lived through the struggle, and took the gold from its hiding-place where it had remained throughout the years of the war. The walnut-timber bank was preserved and has been handed down from one generation to another. It is at present in the keeping of the writer of this book and is highly prized as an heirloom. It is in a perfect state of preservation.

There were many Tories in North Carolina and they hated the Patriots. It so happened that neighbors were often on opposite sides in battle. This was notably true in the battle of Ramsour's Mill in Lincoln county, and at Guilford Court House in Guilford County, North Carolina. Valentin Leonhardt did not escape the malice of the Tories. They were very bitter against him, and planned to take his life. On the second day of

November, 1781, near the close of the war, a band of Tories came to his farm with malice in their hearts. His "Mansion House" was built of immense hewn logs. Its dimensions were forty and thirty feet, two stories. Two long beams, twelve by fourteen inches, ran through the whole length of the house to support the joists of the upper floor. They were hewn with a "broad-axe" almost to perfect smoothness, and the lower edges were nicely chamfered. The logs of the walls were very large, the two bottom ones being twelve by twenty inches. These bottom logs were "rabbeted" on the inner side to receive the joists for the first floor. The joists themselves were worked out of logs with the broad-axe, and are much larger than carpenters now consider necessary. All the nails used in the house were made by hand "wrought iron," as were also the hinges of the doors and window-shutters. The writer has a pair of the hinges that held the narrow shutters in place at one window, as well as the curious hand-made nails that fastened them on. Under the west end of the house was the great cellar, previously referred to in this chapter, partly walled with large rough stones. This cellar was entered by a heavy slanting door on the south side of the house. The immense chimney stood near the middle of the house, with a fireplace on either side below, but with none on the upper floor. The chimney was wide enough to receive wood eight feet long. This width of chimney was so common in those days that it became a custom to cut fire-wood eight feet in length, and the custom was kept up long after such chimneys ceased to be built. A hundred yards distant from the house is a large spring, and three hundred yards to the west flows "Leonhardt's Creek," on which the pioneer built a grist mill, the site of which is still plainly visible. The front door was a double-door after a common pattern used in those days, sawed through the middle horizontally, making an upper and a lower door. Often in mild weather the lower door was closed and the upper one left open.

The old soldier had returned from his day's labor on the farm on this second day of November, 1781, and was quietly resting by the old fashioned open fireplace. Supper was over and the farm hands had gone to their places of rest. The revolutionary Patriot sat peacefully by his own hearth-stone, "under his own vine and fig tree," meditating quietly in the gathering gloom of night. Suddenly, unexpectedly, a gunshot rang out at the open door; the good Christian man, the brave hero, the gallant soldier, fell to the floor mortally wounded. The clean uncarpeted floor ran red with the master's blood. The perpetrators of this black deed, this bloody crime, this gruesome tragedy, were Tories. They hated the man because he was a Patriot and stood for American independence. The cruel murderers, thinking that they had executed their design when they saw the old man fall to the floor, fled into the adjacent forest and escaped. Escape was easy in a sparsely settled country, such as this was at the time. The murderers were never positively identified, though the family and friends had well-grounded convictions as to the primary actors in this foul crime. The murderers fled, thinking that they had killed Leonhardt on the spot. He was in fact mortally wounded, though he lived until the thirteenth of the month, when his spirit took its flight from the fallen temple which had been its home for sixty-three years.

On the same night, the second of November, 1781, a similar murderous tragedy was enacted on the

CAPTAIN CHARLES A. HUNT, Sr., 1843-1925
Confederate Soldier, Lexington Merchant and Cotton Mill Operator

neighboring farm of Wooldrich Fritz. Wooldrich Fritz was also a Revolutionary War soldier. He had enlisted in the army with Valentin Leonhardt, and had returned home with him after the battle of Guilford Court House. While one band of Tories went to Leonhardt's house, another went to the home of Fritz and shot him dead. At the crack of the gun the man fell dead on the spot. The murderers here also made their escape.

The bodies of these two soldiers lie side by side in the old Leonhardt's Church graveyard. Fritz, who was killed on the second day of November, was buried first. When Leonhardt died of his wounds on the thirteenth, his body was buried by the side of his comrade. Soapstone slabs mark the graves of these two Patriots. On the stone at the head of Fritz's grave is the inscription:

Wooldrich Fritz, deceased November the second, 1781, aged 50 years.

> Remember me as you pass by;
> As you are now, so once was I;
> As I am now, so must you be;
> Prepare therefore to follow me.

The stone at the foot of the grave of Fritz has these words on it:

> Lo, here doth lifeless Wooldrich lie,
> Cut off by murder's cruelty.

We have already given the German inscription on the headstone at Leonhardt's grave; on the stone at the foot of his grave are the following lines in English:

> Beneath this stone doth now remain
> An ancient man by murder slain.

This is a quaint inscription. The word "ancient" would seem to indicate that there was an idea in the minds of those who erected the stone that in the years to come, down through many generations, men and women and children would look with reverence upon this grave. This inscription would tell them how the man came to his death. And so it has been; thousands have looked upon the grave, and have read the simple words.

These graves had no other monument to mark the last resting place of their heroic dead until the year 1896, when the citizens of the community decided to erect over them a handsomer and more pretentious stone. Popular subscriptions were taken to defray the expenses, and the people contributed liberally. A tall marble shaft was erected on a broad and strong concrete base. On the north side of this stone is the name of Leonhardt with the dates of birth and death; on the south side is the same concerning Fritz. On the east face of the die are the words: "This monument was erected by citizens A.D. 1896 out of veneration for our brave dead. These men are of those who fought for and gained our liberty. Unveiled with appropriate ceremonies July 4, 1896." On the west face are the words: "The heroes buried in this spot were cruelly assassinated in their own homes by Tories near the close of the Revolutionary War. They were Patriots and bravely fought for American Independence." On the fourth day of July, A.D. 1896, one hundred and fifteen years after the death of these patriots who died as martyrs to American independence, this handsome monument was unveiled in the presence of ten thousand people. The memory of these brave men is fondly cherished not only by numerous descendants, but by the

DAVIDSON COUNTY IN MILITARY SERVICE 251

citizenship of the entire community. Peaceful be the slumbers of the brave heroes who sleep beneath this shaft.

General Z. V. Walser, of this city, possesses one of the best reference libraries in the State and maintains a keen interest in all historical and biographical matters concerning North Carolina. Upon the recent publication in *The Dispatch* of the account of General Greene's stop at the home of Mrs. Spurgeon, in the Abbott's Creek country, which was taken from the second series of Dr. Caruthers's history of North Carolina in 1776, General Walser was reminded that he had some years ago gotten hold of a copy of the first series of this history, published in 1854, or two years before the second series. Referring to this he finds there are several accounts of clashes between Tories and Whigs which took place about midway between Lexington and Denton and in the very southern end of the county.

Dr. Caruthers's account of the incidents follows:

During the period of the war though the precise date is not recollected a number of Tories came to the house of Frederick Goss, who lived in what is now Davidson County, about ten miles southeast of Lexington, and plundered it of all the bed clothing, about seventy yards of homespun cloth, with whatever else they could find that was worth carrying away, and a young and valuable horse. Frederick Goss and his son, Jacob Goss, then only fifteen or sixteen years of age, with a bound boy by the name of Alexander Slader, were in a field at some distance from the house, pulling flax; and when the Tories went to the field for the purpose of making them prisoners, Slader hid himself in the flax, so he escaped notice. Frederick Goss, being somewhat advanced in life, was not made a prisoner; but they took his son, Jacob Goss, who was the father of Jacob Goss, Esq., and carried him away as a prisoner, and his young horse, with the plunder they had taken in and about the house. After night they took the road to a Tory camp, which was distant from any road and in a very secluded place, where they were about to tie Jacob; but one of their number, having some acquaintance with Jacob, persuaded them not to bind him. There came up during the night a hard rain, and they all got very wet. When it was over they made a large fire for the purpose of drying themselves, and on becoming dry, they all fell into a sound sleep, when Jacob went to his young horse, cut him loose, and then jumping on his back, he whipped off and got home safe. The neighbors were soon raised and went in pursuit. Before going far they were informed that the Tories, their enemies, had forded the river near Massey's Ferry, which was not far from the confluence of the Uwharrie and Yadkin rivers. The Whigs were led or commanded by Captain Azariah Merrill, and before getting to the river he met a man who told him that they had crossed. Being conducted by him they went over, and soon came upon the Tories, where they had halted and were lying by. Merrill had a strong company, and leaving them behind, with orders suited to any contingency that would be likely to occur, he went forward himself to reconnoiter, or try if he could discover their precise location; when, passing a hollow or ravine, he came upon one of their sentinels, who raised and cocked his gun; but Captain Merrill shot him down before he had time to fire. This brought on a general skirmish, which was severe but short. Not one of the Whigs, however, was killed, and only one wounded, by a ball in the thigh; for the Tories were attacked so suddenly and furiously that they were not able to get into any kind of order and could take no deliberate aim.

The Tories, it seems, gave only one fire, and that scattering, or given much at random, until they fled and took the boat at Massey's Ferry with the intention of returning to what is now the Davidson or Montgomery side of the Yadkin; but the Whigs were firing on them all the way as they fled across, and they kept jumping out into the water until not more than four or five remained in the boat when it landed. A number of Tories were killed and some of those who jumped into the river were drowned. This made peaceable times in that region of country, and only one man was killed by the Tories from this time to the close of the war.

A man by the name of John Cornelieson, who lived near the lead or silver mines in Davidson County, was killed in his own house, and in a manner which indicated great barbarity. When several of them went in and fell upon him with clubs and swords, he got back under the mantelpiece, when they shot him down and he fell into the fire; but his wife pulled him out. Next morning, Mrs. Ann Briggs, the mother-in-law of Jacob Goss, Esq., who was originally a Miss Collins, from the neighborhood of Wilmington, went over and saw the body of Cornelieson. The hearth was deluged with blood, and the house presented a most frightful scene.

The man who shot Cornelieson was known, and Cornelieson had a relation by the name of Spirey, who was determined to revenge his death. He pursued the Tory who shot Cornelieson, and followed his trail into Tennessee. At length the Tory reached the house of a woman who was a relation of his; and thinking himself out of danger, he stopped there for the night; but Spirey was there and, with the stealthiness of an Indian, was watching round the house, when he heard the murderer tell his relation, the mistress of the house, that he would pull off his clothes to sleep; for he had not had them off since he left North Carolina. While he was stripping and preparing for bed, Spirey, being certain of his man, ran the muzzle of his gun through a crack or opening between the logs, and shot him dead. Spirey then returned to his home in North Carolina; and this affair was the last of the kind that occurred during the struggle for independence. Such scenes present to us the horrors of civil war in a strong light, and while they were the price of our liberties, they should serve as a perpetual warning to guard most vigilantly and strenuously against everything of the kind to the end of time.

Many of the names given in the account of these incidents are now familiar in Davidson County. The Goss family still lives in the county and the name Jacob Goss has been handed down. The Merrill place is about midway between Lexington and Denton. It was owned some years ago by J. D. Holt, of Lexington, and it was handled in sale by Walser & Walser some years ago. The name of Cornelieson is familiar in this section though most of the family now live across the river in Rowan. The Briggses are yet a prominent family in the section of the country where these stirring events of the war for liberty occurred. The name Collins is also well known in the same section.

The historian is indebted also to Zeb V. Walser, Esq., for a sketch of Captain Benjamin Merrill.

Captain Benjamin Merrill is believed to have been a member of Jersey Church in this (Davidson) county

Davidson County in Military Service 255

and to have commanded a company of 300 men, supposed to have been mainly from the Jersey settlement.

Rev. Henry Sheets, in *A History of the Liberty Baptist Association,* says he visited the spot where once stood the residence of Captain Merrill, some four miles south of Lexington, N. C., and about two miles east from Jersey Church. "The venerable oaks standing there, could they but speak, might tell us much of valuable history in the eventful years, now buried forever in the wreck of time." Merrill is said to have been a gunsmith. In the evening he would arrange a barrel for boring, start his crude machinery, and leave it running all night. Little is known of his early history. There were Merrills in the Jersey settlement. Governor William Tryon said Merrill had a wife and eight children. Merrill himself said he had ten children. Nothing is known of the children except one son who had five children. Their names and dates of birth are as follows: Benjamin Smith Merrill, September 10, 1774; Bettie Merrill, May 2, 1776; Azariah Merrill, May 26, 1777; Jemima Merrill, October 6, 1782; Sally Merrill, July 15, 1784. All the Merrills in this section were descended from Azariah Merrill. Deacon Ebenezer Merrill, a member of Jersey Church, and Benjamin Merrill, of Burk Church, Davie County, were sons of Azariah Merrill, a grandson of Captain Benjamin Merrill. Captain Azariah Merrill, who led the Whig forces in a skirmish with the Tories in lower Davidson, was a brother of the subject of this sketch.

The Jersey settlement is believed to have been composed almost exclusively of Baptists. It was from this point that Captain Benjamin Merrill marched toward the battle of Alamance with 300 men, the battle having been fought before his arrival, May 16, 1771. It is said that after the defeat of the Regulators at Alamance more than 1,500 families left this section of the State and that Sandy Creek Church, in Randolph County, was reduced from 606 to 14 souls.

In a letter published in the Boston *Gazette,* October 21, 1771, written by a gentleman in North Carolina to a friend in New Jersey, it is stated that James Hunter and Captain Merrill bore a petition to Governor Tryon to treat for peace. (8 *Col. Rec.* 647.) This statement appears to contradict another statement herein that Captain Merrill did not reach the battle of Alamance. In the foregoing letter it is also stated that Captain Merrill was a man generally esteemed for his honesty, integrity, piety and moral life.

The Trial of Merrill

At a term of the Supreme Court of Oyer and Terminer for the trial of the Regulators in the "Back Country" begun at Hillsborough, May 30, 1771, twelve Regulators were tried and condemned for high treason. Tyron suspended the execution of six. The other six were executed. The *Colonial Records,* Volume 8, page 643, says: "Among these last the most distinguished was Benjamin Merrill who had been captain of militia in Rowan (now Davidson) County." Governor Tryon refused to pardon Captain Benjamin Merrill, Captain Messer, Robert Matear and James Pugh and two others whose names are not known. Over this court Chief Justice Martin Howard presided, together with Associate Justices Maurice Moore and Richard Henderson. Chief Justice Howard concluded the judgment of the court as follows: "I must now close my afflicting duty by

Davidson County in Military Service 257

pronouncing upon you the awful sentence of the law, which is, that you, Benjamin Merrill, be carried to the place from whence you came, that you be drawn from thence to the place of execution, where you are to be hanged by the neck; that your bowels be taken out and burnt before your face; your head be cut off, your body divided into four quarters, and this to be at his majesty's disposal; and the Lord have mercy on your soul."

The trial of the twelve Regulators was held under the eye of Governor Tryon and his soldiery and was a howling farce from beginning to end.

Haywood, a severe critic of the Regulators, on page 146, *Governor Tryon of North Carolina,* says: "The person whose fate probably excited more compassion than that of any other Regulator put to death was Captain Benjamin Merrill, who was an officer of militia in Rowan (now Davidson) and raised a company to join the insurgents. He was largely instrumental in turning back the brigade of General Hugh Waddell. Afterwards he was captured by a force under Colonel Fanning, and his life paid the penalty. It is said that when he was brought to execution one of Tryon's soldiers was heard to declare that if all men went to the gallows with a character such as Captain Merrill's, hanging would be an honorable death."

Rev. Jethro Rumple, in *History of Rowan County,* referring to the foregoing incident, says: "Some time previous to the battle of Alamance Governor Tryon sent General Hugh Waddell to Salisbury with a division of troops from Bladen, Cumberland, and the western counties. These troops were to remain at Salisbury until a supply of powder, flints and blankets

17

from Charleston should reach them. But the Cabarrus Blackboys, as they have been called, intercepted the convoy at Phifer's Mill, three miles west of Concord, unloaded the wagons, stove in the kegs of powder, tore up the blankets and forming a huge pile blew up the whole. The military stores failing to reach him, General Waddell with the 150 men left Salisbury and attempted to join Tryon. But when he reached Potts Creek, about two miles east of the Yadkin River, he was confronted by a large force of Rowan County Regulators who threatened to cut his troops to pieces if he offered to join the army under Tryon. He wisely resolved to fall back across the river to Salisbury. This was on the 10th of May, 1771, six days before the battle of the Great Alamance. A few days after the battle Tryon marched to the east side of the Yadkin and effected a junction with General Waddell."

The point on Potts Creek referred to above is on a farm now owned by Mrs. Zeb V. Walser.

The Place of Execution

The place where the six Regulators suffered death is just beyond the limits of the town of Hillsborough near the historic Eno River. All around is an extensive and well-kept lawn. Everything is beautiful, serene, peaceful, with nothing but the music of songbirds to break the stillness. Were the power of speech given those oaks and the Eno River hard by, how strange a tale would come forth!

> All trees at night like men in thought,
> By poetry to silence wrought;
> They stand so still and they look so wise
> With folded arms and half shut eyes,

> More shadowy than the shade they cast
> When the wan moonlight on the river past;
> The river is green and runneth slow—
> We cannot tell what it saith;
> It keepth its secrets down below,
> And so doth death!

After the battle of Alamance Tryon began his march of devastation into the plantations of the principal Regulators, burning the buildings and laying waste all property.

As already stated, Captain Merrill was taken prisoner by a detachment under Colonel Fanning and brought to Tryon's army encamped at "Jersey Settlement Camp," on Saturday, June 1, 1771, put in chains with other prisoners and dragged through the country to Hillsborough. While on the scaffold he professed faith in Christ, his hope of Heaven, his willingness to go, sang a Psalm very devoutly like the Covenanters in the grass market at Edinburgh and died like a Christian and soldier. He referred feelingly to his wife and ten children saying: "I entreat that no reflection be cast on them on my account." He requested that some part of his estate be spared for the widow and the fatherless.

First Battle for Freedom

Governor Tryon with his own hands fired the first shot at Alamance, the first battle of the American Revolution. The blood shed here made possible the Mecklenburg Declaration. Dr. Hawks says God made the flower of freedom grow out of the turf that covered these men's graves. It was at Alamance, not at Lexington in Massachusetts, where the first patriots defied an army flying a British flag and gave up their life-blood for American liberty and independence.

> No stately column marks the hallowed place
> Where silent sleep, unurned, their sacred dust—
> The first free martyrs of a glorious race,
> Their fame a people's wealth, a nation's trust.
>
> Immortal youth shall crown their deathless fame,
> And as their country's glories shall advance,
> Shall brighter glow, o'er all the earth thy name,
> Our first-fought field of freedom—Alamance!

Should Honor Merrill

More than a century and a half has sped by since Captain Benjamin Merrill gave his life a sacrifice for his country, and no shaft indicates his final resting place. A monument should adorn the public square in Lexington.

Mrs. S. A. Irish, Davenport, Iowa, is a daughter of Zachariah Yarborough of this county. Captain Benjamin Merrill was the great-grandfather of Zachariah Yarborough, a son of Thomas Yarborough. The wife of Thomas Yarborough was Jemima Merrill, a granddaughter of Captain Benjamin Merrill. Mrs. Irish says the name of Captain Merrill's wife was Jemima Stout, Stoutsbridge, Monmouth County, New Jersey. Mrs. Irish left Davidson County in 1846 for Iowa, traveling in a "covered wagon," and lived to be more than ninety years of age. She says she has ridden over much of the west on horseback.

Captain Merrill came from New Jersey, as did a large number of the original settlers in the Jersey settlement.

DAVIDSON COUNTY IN MILITARY SERVICE 261

Lad of Davidson County Helped to Secure Liberty

How a Davidson County woman, wife of a Tory colonel, and her young son performed a service for the army of General Nathaniel Greene, Revolutionary hero more important than the generosity of Mrs. Steele, of Rowan, whose gift of a purse of gold is so well known wherever the history of North Carolina is studied is told in *The Old North State in 1776,* a history prepared by Rev. E. W. Caruthers, D.D. This story is made available for the people of Davidson County by G. W. Clinard, of Wallburg, who now lives on a portion of the plantation made famous by the stay of General Greene and by the generous hospitality of Mrs. Spurgeon. Mr. Clinard borrowed the book from P. P. Motsinger, of High Point, who is a descendant of the Spurgeon family of Abbott's Creek Township.

In the show window of Woodruff's shoe store in Lexington was shown for several days a rare old picture of one of the later Spurgeons, Joseph and his wife. This historical character in 1822, when he was then a man of mature age, assisted in the formation of Davidson County out of Rowan and was one of the early representatives in the Legislature. There is also shown the remains of the old army hat which was worn by Colonel Spurgeon, while he was a member of the British army. It was recently rescued from an attic, where it had lain for twenty years or more. Joseph Spurgeon gave it to the late D. B. Clinard.

In the account following the place mentioned as Possumtown is Bethany community in Midway Township. Many of the older people of that section remember that Bethany was formerly known as Possumtown.

It will be recalled that General Greene had effected a juncture of his army with that of General Morgan, who defeated Tarleton at Cowpens, and this army had been hard pressed from the Catawba, where General Davidson, after whom this county was named, was killed, until the Yadkin was reached at Trading Ford, near where the Southern Railway crosses the river now. General Davidson, according to the historian, was killed by Frederick Hager, a Tory who is thought to have piloted Cornwallis's army across the Catawba. The end of the chase was at Guilford Court House where an important battle was fought. Cornwallis remained on the field but was too badly crippled to follow Greene, so he turned eastward and marched on to Yorktown, where he was hemmed up and surrendered. These facts being considered, Davidson County has an important niche in American history that should be known to all.

Here let Dr. Caruthers's history take up the story:

General Greene Crosses County

From Trading Ford, General Greene, having only a few men with him, and not much encumbered with baggage, took the road which was then commonly traveled from that place to Martinsville, where he had directed General Huger to meet him with the main body of the army. The course was the most direct, but the road was a very bad one. It was never much used after the war, but traces of it may still be seen. Crossing the road which now leads from Lexington to Salisbury, about four miles from the former place, in what is still called the Forahawk Old Field, though now in cultivation, it went by a place called Possumtown, and crossed the road now leading from Greensboro to Salem, about a mile west of New Garden Meeting-House. Any one who has ever traveled through that part of the county, especially the winter season, and was wide awake at the time, knows it must then have been almost impassable, and that, with a heavy baggage train prudence would have dictated another route.

The winter was not one of unusual cold. The one previous had been of unheard of severity, and so intense was the cold that wagons and teams crossed the Yadkin on ice, a thing unknown in this country before or since, until this present time when they are crossing again (January, 1856); but the winter in which the British passed through the State was a comparatively mild one. There were frequent and heavy rains, and it generally cleared off with a "north-wester" which froze the top of the ground for two or three days, and thus, all the time, the roads were in a desperate condition. When the ground was frozen, they were exceedingly rough, and when they were thawed, the mud was so deep that they were almost impassable, either for infantry, or for artillery and baggage.

Mrs. Spurgeon is Hostess

When he came to Abbott's Creek Meeting-House, he halted two or three days to rest his troops, or perhaps to wait for further developments. He made his headquarters at the house of Colonel Spurgeon, who was in good circumstances, and lived about a mile from the church. He was a Tory Colonel, one of those commissioned by Governor Martin, about the beginning of 1776, and had taken quite an active part in favor of the royal cause. Of course he was not at home to receive his guest and "treat him to the best he had";

but his wife, Mary Spurgeon, was as true a Whig as her husband was a Tory, and like Mrs. Steele, in Salisbury, she showed him all the kindness and gave him all the encouragement in her power. On arriving there, the first thing he did was to select his ground for a battle, should one become necessary. It was a very eligible position, elevated, covered with a dense growth of large hickories, most of which are yet standing, and ample enough for all the evolutions that might be necessary, while he would have the buildings to protect him in case of emergency. As this locality was near the house, he told Mrs. Spurgeon that if Cornwallis should overtake him and compel him to fight, she must go into the cellar with her children and remain there until the conflict was over; but fortunately for her and for all concerned, the foe was still prevented from advancing by a higher power. Not having heard a word, however, of Cornwallis or his movements since he left the Trading Ford, he felt very anxious to know whether he would cross there, as soon as the river became fordable, and pursue him, or remain on that side for the purpose of bringing the country into subjection, or cross higher up, with the view of getting between him and Virginia.

In such circumstances, a man of his patriotism and indomitable energy of character could not rest. There was too much at stake, and he was of too noble a spirit to remain long inactive or in a state of suspense, while danger of the most alarming kind was so near. Having no other means of information, and knowing Mr Spurgeon's patriotic spirit, he asked her if she knew of any one in whom he could put confidence as ! wished to send such a one back to the river, for t purpose of procuring some information respecting t movements of Cornwallis. She told him yes, he could put confidence in her son John. Feeling encouraged by this answer, and, at the same time, like a prudent man, fully awake to the perils that beset him, he repeated the question, with a great deal of earnestness:

"Are you sure, Madam, that I can put confidence in John?"

"Yes, sir," was her prompt and womanly reply. "Yes, sir, you can put confidence in John, if he will consent to go, and I think he will."

Lad Serves His Country

That was enough; and John was called. General Greene then told him what he wanted—that he wished him to take his own horse and go back to Trading Ford to see if he could find out anything about the movement of the British, and if he saw nothing of them there, to go up the river for a number of miles. He promptly consented, and set off at once. He rode a fine horse, and with proper vigilance had not much dread. On going to the river, he could neither see nor hear anything of them; but in obedience to orders he went up a number of miles without any better success. He then returned, and General Greene told him he must go again, for he must have the information, and he must have it soon; and if he saw nothing of them, to continue up the river to the Shallow Ford. Young Spurgeon set out again, and on reaching the Shallow Ford, some thirty miles, more or less, from home, he found they were crossing. Then returning as fast as his horse could carry him he reported that they were crossing at that ford. Instantly General Greene ordered his horse, and was off for Martinsville, where he arrived on the evening of the 7th, and found General

Huger there, who had just arrived with the main body of the army. By this time, the designs of Cornwallis were manifest and Greene's situation admitted of no delay; but we ought to observe how much service the wife and son of a Tory Colonel, though a mere lad at the time, rendered at this critical juncture of affairs.

Davidson County Visited by President Washington

The year 1791, when Davidson was still included within the Rowan boundaries, the President made a tour through the South that year in his famous coach, and he was attended by a proper retinue of friends and servants. His first stop in North Carolina was at Halifax, April 16, 1791, about six o'clock in the evening. On the trip down the President stopped at Tarboro, New Bern, Wilmington, and in many private homes. In all the towns and on all the estates where he stopped he was accorded the finest hospitality. On the return from points farther south he reached the border of North Carolina May 27, 1791. He passed through Mecklenburg and Cabarrus counties, and then entered Rowan. A few miles out from Salisbury a company of boys each wearing a bucktail in his hat extended greetings to the chief magistrate of this great country. The incident greatly pleased President Washington. The night was spent in Salisbury, and the company resumed the journey early the next morning. The Yadkin River was crossed at Trading Ford, and late breakfast was served near Reed's Crossroads. Here the horses were given a good rest. The party took dinner farther on in what is now Arcadia Township, at the residence of a Mr. Hege, whose name is thought to have been Christian Hege. Later in the evening the President reached the Moravian town of Salem.

In front of the fine building of Reeds Consolidated School, on the old Salisbury-Salem stagecoach road, at the spot where President Washington and those who were with him on this journey through the county ate a late breakfast, a boulder was erected a few years ago. To this boulder has now been attached by the General William Davidson Chapter Daughters of the American Revolution a bronze tablet with the following inscription: "George Washington Boulder. On this rock President George Washington ate breakfast en route from Salisbury to Salem, May 31, 1791. Erected by General William Davidson Chapter D.A.R., Lexington North Carolina, 1926."

2. DAVIDSON MEN IN THE SPANISH-AMERICAN WAR

In Company D, Second Regiment, North Carolina Volunteers, Captain Gilmer, the following young men were enrolled: George W. Reid, Ellis Wagner, John Anderson, David H. Draughn, Edgar Sink; Company G of the same regiment, Captain Robert L. Durham, Samuel T. Berrier. J. Allen Livengood, Philip F. Hedrick and William H. Trice were in Company L, Captain Hill. First Regiment: Douglass Thompson, Frank Brumley. Others known to have been in the service from Davidson County are Ben Miller, Ben Dickerson, John Welborn, Luther A. Welch, C. D. Hunt, Charles Eastep.

3. CONFEDERATE SOLDIERS OF DAVIDSON COUNTY

Until the present no systematic effort has ever been made to secure a complete roster of the men of Davidson County who served in the great army of the Southern Confederacy. The long period of sixty years has elapsed since the close of the war, making it a difficult matter to gather up from the sparse written records and from the memory of aged men and women still living the honored names of those brave men who enlisted, 1861-65, in the ranks of the armies of the South. But the effort has now been made. The compiler of the list is aware that there have been omissions; this was, under the circumstances, inevitable. But the effort has been sincere and earnest. Appeal after appeal has been made for assistance, and the people from all sections of the county have responded. It was impossible to give names of companies and regiments in all cases and so we give names only.

The A. A. Hill Camp of Confederate Veterans of Davidson County was organized July 8, 1898, in the courthouse in Lexington, sixty-three veterans in attendance. The following were chosen temporary officers: Captain F. C. Robbins, chairman; Charles A. Hunt, Sr., secretary. At a meeting July 16 the following were elected permanent officers for the year: C. M. Thompson, First Commandant; C. A. Hunt, Sr., Second Commandant; Captain F. C. Robbins, Adjutant; Rev. R. H. Parker, Chaplain; H. H. Hartley, Commissary; J. L. Clement, Quartermaster and Orderly Sergeant. This organization has continued down to the present time, holding its meetings annually. For many years the day of meeting has been May 10, Confederate Memorial Day. The members of the United Daughters of the Confederacy are unfailingly courteous to the veterans in their annual reunions and do everything possible to cheer the hearts of this splendid body of men. The annual business meeting of the veterans is always followed by a fine dinner served by the women's organization. Following are the officers of the Camp at the present time: C. M. Thompson, Major Commandant; Captain C. L. Badgett, First Lieutenant; William Fritts, Second Lieutenant; W. L. Myers, Third Lieutenant; Captain F. C. Robbins, Adjutant; Captain C. W. Trice, Treasurer; George Thomason, Commissary; Dr. J. C. Leonard, Chaplain.

THE SWORD OF ROBERT LEE
(From "Father Ryan's" Poems)

Forth from its scabbard, pure and bright,
Flashed the sword of Lee!
Far in the front of the deadly fight,
High o'er the brave in the cause of Right,
Its stainless sheen, like a beacon light,
Led us to Victory.

Out of its scabbard, where, full long,
It slumbered peacefully,
Roused from its rest by the battle's song,
Shielding the feeble, smiting the strong,
Guarding the right, avenging the wrong,
Gleamed the sword of Lee.

Forth from its scabbard, high in air
Beneath Virginia's sky—
And they who saw it gleaming there,
And knew who bore it, knelt to swear
That where that sword led they would dare
To follow—and to die.

Out of its scabbard! Never hand
Waved sword from stain as free,
Nor purer sword led braver band,
Nor braver bled for a brighter land,
Nor brighter land had a cause so grand,
Nor cause a chief like Lee!

Forth from its scabbard! How we prayed
That sword might victor be;
And when our triumph was delayed,
And many a heart grew sore afraid,
We still hoped on while gleamed the blade
Of noble Robert Lee.

Forth from its scabbard all in vain
Bright flashed the sword of Lee;
'Tis shrouded now in its sheath again,
It sleeps the sleep of our noble slain,
Defeated, yet without a stain,
Proudly and peacefully.

The following is the roster of men from Davidson County in the service of the Confederacy:

Andrew, Capt. Daniel
Andrew, Jesse
Anderson, John T.
Anderson, Frank
Adderton, John B.
Adderton, W. S.
Adderton, Stokes
Arner, Charley
Adams, Robert L.
Allred, Clem
Ader, Daniel
Arnold, Rev. J. D.
Badgett, B. R.
Badgett, C. L.
Badgett, W. S.
Badgett, Capt. C. L.
Baker, Rufus
Baker, Wm.
Ball, Henry
Beck, Wm.

Beck, John S.
Beck, David
Beck, T. D.
Beck, Daniel
Beck, H. B.
Beck, Riley
Beck, Sandy
Beck, Alfred
Beck, Lewis
Beck, George F.
Beck, Bert
Beck, Jacob R.
Beck, Jacob
Beck, George
Beck, S. R.
Beck, Obediah
Beck, J. F.
Beck, J. R.
Boney, Daniel
Burkhart, John

COLONEL WILLIAM E. HOLT, 1839-1917
Owner and Operator of Wennonah Cotton Mills at Lexington Until His Death

DAVIDSON COUNTY IN MILITARY SERVICE 273

Burkhart, J. Frank
Burkhart, John W.
Burkhart, Hiram
Burkhart, Obediah
Burkhart, Andrew
Burkhart, Frank
Berrier, Henry J.
Berrier, Thomas
Berrier, William
Berrier, Felix
Berrier, H. R.
Berrier, Jacob
Berrier, Hiram
Boggs, Arrington
Boggs, A. G.
Byerly, Wesley
Byerly, Ephraim
Byerly, Jacob
Byerly, Obediah
Byerly, Andrew
Byerly, George
Byerly, J. F.
Byerly, John
Byerly, Lindsay
Bullybough, Burrell
Brice, Andrew J.
Burrow, Wm.
Burrow, Henry
Buie, Andrew J.
Buie, T. J.
Buie, Nevin C.
Buie, Samuel Jefferson
Buie, A. J.
Beeker, George
Beeker, George W.
Bean, James
Bean, Alexander
Bean, John Kirby
Bean, Otho C.
Bean, Love

Baker, Rufus
Baker, Wm.
Baker, Philip
Baker, George
Bowers, David
Bowers, Julius
Bowers, Erastus
Bowers, L. W.
Bowers, Wm.
Bowers, Wm. H.
Brinkley, Britt
Brinkley, Henry B.
Bailey, John
Bailey, S. S.
Bailey, John F.
Beall, T. B.
Beall, Maj. Dr. James F.
Brassington, S. W.
Brittingham, John W.
Billings, M. B.
Billings, J. L.
Billings, R. A.
Blair, Joseph
Blair, Madison
Blair, Array
Blair, Emsley
Broadway, David
Broadway, W. R.
Broadway, A. A.
Broadway, W. H.
Broadway, Wm.
Barnes, Richard
Barnes, C. A.
Barnes, Alexander
Britt, ?
Bryant, Tom
Bryant, Wm.
Bryant, Cornelius
Bryant, Kelly
Benister ?

18

Babcock, Edward
Bodenhamer, Pleas
Bell, Z. T.
Benson, Wm. F.
Barger, Jacob
Biggers, W. D.
Brooks, H. M.
Black, J. W.
Black, Robert
Black, Felix
Black, George
Brown, Wm.
Brown, Silas
Clinard, Samuel
Clinard, John Wilson
Clinard, S. Z.
Clinard, Francis
Clinard, John
Clinard, Aihart
Clinard, A. C.
Clinard, Alex
Clinard, Randall
Clinard, Philip
Crouse, Wm. (Joe)
Crouse, Thomas M.
Crouse, Geo. W.
Crouse, Wiley
Craver, James
Craver, John Davidson
Craver, Burgess
Craver, James W.
Craver, A. Burgess
Craver, Newton
Craver, Ad
Craver, J. A.
Craver, Lee P.
Carter, Wm. C.
Carter, Abram H.
Carter, H. H.
Cross, Silas

Cross, Jackson
Cross, Henry Giles
Cross, D. H.
Cross, Alexander
Cross, James
Cross, Moses H.
Cross, A. R.
Cross, E. H.
Cross, G. W.
Cross, H. J.
Cook, Darling
Cook, George W.
Cook, Calvin
Cecil, Wesley
Cecil, Thomas
Cecil, S. L.
Cecil, T. S.
Cecil, Burrell
Clodfelter, Hugh
Clodfelter, Dougan
Clodfelter, Wm.
Clodfelter, David
Clodfelter, Joe
Coldfelter, Jacob
Clodfelter, David
Clodfelter, Solomon
Clodfelter, Hamilton L.
Clodfelter, Adam
Clodfelter, Adam (of Joly)
Clodfelter, George
Clodfelter, Ransom
Clodfelter, D. A.
Clodfelter, J. C.
Clodfelter, A. E.
Clodfelter, A. W.
Clodfelter, Joseph
Clodfelter, Samuel W.
Clodfelter, Lemuel
Cox, Solomon
Cox, Ebenezer

Davidson County in Military Service

Cox, John F.
Collett, Albert
Collett, Henry
Collett, Wm.
Collett, John
Carmalt, Thomas J.
Carrick, Otho
Carrick, J. F.
Carrick, J. D.
Carrol, Alsy
Carrol, Benjamin
Carrol, Peter
Carrol, Stephen
Carrol, W. J.
Cameron, J. W. R.
Conrad, Daniel W.
Conrad, Henry G.
Conrad, James N.
Conrad, Wm.
Conrad, Joseph
Conrad, James
Conrad, L. L.
Conrad, H. L.
Conrad, J. M.
Cooper, Henry A.
Cooper, Robert
Cristman, Allen T.
Cornelison, Burgess
Cornelison, George
Cutting, L. O.
Chapell, Wm.
Cole, Bennett
Cole, B. C.
Cranford, Wm.
Cranford, Wilburn
Cranford, Elias G.
Cranford, J. D.
Cranford, J. H.
Cranford, Joel
Copley, John

Coggins, Roby
Coggins, John
Coggins, Milas
Crotts, David
Crotts, Andrew
Crotts, Will
Curry, Calvin
Curry, James S.
Cope, John
Clement, J. S.
Clement, J. L.
Clement, H. A.
Copple, Joshua
Caudle, H. H.
Charles, R. T.
Dodson, George P.
Dodson, George F.
Dusenberry, Dr. E. L.
Durkins, W. Lindsay
Davis, Ivy
Davis, Joe
Davis, Henry
Davis, Wm.
Davis, Wyatt
Davis, S. R.
Davis, Ed
Davis, Hack
Davis, Henry
Davis, H. Jack
Davis, Woodson
Davis, Travis
Davis, Dow
Davis, Tucker
Davis, Dougan
Davis, S. L.
Davis, T. D.
Davis, E. P.
Dickens, Ephraim
Dickens, Thomas
Dickens, B. E.

Doty, Jake
Doty, Ben
Delap, John S.
Delap, Valentine
Delap, John
Delap, Felix
Doby, Wm.
Doby, Alex
Doby, Daniel
Doby, J. P.
Doby, J. D.
Dorsett, Leonard
Dorsett, Martin C.
Dorsett, Wm.
Dorsett, Ivory
Dorsett, Henry
Dorsett, David
Dorsett, Wesley
Darr, Henry
Darr, Solomon
Darr, George
Darr, Samuel
Darr, W. Andrew
Darr, Irenius
Darr, Socrates
Darr, J.
Daniel, Murphy
Daniel, J. H.
Daniel, Travis
Elberson, John Ham
Elliott, L. W.
Edinger, George
Edinger, Ransom
Edinger, Wm.
Edinger, Philip
Edinger, Daniel
Edinger, John R.
Edinger, George W.
Edinger, Philip H.
Edinger, Wm. M.

Edinger, David
Edinger, D. W.
Ellington, George
Ensley, Sam
Eller, John
Eller, Lorenzo
Eller, Samuel
Eller, George
Evans, Alexander
Evans, David
Evans, J. R.
Evans, Daniel
Evans, Michael
Epps, Bedford
Epps, Elisha
Epps, Morrel
Epps, James
Epps, Wm.
Epps, Thomas
Everhart, Felix
Everhart, Eli
Everhart, Robert
Everhart, Jake
Everhart, Andrew (of Jacob)
Everhart, Ambrose
Everhart, W. H.
Everhart, F. H.
Everhart, H. W.
Everhart, Michael
Everhart, Kelin
Everhart, A. C.
Everhart, Michael
Everhart, Hamilton
Everhart, Andrew
Everhart, Emanuel
Everhart, Christian
Everhart, Lewis
Everhart, Daniel
Everhart, Louis
Earnhart, R. T.

THE CONQUERED BANNER

"The warrior's Banner takes its flight
To greet the warrior's soul."

Earnhart, Whitt
Essick, John
Essick, Wm.
Essick, Thomas
Essick, Daniel
Essick, W. R.
Essick, Ransom
Essick, Jacob
Easter, George
Easter, Michael
Fine, Gabriel
Fine, J. S.
Floyd, Isam
Floyd, James
Floyd, Roby
Floyd, Squire
Floyd, Frank
Floyd, J. M.
Floyd, J. R.
Frank, John
Frank, Martin
Frank, P. M.
Frank, Jesse M.
Frank, Alex
Frank, George
Frank, George W.
Fritts, Adam
Fritts, Hiram
Fritts, Jesse
Fritts, Wm.
Fritts, Amos
Fritts, Daniel
Fritts, Frank
Fritts, George
Fritts, Hence
Fritts, Henry
Fritts, Smith
Fritts, Henderson
Fritts, H. G.
Fritts, Felix

Fowler, Thomas
Freedle, Frank
Freedle, Wm.
Freedle, David
Freedle, Lemuel
Freedle, S. R.
Farabee, Joe
Farabee, B. L.
Farabee, P. L.
Forshee, Wm.
Forshee, George
Forshee, Kearney
Forshee, Carey
Freeman, Jim
Freeman, Rev. J. W.
Ferrill, Emsley
Ferrill, Winburn
Foust, ?
Foust, Absalom
Faulkner, Jim
Foard, W. F.
Foard, Frank
Finch, S. J.
Fagg, J. C.
Fitzgerald, John A.
Fitzgerald, J. B.
Fouts, Erastus
Feezor, H. B.
Gordon, Ransom
Gordon, Amos
Gordon, David
Gordon, Jodie
Gordon, Roswell
Gordon, A. T.
Gordon, Joseph
Gray, John W.
Goss, D.
Goss, Daniel
Goss, Cicero
Garner, Solomon

Garner, Wm. H.
Garner, J. I.
Grubb, Henry
Grubb, Andrew
Grubb, Alex
Grubb, Daniel
Grubb, Dave
Grubb, Wm.
Grubb, Ambrose
Grubb, John
Grimes, A. L.
Grimes, J. T.
Grimes, Jacob
Grimes, T. W. S.
Grimes, George
Grimes, R. H.
Grimes, Lindsay
Grimes, Hamilton L.
Grimes, Allison
Grimes, Capt. Jack
Grimes, W. L.
Green, Solomon
Green, Shepard
Green, Smith
Green, B. F.
Green, Lindsay
Green, Obediah
Gobble, Dave
Gobble, Wm.
Gobble, Henry
Gobble, Robert
Gobble, Wash
Gobble, James
Gobble, Hub
Gobble, Philip
Gobble, Will
Gobble, B. C.
Gobble, Hiram
Gallimore, Wilson
Gallimore, B. F.

Gallimore, D. W.
Gallimore, Ebenezer
Gallimore, O. A.
Gallimore, B. L.
Guyer, Andrew
Guyer, A. D. C.
Gentle, R. B.
Haley, Harrison
Haley, W. H.
Hanes, John
Hanes, Capt. Lewis C.
Hanes, Jonathan
Hedrick, Adam
Hedrick, Moses (of Michael)
Hedrick, Benjamin F.
Hedrick, Levi
Hedrick, George W.
Hedrick, Jesse
Hedrick, Jacob W.
Hedrick, Valentine
Hedrick, Joseph
Hedrick, Michael
Hedrick, Washington
Hedrick, Sam
Hedrick, Daniel K.
Hedrick, Bill
Hedrick, John
Hedrick, Rev. M. L.
Hedrick, Moses (of Jesse)
Hedrick, Wm. (of Valentine)
Hedrick, Franklin
Hedrick, George A.
Hedrick, Jefferson
Hedrick, Lindsay
Hedrick, Jake
Hedrick, Ezekiel
Hedrick, Philip E.
Hedrick, B. F.
Hedrick, G. Washington
Hedrick, Samuel C.

Davidson County in Military Service 281

Hedrick, Michael (of Jacob)
Hedrick, G. M.
Hedrick, J. F.
Hedrick, Adam S.
Hedrick, J. L.
Hedrick, George Frank
Hedrick, David
Hedrick, Lafayette
Hedrick, Daniel R.
Hilliard, Benjamin F.
Hilliard, Sike
Hix, Richard D.
Hix, W. W.
Hix, Thomas F.
Hix, J. M.
Huff, Barton E.
Heath, John
Hughes, Jacob S.
Hughes, Philip S.
Hughes, James
Hall, M. N.
Hall, Wm.
Hall, B. D.
Hall, R. B.
Hall, John A.
Hill, Milbury
Hill, Henry
Hill, Hiram
Hill, Leopold
Hill, Wm.
Hill, Capt. Dr. A. A.
Hill, George
Hearne, Solomon
Hopkins, J. H.
Hopkins, Anderson
Harris, E. L.
Harris, J. F.
Harris, Capt. H. J.
Harris, Hammet
Harris, Gray
Harris, J. E.
Harris, T. M.
Harris, C. G.
Harris, Giles
Harris, Turner Mc.
Home, Cornelius
Hunt, Obediah
Hunt, David
Hunt, Wm. H.
Hunt, Osburn
Hunt, Wm.
Hunt, Capt. C. A., Sr.
Hunt, Andrew
Hunt, Rev. Geo. E.
Holt, Dr. Wm. R.
Holt, Wm. N.
Holt, Col. Wm. E.
Holt, Eugene R.
Holt, Wm. Michael
Heitman, Capt. A. M.
Heitman, Capt. John F.
Heitman, Capt. Frank
Heitman, Wm.
Heitman, Rev. Henry
Hiatt, John
Hiatt, Joseph
Hiatt, Mack
Hiatt, J. A.
Hoover, Frank
Hoover, Capt. P. A.
Henderson, Henry
Henderson, Wm. F.
Howell, ?
Hepler, Thomas
Hepler, D. Henderson
Hepler, Lindsay
Hepler, R. B.
Hargrave, Frank
Hargrave, John H.
Hargrave, Robert B.

Hargrave, Col. Jesse
Higgs, P. F.
Hilton, Randall
Hilton, Jesse
Hilton, Evans
Hilton, J. Truman
Hilton, Jacob
Hilton, Lorenzo
Hilton, Clark
Hogan, Wm. Gray
Hamner, Columbus
Hamner, Wm. B.
Harrison, Joseph
Harrison, Henry
Harrison, J. C.
Harrison, Harris
Harrison, John
Hartley, Wesley
Hartley, Wm. W.
Hartley, H. H.
Hartley, James K.
Hartley, James F.
Helmstetler, H.
Hunnicut, J. A.
Hartman, J. A.
Hinkle, J. S.
Hinkle, John
Hege, Alex
Hege, Christian
Holmes, C. K.
Harman, H. V.
Hampton, W. B.
Hunter, A. C.
Hunter, A. G.
Hough, Obediah
Hayworth, S. S.
Hasten, Thomas
Hamm, Bill
Hanner, Daniel J.
Idol, John

Imbler, Hardee
Imbler, Stephen
Imbler, David
Ingram, H. C.
Ingram, W. S.
Ingram, Andrew
Ingram, J. W.
Jordan, A. G.
Jordan, John
Jones, Henry
Jones, Samuel S.
Jones, John
Jones, Robert
Jones, Si
Johnston, Rev. Frontis H.
James, John
Johnson, John H.
Johnson, A. G.
Johnson, Titus W.
Johnson, Eli W.
Johnson, Will
Jarrett, Addison
Jarrett, Julius
Jarrett, Wm.
Jenkins, D. A.
Jenkins, Henry
Jackson, Daniel
Kindley, Franklin
Kepley, John
Kepley, Peter
Kepley, Jacob
Kepley, Leonard
Kepley, Andrew
Kepley, David
Kepley, Henry
Kepley, George
Kepley, Jake
Kepley, Peter
Koonts, Jesse
Koonts, Jack

DAVIDSON COUNTY IN MILITARY SERVICE 283

Koonts, Capt. Jake
Koonts, Absalom
Koonts, Casper
Koonts, Philip
Koonts, John
Koonts, Andrew
Koonts, Ezekiel
Koonts, Zwingli
Koonts, K. Z.
Koonts, Aps
Koonts, Henry
Koonts, Franklin
Koonts, Jackson
Koonts, George
Koonts, H. F.
Koonts, Daniel
Koonts, David
Koonts, Capt. J. H.
Kennedy, Charles
Kennedy, Wm.
Kennedy, J. C.
Kennedy, Calvin
Kennedy, James
Kennedy, Isaac
Kennedy, Sim
Kennedy, Daniel
Kennedy, Wm. J.
Kennedy, A. J.
Kinney, Jerome C.
Kinney, W. P.
Kinney, D. F.
Kinney, Benny
Kinney, Roby
Kinney, A. D.
Kinney, George
Kesler, Robert E.
Kesler, A. K.
Kesler, Alfred
Kesler, Daniel
Kanoy, Wm.

Kanoy, John
Kanoy, Henderson
Kanoy, Samuel
Kanoy, Jones
Ketchie, Steve
Kinsey, J. A.
Kinsey, George
Kern, John R.
Kearns, John
Loflin, M. G.
Loflin, A. A.
Loflin, H. L.
Loflin, W. J.
Loflin, T. C.
Loftin, Jeremiah
Loftin, Cornelius
Loftin, Gray
Loftin, Wm.
Loftin, David
Loftin, J. C.
Loftin, Wilburn
Loftin, W. C.
Loftin, James G.
Loftin, Judethin
Loftin, Mal
Lookabill, F. D.
Lookabill, Jake
Leonard, John
Leonard, Riley
Leonard, Lee N.
Leonard, Wiley
Leonard, Solomon
Leonard, John (of Joe)
Leonard, Joe B.
Leonard, Henry C.
Leonard, John A.
Leonard, John R.
Leonard, Willie
Leonard, Wiley B.
Leonard, Riley W.

Leonard, Aps
Leonard, Samuel
Leonard, Ham
Leonard, D. S.
Leonard, Joseph A.
Leonard, Ransom
Leonard, Alex
Leonard, Henderson
Leonard, Valentine
     (of Jacob)
Leonard, H. J.
Leonard, Burgess
Leonard, W. H.
Leonard, George H.
Leonard, G. H.
Leonard, Jacob
Leonard, J. F.
Leonard, George W.
Leonard, Alvearn
Leonard, John H.
Leonard, Daniel
Leonard, John A.
Leonard, George
Leonard, Joseph
Leonard, Jesse
Leonard, A. L.
Leonard, Valentine (of Alex)
Lanning, Wm.
Lanning, John
Lanning Obediah
Lanning, T. F.
Lanning, Thomas
Leach, Gen. J. M.
Leach, J. A.
Lewis, Capt. ?
Lewis, J. L.
Lohman, Hub
Lanier, Isaiah
Lanier, D. G.
Lanier, Thomas F.

Lanier, W. D.
Lanier, Philip
Lanier, James C.
Lanier, Franklin
Lanier, James
Lanier, E. L.
Lanier, Daniel
Lanier, Clement
Long, Jess
Long, J. M.
Long, George
Long, Joseph
Long, Wm. D.
Long, Rev. Thomas
Long, Henry
Long, Lorenzo
Long, John P.
Long, Solomon
Long, John
Long, Wesley
Long, Charles
Lindsay, Dr. Wm. Dillon
Lindsay, Robert Wilson
Lindsay, Alpheus
Lambeth, David H.
Lambeth, Samuel
Lambeth, Maj. J. H.
Lambeth, L. D.
Lambeth, D. H.
Lambeth, J. H.
Lambeth, Jones
Louia, Wesley
Louia, R. L.
Lomax, Ira
Lomax, John
Lomax, Wm. C.
Lomax, Pink
Lomax, John
Lethco, James P.
Leatherman, Elijah

DAVIDSON COUNTY IN MILITARY SERVICE 285

Leatherman, John
Leatherman, Wm.
Lamb, James
Lamb, Moses
Lopp, Jacob
Lopp, Tice
Lopp, Peter
Ledford, P. L.
Lyons, Charles
Lee, J. W.
Morris, Shepard
Morris, S. G.
Morris, A. S.
Morris, Jesse W.
Morris, Wm.
Morris, J. R.
Morris, John
Morris, Jack
Morris, John W.
Morris, Thomas
Morris, Allen
Morris, James
Morris, Frederick
Myers, Wm. Ambrose
Myers, J. C.
Myers, Caanan
Myers, D. Welsey
Myers, Wm.
Myers, Tyson
Myers, Andrew
Myers, Felix
Myers, Willie
Myers, Isaiah
Myers, J. A.
Myers, R. B.
Myers, B. D.
Myers, H. F.
Myers, W. L.
Myers, Kenneth C.
Myers, Jesse W.

Myers, Frank
Myers, Ambrose
Myers, Henry
Myers, Wm. A.
Myers, Robert
Myers, Barton
Myers, Albert
Myers, Jim
Myers, Giles
Myers, Junius L.
McCrary, John W.
McCrary, Levi
McCrary, John C.
McCrary, Press
McCrary, Frank
McCrary, Reuben
Mock, J. A.
Mock, George
Mock, L. N.
Mock, David
Mendenhall, J. L.
Mendenhall, John
May, Benjamin
May, Elias P.
May, Henry
May, Peter
May, Joe
May, Thomas
May, Robert
May, J. L.
Mays, Tom
Miller, James
Miller, H. V.
Miller, Obediah
Miller, Washington
Miller, W. L.
Miller, L. F.
Miller, Capt. John H.
Miller, Felix
Miller, Henry

Miller, Eli
Miller, Frank
Miller, Alexander
Miller, David
Miller, Alfred
Miller, John
Miller, Mike
Miller, James
Miller, John B.
Miller, Lovelace
Miller, J. H.
Miller, John Q.
Miller, Frank
Miller, Elijah
Miller, Alexander
Miller, Daniel
Miller, James
Miller, W. F.
Miller, O. C.
Michael, Valentine
Michael, Henry
Michael, Philip
Michael, John
Michael, W. R.
Medlin, Henry
Medlin, Jess
Medlin, Nathan
McCutcheon, E. H.
McCutcheon, Robert
Murphy, Joseph
Murphy, Pleasant
Murphy, J. R.
Meredith, John
Mallard, Bob
Mabry, Capt. John H.
Merrell, Paul W.
Merrell, Samuel L.
Minor, John
Mills, Wm.
Maley, ?

Myrick, Jesse
Myrick, John S.
Mize, Burgess
Mize, John
McGuire, Ham
McDonald, John
Moore, Jones, Sr.
Moore, Jones, Jr.
Moore, Capt. W. T.
Meadows, Jim
McBride, W. A.
McCarn, Abram
Morton, Rev. H.
Musgrave, George
Massey, Daniel
Massey, D. W.
Maslin, Wm.
Nooe, Thomas
Nooe, John
Nooe, Bennett
Nooe, Wm.
Newsome, N. H.
Newsome, J. Frank
Newsome, John
Newsome, C. C.
Newsome, Wm.
Newsome, A. H.
Nance, Lyndon
Nance, W. E.
Nifong, Wiley
Nifong, Samuel
Nealy, Jesse
Newell, Jim
Nelson, James
Newby, H. B.
Owen, B. L.
Owen, Wm.
Owen, Anderson
Owen, Michael
Owen, A. A.

DAVIDSON COUNTY IN MILITARY SERVICE 287

Owen, Alfred
O'Daniel, Wm.
Oaks, J. A.
Oaks, P. C.
Osborn, Zacharias
Odell, Wm.
Perry, James M.
Perry, Hezekiah
Perry, J. M.
Perdue, Henry H.
Perdue, Ransom
Parish, Ansil
Parish, James A.
Peace, L. A.
Peace, L. E.
Proctor, Randall
Proctor, Mike
Proctor, John A.
Petree, J. F.
Perry, Hezekiah
Parks, John
Parks, J. A.
Payne, Joseph
Payne, Rev. Dr. Chas. M.
Payne, Alfred
Payne, Dr. R. L.
Phillips, Sanford
Phillips, Wesley
Phillips, H. T.
Phillips, W. A.
Pope, George
Pope, Alexander
Palmer, H. J.
Palmer, George W.
Palmer, H.
Palmer, J. B.
Penry, Dick
Penry, Richard A.
Pool, Meredith
Penaluna, George

Pugh, James A.
Powers, E. L.
Pickett, Alex
Pickett, Ralph
Powell, ?
Paugh, ?
Perrell, D. C.
Parker, Rev. P. E.
Prim, J. M.
Peacock, W. G.
Peacock, Wm.
Peacock, John L.
Pickle, F. A.
Roach, Sidney
Roach, James
Rothrock, Henry
Riley, James
Riley, H. C.
Richard, I. J. E.
Richard, Wm.
Richard, Eli
Redwine, Capt. Thomas
Redwine, G. D.
Redwine, J. M.
Redwine, Dave
Redwine, Henry
Redwine, Wash
Redwine, David H.
Reid, Jesse
Reid, John
Reid, Calvin
Reid, George W.
Russell, Pleasant
Rhodes, John A.
Rhodes, Franklin
Rhodes, Zachariah
Rhodes, Daniel
Roland, John W.
Rush, Abner E.
Rickard, Emanuel
Rickard, N. L.

Rickard, John Lewis
Rickard, B.
Rickard, Addison
Rickard, J. A.
Rickard, P. S.
Robbins, M.
Robbins, H. J.
Robbins, Capt. F. C.
Raker, David
Reinhardt, H. W.
Reeves, E. M.
Reeves, C. M.
Regan, J. M.
Raper, Elisha
Ratts, T. O.
Ritchie, S. C.
Stokes, W. C.
Stokes, T. B.
Stafford, George W.
Shemwell, J. F.
Shemwell, L. D.
Sills, W. H.
Stewart, Samuel
Stewart, Henry
Stewart, Andrew
Surratt, Gorrell
Surratt, Ivy
Surratt, Daniel
Surratt, Beverly
Surratt, Moton
Surratt, J. G.
Surratt, A. G.
Surratt, Dr. L., Sr.
Surratt, Whitson
Surratt, B. A.
Surratt, Travis
Surratt, Payton
Surratt, Allen
Surratt, George
Sechriest, James

Sechriest, H.
Sechriest, Daniel
Sechriest, Eli K.
Simon, James
Sink, Gesham
Sink, Jacob
Sink, Reid
Sink, Wm.
Sink, John
Sink, Tice
Sink, Noah
Sink, Solomon
Sink, Samuel
Sink, Wilson
Sink, Adam
Sink, Wm. A.
Sink, Samuel P.
Sink, Matthias
Sink, Joseph
Sink, Jacob
Sink, Andrew
Sink, Travis,
Sink, David
Sink, Henry
Sink, George
Sink, Solomon A.
Sink, O.
Sink, H. L.
Sink, M.
Shaw, Henry
Shaw, Enoch
Shaw, John
Shaw, Enoch (of Jesse)
Shaw, Obediah
Shaw, Jake
Shaw, Jesse
Strange, Burgess
Strange, R. S.
Sullivan, Wesley
Sullivan, Wm.

DAVIDSON COUNTY IN MILITARY SERVICE   289

Sullivan, Clark
Sullivan, J. C.
Sullivan, W. A.
Sullivan, Wm. H.
Smith, Y. H.
Smith, B. F.
Smith, Ham
Smith, John
Smith, Maj. S. H.
Smith, Peter
Smith, Alfred
Smith, Capt. Benj. C.
Smith, David
Smith, Capt. G. F.
Smith, Kirby
Smith, James
Smith, Thomas
Smith, C. M.
Smith, J. H.
Smith, P. T.
Smith, A. A.
Smith, Emanuel
Smith, George H.
Smith, L. F.
Smith, M. L.
Shackelford, Terry
Shackelford, ?
Snider, Elijah
Snider, Solomon F.
Snider, Frank
Snider, Lewis Wesley
Snider, Peter
Snider, Henry Nelson
Snider, Amos
Snider, A. P.
Snider, Wm.
Snider, John L.
Snider, J. N.
Snider, G. W.
Snider, John S.

Snider, D. H.
Snider, Solomon
Sowers, Michael
Sower, Felix
Sowers, Jesse
Sowers, Joe
Sowes, Jake
Sowers, Wm.
Sowers, Philip
Sowers, Humphrey
Sowers, Ambrose
Sowers, Christian
Sowers, George
Swicegood, Alfred
Swicegood, Sandy
Swicegood, J. H.
Swicegood, John H.
Swicegood, R. S.
Simerson, Samuel
Simerson, Burrell
Sheets, Milton
Sheets, T. C.
Sheets, George
Swift, Benjamin
Stimpson, Jim
Stimpson, Ed
Stimpson, J. P.
Siceloff, Alfred
Siceloff, John
Siceloff, Joe
Siceloff, Philip
Siceloff, D. Lumsden
Sappenfield, Dave
Sappenfield, Andrew
Shoaf, Alfred
Shoaf, Washington
Shoaf, Levi
Shoaf, John
Shoaf, Rich
Shoaf, Eli

19

Shoaf, Ross
Shoaf, John T.
Shoaf, Dave
Shoaf, Henry
Shoaf, Jake
Shoaf, Sherman
Shoaf, Henderson
Shoaf, M. R
Shepard, John
Stone, Monteville
Stone, John
Stone, Joseph
Stoner, W. F.
Suggs, John
Swing, Cicero
Swing, Anderson
Swing, John D.
Swing, Franklin
Swing, James F.
Swing, Obediah
Swing, J. H. C.
Swing, Alfred
Swing, John Henry
Swink. A. W.
Styers, Jesse
Styers, S. Mibby
Shipton, George, Sr.
Sanes, Nathan
Star, J. D.
Saintsing, G. W.
Skeen, J. C.
Scott, T. J.
Scott, B. F.
Scott, G. W.
Scott, Robert
Scott, Front
Scarborough, Benj. L.
Sumner, J. E.
Sumner, Bill
Sharpe, A. W.

Sharpe, R. L.
Seal, Jonathan
Taylor, Travis
Taylor, Franklin
Taylor, Christian
Taylor, Caswell
Taylor, Frank
Taylor, Dewitt
Taylor, Wilson
Taylor, John
Thomas, L. L.
Thomas H. Clay
Thomas, James
Thomas, Frank E.
Thomas, John C.
Thomas, Lewis
Thomas, Wess
Thomas, Newton
Thomas, Ped C.
Thompson, W. E.
Thompson, Capt. C. M.
Thomas, J. H., Sr.
Thomas, Frank
Thomas, W. L.
Thomas, J. F.
Trantham, Daniel
Trantham, Francis
Trantham, Henry
Trantham, Alex
Trantham, H. A.
Tussey, Zeno B.
Tussey, John
Tussey, Franklin
Tussey, David
Tussey, Frank
Teague, John
Tysinger, James
Tysinger, P. W.
Tysinger, Alex
Tysinger, Fourney

DAVIDSON COUNTY IN MILITARY SERVICE 291

Tysinger, Robert
Tysinger, P. N.
Tysinger, W. G.
Turner, Wm.
Turner, Lee
Turner, Eli
Turner, J. S.
Turner, A. W.
Turner, E. D.
Tesh, Theophilus
Tesh, J. A.
Tesh, Solomon
Tesh, Frank
Tesh, George
Tesh, Levi
Tesh, ?
Todd, Milo G.
Trexler, D. L.
Trice, Capt. C. W.
Thomason, Jesse
Thomason, George A.
Thomason, J. A.
Thomason, Richard
Thomason ?
Ward, W. W.
Ward, Wm.
Ward, Peter
Ward, Frank
Ward, Griffith
Ward, Elwood
Underwood, C. C.
Underwood, Sidney G.
Veach, Frank
Vanstory, ?
Varner, Herbert
Varner, Eli C.
Varner, J. G.
Varner, Senos
Varner, Tub Bill
Varner, John

Varner, Doder Bill
Varner, Andrew
Varker, Wm.
Wilson, Wm.
Wilson, James W.
Wilson, Henry
Wilson, Giles
Wilson, H. W.
Wilson, J. H.
Watford, S. C.
Watford, Green P.
Wright, McAjor
Wright, Amos
Wright, Joe
Wagner, John
Wagner, Scott Dan
Wagner, Emanuel
Wagner, Jacob
Wagner, R. J.
Wagner, Peter
Wilborn, K. C.
Wilborn, John
Wilborn, J. C.
Wilborn, Lem
Wilborn, Madison
Wilborn, Dock
Wilborn, W. M.
Workman, J. I.
Workman, James E.
Workman, A.
Woodard, John
Woodward, John
Westmoreland, D. S.
Westmoreland, Wm. J.
Westmoreland, Wm. F.
Westmoreland, John
Warner, Hubbard
Warner, Henry
Watson, H. P.
Watson, John Thomas

Watson, Wm. A.
Watson, A. Alexander
Watson, James G.
Watson, Charles Rankin
Watson, Albert B.
Whitehart, Wm.
Whitehart, Willis
Worley, E.
Wood, Spencer
Wood, Richard W.
Wood, James
Walker, Wm.
Walker, Washington
Walker, Jarrett
West, Alexander
Weaver, H. N.
Weaver, P. J.
Weaver, Elias
Weaver, Wm.
Wallingford, J. A.
Womack, Roswell
Womack, James C.
Wharton, A. C.
Walser, Albert
Walser, Burton
Walser, J. H.
Walser, Herbert
Walser, Gaither
Walser, Roland
Walser, Maj. Henry Clay
Williams, L. H.
Williams, Martin Henry
Williams, George
Williams, A. M.
Williams, Hiram
Warford, J. E.
Wall, Samuel W.
Weisner, E. L.
Weisner, ?

Walton, J. H.
Walton, H. P.
Worrel, John
Watkins, John
Whirlow, Jesse
Wren, Wm.
Wren, John
Whitlow, Jesse
Yokeley, Mack
Yokeley, John
Yokeley, Samuel L.
Yokeley, Samuel
Yarborough, John T.
Yarborough, Robert
Yarborough, Green
Yarborough, C.
Yarborough, P. A.
Yarborough, R.
Yarborough, Addison
Yarborough, John
Yarborough, Charles
Yarborough, J. D.
Yarborough, M. N.
Young, James J.
Young, Franklin
Young, Philip
Young, Rev. James A.
Young, Jacob
Young, R.
Young, B. B.
Young, A. J.
Younts, Wm. C.
Younts, John F.
Younts, Frank
Younts, Ike
Younts, R. A.
Younts, Luther
Younts, Isaiah
Yearby, Allen

The Conquered Banner

(From "Father Ryan's" Poems)

Furl that Banner, for 'tis weary;
Round its staff 'tis drooping dreary;
Furl it, fold it, it is best;
For there's not a man to wave it,
And there's not a sword to save it,
And there's not one left to lave it
In the blood which heroes gave it;
And its foes now scorn and brave it;
Furl it, hide it—let it rest.

Take that Banner down! 'tis tattered;
Broken is its staff and shattered;
And the valiant hosts are scattered
Over whom it floated high.
Oh! 'tis hard for us to fold it;
Hard to think there's none to hold it;
Hard that those who once unrolled it
Now must furl it with a sigh.

Furl that Banner! Furl it sadly!
Once ten thousands hailed it gladly,
And ten thousands wildly, madly,
Swore it should forever wave;
Swore that foeman's sword should never
Hearts like theirs entwined dissever,
Till that flag should float forever
O'er their freedom or their grave!

Furl it! for the hands that grasped it
And the hearts that fondly clasped it,
Cold and dead are lying low;
And that Banner—it is trailing!
While around it sounds the wailing
Of its people in their woe.

For, though conquered, they adore it!
Love the cold, dead hands that bore it!
Weep for those who fell before it!
Pardon those who trailed and tore it!
But, oh! wildly they deplore it,
Now who furl and fold it so.

Furl that Banner! True, 'tis gory,
Yet, 'tis wreathed around with glory,
And 'twill live in song and story,
Though its folds are in the dust;
For its fame on brightest pages,
Penned by poets and by sages,
Shall go sounding down the ages—
Furl its folds though now we must.

Furl that Banner, softly, slowly!
Treat it gently—it is holy—
For it droops above the dead.
Touch it not—unfold it never,
Let it droop there, furled forever,
For its people's hopes are dead.

Monument at the Graves of the Revolutionary War Marytyrs, Wooldrich Fritz and Valentin Leonhardt in the Leonard's (Pilgrim) Church Graveyard, Erected in 1896

4. DAVIDSON COUNTY IN THE WORLD WAR

We give herewith the roster of the Davidson County World War veterans. A total of 932 men were called to the colors from Davidson County. Of these brave men the county lost thirty-nine.

The Dead

The following names of those who died in the conflict appear on the memorial tablet on the court square:

Jesse L. Barkley, Odell Barnes, W. M. Bazemore, Harvey Briles, George W. Broadway, C. C. Cook, Ben W. Cornelius, Fritz Creakman, D. C. Culbreth, John H. Easter, Raymond Elliott, Robert Lee Fritts, Ernest Gurdner, H. D. Harris, Charles W. Harrison, N. M. Hopkins, Arthur R. Howell, Lloyd Irvin, Albert A. Lineberry, Carl Link, Fred C. Lookabill, John Carl Miller, William Albert Miller, Jno. A. Myers, Thomas Gurney Nance, Ira Poston, Nelson Rayfield, Adlai Stevenson, Harrison Sullivan, J. R. Surratt, W. P. Surratt, Oliver Thomason, Travis Thompson, Henry V. Traynham, Ernest Weaver, Fred Welch, Haymore Westmoreland.

Colored—Will Hargrave, James Franklin Lopp.

Roster of Whites

G. L. Adams, R. G. Adams, Jesse Adderton, David Almond, Henry Allen, James R. Allen, Obie D. Allen, T. Frank Allred, Byron T. Andrew, Paul Andrew, Raymond O. Arnold, Stephen W. Ashley, Elihu Auman, Smoten Auman.

S. H. Badgett, A. J. Bailey, John Bain, McLaurin Baker, Jacob E. Ball, A. B. Barkley, J. L. Barkley, Luther Barnes, Odell Barnes, W. G. Barnhart, Baxter Bates, Robert Baucom, Carl Bean, C. H. Bean, E. H. Bean, H. C. Bean, H. E. Bean, Alexander Beck, C. H. Beck, Edison Beck, Wesley O. Beck, C. G. Bedford, Geo. W. Beeker, Albert S. Berrier, J. T. Beverly, C. Lee Black, Franklin Bodenheimer, Grady W.

Bowers, Dr. M. A. Bowers, Ray Bowers, Roy Bradley, U. U. Bradley, Charles A. Brewer, J. C. Brewer, John Brewer, D. W. Biggerstaff, H. L. Briles, E. E. Briles, J. M. Briles, Roscoe Briles, H. H. Briles, John Lee Brinkley, G. W. Broadway, Marvin Brown, R. F. Brown, Andrew L. Buie, J. J. Burkhead, John H. Burris, A. G. Burton, J. S. Burton, Levi C. Burton, Emery Byerly, K. W. Byerly, M. A. Byerly.

Tony S. Cain, C. M. Cameron, Robt. F. Cameron, Richard Campbell, W. C. Canup, Joe Carlton, John Carlton, W. C. Carlton, W. Avery Carroll, W. M. Carroll, S. G. Carmichael, L. A. Carswell, Edward W. Cates, Jr., Lee Caton, D. P. Causby, Harold Cecil, Harold O. Cecil, Joe K. Cecil, John W. Cecil, C. L. Charles, Gurney Lee Charles, J. D. Charles, N. L. Charles, C. E. Childers, J. B. Clemons, G. G. Clinard, C. W. Clodfelter, D. W. Clodfelter, I. Clodfelter, Thurman Clontz, Ottis Cloyd, George H. Coggins, Clarence Conrad, C. C. Conrad, Flavius C. Conrad, G. C. Conrad, H. P. Conrad, Robert L. Conrad, Romas L. Conrad, W. G. Conrad, Charles C. Cook, Odius Cook, Oscar Cooksey, John Cope, LeRoy Coopley, B. Cornelius, F. M. Cox, W. C. Craven, Marvin J. Craver, M. M. Craver, M. O. Craver, W. W. Cranford, F. A. Creakman, Claud E. Crook, Jacob F. Crook, John T. Cross, Marvin Crouse, D. C. Culbreth, Geo. W. Curry, Wm. Lee Curry, K. H. Crutchfield, Elwood Curtis.

Erle Dale, Robert G. Daniels, Sam J. Darr, Charles B. Davis, E. H. Davis, Richard Davis, R. E. Davis, Wm. Clyde Davis, W. F. Davis, V. G. Davis, Jno. S. Delap, W. C. Dennis, Tom DeVane, George DeVine, Fred Disher, Arvil Disher, W. W. Dixon, Homer C. Doby, C. L. Dodson, Gladstone C. Donovan, Archie Dorsett, Fletcher Dorsett, E. C. Dorsett, Jno. W. Dorsett.

R. P. Earnhardt, J. H. Easter, J. L. Easter, Fred Lee Eddinger, Olin J. Eddinger, James H. Eddings, G. F. Elliott, R. V. Elliott, M. L. Embler, J. H. Essick, N. M. Essick, Howard Lee Evans, Avery Everhart, Arvel F. Everhart, Clewell R. Everhart, J. A. Everhart, J. L. Everhart, J. M. Everhart, J. O. Everhart, R. F. Everhart, R. H. Everhart, Silas Everhart, Wm. B. Everhart, Wm. F. Everhart, W. M. Everhart, H. C. Euring.

DAVIDSON COUNTY IN MILITARY SERVICE   299

D. I. Feezor, J. B. Feezor, Jas. B. Feezor, Peter Lee Feezor, C. W. Ferguson, Jno. T. B. Fesperman, P. M. Fields, A. B. Finch, Edward W. Finch, J. M. Fishel, Jr., Luther S. Fishel, Wm. A. Fishel, W. C. Fitzgerald, J. W. Fletcher, A. C. Fluck, H. M. Flynn, Frank Forrest, Frank Forshee, G. E. Forshee, D. C. Foust, Jno. W. Foust, W. E. Fouts, Henry H. Frank, W. E. Frank, H. F. Fraylick, E. F. Freedle, Hugh E. Fritts, J. M. Fritts, Robert Lee Fritts.

E. A. Gallimore, H. A. Gallimore, M. A. Gallimore, O. W. Gallimore, Vance Garrett, H. M. Garrison, H. C. Gibson, Sam Gibson, Clyde E. Glasscoe, Clyde C. Gobble, O. L. Gobble, Charles Goins, Tom Gooding, A. C. Gossett, Fred B. Gray, George Gray, J. H. Gray, Hobert L. Green, Hugh LeRoy Green, H. O. Green, Jesse S. Green, O. Green, Paul Green, Robert L. Green, Wm. R. Green, Wm. Tate Green, Paul I. Grimes, Jesse Gurdner, Ernest Gurdner.

Charles W. Hackney, Lewis R. Hall, Pearlie Hall, P. M. Hall, W. S. Hall, Barney Hambrick, Clarence Hamilton, C. R. Haneline, Charles Hanes, Jackson H. Hanes, Wm. B. Hankins, Z. V. Hannah, Wm. B. Harkey, Branson Harrelson, Charles Harris, H. D. Harris, I. H. Harris, Sam P. Harris, C. W. Harrison, G. M. Hartley, L. P. Hartley, Sam Hartley, Jack Harvey, Noah L. Heitman, Lewis F. Harvey, Roy Harvey, J. C. Hathcock, B. M. Hayes, J. P. Hayes, Dennie Hayes, J. W. Hayes, John Lee Hearne, Jas. Lee Hedgecock, C. J. Hedrick, Charles R. Hedrick, L. L. Hedrick, Ottis Hedrick, Ted. L. Hedrick, W. O. Hedrick, Joe H. Hege, J. H. Helmstetler, J. E. Henry, O. C. Herman, J. F. Hiatt, R. F. Hiatt, M. W. Higgans, Francis L. Hill, H. L. Hill, Henry S. Hill, S. M. Hill, Lester Hilton, Raymond Hilton, C. C. Hinkle, D. R. Hinkle, Grover C. Hinkle, Paul Hinkle, R. C. Hinkle, I. R. Hinson, Chas. C. Hix, Jno. M. Hobbs, Frank Hoke, D. C. Holder, Jas. W. Holder, Chas W. Hoover, Henry Hoover, N. M. Hopkins, Carl Hudspath, J. C. Huffman, W. H. Hulin, Earl Hunberry, H. D. Hunt.

J. V. Ingram, F. H. Imbler, Bob Ivey, L. C. Irving.

Carl Jackson, Ernest James, Albert Johnson, Bob Johnson, Carb Johnson, D. R. Johnson, E. S. Johnson, Henry James Johnson, O. F. Johnson, R. B. R. Johnson, Ray Johnson, Doland Jones, Wm. A. Julian, Cramer Julian.

J. A. Kanoy, Joseph Wm. Kanoy, Murphy Kearns, J. E. Kearns, J. E. Kendall, Edward Kennedy, Fred N. Kennedy, J. Lee Kennedy, Robert W. Kennedy, R. Wilson Kennedy, Wm. C. Kennedy, J. H. Kepley, Jas. C. Kesler, Jno. M. Kesler, Dr. W. L. Kibler, C. E. Kiger, Ed. Kindley, Grover King, N. L. King, Eugene Kirk, Clyde Kirkman, J. A. Klass, A. Wade Koonts, C. H. Koonts, C. P. Koonts, Hoyle Koonts, Eddie Krites.

Ernest Lambeth, J. M. Lambeth, R. Lambeth, Walter Lambeth, Charles G. Lancaster, J. E. Landert, Marvin A. Lanning, Walter A. Lanning, W. G. Lanning, Speight Laughlin, Edward H. Layden, R. R. Lawrence, F. L. Layton, Jay Layton, Chas. E. Lee, Chas. S. Leigh, A. V. Leonard, Aldrich O. Leonard, Arthur J. Leonard, Carl Leonard, Charles E. Leonard, Clarence G. Leonard, Cletus Leonard, D. C. Leonard, E. H. Leonard, Fred B. Leonard, G. H. Leonard, Hubert Ray Leonard, James A. Leonard, James B. Leonard, James G. Leonard, Jesse Leonard, J. F. Leonard, Joseph H. Leonard, M. H. Leonard, M. M. Leonard, R. L. Leonard, Shelly W. Leonard, Sidney A. Leonard, Thos. A. Leonard, V. C. Leonard, Albert R. Link, Carl Link, Jesse O. Link, Henry D. Litaker, Oliver M. Litaker, R. O. Little, R. S. Loflin, Ivey W. Lohr, John H. Long, Paul H. Long, Earl Lomax, O. L. Lookabill, J. W. Lookinbee, John A. Lopp, John S. Lopp, Cletus Lopp, F. M. Lloyd.

Jesse Mann, Burton L. Manning, J. P. Mathews, Wm. B. May, W. C. May, J. W. Meacham, Wm. B. Meares, Ed Medlin, Darcus E. Meredith, D. L. Meredith, J. R. Meredith, A. W. Michael, C. L. Michael, Edgar D. Michael, E. L. Michael, G. Michael, H. G. Michael, J. E. Michael, R. C. Michael, Tom Michael, C. W. Miller, R. B. Miller, Jr., R. S. Miller, W. A. Miller, W. A. L. Miller, Walter H. Miller, Arthur A. Miller, J. R. Milton, Kenneth Mountcastle, M. A. Mooneyham, Levi B. Moore, H. W. Moore, C. A. Morgan, E. G. Morgan, McKinley Morgan, S. J. Morgan, Walter Morgan, B. V. Morris, C. Leach Morris, E. V. Morris, Jim Morris, Lacy Morris, Lowe Morris, Frank B. Moser, Carl Motsinger, Chester Motsinger, G. W. Murphy, H. H. Murphy, J. T. Murphy, Ben. F. Myers, E. A. Myers, Elmer Myers, E. H. Myers, G. L. Myers, J. E. Myers, J. Lee Myers, J. J. Myers,

Lowe Myers, N. F. Myers, R. D. Myers, R. P. Myers, S. A.
Myers, W. E. Myers, Y. B. Myers, Z. W. Myers
O. C. MacQuage, Joe L. McCrary, M. M. McCarn, V. V.
McDaniel, C. L. McDonald, John McDonald, W. F. McGee,
Bascom McNeil, Don C. McRea, Ben C. McSwain.

F. L. Nance, Thos. G. Nance, Grady Nail, Otha H. Nifong,
Walter E. Nifong, David A. Nifong, C. H. Newby, R. D.
Newby, B. H. Newsom, L. E. Newsom, Paul C. Newton.

W. G. O'Daniel, C. T. O'Mara, R. P. Osborne, F. R. Owen,
Marvin J. Owen, Mansfield Owen, Norman Owen.

R. T. Palmer, Wm. J. Parker, Conroy Parks, J. C. Parrish,
A. L. Payne, Alfred S. Payne, D. S. Penninger, H. A. Penninger, Willie R. Perrill, J. M. Perryman, M. C. Perryman,
Robah L. Perryman, H. G. Peters, R. E. Peters, James Peterson, C. G. Phibbs, Clifford Phillips, Wade H. Phillips, James
Phelps, C. W. Phifer, Carl Pickard, Cary Pickard, L. D.
Player, Ben. H. Porter, Ernest Potts, K. B. Potts, W. G.
Potts, G. C. Pressley, J. T. Prichard, Wm. Luther Propst.

Wm. A. Queen.

H. J. Ramsey, Cletus Raper, Joe Raper, Julius R. Raper,
Wm. E. Raper, R. C. Rapp, Nelson Rayfield, J. A. Redmon,
W. C. Redwine, Welborn Reid, J. H. Ribelin, Jno. W. Rice,
Robert T. Riley, Hoyle C. Ripple, John H. Ripple, Van B.
Rickard, Fred Roach, J. F. Roach, F. L. Robbins, Roswell
Robbins, W. W. Robinson, John Rogers, Aubry Rothrock,
C. Bruce Rothrock, E. H. Rothrock, Max Rothrock, John L.
Rowe, Lester B. Rule, S. A. Russell, Charles R. Russell.

D. M. Sanders, W. S. Sanders, F. W. Sanford, Watson
Saintsing, Wm. Fred Saintsing, F. F. Saunders, C. L. Sechriest, C. S. Sechriest, J. B. Sechriest, Marvin Sechriest,
Ray Sechriest, R. G. Sechriest, H. Senter, Daniel M. Sexton,
Buren Shaw, James Shaw, R. G. Shaw, Richard Shaw, R. Y.
Shaw, A. W. Shirley, W. L. Shirley, George Shipton, Albert
Shoaf, Harvey R. Shoaf, H. W. Shoaf, P. H. Shoaf, Walter
Ray Shoaf, J. H. Shytle, R. H. Shytle, Cletus A. Sink,
Garland B. Sink, H. Hoyle Sink, Homer C. Sink,
Herbert O. Sink, J. H. Sink, Jr., J. O. Sink, L. Franklin Sink, Luther G. Sink, R. N. Sink, F. F. Skeen,
W. C. Skeen, F. Lee Smith, Henry R. Smith, Hill
Smith, J. B. Smith, J. G. Smith, Jno. I. Smith, J. Lee

Smith, J. P. Smith, N. D. Smith, Robert H. Smith, R. S. Smith, Stokes A. Smith, S. H. Smith, W. L. Smith, Albert L. Snider, A. M. Snider, C. E. Snider, Luther Snider, R. B. Snider, Thos W. Snider, F. M. Sowers, Fred Sowers, Jake J. Sowers, J. L. Sowers, R. G. Sowers, W. R. Sowers, Wiley Spencer, J. W. Spoolman, Thos. Spry, J. H. Spurgeon, Hamlet J. Spurrier, Joseph Stewart, Moses Stewart, Grady Stinson, B. C. Stokes, H. B. Stokes, S. H. Stokes, A. E. Stone, L. W. Stone, M. W. Stone, R. H. Stone, W. B. Stone, Wayland D. Stone, C. L. Stoner, Walter Stoner, Mod Stout, J. A. Stratton, Carl Suggs, F. L. Sullivan, H. E. Sullivan, J. G. Surratt, J. E. Surratt, J. R. Surratt, W. P. Surratt, B. C. Swain, A. R. Swaim, Dewey W. Swicegood, Ralph J. Swicegood.

R. B. Talbert, D. L. Taylor, Harvey Lee Teague, J. R. Teague, Clyde Tesh, H. A. Tesh, Mickie Tesh, W. B. Tesh, Ivory Thomas, N. P. Thomas, G. Arthur Thomason, George Ira Thompson, Lloyd Thomason, Oliver Thomason, Gilmer Thompson, John G. Thompson, J. M. Thompson, Travis Thompson, John Tillett, C. M. Tomlinson, John Totten, Roland Totten, J. F. Traynham, W. Traynham, C. A. Trexler, John M. Trexler, John Trice, Propst Trice, Paul Tucker, Jesse Lee Turner, D. L. Tussey, E. L. Tussey, H. C. Tussey, C. J. Tysinger, D. L. Tysinger, George Tysinger, Henry C. Tysinger, R. L. Tysinger.

Henry M. Underwood.

A. E. Varker, A. H. Varner, B. E. Varner, Grover C. Varner, H. G. Varner, D. C. Veach, Paul Veach.

Chas. A. Wade, E. A. Warfford, Evans Wall, Fletcher H. Wall, Harris Wall, L. O. Walser, Raymond C. Walser, Roscoe M. Walser, Z. V. Walser, Jr., E. J. Ward, H. W. Ward, John Ward, Raymond Ward, Will Ward, W. L. C. Warner, J. A. Watson, Ernest Weaver, Jesse Weaver, O. H. Weaver, Rome Weaver, W. Zeb Weaver, C. M. Welborn, Guy E. Welborn, L. H. Welborn, S. J. Welborn, A. W. Weisner, C. R. Welch, Fred Welch, Levie West, Haywood Westmoreland, R. J. Westmoreland, Stewart Westmoreland, W. R. Westmoreland, J. M. White, A. E. Whitesides, G. L. Wicker, C. M. Williams, Ray Williams, R. F. Williams, W. L. Williams, J. C. Williamson, J. G. Williamson, R. D. Williamson,

DAVIDSON COUNTY IN MILITARY SERVICE 303

M. Willhoyt, Amos Willis, Charles Lee Wilson, Ray Wilson, Willie N. Wilson, W. S. Wilson, E. L. Wood, J. A. Wood, Jesse Wood, Shelton Woodson, R. P. Woosley, C. C. Workman, James E. Workman, J. S. Workman, W. T. Workman, Marvin M. Wyre.

Grady Yarborough, Iredell Yarborough, M. A. Yarborough, Robert Yarborough, R. G. Yarborough, R. Sam Yarborough, J. D. Yates, Will Yates, Robert H. Yokeley, Jno. G. York, A. E. Young, B. A. Young, Bert Young, B. S. Young, Jno. E. Young, Wm. A. Young, Burdett Young, H. O. Younts, Walter G. Younts, Walter R. Younts, W. R. Younts.

R. E. Zimmerman.

Roster of Colored

J. B. Adams, Jesse Adderton, Arthur Alexander, Jesse Anderson.

Robert Bailey, Wallace Ball, Shepard Barber, Charles I. Barringer, Theo. Boger, Cheran Bordin, Stacy Bost, Albert Bostic, David Brace, Sam Brown, Sandy Brown, Ezelle Bruster, Geo. Bynum.

Will Carson, John H. Carter, James A. Chavis, Robert Clark, Willie I. Clemons, Mills Clowney, W. A. L Cooper, LeRoy Cross, Pud Cross, Reed Cross, Ezra Crump, James A. Crump, James W. Crump, Ben F. Curry, Daniel E. Curry, Thomas L. Curry, J. A. Curry.

Babe Davis, Geo. N. Davis, Clem Davis, Lindsay Davis, Sam Dean, Will Dorsett, Sam Duley

Bud Ellis, Eddie Ellis, Robert D. Ellis, Mod Everett.

Jerry Foster, Allen Fuller.

Thurla Gaither, Henry Gary, Alvin Gilchriest, Andrew Gilchriest, James B. Gilchriest, Arch Green, Dewey Green, Will Green, Weldon Grice,

William Haden, Curtis Hargrave, Richard Hargrave, Will Hargrave, David Harper, Frank Harper, Green Harper, Isaac Harper, Lonnie A. Harris, Howard Henderson, Wm. C. Henderson, Alex. Herring, Grady Holmes, Jesse Holmes, Frank Holt, Giles Holt, Norman Hoover, Walter T. House.

Geo. Johnson.

John Kendall, Murphy Kearns, Thomas King, James Knox, Carl Koonts.

Elbert Lambeth, Robert Lee, Rastus Lee, Albert Loney, Olphus Long, John A. Lopp, J. Frank Lopp, James A. Lowe, Odell Lowe, Ray L. Lowe, Rogers Lowe.

Artis March, Clyde Martin, Lewis Martin, Curry Mitchell, Greedy Mitchell, Jesse Mock, Robt. E. Myers, Zed Myers, Dorsey McRea, Percy F. McCrary, Robt. McCullough.

Clyde Nelson, W. N. Nelson, Richard Nicholson, Ellis Nixon.

Robert Owen.

Albert R. Payne, Delos L. Payne, James Payne, J. W. F. Payne, Roby Payne, Schofield Peck, Clarence Perryman, Lewis Perryman, Clarence Powell.

Percy Raper, Daniel W. Reid.

Robt. M. Scott, Clyde Siler, Martingale Simmons, Willie Simmons, Geo. W. Smith, Willie C. Smith, Tony Smith, Hazel Springs, Walter Springs, Rufus Steed, Burt Stevenson, H. N. Sullivan, Foster Streater.

John A. Thomas, W. B. Thomason, J. W. Turner, Frank Twine.

Ellis Waddell, Coy Welborne, Wm. A. Welborne, Arthur Wells.

Earl Young.

CHAPTER XV

LEXINGTON, CAPITAL OF DAVIDSON COUNTY

1. Facts and Figures

Age, 104 years.

Area, 3.27 square miles.

Elevation, 811 feet.

Population, 1920, 5,254; 1926, 12,000 with 8,519 within city.

County seat of Davidson County and geographical, financial, wholesale and retail, educational and social center of the county.

Average temperature the entire year 57.5 degrees.

Abundant supply of water—pure and unlimited for both drinking and manufacturing purposes. One of the few cities in the drought belt of 1925 that did not have to limit the supply of water.

Population, 90 per cent white, All-American stock.

Wide streets, wider than generally found in cities many times as large.

Manufacturing plants number 57.

Value of manufactured products annually, $18,-000,000.

Manufacturing plants employ approximately 4,500 and have an annual payroll of about $3,000,000.

Five cotton mills, including the giant Erlanger mills which make all the cloth for the famous B. V. D. underwear, are located here.

Six of the South's leading chair and furniture factories, box shook factories, veneer plant, five large lumber concerns, mattress factory, three upholstering plants, mirror factory, panel factory, large bleachery located near the city, candy factory, hosiery mills, successful here for many years and are only tokens of what others can do.

Cheap real estate, competitive railway service, abundance of hydro-electric power, coal at low cost, large supplies near at hand for all kinds of manufacturing.

Two splendid banks with assets of several million dollars.

Within twelve miles of the largest steam-electric power plant in the world, located on the Yadkin River bordering our county.

Plans well advanced, land secured and work under way for the world's largest artificial lake with 75,000 to 100,000 H.P. hydro-electric dam, assuring not only an abundance of power but a fishing paradise.

Located in the heart of the Piedmont section and center of the industrial belt of North Carolina.

Located on the main line Southern Railway, midway between Washington and Atlanta, at the intersection of the Winston-Salem Southbound Railway, a connecting link between the Norfolk and Western, the Atlantic Coast Line and the Seaboard Air Line.

Adequate transportation facilities, hourly bus service between all the leading cities of the State, fine railroads, jitneys and taxis.

Seventeen thousand freight cars are loaded and unloaded annually in the city.

Many available industrial sites are located in the city along railroad sidings at extremely low prices.

Assessed valuation of city, $9,000,000; township, $16,000,000.

LEXINGTON, CAPITAL OF DAVIDSON COUNTY 307

Capital stock in banks $400,000.
Number of business houses, 150.
Number of dwellings, 3,000.

Lexington's city water unsurpassed in State as shown by records and tests of the North Carolina State Board of Health.

City has second class fire insurance rating as laid down by Southeastern Underwriters. Only requirements to place city in first class rating would be the employment of only a few more all-time firemen. The city is equipped with Gamewell fire alarm system covering entire city.

Living conditions are found cheaper here than in many near-by towns and far cheaper than in most cities and towns farther north.

Farm lands in the vicinity of Lexington are rich in natural resources and are inhabited by scientific and practical farmers. Agricultural wealth of county is unlimited.

All highways leading out from the city are either hard-surfaced or of the improved type.

The city is located within seventeen miles of Winston-Salem, the largest city in the State, seventeen miles of High Point, the South's leading furniture market, seventeen miles from Salisbury, midway between Charlotte and Greensboro, midway between Asheville and Raleigh, midway between all the industrial cities of the State and directly connected with them by hard-surfaced highways and without a doubt the best road system in the entire South.

Miles of paved highways around city total fifty.
Fifteen miles of paved streets in city.
Thirty miles of improved sidewalks.

Site of the new branch National Junior Order Orphans' Home, designed for million dollar plant and one thousand children. Located on fine three hundred acre tract donated by citizens at a cost of thirty thousand dollars and planned to be one of America's best.

School facilities almost unsurpassed in the State. Over sixty teachers are employed in the city schools teaching 2,200 pupils in five modern school buildings. Lexington's schools led the State in 1925 with 91.7 per cent average daily attendance. Twenty-five per cent of the total population of the city are enrolled in the city schools.

Recreational facilities are second to none. All-time recreational directors are employed the year through. New city athletic field recently opened near heart of city with full equipment, three large playgrounds well equipped for all the children of the city, city park, large and spacious, within three blocks of the heart of the city. The Boy Scouts hut is located in this park and was built for the Scouts by the local Rotary Club. A large bathing pool has recently been completed and swimming lessons are being taught free to any one in the town. High school gymnasium with full equipment for indoor sports. Country Club within few miles of city with nine hole golf course, club house, lake and many other features under development.

Cemeteries, squares, school lawns and all public lots are beautified through efforts and work of one of the city's leading attorneys, J. R. McCrary, who receives no compensation for his services, and his service is second to none.

HOLLAND E. SHOAF, Lexington
Manufacturer, President Shoaf-Sink Hosiery Mill Company

LEXINGTON, CAPITAL OF DAVIDSON COUNTY

A city that compares favorably with other cities in regard to living conditions, industrial progress and steady growth.

A fine hospital owned and operated by Dr. J. A. Smith.

The above statements were issued by the Lexington Chamber of Commerce in 1926.

2. SOME LEXINGTON FACTORIES

Grimes Brothers' Mill was started in 1879 by the late J. D. Grimes and his brother, Thomas J. Grimes, and it was the first roller process flour mill ever operated in North Carolina. The mill is located on the same spot where it was first built, and even the same building is being used with additions. Of course the machinery has been changed. After the death of J. D. Grimes in July, 1918, his son L. M. Grimes, bought the interest of Thomas J. Grimes and now runs the mill under the same name. The capacity of the mill has increased from forty barrels per day to one hundred and twenty-five barrels.

The Model Mill was built in 1896 by F. L. Hedrick & Co., and was operated under the management of F. L. Hedrick. Later the mill was sold and R. L. Penry was manager for some years. W. G. Hinkle then took charge of the mill. In February, 1913, L. M. Grimes took charge and operated it until January, 1919, when Thomas F. Grimes took charge and the mill is now being operated under his management. The capacity of this mill is fifty barrels per day.

The Star Milling Company is Lexington's youngest flour mill, and is located on Seventh Avenue East and Southern Railway. Its wareroom has enough storage space for 10,000 bushels of wheat. The mill has a capacity of one hundred barrels per day and employs six men. Harvey R. Shoaf was the main promoter of the mill, and is now in charge of it. The officers are C. A. Snider, president; H. A. Leonard, vice president; H. R. Shoaf, secretary and treasurer. The following compose the board of directors: J. S. Snider, H. L. Leonard, H. A. Leonard, D. T. Fritts, C. F. Crouse, C. A. Snider, H. R. Shoaf, T. S. Eanes, J. B. Evans and B. G. Robbins.

In 1907 the Valley Tie and Lumber Company, a Virginia corporation, was awarded the contract to provide crossties for the construction of the Winston-Salem Southbound Railroad. It was deemed advisable to open an office in North Carolina. Due largely to the active interest of Colonel H. B. Varner, it was decided to locate it at Lexington. Lumber and crossties are now purchased and shipped by the local company from points throughout the South. A. D. Lusk is local manager, and James L. Gordon is secretary-treasurer.

The Davidson County Creamery Company was organized in 1915, due to the efforts of R. L. Coons. A site was secured on Church Street and a brick building erected. In 1916 Mr. Coons resigned as general manager and Glenn Yoder was elected to fill the vacancy. In 1918 Mr. Yoder resigned and since that time Mrs. Charles Young has acted as secretary and general manager. Since the creamery has been in operation

DAVIDSON HOSPITAL, LEXINGTON
Dr. J. Alex. Smith (Insert)

hundreds of thousands of dollars have been paid to the farmers of Davidson and adjoining counties for butterfat, which has been made into butter and shipped mainly to the eastern part of North Carolina. The present officers are J. W. Bowers, president; C. M. Yokley, vice president; T. S. Eanes, treasurer; Mrs. Charles Young, secretary. The directors are H. J. Sink, A. H. Kepley, F. H. Beall, Mrs. Charles Young, T. S. Eanes, C. M. Yokley, Will L. Smith and Wade H. Phillips.

The Wennonah Cotton Mills are the oldest in the county. They were built in the years 1884 and 1892. The success of the Wennonah Mills is due to the untiring efforts of the Holts. W. E. Holt is now president of the mills; R. L. Tate, vice president; J. V. Moffitt, secretary and treasurer; A. L. Pickard, superintendent. The capital stock is $100,000. The equipment consists of 12,568 spindles and 454 looms. Chambray, shirting and ticking are manufactured.

The Dacotah Cotton Mill was founded in 1910, and has not changed hands since it was organized. The officers are C. A. Hunt, Jr., president and general manager; C. M. Thompson, vice president; W. H. Mendenhall, secretary and treasurer; and J. H. Mattison, superintendent. The mill has a capital stock of $600,000, with 22,000 spindles and 650 looms. The product is chambray and 350 people are employed. It is located on the main line of the Southern Railway in the southern part of town.

The Nokomis Cotton Mill was built in 1900 and was Lexington's third mill, the Wennonnahs being the first two. Its officers at the organization were C. A. Hunt, Sr., president; C. M. Thompson, vice president; D. H. Hinkle, secretary and treasurer. The mill is situated in the eastern part of town. It manufactures convertible cotton goods. It has 15,296 spindles and employs about two hundred and fifty hands.

The Erlanger Cotton Mills Company began operations March 28, 1914, as producers of the cloth used in making the "B.V.D." underwear. It has 46,000 spindles, 1,240 cloth looms and employs 800 hands on two shifts a day. The mill is situated in the center of a model village of 325 modern bungalows, the village having a population of about 1,700. A community club house, day nursery, kindergarten, primary and grammar schools, dairy and church are included in the Welfare Department. When the mill first began operations, it had an annual output of 8,000,000 yards. Today its output is 20,000,000 yards.

The Shoaf-Sink Hosiery Mills Company was organized in 1920 by I. L. Sink and H. E. Shoaf, and began business in March, 1921. The plant was first located in the old Bailey block on Court Square, but business grew rapidly and in 1923 a new site was secured on Railroad Street on which its new building was erected. This building is the most modern and up-to-date building of its kind to be found anywhere. Approximately 150,000 dozen pairs of hose are manufactured yearly, and seventy-five hands are employed. The mill has 101 knitting machines, twenty-two looping

DACOTAH COTTON MILLS, Lexington
C. A. Hunt, Jr., President and General Manager

machines and eight sewing machines, and a complete dyeing equipment, including 144 Paramount forms. H. E. Shoaf is president, and I. L. Sink is secretary and treasurer.

The Wabena Mills Company is one of Lexington's youngest manufacturing plants. It was organized in 1923, the main promoters being W. H. Mendenhall, D. M. Myers and Raymond Earnhardt. The mill is located on Tenth Avenue and the Southbound Railway, and manufactures approximately one-half million pounds of yarns per year for the carpet trade. About thirty hands are employed in the mill. Joe H. Thompson is president; D. M. Myers, vice president and manager; R. P. Earnhardt, secretary; W. H. Mendenhall, treasurer.

The Lexington Ice and Coal Company, successors to T. S. Eanes, who had been handling ice and coal, ice having been shipped in and distributed by him, was organized in 1914. Realizing Lexington's need for an ice plant, Mr. Eanes erected one in the spring of 1914. Not until the plant was making ice and was a reality in every detail did Mr. Eanes attempt to interest his friends to invest money in the proposition. About July of the same year the company was incorporated and H. B. Varner was elected president; A. M. Neese, vice president; T. S. Eanes, treasurer and general manager. The present officers are A. M. Neese, president; G. W. Leonard, vice president; T. S. Eanes, treasurer and general manager. The following compose the board of directors: T. S. Eanes, W. H. Phillips, G. W. Leonard, A. M. Neese and J. C. Bower. The plant has a capacity of thirty tons per day and employs about thirty-five hands. In addition to the manufacture of ice, this company supplies a large part of the coal needs of the town and has built up a large business.

During the year 1914 J. C. Grimes and his brother, W. T. Grimes, purchased the little bottling business operated by L. A. Young and began business under the name of the Lexington Coca Cola Bottling Company. At that time the plant was located in a small building in the rear of Conrad Hardware Company. Realizing that their business would soon outgrow this small building, Mr. Grimes, in 1915, purchased the property where their two-story brick building is now located. In 1917 a large addition was built to the main building and the Grimes Ice Cream Company was organized and installed in the new building. Then, in 1921, a large two-story building planned especially for the manufacture of ice cream was built just back of the main building. The business has developed wonderfully under the management of J. C. Grimes, who is now sole owner of both the Lexington Coca Cola Bottling Company and Grimes Ice Cream Company, and he has one of the largest bottling and ice cream plants in the State, employing fourteen people.

The Peerless Mattress Company started business in 1907. The plant is located on Seventh Avenue and State Street, and it is owned and controlled entirely by Joe V. Moffitt. It is one of the most modern equipped factories in the Carolinas and manufactures all grades of mattresses and pillows, which are shipped to North Carolina, South Carolina, Virginia, West Virginia,

IRVIN L. SINK, Lexington
Manufacturer, Secretary and Treasurer Shoaf-Sink
Hoisery Mill Company

Tennessee and Florida merchants. The capacity is 150 mattresses per day, and thirty-five hands are employed. This concern also jobs springs, beds, pillows, upholstery, etc.

The Lexington Mattress Company was started in October, 1920, in a very small way, in two rented rooms up stairs in the old building recently torn down for the erection of the new Jule C. Smith block. A. L. Disher, now manager of the plant, did all the work of making the mattresses, except the making of the ticks. In a few weeks a colored boy was employed to assist in the work. Sales gradually grew, until more room was required, and in May, 1921, the present two-story building was erected. Several persons are now employed regularly and two salesmen are on the road. During the year ending July, 1926, forty thousand dollars worth of mattresses were sold, and it is the hope to reach fifty thousand during the next year. This concern is owned by Miss Roxie Sheets, who does all the book work connected with the business, and is managed by A. L. Disher, an experienced mattress man, who knows the business thoroughly. [Later this business was purchased by A. E. Smith and Lloyd R. Hunt.]

In 1907 the Lee Veneer Company was organized, the main promoters being L. V. Phillips, Wade H. Phillips and others. In 1910 D. W. Phillips purchased the bulk of the stock, and he, with three or four others, owned the business until 1920 when Mr. Phillips purchased all outstanding stock, and he continued running the business until his death in 1922, after which it was run a year by the D. W. Phillips estate. In 1923 it was burned, but was rebuilt at the same site—in the southern part of town on the Southbound Railway— and the name was then changed to the Lexington Veneer Company. In 1925 this plant was purchased by the Linwood Manufacturing Company, which was organized in 1902 by Lee V. Phillips at Linwood; Mr. Phillips continues as secretary and treasurer of the corporation.

The Lexington Chair Company was organized in the spring of 1911 by George L. Hackney, G. W. Mountcastle, W. E. Holt, F. S. Lambeth, of Thomasville, and Frank M. Weaver, of Asheville. Changes were made in the plant formerly operated by the Oneida Chair Company, located on the Raleigh road and the Southern Railway, which property the new company acquired. Charles Prevost was made superintendent and served for about two years, when he resigned and was succeeded by Fred R. Hackney. The business has steadily grown and each year has brought many new improvements. When running at normal, the plant employs about 85 men and manufactures about $200,000 worth of chairs yearly, which are shipped not only to the entire South, but to the West and Northwest and some even to Cuba, South America and South Africa. In the fall of 1919 George L. Hackney purchased the interest of his associates in the business and is now sole owner.

The Southern Upholstery Company was organized in 1916 by J. G. Hege, H. B. Davis and Miss Dell Watson. The business was started on Main Street in the old Opera House. The business grew so fast that

GEORGE L. HACKNEY, Lexington
Owner and Operator of the Lexington Chair Company

larger quarters were secured on Depot Street in the old brick building just opposite the Coca Cola Company's plant. In 1919 Mr. Davis and Miss Watson sold their interest to J. C. and T. J. Grimes. The present officers are T. J. Grimes, president; J. G. Hege, vice president; J. C. Grimes, secretary and treasurer. The company specializes upon upholstered furniture and employs about fourteen hands.

During September, 1920, B. C. Philpott, J. D. Bassett and T. V. Kirkman purchased the plant of the old Atlas Furniture Company, which is located on the Southern Railway, opposite the new depot, and began the organization of the United Furniture Company. Active work was started January, 1921, and great improvements have been continually going on. The company specializes upon bedroom furniture, making it in walnut and ivory finishes. Under normal conditions the plant employs from 150 to 175 men. B. C. Philpott is president; J. D. Bassett, of Bassett, Va., vice president; and T. V. Kirkman, secretary-treasurer and superintendent.

The Elk Furniture Company was organized in 1902. Its first officers were Dr. E. J. Buchanan, president; R. L. Burkhead, vice president; D. F. Conrad, secretary and treasurer; and J. W. Crowell, superintendent. Since that time several changes have taken place in the personnel of the officers. In 1912 G. F. Hankins was elected president; W. J. Lancaster, superintendent; J. L. Gallimore, secretary and treasurer. In March, 1923, the larger part of the plant was destroyed by fire and the company was reorganized with the following officers: J. T. Hedrick, president; B. C. Philpott, vice president; T. E. McCrary, second vice president; W. N. Kinney, Jr., superintendent; J. L. Gallimore, secretary and treasurer. The plant was immediately rebuilt on the same site, which is located near the Southern Railway freight station. The company specializes on bedroom furniture, in period designs, which are finished in American walnut and French walnut. Under normal conditions the company employs about one hundred and fifty men and the output is sold in practically every state in the Union and bears a high reputation.

The Lexington Upholstery Company was incorporated in March, 1903. The officers were W. H. Walker, president; E. J. Buchanan, vice president; L. J. Peacock, secretary and treasurer and general manager. This concern started business in a small storeroom on Main Street, later buying lots on Salisbury and Foster streets, on which were erected two two-story buildings. The output grew from a few thousand dollars per annum to over $100,000 per annum. In January, 1922, L. J. Peacock bought all outstanding stock and dissolved the corporation. This concern paid the original stockholders several times over in dividends the amount invested, and when they sold out they were paid one and one-half times the amount invested.

Dixie Furniture Company was incorporated January, 1901, with the following officers: E. J. Buchanan, president; P. J. Leonard, vice president; W. H. Walker, secretary and treasurer; J. W. Crowell, superintendent. The plant was built in the spring of 1901, beginning

J. CLARENCE GRIMES, Lexington
Owner and Operator of Lexington Coco Cola Bottling Company and also Grimes Ice Cream Plant

operation in April of that year. The machine room fell under heavy weight in September of same year. This was rebuilt and operation resumed. A line of plain oak bedroom furniture was made with an output of about $100,000 per year. The entire plant was burned down in April, 1904. The company immediately rebuilt the present plant with exception of several additions, and resumed operation September the same year, the output being increased to about $175,000 per year, having added quartered oak bedroom furniture to the line. In 1907 a line of American quartered oak, or printed furniture, was added to the line, and continued making plain oak, quartered oak and American quartered oak, until 1920, when the line was changed to walnut and mahogany. The plant now makes only walnut in high grade period bedroom suits, the line being marketed, in almost every state in the Union. Dr. E. J. Buchanan has been president of the company since organization. P. J. Leonard has been vice president since organization. W. H. Walker was secretary and treasurer from organization until his death February, 1913, A. A. Neese succeeding him and holding the place until January, 1916. The present secretary and treasurer, W. F. Sparger, was elected on Mr. Neese's resignation. J. W. Crowell was superintendent from organization until January, 1911, being succeeded by M. H. Conrad, who has been superintendent ever since. The present output is about $425,000 per year. The capital stock of the company has been increased from time to time and now has an authorized capital stock of $200,000 common stock, and $100,000 preferred stock, with common stock of $100,000 and preferred stock of $28,000 paid up.

In the fall of 1909, the old Eureka Trouser Company suspended business and D. S. Siceloff, who had been working for the company, organized a pants factory of his own, taking over part of the machinery of the old organization. Since that time Mr. Siceloff has increased his business over twelve hundred per cent. The old business was conducted in the old brick building on Depot Street, but during 1915 Mr. Siceloff purchased a lot on South Pugh street, on which he erected a modern factory. The Siceloff Manufacturing Company manufactures overalls and work pants, and employs about ninety people.

The Lexington Mirror Company was organized in 1906 by Thomas Gallagher, of Pennsylvania. For several years it was operated under his management; then A. G. Jonas took charge and it was operated under his management until about 1914, when it was sold to the Southern Mirror Company, of High Point. In 1916 the Elk and Dixie Furniture companies bought it, and since that time it has been operated under the management of these two plants, running under the name of the Piedmont Mirror Company. The output is used entirely by the furniture factories in this city.

The Standard Parlor Furniture Company was organized in 1919, M. H. Conrad being chief promoter. In 1922 George McCarn purchased all outstanding stock and the plant was owned and controlled entirely by him until it was destroyed by fire. Mrs. McCarn was president; Miss Virginia McCarn, vice president, and Mr. McCarn, secretary and treasurer. The plant was located on Fifth Avenue East and Railroad Street,

JOHN H. COWLES, Lexington
Superintendent Lexington City Schools

and employed about twenty-five hands. A line of parlor and living room suits was manufactured and shipped to practically every southern state.

The Art Upholstery Company, manufacturers of living room and parlor suits, davenetts, odd rockers, etc., was organized in 1923. The plant is located on Main Street in the old Opera House. Its officers are G. W. Pugh, president; E. G. Rhodes, secretary; and H. B. Davis, treasurer. Its output it shipped to points in North Carolina and Virginia.

In 1869, J. H. Thompson, Sr., and his son, C. M. Thompson, went into the business of manufacturing plows and all kinds of agricultural implements in the little village of Tyro. In 1872 Mr. Thompson died, leaving his shop to his three sons, C. M., P. H. and F. M. Thompson, who continued running the business until 1879, when C. M. Thompson bought F. M. Thompson's interest, and the shop was moved to Lexington in a building just opposite the old Southern passenger station, which has long since been torn down. In 1882 or 1883, the two brothers went into the lumber business, and in 1886 C. M. Thompson bought his other brother's interest. He then purchased a lot on Depot Street, erecting a building which still stands. About 1889 Mr. Thompson went into the lumber business exclusively and from that time this plant has been turning out all sorts of building materials such as sash, doors, blinds, etc. In 1910 Mr. Thompson retired from the business, turning the plant over to his two sons, Cliff H. and Joe H., who are continuing the business at the same place, running under the name of C. M. Thompson's Sons.

3. Lexington Schools

The graded school system in Lexington only extends back to the year 1901. There were schools in the town through all the years of its history. Many teachers of note had charge of the schools, remaining longer or shorter periods. There were public schools here from the date of the organization of the public schools by the Legislature of the State. There were at different periods private schools and academies conducted here. The Lexington Academy was favorably known for a long time under a number of instructors. For this school a brick building was erected on Main Street about the year 1850. It is still standing, though not used for school purposes for many years. In 1883 Captain S. E. Williams, then a young barrister who had just hung out his shingle in the county seat of Davidson, taught a school for boys in this building. At the same time he was Superintendent of the Davidson County public schools. Among his pupils in that building was the author of this history. In this building the "Southern Normal," later transferred to a new building a little farther up town, now occupied as the residence of the late Sheriff A. T. Delap's family, was conducted by Prof. S. H. Thompson. He was succeeded by the brothers L. E. and P. O. Duncan. Their school was very successful and was attended by most of the boys and girls of the town as well as by numerous others from the county and beyond its bounds. Prof. Allen Jones was a well-known teacher of the years following. Miss Laura Clement was a successful teacher of boys and girls in these years preceding the coming of our graded schools. Prof. Edgar, with a

ERLANGER COTTON MILLS, ERLANGER
Joseph M. Gamewell, General Manager

corps of assistants, taught many of our young people for several years in the early eighties. Prof. W. B. Dove, a graduate of Catawba College, later Secretary of State in South Carolina for many years, was principal of the school conducted in the building erected in 1884, still standing as a part of our present Robbins School building.

Rev. Jesse Rankin, a Presbyterian minister, was a noted school-teacher in the community for a long period prior to the schools and teachers above named. His work dates back to about 1834. Besides school work he took quite an interest in agriculture and cattle raising. In order to produce better pasturage for cattle and sheep, he introduced from elsewhere a grass known ever since as "Rankin grass." He thought he was doing the county a great favor; but many farmers would be glad if "Rankin grass" had never been heard of, because it is difficult to get rid of when once it takes root in the soil.

The graded schools of Lexington were organized in 1901. At the regular town election that year the following were elected members of the school board: F. C. Robbins, Dr. Joel Hill, J. B. Smith, Dr. E. J. Buchanan, H. P. Gallimore, S. E. Williams. Captain Robbins was elected chairman and Captain Williams secretary. The official title was recorded as follows: "The Board of School Commissioners for Graded Schools in the School District of the Town of Lexington for White and Colored Schools." The "Lexington Seminary" property was purchased from J. D. and T. J. Grimes for the sum of $2,800, plus a small sum of interest due them on their original purchase. This is the present site between Fifth and Sixth avenues. A lot was at the same time purchased for the colored schools on "Factory Row" for the sum of $290.

Graded school superintendents have been the following: J. B. Spillman, 1901-1903; W. M. Brown, 1903-1909; A. H. Jarrett, 1909-1912; O. V. Woosley, 1912-1918; J. H. Cowles, 1918-

In 1915 a frame building was erected on the school grounds with three large rooms to accommodate the overflow of pupils. The committee having this work in charge consisted of Dr. J. C. Leonard, E. B. Craven, Dr. E. J. Buchanan and Prof. O. V. Woosley. After being in service several years this building was destroyed by fire. The Hege building on the northeast corner of the public square was then rented for school purposes and it was used until the new High School Building was ready for occupancy.

May 9, 1919, Dr. J. C. Leonard, W. J. Lancaster, Dr. E. J. Buchanan and Prof. J. H. Cowles were appointed a committee to find suitable lots for a new school building. This committee selected the Dobson and the Grimes properties at the corner of State and West Second streets, and their choice was approved by the whole board in subsequent session. The total cost of the lots was about $6,000. The same committee purchased a new site opposite the Nokomis Cotton Mills, known as the "Pinnix Hall Property," for the colored schools of the city. The building committee for the construction of the new building on the Dobson and Grimes lots consisted of Dr. J. C. Leonard, Zeb V. Walser, Esq., L. F. Barr, Dr. E. J. Buchanan and J. D. Redwine. Later the "Lexington High School District," consisting of the city of Lexington and several outlying districts, was created. Bonds were voted by which this new district took over the new building.

B. CABELL PHILPOTT, Lexington
Manufacturer, President United Furniture Company

The cost of the High School building without the auditorium was $170,000. The auditorium cost about $75,000. The whole plant means an outlay of $250,000. The new colored school building was constructed at the cost of $55,000. The Cecil School property on East Center Street involved an investment of $180,000.

CHAPTER XVI

THOMASVILLE, A THRIVING CITY

1. A Davidson County Asset

Davidson County is famous for many of its great assets, but in none does it excel more than in the possession of Thomasville, North Carolina's and the South's largest chair manufacturing center, a city which holds a record for steady, substantial growth, and a community of many and diversified industries situated in the heart of Piedmont North Carolina and the trade center of a rich agricultural center.

Incorporated in 1852, Thomasville remained a village for half a century until the possibilities of its industrial advancement were recognized. Its population in 1900 was 751, but by 1910 it had grown to 3,877 and by 1920 to 5,676. Its phenomenal growth in the last ten years represents an increase in population of 46 per cent, and for a twenty-year census period of 655 per cent, a record perhaps unequaled outside of mushroom towns.

Thomasville today is one of the most modern cities in the South for its size. It has a complete water and sewer system, paved streets, electric lights and electric power. Its industries include: seven chair factories, two furniture factories, two knitting mills, one finishing mill, two panel factories, one box and shook factory, one packing pad factory, one excelsior plant, one concrete products plant, one roller mill, one machine shop, two banks, thirty-six stores.

The city is situated on the main line of the Southern Railway, and has the High Point, Thomasville and

FESTUS E. SIGMAN, Thomasville
Davidson County Register of Deeds, 1916-1921, Thomasville Postmaster 1921—

Denton Railroad to High Rock on the Southbound Railway. It has a belt line of side tracks, giving all industries complete transportation service; it is located on an excellent system of State highways, now being hardsurfaced, and is connected with the county highways in all directions. The school system of Thomasville is modern and up-to-date in every way, being recognized as one of the best in the State. The new school building cost half a million dollars.

It is the home of the Baptist Orphanage, and has representative religious denominations which give the city an air of refinement, with many handsome edifices which would do credit to a much larger city. One of these is the New Methodist Protestant Church and Community Building erected through the generosity of C. F. Finch, Thomasville manufacturer and philanthropist, "to meet not only the demands of spiritual development but the natural demands of children for social and physical exercise."

Thomasville has the city manager form of government, and its municipal progress is excellent with a comparatively low tax rate. It has an automatic telephone system, Rotary and other civic clubs, many beautiful homes, civic pride, thrift and industry. It is truly a city for a homeseeker, the investor or the manufacturer.

Thomasville has been truly described as "industrious, progressive, aggressive and democratic,"—a city which is an asset to the county, State and Nation, and one of the greatest contributing factors in the industrial development of the South.

2. A Bird's-eye View

[In the issue of *The Thomasville Times* for August 10, 1922, the following article was published under the heading. "Thomasville Told Tersely," written by George Claiborne Simms:]

Mother Nature placed in her galaxy no fairer scene than the environs of Thomasville, nestling snugly in the foothills of the Blue Ridge mountains, a site both picturesque and healthful. Thomasville is laid out along liberal lines of ample ground surrounding all homes. It has sparkling clear pure mountain limestone water and a delightful blending of pure country breezes and Carolina sunshine.

By day this ideal community is in a fever-heat of business activity. At night it is a typical peaceful Southern night-setting that no stage director has ever been able to show in replica. The hills, their shading of pine fringe, the vales and pasture lands, good homes, soft Southern moonlight, balmy evening breezes freshened and perfumed by the scented breath of flowers, slowly floating billowy white cloud featherings, the evening star surrounded by a countless ensemble of smaller shining orbs, make a night picture never to fade from the memory. Where the trail of the Chowan and Catawba Indians led now races the steel horse of the palefaces, with the speed of an arrow in flight. Thomasville is on the main line of the famous Southern Railway and has exceptionally good train service.

The town was not founded until 1852, when a village was projected by Senator John W. Thomas and Dr. Rounsaville and they combined their two names into Thomasville as the title of the settlement. It was

WILLIAM G. HINKLE, THOMASVILLE
Owner and Operator of the Thomasville Roller Mills

incorporated as a town in 1854, and in 1857 the North Carolina Railroad was constructed. Thomasville is 852 feet above the sea level and is one of the prettiest of all Carolina towns. Its chief industrial pursuit is the making of chairs, which had its start in the early '70's when D. S. Westmoreland began making chairs here. It is now known as "The Chair Town," being the second largest in this enterprise in America. It has numerous diversified industries, chief among which are furniture factories, veneer works and cotton mills. The town is steadily growing at a healthy pace. In 1900 it had but 751 inhabitants, which is now increased to 5,676 people. It is in the rich Piedmont section and has wonderful natural resources in agricultural adaptability, deposits of raw materials and a truly wonderful climate. Thomasville is especially adapted as a manufacturing location from an all-round viewpoint.

It has the city manager form of municipal government. The city's official family consists of the following: Mayor, T. E. Jennings; City Manager, T. F. Harris; City Attorney, H. R. Kyser; City Clerk, Miss Belva Harris; Judge Recorder's Court, Judge W. S. Bogle; Prosecuting Attorney, J. T. Jackson; Chief of Police, G. W. Wimberly; Fire Chief, Charles L. White; Councilmen, C. F. Lambeth, R. L. Pope, Dr. Crews, F. B. Hamrick and D. R. Connell.

The community is not only law abiding but of high moral attainment, and there is almost no need of a jail. The town is well supplied with churches in the Baptist, Methodist, Lutheran, Reformed, Presbyterian, and Methodist Protestant faiths. It is here that the Baptists of North Carolina have built their great orphanage for both boys and girls, where they are properly reared and instructed, each being taught a vocation.

Thomasville has good schools, although having the misfortune to recently lose its magnificent $100,000 graded school structure through fire, but which has been rebuilt, larger and better.

Labor is plentiful here. Good wages are earned and paid. The city has a modern water system and sewerage and is lighted by the Southern Public Utilities Company, which gives excellent service.

Thomasville's commercial houses number approximately 250 representative, enterprising and progressive firms. It is a good business town, and the First National Bank has resources of over a million and a quarter dollars. Two flourishing building and loan associations are a helpful constructive element in the community.

Several good dairies are maintained, and farmers generally are showing new interest in better livestock and in dairying. One noticeable feature of the county is the absence as well as need of sheep on the farms. There appears to be a future ahead for those who pioneer the way in wool growing.

Thomasville needs a chamber of commerce, a real theater, a paid fire department, several apartment houses, several hundred new dwellings, a public library, more asphalt streets and good roads, many more storerooms and last, but not least, less taxes.

3. THOMASVILLE IN ITS BEGINNING

[The following article from the pen of the late Mrs. John T. Cramer appeared in *The Chairtown News* Thursday, July 28, 1921:]

JOHN W. LAMBETH, THOMASVILLE
President and General Manager of the Lambeth Furniture Company

Thomasville is the largest town in Davidson County, the census of 1920 giving the town a population of 5,676, having grown from 3,877 in 1910. This city has the largest chair factory in the country. John W. Thomas, my father, who was the founder of Thomasville, N. C., lived at "Fair Grove" when the North Carolina Railroad was surveyed. He was in the State Senate when the charter was granted, and gave it his strongest support. He came here and bought about four hundred acres of land from Jonathan Winston, with a view of establishing a town. He always told us "there was nothing here when he came but a burned hogpen." It was an old camping ground known as the "Whitehart Hog Crossing," where the college now stands. The campers used water from the spring at the Cramer factory. Later a sawmill was built near it, which furnished lumber for building houses and the plank road between Greensboro and Salisbury. Hill and Winston first owned it, but sold to my father.

About 1850 the Winslow house was built where L. W. Elliott now lives. After occupying it for some time L. L. Thomas rented it and moved here to keep boarders while the hotel was being built, the house we now live in. Some log cabins were erected for workmen to use, who cleaned up the forests and worked any and everywhere for the advancement of the prospective town. John W. Thomas's store was completed in 1852 and was considered a marvel of skill and architecture, and drew the country people like a magnet. David Lambeth owned it when it was burned a few years ago, and from its ashes has arisen one of the handsomest brick blocks of our new town. The Rounsaville house was building at the same time the Lewis Thomas

Hotel was going up and the William Foster house opposite. Then the John W. Thomas house was built by Winslow and Foster and was considered a grand mansion in those times. About this time my father took the contract for building six miles of the North Carolina Railroad, beginning here and going toward Lexington, while Valentine Hoover and others went toward High Point.

The first child born in the new town was William Bascom Thomas, son of Lewis Thomas. The first death was Nelson Foster, brother of William, and the next was David Hill Thomas, my brother. They were buried back of our Methodist Church, and in after years were moved with many others to the new cemetery.

While the railroad was being built the town was progressing every way and many desirable citizens were moving their families here. When the railroad was completed Thomasville put on her gala attire and prepared a big "barbecue" to welcome the first passenger train and its operatives coming from the south. The whole country for miles came to do honor to such a grand occasion and the variety of vehicles, to say nothing of the style, would do credit to any curiosity shop in existence. Long before time for the arrival of the train runners were stationed down the track to give warning, and when she hove in sight they had to run over each other getting out of the way yelling "She's a comin'." Just as the people were thinking of dinner there was a roar like an earthquake and before the last toot of the engine was over the inhabitants and horses were flying to the woods and it was said many never came back to enjoy the dinner. The first engine used here to haul dirt, sills and iron was the "Traho," Capt.

W. B. Lewis, engineer. The first agent appointed was Lewis L. Thomas and the ticket office was in the room where our parlor is. The train stopped in front of the hotel at a long platform. The passengers took their time to eat, and when the conductor got through he hunted them up and off they went, never dreaming of the days when they must eat by the minute and if you were not on hand you were left.

In 1855 C. M. and G. Lines moved here from Bush Hill (now called Archdale). They built a factory for making leather belts and brogan shoes for farmers. The shoes became famous all over the South, and so the Lines Company was induced to add a nice grade for men and women to their mammoth trade. Northern workmen came down and many men in town went into the shop to work, which was easy, as well as good pay. Then a fine boot and shoe factory was opened where Mr. Cates's store now stands, operated by Lewis Thomas, and the town was called the "Lynn" of the South.

At this time it became necessary to name the town, which my father did, calling it Thomasville after himself, and it was well supported by his six sons living here as they grew up and married. Progress and thrift were manifest. The farmers were busy getting "crossties" as they were called then. It was a close race between them and the shoes as to which should be the chief stock in trade. The Whitehearts of "Pine Woods" made split-bottomed chairs in a crude way by hand and it was said that "Long Bill" Whitehart could pack eighteen chairs on his back and tramp all the way to Bush Hill with them. D. S. Westmoreland manufactured these same split-bottomed chairs in 1865 just across the creek, and made money. It was said he raised his own help! And is it any wonder this should be such a great chair town when such stalwart men laid the foundations? They little dreamed what it would become in after years. What a pity we allowed our magnificent forests to be cut down and shipped to other towns in needless waste, when we have one of the grandest openings, for wood manufacturing in the South! We are forty years too late finding out our mistake.

In 1856 my father decided to build a college, which he did with his own slaves under the supervision of Robert Gray, a fine mason and contractor. There was a female school about one mile from here, established and run by Charles Mock and wife, two great educators of that day, who afterwards sold it to Dr. Charles F. Deems, pastor of the "Church of the Strangers" in New York City. He gave it the name of "Glen Anna" for his wife. Dr. Deems sold it to my father, and in 1857 he moved it up here, and called it Glen Anna Seminary. The first music teacher was Miss Ellen Morphis, who afterwards married Rev. Marcus L. Wood and went to China as a Methodist missionary. She died there and he returned, bringing two little boys with a Chinese nurse, and now lives in Surry County, an old man. The first graduates of the seminary were Linnie Gray, Corinna Whitaker, Lon Frazier, Miriam Clifton and Jennie Thomas. The diplomas were delivered by Dr. Craven, of Trinity College. Before the seminary was completed the Methodists held their services in the Lines Shoe Shop, afterwards in the new depot, and at last in the chapel of the seminary.

In 1861 the great Civil War began, demoralizing everybody and everything. I will not attempt giving a

T. A. FINCH, THOMASVILLE
President and General Manager of the Thomasville Chair Company

description of those horrible times. History's pages are full of the facts. Thomasville furnished a company, and the ladies made the uniforms. Miss Dart, a northern teacher in the seminary, painted the flag, a rattlesnake coiled ready to strike. Her tears fell while she painted, yet she would not stop until it was finished. Times were hard and we had to undergo many privations, but thanks to my mother we escaped much. As soon as war was decided she had all the sugar, coffee, groceries and dress goods taken from our store to her storeroom in the house, and then she had a friend who ran the blockade and always brought her a mat of Java coffee, but many people during the four years had to use parched wheat, dried sweet potatoes and other stuff, which was as good as Postum I imagine. At the close of the war the wounded from the battle at Bentonville were brought here and filled the Methodist and Baptist churches and the Pinnix tobacco factory. The commissary stores were here in the care of Dr. Baker, and the people threatened to raid the "tithes" that had been collected, so he called for a guard, and Mr. Cramer's company from Greensboro was sent here. Their tents were in front of where we now live, and the officers took their meals in my room. There was a great flag-raising here and Jack Leland's celebrated band from Cleveland, Ohio, with many high officers of the Northern army came down from Greensboro. My father, who always made the best of everything, invited them to stop at our house and no one knows to this day how Mr. Cramer managed to get himself invited with them, but that was the beginning of our romantic courtship. One day a train load of soldiers on their way north stopped in front of my father's, and piled out and ran to some red, ripe cherry trees. The officers at the quarters saw them and Mr. Cramer with sword and red silk sash came dashing up and the soldiers flew for the train, but one fellow more bold had come to the front porch where Pat Lewis and I were standing, and began taunting us with being whipped, which we stoutly denied and "sassed" him good fashion. By this time Mr. Cramer with two of his orderlies had gotten up the walk and in stentorian tones said "What are you doing here, sir?" So he slunk away amid the peals of laughter of the soldiers. Of course I had to write a note of thanks after that, and then he must call, and kept calling, and that is the way the world goes.

During the days of reconstruction everything was uncertain and there was very little progress in our town. Houses were built, people married and died, and in 1871 the founder of Thomasville died with a disease of the heart, angina pectoris, mourned and missed by all who knew him.

4. Some Thomasville Factories

Thomasville is known the world over as the "Chair Town," and boasts of the largest chair in the world, which is near the Southern Railway, mounted on a pedestal, so every traveler can see what Thomasville makes.

The first plants to be built were a sawmill and a flour mill by the founder, John W. Thomas. The sawmill furnished material for newcomers to build homes. Burrell and Tom Lambeth were the millwrights and for many years operated these plants successfully.

C. M. & G. Lines came to Thomasville in 1856 and built a shoe factory, making shoes for men, women and children. They made four hundred pairs per day and employed three hundred men and women. This plant was very successful for many years.

J. W. Jones owned a tan-yard just back of his home and furnished a great deal of leather to the shoe factories.

J. W. Gray had a sash and blind factory on Randolph Street which was a great help to the contractors.

M. H. Pinnix & Bros. owned a tobacco factory on Main Street below the freight depot. They manufactured chewing tobacco. During the war they allowed the soldiers to be carried there and their plant used as a hospital.

J. A. Leach Company operated a cigarette factory on Guilford Street. Mr. Frank Ware was superintendent and made millions of cigarettes which were shipped North.

The Lee Manufacturing Company was owned by Major J. H. Lambeth & Sons. They made chairs, tables and roller-top desks. This firm had the misfortune to be burned out twice, but each time they built larger and better plants which were run until the death of Major Lambeth.

Thomasville Furniture Company is owned by Robert Lambeth, president and general manager, John R. Myers, secretary and treasurer; incorporated for $150,000. This plant is one of the best in town. They make beautiful bedroom suites, using twelve thousand feet of lumber per day, working 135 hands, shipping two cars per day. Charles Stone is the efficient superintendent of the finishing department.

Thomasville Bottling Works are owned by J. W. Boyles. This splendid plant was founded in 1907, making about fifty cases per day. In 1923 the amount per day had increased to 250 dozen. Mr. Boyles added a cold storage and ice plant, making fifteen tons every day and employing ten men. Mr. Boyles deals in coal, ice and ice cream. This is another pride of Thomasville.

Thomasville Shuttle Block Factory was built by Mr. White and made shuttles which were sent to Elwood Cox at High Point.

Thomasville Roller Mills were built by the late George A. Thompson in 1884, who operated for some time and then sold to George Miller. The latter sold to Captain Sumner who was successful until his death. This mill is now owned by W. G. Hinkle, who has enlarged and improved it until he has one of the most modern plants in Davidson County.

The Lambeth Furniture Company, owned by John W. Lambeth, was built in 1901 and incorporated for $98,000. This plant uses ten thousand feet of lumber per day making kitchen cabinets. They employ one hundred men and ship goods all over the states.

The Kindergarten Chair Factory is owned by E. F. Perryman and employs eighteen men, making beautiful little chairs for children.

The Hoover Chair Factory was built and owned by Charles and Marshal Hoover. These gentlemen made beautiful chairs and employed a large number of men. They had the misfortune to be burned out. Later they moved to Lexington where they are making a wonderful success.

The Thomasville Manufacturing Company was owned by Dr. R. W. Thomas, T. J. Finch and George A. Thompson. Chiffoniers and dressers were made and shipped to all parts of the United States. H. E. Clement was superintendent and worked a large number of hands.

A. H. RAGAN, THOMASVILLE
President and General Manager of the Ragan Knitting Company

Columbia Panel Manufacturing Company, R. R. Ragan, president, J. C. Connolly, vice president, S. E. Tucker, secretary and treasurer, was incorporated for $40,000. This factory makes the beautiful built-up stock which is taken to High Point and made into high-class furniture. It employs about sixty men and is another one of our successful plants.

The Bard Chair Company was built in 1907 by McKoy & Lance. Box seat dining chairs and rocking chairs were made. Incorporated for $25,000; number of hands, 35.

Ragan Knitting Mills are owned by Adams & Ragan, incorporated for $40,000. These gentlemen use 1,500 pounds of yarn per day and employ 130 hands, making fifteen hundred dozen pairs of hose a day.

The North State Veneer Plant is owned by E. C. & R. C. Jones. Incorporated for $10,000. All kinds of veneer are made at this factory and quite a few skilled hands are employed turning out beautiful material.

The Gray Concrete Company is owned by Fred and Julius Gray. These young men make all kinds of building blocks, tile and culverts which are used very sucessfully in many places in buildings of all kinds.

The Amazon Cotton Mill was built in 1910 and is incorporated for $525,000. It is owned by the late J. W. Cannon estate and C. G. Hill. There are 13,000 spindles in the mill and there are 175 hands making combed knitting yarns. The mill is being greatly enlarged and will be more than doubled. A great many new houses are being constructed which will help to house their operators.

Jewel Cotton Mill is one of the best equipped plants in Thomasville. It makes yarn and employs many skilled laborers. This mill is on East Main Street, and it is a very impressive structure which Thomasville is very glad to welcome under her domain.

The Thomasville Baptist Orphanage has a woodworking plant that supplies its own building material, requiring an enormous amount of lumber. This splendid institution is arranging to make all kinds of material and teaches the boys trades. Mark Stone is the superintendent and has been there for years.

The Standard Chair Company was organized in 1898, and was incorporated in 1901 for $125,000. Capital, $70,000. Charles F. Lambeth, president, James E. Lambeth, vice president, Frank S. Lambeth, secretary and treasurer. This plant is one of the largest in town, and makes 2,000 chairs per day and employs 300 men and 500 weavers who bottom chairs. This is the largest assorted plant in the South. They make a specialty of porch furniture. Their goods are shipped to every state in the Union and to Cuba.

Jennings Manufacturing Company is another successful plant. Eugene Jennings is the efficient president and Will Peace is manager.

Thomasville Chair Company, T. J. Finch, president, T. A. Finch, secretary and treasurer, Charles F. Finch, manager. Four factories make all kinds of chairs, turning out 4,000 per day and employing over 700 people. This is the largest plant in Thomasville. Another plant makes pads and panels. Excelsior pads and all kinds of built-up chair stock are produced. Another plant under this organization is Glen Anna Veneer Plant, making veneer of every kind.

5. Thomasville Graded School

The Thomasville graded school was organized in 1901. At that time Thomasville was one of the smallest towns in the State to take this forward step. The special charter, passed by the Legislature that year, provided for a school board consisting of five members who should establish and carry on a graded school for each race in the town of Thomasville. The names of the persons chosen to compose the first board were as follows: F. S. Lambeth, Archibald Johnson, W. C. Harris, D. C. Moffitt and Peter Cates. F. S. Lambeth was made chairman and served in that capacity a number of years. Since then the chairmanship has been held by Archibald Johnson, John R. Myers and C. F. Lambeth, the present incumbent.

The first superintendent was J. T. Henry, who organized the school and directed its activities one year (1901-02). The first teachers in addition to the superintendent were Miss Lizzie McCall, of Statesville, and Miss Elizabeth Allen, of Goldsboro. Miss McCall taught only until Christmas and was succeeded by Miss Annie Hoover, of Concord. On the resignation of Superintendent Henry in 1902, J. N. Hauss was elected his successor and has served as superintendent since that time.

The growth of the school has been steady, keeping pace with the growth of the town. The average daily attendance in the white school during the first year of its history was ninety-six. In the year 1925-26 it had increased to 1,213. From a course of study consisting of six elementary grades it has advanced to a complete elementary school and a high school that is accredited both by the State and the Southern Association of Colleges and Secondary Schools.

The school was first conducted in temporary quarters. The lower floor of the old Masonic building on Randolph Street furnished two classrooms and the Hanner shoe shop on the corner of Randolph and Mill streets was converted into a third classroom. In 1902 a lot was purchased on Main Street and a brick building was erected. It was thought at the time that this building would furnish sufficient room for years to come. Before long, however, all the space was being used and even the chapel was carved into classrooms. In 1915 a large addition was erected in the rear of the old building, thereby furnishing six more classrooms, an excellent auditorium, and furnace room.

In April, 1922, the entire plant was destroyed by fire. However, with remarkable coöperation on the part of the community the school was enabled to complete the year's work without the loss of a single day and to continue throughout the following year principally in the Sunday school rooms of churches. In the fall of 1923 a new, fireproof structure, conveniently arranged and with modern equipment was occupied. It contains twenty-nine classrooms, auditorium with seating capacity of 1,000, large gymnasium with shower rooms attached, manual training room, cafeteria, food laboratory, sewing room, science laboratory, library, offices, rest rooms, etc. The building committee was composed of John R. Myers, chairman, C. F. Lambeth and T. A. Finch. This new building was erected at a cost of a quarter of a million dollars and stands as a testimony to the progressive spirit of the citizens of Thomasville.

The names of the present school board are as follows: C. F. Lambeth, chairman, Mrs. C. M. Howell, secretary, Dr. C. A. Julian, J. W. Boyles, H. S. Hankins.

J. N. Hauss is superintendent, and P. C. Newton is principal of the high school.

CHAPTER XVII

RELIGIOUS FORCES OF DAVIDSON COUNTY

1. GENERAL STATEMENT AND STATISTICS

[The author is greatly indebted to the following gentlemen for assistance in the preparation of this chapter: Revs. N. G. Bethea, B. S. Brown, Jr., W. R. Shelton, W. B. Harrell, J. W. McCuiston, J. R. McGregor, W. S. Holmes, Dr. Archibald Johnson.]

The character of the people counts more than all else in the building of a great county. This year (1922) Davidson County is celebrating its centennial. That which in these hundred years has contributed most to the making of the county really great has been the religious devotion and Christian piety of a large element of its population. In the early years came the devoted followers of the lowly Nazarene. They were Swiss, French, English, German and Scotch-Irish—the latter two nationalities predominating. These Christians brought with them from the old countries their Bibles, catechisms and hymn-books. They also brought with them their school-teachers and their pastors. Wherever they made a settlement they built a church and a schoolhouse. These were humble places of education and religious worship, but how great is our debt to them! They laid the foundations of education and religion. Others have built upon the foundation laid by them, and as a consequence Davidson County is very markedly under the influence of genuine piety and religion in this good day.

Various denominations were found among the early comers to this section of North Carolina. But since the Germans, the Scotch-Irish and the English were most numerous, the denominations prevalent in the home countries predominated here, such as the Moravians, Episcopalians, Presbyterians, Reformed, Lutherans, and later Methodists and Baptists. It happened in the territory now covered by Davidson County that there were more German settlers from about 1740 to 1775 than any other nationality. For this reason the Reformed and Lutheran churches were quite strong in the early years, and throughout the history of the county these churches have maintained their organizations. In later years the Methodists and Baptists gained a very strong following. The oldest church in Davidson County is that at Pilgrim whose origin was prior to 1757. Other old churches are Bethany (originally union Reformed and Lutheran), St. Luke's Lutheran, Beulah Reformed, Beck's Reformed and Lutheran. Pilgrim was originally called "The Dutch Congregation on Abbott's Creek." It was also called "Leonard's Church," in honor of one of its leading families. Valentine Leonard, who was born in the Palatinate in 1718, came to North Carolina in 1746 and settled on the stream still bearing his name, "Leonard's Creek." The church was located on a tract of land adjoining his numerous acres. He was a devoted Christian; he was also a strong patriot and a brave soldier in the war of the Revolution in which he sacrificed his life. His ashes are buried in the graveyard at his home church. By his side also sleeps another brave soldier, Wooldrich Fritts, founder of the Fritts family in this county, who was also killed in the Revolution. A grateful citizenship in the year 1896 erected over the graves of these Revolutionary patriots a handsome monument.

The early history of the several denominations in Davidson County is full of deep interest. Some of the congregations were very careless in keeping their records, and much valuable history has been lost. Pilgrim Reformed Church (Leonard's Church, or the Dutch Congregation) has in a good state of preservation its first record book, dating from 1757. The Lutheran Church in the same community is also very old. Rev. C. E. Bernhardt, according to Dr. Bernheim, was its first resident minister, his pastorate dating from 1787. The first Lutheran minister in North Carolina located in a regular pastorate was Rev. Adolph Nussman, who arrived in 1773; he became pastor of churches in Cabarrus and Rowan counties west of the Yadkin River. Beck's union Reformed and Lutheran church dates from 1787. The union Reformed and Lutheran church at Bethany goes back to 1789. The first outstanding preacher of the Methodist denomination in early days was the Rev. Peter Doub, who preached over a large section of the county wherever he could find hearers. About 1848 the Methodist church in Lexington began to take on real strength. Its first house of worship was on the site of the present colored M. E. church. In 1873 a new house of worship was built at the present location. The Presbyterian Church was organized in 1827, nearly a hundred years ago. The activities of this denomination in Davidson County have been confined mostly to Lexington, though several years ago a congregation was organized in Thomasville. The Episcopal Church had its origin in 1835. The Baptists began their work in Lexington in 1879, though there were congregations in the county much earlier than that date. The Reformed church organized its first congregation in Lexington in 1901, and the Lutherans came in 1905.

Statistics of Churches

The following statistics of all the churches in Davidson County are given: White churches—Baptist: 25 churches; 4,025 members; 3,571 in Sunday school; $40,571 contributed; $130,700 value of church property. M. E. South: 29 churches; 4,987 members; 4,974 in Sunday school; $75,598 contributed; $224,327 value of church property. Episcopal: 1 church; 38 members; 39 in Sunday school; $4,597 contributed; $16,000 value of church property. Presbyterian: 3 churches; 300 members; 437 in Sunday school; $16,083 contributed; $75,000 value of church property. Methodist Protestant: 22 churches; 2,222 members; 2,350 in Sunday school; $30,582 contributed; $55,200 value of church property. Lutheran: 9 churches; 855 members; 679 in Sunday school; $7,695 contributed; $70,400 value of church property. Moravian: 2 churches; 550 members; 484 in Sunday school; $2,000 contributed; $22,000 value of church property. M. E. (North): 4 churches; 300 members; 400 in Sunday school; $800 contributed; $8,000 value of church property. Reformed: 15 churches; 2,371 members; 2,724 in Sunday school; $155,855 contributed; $105,500 value of church property. Total figures for the white churches of the county: 110 churches; 15,648 members; 15,658 in Sunday school; $333,781 contributed; $708,127 value of church property.

Colored churches—Baptist: 9 churches, 1,040 members; 600 in Sunday school; $2,500 contributed; $15,000 value of church property. A. M. E. Zion:

5 churches; 350 members; 200 in Sunday school; $1,000 contributed; $8,000 value of church property. Presbyterian U. S. A.: 2 churches; 132 members; 155 in Sunday school; $2,069 contributed; $10,000 value of church property. Methodist Episcopal: 5 churches; 600 members; 450 in Sunday school; $2,000 contributed; $20,000 value of church property.

Total statistics for all the colored churches: 21 churches; 2,122 members; 1,405 in Sunday school; $8,569 contributed; $53,000 value of church property.

Total for all churches white and colored: 131 churches; 17,770 members; 17,063 in Sunday school; $342,350 contributed; $761,127 value of church property.

In addition to the above tabulated figures there are some members of the Friends, Dunkards, Primitive Baptists, Holiness, and other denominations, whose figures could not be secured.

This brief recital of church history shows that the county of General William Davidson has a citizenship of religious people. The leading denominations except Roman Catholic are found here, and the members are doing aggressive work in the Master's Kingdom. Religion is of more value to Davidson County than all other things combined. The Christian people of Davidson County make it a fit place in which to live. Our religious forces are our greatest asset. A converted man is a safe man. A Christian is a good citizen. The more Christians we have, the deeper the piety of our Christians, the stronger and more reliable will be the moral worth and integrity of our people.

2. LUTHERAN CHURCHES

General History

Among the early settlers of that part of North Carolina which is now called Davidson County were quite a number who were of German descent. These people came, not in general directly from Germany, but mostly from Pennsylvania and were popularly known as Pennsylvania Germans. They were attracted to this part of the country by the abundance, fertility and cheapness of the land. Many of these settlers came to North Carolina as early as 1750 and some prior to that date, and soon, by industry and thrift, had attained a position of prosperity and influence.

The religious faith of these early settlers was chiefly that of the Moravian, Reformed and Lutheran churches. As the development and activities of the former are considered elsewhere, special reference is now confined to the organization and growth of the Lutheran congregations.

Owing to the fact that few early records have been preserved, much of the history of the Lutheran congregations in the county is uncertain and incomplete. That congregations were organized prior to the year 1790 is evident from references made in the correspondence of the time. Perhaps the most interesting is that contained in a letter of the Rev. Arnold Roschen who had come from Germany to labor in the new country. The following excerpts have to do specifically with the work in Davidson County:

"North Carolina, Rowan County, near Abbott's Creek; in the midst of the forests of North America, sixty-six miles from the Blue Ridge Mountains, eighteen miles from Salem; from April 29th to June 21st, 1789.

". . . At length we arrived in Salisbury, where Pastor Storch resides, whom I esteem and love as a friend, and who rendered me very important services, where we were as kindly received as we could have expected. Upon the first intelligence of our arrival, the deacons of one of the nearest of my congregations, together with some wealthy planters residing there, came to the town to welcome us. The people here know nothing of compliments, but express their opinions in a manner that indicates good thinking faculties. They informed us that we would not find a dwelling-house as yet prepared for us, because, upon consultation, it was thought best to wait until my arrival, so that I could myself direct the building of the same. And now the whole train moved along, increased by Pastor Storch's accompanying us, until we came to the place appointed for me, situated on Abbott's Creek, a small stream that empties itself about twelve miles distant into the Yadkin River. A deacon of my central congregation took me to his home, where we remained for several months, until we moved to our own plantation of two hundred acres of land, which we have purchased advantageously, assisted by several upright planters of this place; we were advised to take this step by Pastor Nussman, who came to meet us in Salisbury, in which advice Rev. Storch also joined.

"As soon as we arrived, the deacons out of three congregations came to visit us. A fourth congregation, which is now almost the largest, also placed itself under my ministry. So now I am the pastor of four churches. The people from all parts of the country brought us abundantly flour, corn, hams, sausages, dried fruit, chickens, turkeys, geese, etc., so much so, that there has been scarcely any necessity to spend one farthing for our housekeeping up to this time."

A report of Pastor Roschen made to authorities in Germany a little while after he had settled in his new field of labor is quite interesting and is given here in abridged form:

"In my middle congregation I have confirmed twenty-four persons; in the congregation situated toward the Yadkin River I confirmed twelve and in the others I have this duty yet before me. . . .

"Marriages are here performed in two modes; the one according to the rules of the Church requires to be announced three times; the other is managed as follows: The groom gets a certificate from Salisbury, rides, accompanied by his friends, with his bride to the minister, or, if none is in the place, to the magistrate, where the marriage takes place. The first questions of the minister are, Whether he has taken his bride without her parents' knowledge?—this occurs frequently—and, whether the parents have given their consent. If any one has stolen his bride and has a certificate from Salisbury, then the objections of the parents avail nothing. Upon the whole, in this free country, a son, whenever he has arrived at his twenty-first year, and a daughter as soon as she is eighteen years old, is no longer under the parents' control. Persons generally marry very young, because they need not be much concerned for the future.

He that will work can soon have a plantation; and poor people are not to be met here at all. A person can often meet with families that have thirteen or fourteen children, nearly all living. I myself am acquainted with a planter here, who has had a family of twenty-three children, born of one mother, and who, with the exception of two, are all living and well.

"My catechumens, whom I have instructed three days in every week for seven weeks, consist partly of married persons, some of them as old as thirty years, and young persons from sixteen to twenty years of age. Among other things, I advise them not to intermarry with persons of other nationalities, because such mixed marriages are generally unhappy, and sometimes occasion murder and homicide, and because the English in these regions belong to no religious denominations, and do not permit their children to be baptized, nor send them to school.

"We ministers are treated with a respect such as is shown to no other person. There is no difference in rank acknowledged here, and yet no one has ever spoken with me, who did not hold his hat in his hand. I must say the same of Storch; he is treated with such love and respect by his congregations, as few ministers in Germany are treated. . . . We all preach in black clothes and collar, but mostly without a gown, and oftentimes in our overcoat during bad weather in winter.

"I endeavor to make the Divine service as impressive as possible, and suitable to the occasion, but as simple as I can. I dare not make my discourse shorter than three-quarters of an hour, because there are members who have ridden eighteen miles to church, and in each church there is service only once every four weeks. Baptisms take place after the sermon and in the presence of the whole congregation. Whenever the communion is administered on Sunday the preparatory service takes place on Friday or Saturday preceding. Nothing is known here of private confession."

Very little is known of the work of Mr. Roschen except that he remained in this field until the year 1800, when he returned to Germany. That there were others before him is evident from the fact that he found the work so well organized when he came. One of these was Rev. Christian Eberhard Bernhardt who was born, educated and ordained in Germany and came to this country in 1786. In 1787 he came to Rowan County and labored in churches located east of the Yadkin River in what is now known as Davidson County for one year, when he took charge of churches in Stokes and Forsyth counties. If there were others who labored before him, there are evidently no records of their activities.

In the year 1800 Rev. Paul Henkel, a great-grandson of Rev. Gerhard Henkel who was one of the first Lutheran ministers to come to America, took charge of the churches left without a pastor by the removal of Pastor Roschen. He was born near what is now Salisbury in the year 1754, but had been a resident of Virginia for the past forty years. Something of his activities may be seen from the following extract from the German minutes of a Virginia Conference, held in Roeder's Church, in Rockingham County, in 1806:

"In Rowan County (now Davidson) on Abbott's Creek, we find three joint and one Lutheran Church on the Sandhills. These were served by the Rev. Paul Henkel from the year 1800 to 1805, when he was necessitated to resign this charge, on account of the failure of his own and his family's health; he therefore introduced the Rev. Ludwig Markert as candidate preacher in these congregations, which he was himself compelled to leave."

Mr. Markert continued to serve these congregations until 1816 when he removed to Indiana. Synod then appointed Rev. G. Shober to serve two congregations, while the other two were placed under the care of Rev. J. W. Meyer. In 1817 Rev. Daniel Walcher was sent by Synod to labor in the vacant churches. He remained until 1821. The four congregations mentioned above were probably Pilgrim, Beck's, St. Luke's (first known as "Swicegood's Meeting House" and later as "Sandy Creek"), and Bethany, now no longer in existence as a Lutheran congregation.

From the minutes of the North Carolina Synod the following facts are gleaned: In its third convention Synod met at Leonard's (Pilgrim) Church near Lexington. The Rev. Ludwig Markert was licensed at Abbott's Creek Church October 22, 1804, and was ordained at the same place October, 1808. Synod met at Pilgrim Church (called Ebert's Creek at one place) in the years 1804, 1808, 1813, 1817 and 1822.

The foregoing references indicate that the original Synodical connection of these churches was with the North Carolina Synod. Their pastor, Rev. Paul Henkel, was one of the ministers participating in its organization, and it is probable that Beck's, Pilgrim, and St. Luke's were among the fourteen congregations that took part in the organization. In 1819 came the unfortunate rupture, due to personal and practical differences rather than to doctrinal ones; and in at least two instances this rupture manifested itself in the life of local congregations with the result that there were two organizations, the one connected with the newly formed Tennessee Synod and the other with the North Carolina Synod. In 1921 the two synods were reunited, and since then all the Lutheran churches of the county have been connected with the United Evangelical Lutheran Synod of North Carolina and are working together most harmoniously.

According to the statistics of the year 1925 there are eight congregations in the county with a baptized membership of 1,438 and a confirmed membership of 863 and an enrollment of 1,111 in the Sunday schools. These congregations have property valued at considerably more than $75,000. Further interesting facts are given in the sketches of the individual congregations.

Pilgrim Lutheran Church

Pilgrim is probably the oldest Lutheran congregation in Davidson County. The exact date of its organization is not known, but it must have been prior to 1787 when Rev. C. E. Bernhardt became its first regular pastor. That there were many Lutherans among the early German immigrants to this section is most probable, and that these Lutherans formed some sort of an organization is equally probable. Revs. Adolph Nussman and John Arndt came over from Germany in 1773 and settled on the south side of the Yadkin River, but their activities were by no means confined to that immediate section. We are told that

Arndt especially made many missionary tours, preaching, baptizing, confirming and organizing wherever it was practicable, and he certainly did not neglect his neighbors on the north side of the Yadkin.

Mr. Bernhardt remained but one year and was succeeded in 1788 by Rev. Arnold Roschen who continued to serve the congregation till 1800. He was a polished scholar and a much beloved pastor. To him we are indebted for all the early records which we possess. It has been stated that there were fifty-two families in the Lutheran congregation at Pilgrim in 1792, nearly as many as the combined membership of the three oldest congregations south of the Yadkin. This would indicate an organization much earlier than the coming of the first pastor in 1787.

Rev. Paul Henkel, who became pastor in 1800, was a man of oustanding ability whose influence was exerted not only in his own congregation but throughout the State and Nation as well. He left the work in splendid shape for his successor, Rev. L. Markert, who followed him in 1805 and continued to serve the church at Pilgrim until 1816.

With the formation of the Tennessee Synod in 1820 there came into existence a second definite Lutheran organization at Pilgrim. One of the groups continued its relationship to the North Carolina Synod while the other was numbered among the congregations of the new synod. For the next eighty-three years each congregation maintained its own organization and had its own pastor, but both used the same house of worship which was also used by the Reformed congregation. The period was not fruitful of outstanding events or developments, but it was one in which each congregation continued to make its own contribution to the life of the community and to the production of a well-rounded Lutheranism in the county and State.

There were two buildings prior to the one erected in 1882, the first a log house, followed by a frame building two stories high with a gallery around two sides and one end, which was erected in 1807. An old tradition says that Gottlieb Greim (Grimes) struck the first blow of the axe in preparation for this building, and that seven years later he performed the same office for the new congregation at Emanuel. This second building continued to be used till 1882 when Lutheran and Reformed congregations united to build a third, which is still standing.

In 1903 a discussion arose between the Reformed and Lutherans about the title to property which both had occupied for so many years. The claim of the Reformed was that originally the property belonged to them alone. Finally, however, an agreement was reached whereby the Reformed congregation was recognized as entitled to a half interest in the property and the two Lutheran congregations to a half interest. It was further agreed that the property should be sold at auction. The two Lutheran congregations agreed before the sale that they would bid as one and that each should be entitled to half of their part of the property or money as the case might be. Soon after the sale, which resulted in the purchase of the old property by the Reformed, the two Lutheran congregations united under the name "Pilgrim Evangelical Lutheran Congregation of the Synod of North Carolina," bought a site half a mile from the old church and built a beautiful house of worship at a cost of more than three thousand dollars. It was ready for occupancy, save for the pews, when on October 9, 1903, it was burned. The loss was complete as the building had not been insured. This was a terrific blow, but the members rallied to the call of their church and immediately rebuilt. This second house, which cost $3,500, was dedicated on April 17, 1904.

It has been a rather difficult task to compile a full list of pastors. In most instances names and dates have been taken from the Baptismal record of St. Luke's which was in the same pastorate. The following list is practically complete:

Christian E. Bernhardt	1787-1788
Arnold Roschen	1788-1800
Paul Henkel	1800-1805
Ludwig Markert	1805-1816
Gottleib Schober	
J. W. Meyer	1816-1817
Daniel Walcher	1817-1821
Jacob Miller	1824-1827
David P. Rosemiller	1830-1831
Daniel Jenkins	1833-1834
Benjamin Airey	1837
Jacob Crim	1839-1842
J. B. Anthony	1847-1848
L. C. Groseclose	1849-1854
W. A. Julian	1853-1863
W. H. Cone	1864-1865
A. D. L. Moser	1867
J. D. Bowles	1871-1874
C. H. Bernheim	1874-1878
W. A. Julian	1879-1885
J. M. Hedrick	1885-1886
D. W. Michael	1887-1891

W. Kimball..1892-1894
T. H. Strohecker..1896
P. J. Wade..1898-1905
G. H. L. Lingle..1906-1910
J. L. Smith..1911-1912
N. D. Bodie...1912-1913
W. C. Buck..1914-1918
M. L. Kester..1918-1919
C. H. Day..1920-1921
C. R. Pless..1922

TENNESSEE PASTORS

Henry Goodman.......................................1832-1849
A. Efird..1849-1854
J. M. Waggoner.......................................1854-1860
J. E. Seneker..1860-1861
I. Condor..1861-1866
Thomas Crouse.......................................1868-1875
C. H. Bernheim......................................1877-1882
W. P. Cline...1883-1891
Jacob Wike..1891-1893
A. R. Beck..1893-1895
J. L. Deaton (supply).............................1897-
C. L. Miller..1898-1903

St. Luke's Lutheran Church
(Sandy Creek)

A great deal of history is sometimes revealed in the names by which churches have been known. The congregation eight miles west of Lexington, now known as St. Luke's, has at one time or another been called Sandy Creek Meeting House and Swicegood's Meeting House. The first name locates the congregation and the second gives the name of the original donor of the land on which the church was built. The investigator finds this verified by the original deed to the property which is recorded in the courthouse at Salisbury. A part of this deed is here given:

This DEED made the eighth day of January in the year of Our Lord 1790 between Adam Swicegood and Mary Cathron his wife of the County of Rowan and the State of N. Carolina, Planter, of the one part and HENRY CLEMMENTS and JOHN GOBEL of said County and State, Trustees for the Congregation that upholds the German Meeting House known and designated by the name of Sandy Creek Meeting House on the waters of Sandy Creek; Witnesseth that for and in consideration of the good will and regard that the said Adam Swicegood and Mary Cathron his wife hath for the propagation of the Gospel and sundry other reasons moving thereto together with five shilling sterling by the said Henry Clemments and John Gobel, Trustees for the Sandy Creek congregation in hand paid by the trustees in behalf of the said congregation to the said Adam Swicegood and Mary Cathron his wife at and before the sealing of these presents the receipt and payment whereof is hereby acknowledged hath granted, bargained, sold, aliened, enfoeffed, convey and confirm unto the said Henry Clemments and John Gobel trustees of the aforesaid congregation forever—(here follows a description etc., of the land.)

The unavoidable inference from this is that prior to the year 1790 there existed in this community an organization known as "Sandy Creek Meeting House." Another inference based on the double use of the word "Meeting House" is that there had been a building in existence even before this, but the peculiar use of terms prevalent at that time makes this uncertain. A third inference based on the wording of the deed and upon strong tradition is that the Lutheran congregation was the only one represented and that it has always been the sole owner of the property.

Rev. C. E. Bernhardt and Rev. Arnold Roschen were the first pastors of the congregation. The first building was a rude log structure 24 x 30 feet which was destroyed by fire; the second was a reproduction of the first; the third was a frame building of the same size erected in 1835; and the fourth is a frame building 35 by 58 feet which has undergone various remodelings. The congregation now has under construction an attractive brick church designed to meet the needs of modern church life. It is located half a mile from the original site.

In 1854, under the pastoral direction of Rev. L. C. Groseclose, the pastorate consisting of St. Luke's, Pilgrim, Beck's and Bethany erected a parsonage on land adjoining the St. Luke's property at a total cost of $350. This too, has been remodeled several times. The land for the parsonage was given by J. H. Thompson and John Sharp.

In 1880 the congregation extended its activities to cover the sphere of general education. An academy was built on land donated by R. F. Thompson and his mother. This institution was under the direction of a board of trustees appointed by the church, and for a number of years it contributed much to the development of the community.

Some idea of the life of the times and of the strict discipline which prevailed in the earlier days of the congregation's history may be gained from the following extract from the records:

December 1, 1831. The Church Council convened this day to take cognizance of the conduct of.................................and
....
It was resolved, 1st that the said................... ....as he was lately intoxicated and engaged in fighting, be suspended from membership in the church for six months.
2nd. That the said J................... ...., inasmuch as he has tolerated riot and reveling at his house, that he also be suspended during the term of six months.
3rd. That .... inasmuch as he has been intoxicated and engaged in wrestling on the Sabbath day, be finally excluded from the church.
4th. Resolved that Public notice be given to......................
....and................... ....that if they do not reform their lives and attend the preaching of the Gospel for the next six months, that they shall be excommunicated from the church.

St. Luke's was most probably one of the fourteen congregations which united in the organization of the North Carolina Synod, and it has always maintained its relationship with that body. The minutes of 1810 give the following as Elders and Deacons of Sandy Creek Meeting House: Elders—Adam Schweisguth and John Gobel; Deacons—Henry Ratz and Philip Beck. Synod met with the congregation four times during the nineteenth century. In numbers St. Luke's is the largest Lutheran congregation in the county. It now has a confirmed membership of 195 and a Sunday school enrollment of 269. That it is still vigorous after more than 135 years of activity is indicated by the large Sunday school and by its determination to procure a house of worship which will be adequate for its needs.

As St. Luke's has always sustained a pastoral relationship with Pilgrim, it will not be necessary to give a list of pastors here. Such a list will be found in the sketch of Pilgrim.

Beck's Lutheran Church

One of the older Lutheran congregations in Davidson County is Beck's situated six miles southeast of Lexington. November 5, 1787, Dr. John Billings, L. Smith and others deeded to the "Trustees of the Congregation of the Profession of the Church of England and the Congregation of the Profession of the Church of the Dutch Settlement on Abbott's Creek" fifty-three acres of land to be used for religious purposes by the two congregations. There has never been a question seriously raised that these two congregations mentioned were not Lutheran and Reformed. The description, "The Profession of the Church of England," was doubtless due to the fact that the Lutherans, like the Episcopalians, used a liturgical service. The description, "The Profession of the Church of the Dutch Settlement on Abbott's Creek," described the Reformed congregation as like the one already named in earlier records in the deed for the Pilgrim (Leonard) church lands. The trustees named for the Lutheran congregation were Martin Frank and Frederick Billings, and those for the Reformed congregation were David Smith and Henry Lookinbee. The consideration paid was the nominal five shillings.

A church was soon built on the property, and with the coming of Pastor Arnold Roschen the Lutheran congregation began to assume real importance. In one of his reports to the authorities in Germany Pastor Roschen says that he confirmed twelve in the congregation toward the Yadkin River. It is very likely that Beck's was one of the fourteen original congregations of the North Carolina Synod. In the minutes of Synod for the year 1810 the following officers of the congregation are given: Elders—John Beck and David Beyrer; Deacon—Ephraim Gass.

For many years after the formation of the Tennessee Synod two Lutheran congregations existed at Beck's. The North Carolina Synod congregation joined with the other congregations of that Synod in the county in the erection of a parsonage at Tyro in 1854, and North Carolina Synod pastors seem to have served there at least as late as the time of Rev. J. D. Bowles. For a number of years prior to the merging of the two synods in 1921, however, the sole congregation had been that one having connection with the Tennessee Synod. Lists of pastors who served the two congregations may be found in the sketch of the Pilgrim congregation.

About the year 1875 the Tennessee Synod Lutherans decided that each congregation should have a church of its own, and in order that the two buildings might not be too close together, George Hedrick gave the Lutherans one-fourth acre of land adjoining the original tract. Upon this they built a church which is still in use. For some reason the Lutherans failed to maintain a regular succession of trustees for the original property, and when the question was raised the courts decided that the Lutherans of the Tennessee Synod had no legal right to it.

Beck's Church now has a confirmed membership of 125 with a Sunday school enrollment of 130. New Jerusalem, Lebanon, and to a certain extent Holly Grove, are children of this congregation.

Bethany Lutheran Church

Had the history of Bethany Lutheran Church been written a quarter of a century ago it might have been fairly complete; but at the present time the records are not available, and most of those who could have given valuable information are dead. Immigrants settled in this section during the latter part of the eighteenth century, and they soon organized a union congregation. The old deed was made to the "inhabitants of Brushy Fork belonging to the Societies of the Church and Presbyterian parties." The Rev. Mr. Roschen, in his report of 1789, refers to the fact that he was pastor of four congregations. This indicates that the congregation was organized prior to that date. The Rev. Mr. Henkel's report in 1805 also refers to four churches in what is now Davidson County. The "Church party" was the Lutheran Church and the "Presbyterian Party" was the Reformed Church.

The first church was of log construction. Mrs. M. R. Shoaf, who was confirmed in this congregation in 1854, says that the building at that time was a log structure. She also says that when a frame building was erected in 1861 the name Bethany was given to the congregation. Before this it was known as Fredericktown Church, and the minutes of the North Carolina Synod show that the Synod met with a congregation of that name in 1855.

For many years a strong Lutheran congregation was maintained, but for various reasons it gradually became weaker and was finally abandoned entirely in the early years of the present century. The congregation was in a pastorate with Pilgrim and St. Luke's and had an interest in the parsonage at Tyro.

Emanuel Lutheran Church

One of the first Lutheran churches organized in the nineteenth century was Emanuel, located south of the town of Thomasville, having its origin in 1813. In that year three acres of land were deeded to Philip Kanoy, Jacob Myers and John Bowers, "Elders of the Presbyterian and Lutherian German Churches or their successors in said churches," by John Myers and his wife Elizabeth for a consideration of five dollars. These peculiar titles mean the Reformed and Lutheran (German) churches. In 1814 the two denominations built a union house of worship. An interesting legend has been handed down to the effect that Gottleib Greim (Grimes at present) had struck the first blow with the axe in felling a tree seven years earlier for the second church at Pilgrim, and that he performed a similar service for Emanuel Church. This gentleman became a staunch supporter of the Lutheran congregation at this place. For many years the congregation rendered valuable service to the community and to the church at large. It was served by pastors connected with the pastorate belonging to the Tennessee Synod and a list of them will be found in connection with the history of Pilgrim. December 12, 1901, the first building was burned and a new and handsome church was erected by the Lutheran and Reformed congregations the next year. This house, with some improvements, is still used by the Reformed.

Modern methods of travel have made it possible for the Lutherans of the community to attend services either at Thomasville or Holly Grove, and in 1925 the Lutheran congregation was dissolved and the fifty members were transferred to Grace and Holly Grove. Their share of the property was sold to the Reformed for $400. Thus, after more than 100 years of activity, the Lutheran congregation ceased to exist; but its influence and service will be continued in the more effective work which the other congregations will be able to do. A splendid example has been set for further consolidation in keeping with conditions existing at the present time.

New Jerusalem Lutheran Church

On August 28, 1856, Levi Beck, a Lutheran, deeded to Daniel Foust, A. J. Ward, David Beck and David Swing, trustees, a tract of land in eastern Davidson County to be used by the Evangelical Lutheran, Reformed, Methodist and Baptist churches as a site for a church building. This building was immediately erected by Lutheran and Reformed, and the history of New Jerusalem dates from that time. Peter A. Kepley, who is still living, was a charter member. Rev. J. M. Waggoner was the first pastor.

In 1910 the old building was torn down because it had become unsafe and the present church was erected by the Lutheran, Reformed and Methodist Protestant congregations. The Baptists seem never to have had an organization.

The Lutheran group, which came originally from Beck's congregation, has always been the strongest of the coöperating congregations, but it has never been large. At present there is a confirmed membership of forty. Until the merging of the North Carolina and Tennessee synods it was connected with the latter, and with the exception of a few years about 1900 when that synod had two pastorates in the county, it has been a part of the Holly Grove pastorate. During this brief period a parsonage was erected at Cid, but this was later sold. A Sunday school has recently been organized and the congregation seems to be taking on new life.

Holly Grove Lutheran Church

Since Holly Grove Church is an outgrowth of the academy of the same name, the beginnings of its history are inseparably connected with that institution. The first place of worship was the auditorium of the school and the first service was held on Christmas day, 1885, and the building was dedicated on the second Sunday in May of the following year. The membership was largely made up of members from Pilgrim, Becks and New Jerusalem congregations. The land for the school and church was donated by Eli Younts.

For a number of years the need of a more adequate and churchly house of worship was keenly felt, but this feeling did not crystallize into definite action until after Mrs. Eliza Hedrick had left a bequest of $500 to be used toward the erection of a new church. The definite decision to build was made on Thanksgiving Day, 1913, and the cornerstone was laid one year later. The new church, which was erected during the pastorate of Rev. J. M. Senter, is a beautiful brick structure which would be a distinct credit to a much larger congregation.

Holly Grove from its beginning was connected with the Tennessee Synod. It now has a membership of 165 with a Sunday school enrollment of 190. The congregation is comparatively young and still has the vigor of youth. At present it is engaged, with the other congregations of the pastorate, in the erection of a beautiful brick-veneer parsonage which will be equipped with all modern conveniences. This is situated near the church, and the two together make an unusually fine rural church plant.

The pastors of this church have been the following:

W. P. Cline	1883-1891
Jacob Wike	1891-1893
A. R. Beck	1893-1895
J. L. Deaton (supply)	1897-
C. L. Miller	1898-1903
W. P. Cline (supply)	1904-1905
A. L. Bolick	1906-1909
J. F. Deal	1910-1911
J. M. Senter	1912-1918
R. B. Sigmon	1919-

Lebanon Lutheran Church

Some time prior to the year 1860 Peter Owen donated to the Lutheran Church for use as a site for religious services two acres of land lying a mile or more south of Abbott's Creek. An arbor was built and for many years occasional services were held by pastors from both the North Carolina and Tennessee synods. Some sort of organization prevailed at various times, but no effort was made to build a church until 1890. Work proceeded slowly, or not at all, until 1899 when, under the pastoral direction of Rev. C. L. Miller, the congregation was reorganized and the building completed. Mention should be made in passing of the loyal support which Franklin Younts gave to the work at this place both before and after the building of the church. This church is located on the Winston-Salem Southbound Railroad near the site of the Junior Orphanage, and has a membership of twenty-seven with a Sunday school of thirty-five. It is now a part of the Holly Grove pastorate.

First Lutheran Church of Lexington

The history of Lutheran activity in Lexington dates back to the year 1827, five years after the town became the seat of government for the new county of Davidson. In that year Rev. D. J. Hauer, a recent graduate of the Theological Seminary at Gettysburg, conducted services in the courthouse and preached sermons in both English and German. Some sort of an organization was effected, a Sunday school was organized and plans were started for the erection of a house of worship. For some reason this house was never built, and for the next three-quarters of a century the activities of the Lutheran Church in Lexington were confined to occasional services held by neighboring pastors.

Early in the year 1905 Rev. Edward Fulenwider, Synodical Missionary of the North Carolina Synod, began holding services in Hedrick's Hall, and on July 30 of that year organized a congregation with sixteen charter members. Fourteen others had applied for letters but did not get them in time to be received at this service. The officers of the new congregation were: Elders—C. M. Thompson, H. L. Propst and Jackson Sink; Deacons—D. A. Shoaf, George W. Crouse and M. H. Conrad. A building committee was appointed consisting of C. M. Thompson, George W. Crouse, H. L. Propst and Rev. Edward Fulenwider.

The erection of a church building was soon begun and at a special service held June 9, 1906, the cornerstone, a gift of H. J. Hege of the M. E. Church, South, was laid. The first service in the new church was held November 25, 1906, and the formal opening on January 13, 1907. At a special meeting held December 31, 1909, the announcement was made that the church property, valued at more than $12,000, was free of debt. This accomplishment was due, in no small measure, to the generosity and tireless activity of C. M. Thompson. The church was formally dedicated on the first Sunday in April of the following year. Rev. V. Y. Boozer, who had been pastor of the congregation for the past six months, was assisted in the service by Dr. M. M. Kinard of Salisbury.

The congregation continued to grow until additional Sunday school equipment became an imperative need, and once more the generosity of Mr. Thompson made the meeting of this need a possibility. Early in 1926 additional Sunday school rooms were erected at a total cost, including equipment, of approximately $5,000. Mr. and Mrs. Thompson contributed the amount necessary for the construction of the rooms themselves and the congregation provided the funds necessary for their equipment.

The growth of the congregation has not been unusual, but it has been substantial. The original sixteen members have increased to one hundred and seventy-two, and the Sunday school has an enrollment of one hundred and seventy-five. The congregation is making its influence felt both in the local community and in the church at large.

The following ministers have been in charge of this church:

Edward Fulenwider..1905-1908
G. W. Spiggle..1909-
V. Y. Boozer..1909-1916
P. J. Bame...1917-1924
B. S. Brown, Jr...1924-

Grace Lutheran Church of Thomasville

Some time during the spring of 1905 Rev. Edward Fulenwider, Synodical Missionary of the North Carolina Synod, made a survey and found that there were twenty-eight Lutherans living in and around the town of Thomasville, but the outlook was not deemed sufficiently bright to warrant the development of the work. No further effort was made until the summer of 1911 when Rev. V. Y. Boozer, pastor of the First Lutheran Church of Lexington, was instructed by the Executive Committee of the North Carolina Synod to begin definite work there. This he did, and on November 5, 1911, he organized Grace Lutheran Church with a charter membership of twenty-eight. The new congregation was supplied by neighboring pastors until September, 1917, when Rev. J. B. Moose, Synodical Missionary, was located at Thomasville. He was succeeded by Rev. N. D. Bodie, who became Synodical Missionary on September 11, 1918. In 1921 Mr. Bodie became the regular pastor and continued in that capacity ever since.

For the first ten years of its history the congregation had no house of worship but held its services in the Reformed and Presbyterian churches, and later in the Masonic Hall. In the spring of 1921 the property on Salem and West Guilford streets on which the present church building and parsonage stand was secured from Dr. J. W. Peacock in exchange for property which the congregation owned, and an additional $5,000. On April 20, 1921, in connection with a unique service, ground was broken for the new church. The congregation began to use the basement for services in February, 1922, but the building was not completed until June of the same year. The church was formally opened on July 2 with a sermon in the morning by Dr. J. L. Morgan, President of Synod, and another in the evening by Rev. A. D. R. Hancher of the United Lutheran Church Home Mission Board. The building was erected at a cost of approximately $18,000, and the total cash expenditure for the church and parsonage was more than $27,000. The congregation was organized in 1911 with a membership of twenty-eight, and when the present pastor took charge the membership was still twenty-eight. Since that time the growth has been steady, and the membership at the present time, January, 1926, is 111 with an enrollment of 158 in the Sunday school. The prospect for future development is indeed bright.

3. BAPTIST CHURCHES AND THOMASVILLE BAPTIST ORPHANAGE

Abbott's Creek Church

So far as the records go, Abbott's Creek is the oldest Baptist Church in Davidson County. It was constituted in the year 1757 and the gospel was preached there until the year 1832, when, on account of a division of the members, on the question of world-wide missions, the congregation separated into two groups. The majority retained the house, and the minority moved across the road and built for themselves. There are two houses of worship and two congregations still in existence, the one known as Primitive Baptist and the other as Missionary Baptist. Daniel Marshall, George Pope and Ashley Swaim are the only pastors on the record of the church for the first seventy-four years of its existence. Mr. Swaim was the pastor at the time of the division. Beginning in 1832 the following pastors have served the Abbott's Creek Missionary Baptist Church; Eli Phillips, Josiah Wiseman, Enoch Crutchfield, Benjamin Lanier, William Hamner, William Turner, John Robertson, Amos Weaver, J. B. Jackson, J. B. Richardson, G. W. Harman, R. R. Moore, S. F. Conrad, S. H. Thompson, J. N. Stallings, J. M. Hilliard, Thomas Carrick and E. F. Mumford. The church is a vigorous and loyal body. It is in hearty accord with the denominational policies, has a flourishing Sunday school and various missionary agencies. It is reputed to be the wealthiest of the country Baptist churches in this section of the State.

Jersey Church

This church takes its name from a colony from New Jersey which settled in this fertile valley of the Yadkin long before the Revolutionary War. Benjamin Miller, a native of the State of New Jersey, was the first preacher, so far as the records show, who ever ministered to the colony. He was here as early as September, 1755. Of his early life little is known. It is supposed he followed his friends to the Jersey settlement to look after their religious welfare. He did not remain long, however, but returned a few years later to his New Jersey home where he died in 1781. So far as we know Benjamin Miller did not organize the Jersey Church but preached for the settlement for a time. He had a friend, John Gano, who was also a citizen of New Jersey and who was induced to come to North Carolina. He constituted the Jersey Church, probably in 1757, but after doing fine service left the settlement and returned to New Jersey on account of the constant menace of the Cherokee Indians which made life unpleasant.

After a few years the church disbanded and the members scattered to other churches. On October 16, 1784, the scattered members came together and under the leadership of Rev. Drury Sims and Rev. William Hill reorganized the church with fourteen members. Drury Sims was installed as pastor of the church. From that date until the present date this church has been doing business for the Lord, and worships now in a substantial brick building near Linwood station. John Gano was a remarkable man. Although he lived and labored only about two years and a half in North Carolina, he left an impress upon this section of the State that has never faded away. He was an intimate friend of George Washington, who was greatly influenced by the preaching of Gano, who for twenty-six years was pastor of the First Baptist church of New York City.

Holloways

There is no exact date as to when Holloways church was constituted though it was probably established in 1831. However, it was what was called in those days an "arm" and preaching services were held there long before this date. "The Yadkin Association was appointed to meet with Jersey Church October, 1799, but the church having no house that year, the body held its session with the 'arm' at Holloways." (Sheets's *History of the Liberty Association,* page 89.) As is well known, before the Civil War, slaves that were church members held their membership in white churches. Holloways's record shows twenty negro members prior to 1861. This church has always maintained a good reputation for loyalty to the general work of the denomination. It stands with Jersey among the earlier churches for its efficient work and its loyal fellowship with other churches. Rev. Eli Carroll was the pastor at Holloways when the great division in 1832 occurred, and he remained as pastor for eleven years. The name of sixteen pastors since Carroll are recorded on the church book.

Lick Creek

No records show the day or the year when Lick Creek was constituted. It is situated in the extreme southern part of the county, near High Rock. It is, however, one of the oldest churches in the Liberty Association. The Abbott's Creek Church records give this information: "August, 1787, the church received a petition from Lick Creek church for helps, etc." (Sheets's *History of Liberty Association,* page 87.) The body was evidently doing business as an "arm" at that date and "help" was as welcome then as now. This is the oldest record known concerning this church. On August 7, 1808, the church petitioned the Jersey Church for help to constitute them into a church. It is probable that the church was constituted in that year. There have been fifteen pastors of this church since it was constituted, whose names are on record. Rev. Eli Carroll was the pastor at the time of the division.

Liberty Church

This church, which is situated seven miles south of Thomasville, was organized August 22, 1829. It began with twenty-five members, has had twenty-two pastors and has just completed a beautiful house of worship. A test of loyalty was made in this church in 1832. Two preachers, Rev. Eli Phillips and Rev. Ashley Swaim, disagreed on several points of church order. Mr. Phillips held that the minister should be supported by the church, while Mr. Swaim contended that ministers ought to preach without pay. The debate, like that between Paul and Barnabas, grew quite sharp. Finally Mr. Swaim arose and walked out, inviting those in sympathy with him to follow. Six or seven went out. The others remained and the church has maintained an orderly walk ever since that day.

New Friendship Church

This church is situated in Forsyth County, four miles south of Winston-Salem. The formal organization of this church occurred on Saturday, January 27, 1827. The pastor was William Dowd. The church at Jamestown, now extinct, furnished the "helps" necessary for the constitution of the church. The name of New Friendship was given in honor of a church in Moore County. The early records of the church were lost about the time of the division in 1832. The church was blessed in its early history with notably strong men as pastors. Rev. William Turner served this church six or seven years and Rev. F. H. Jones's pastorate covered thirty-three years. During the pastorate of Rev. Henry Sheets, which covered nine years, the present commodious brick edifice was built as a memorial to Pastor F. H. Jones.

Reeds Cross-Roads Church

This church, located in a splendid community, near Lexington, was an "arm" of the Jersey Church for more than forty years, but was not organized into an independent Baptist Church until the 12th day of October, 1839, beginning with a membership of twenty-five. Twenty pastors are recorded as ministering to this church since it was established. Its membership has always been composed of substantial farmers, and has maintained to this day that fine type of citizenship. For many years a good school has been supported at this point, and the church has exerted a fine influence upon the lives of the youth enrolled in this institution.

Churchland

On May 17, 1837, a body of believers met at what is now Churchland and organized a church which they called Pine Meeting House and which bore that rather unattractive name until a few years ago when it was changed to Churchland, the name the flourishing school at that point gave to the pretty village located in the northwestern section of the county. Large congregations attend the services of this church which has been served by eighteen pastors. It is in a flourishing condition and occupies a very important field on account of the excellent school to which it ministers in spiritual things.

First Baptist Church of Thomasville

This church has had a checkered experience. It was organized and received into the fellowship of the Liberty Association in 1859. The town was almost dead and the church had no new life in the town. For a little while the Thomasville Female College quickened somewhat the church life, but it never at its highest tide reached a membership above forty. About the year 1900 the town began to feel the thrill of new life. Manufactories were established. The business volume rapidly increased. Old things passed away and all things became new. The church grew in favor and strength with the town, but its building was shabby. Under the pastorate of Rev. G. A. Martin a beautiful temple of worship was erected. The church at last after forty years of feeble struggle stood out prominently. The first signs of new life were seen during the pastorate of Rev. J. B. Richardson. It continued to grow, led by such men as George P. Harrill and T. S. Crutchfield; when under Pastor Martin the church house, which was a splendid one, was built, it burst into bloom. Dr. I. U. Mercer succeeded Pastor Martin and paid off the debt that held the church down. Dr. J. S. Hardaway by his loving ministry harmonized the body and made it solid, and the present pastor, the Rev. Mr. Alexander, is reaping a great harvest by his virile and enthusiastic leadership. The membership now numbers about 375 and the skies are radiant with great hope.

First Baptist Church of Lexington

The Baptists long neglected the capital of Davidson County. Other denominations preëmpted the ground and several other churches were well established long before the Baptists entered the field. Occasionally a Baptist preached, held a service wherever he could gather a group of people, but nothing like regular preaching services was attempted. In the year 1879 a missionary of the Liberty Association was passing through the town and was invited to spend the night and hold a service. This was the small beginning of what has developed into the great church that now holds its place among the leading churches of Lexington. Rev. S. F. Conrad was engaged to preach regularly for the Baptists of Lexington. This was in 1881, and on July 3 of that year the church was constituted with eighteen members. The presbytery in the organization of the church consisted of Revs. W. H. Hamner, J. B. Richardson, S. F. Conrad and Prof. H. W. Reinhart. The lot on which the present edifice stands was secured that year. Many eminent ministers have served this church. Its growth of course was slow at first but it has been steady and sure. Like its older but smaller sister in Thomasville, the church grew with the wonderful growth of the town. The membership now numbers 602, with Dr. C. A. Owens vigorously leading the church into larger things. This church is the largest and wealthiest church in the Association and its generosity corresponds with its financial ability.

Oak Hill

Oak Hill is a small church located about four miles southeast of Thomasville. It was constituted October 12, 1884, with a membership of fourteen. Rev. Henry Sheets was the first pastor of this church, and six other ministers have served as pastors. Its present membership is forty.

Summerville

This church, four miles south of Denton, was constituted July 6, 1873. Rev. A. P. Stoker was its first pastor, and served the church for fourteen years. The church was received into the Liberty Association in the year 1874 at which time its membership numbered thirty-seven. The present membership is 266.

Denton

The village of Denton is in the southeastern part of Davidson County, on the High Point, Thomasville and Denton Railroad. The Denton Baptist Church was organized August 30, 1891. Rev. Hezekiah Morton was the first pastor of the church. Six pastors have served this church, and its present membership is 216.

The Orphanage Church

April 28, 1891, the Orphanage Baptist Church was constituted. This church is unlike any of its sister churches in that its membership is composed wholly of the employees of this institution and the children under its care. This church has for many years been very liberal in the giving of its adult membership *per capita*. Last year the members having an income gave on the average of $60 per capita. The children are there brought up in the atmosphere of Christian giving. Nine pastors have served this church since it was organized. The present membership is 388. The total contributions for the year ending September 1, 1923, were $3,951.46. Of this amount $530.22 was given for the support of the orphanage.

Rich Fork

This church is located three miles southeast of Thomasville, near the home of the late John H. Mills, through whose efforts mainly the church was organized December 30, 1884. Eighteen members were enrolled in the organization, and the first pastor was Rev. Hezekiah Morton. Ten pastors have served the church since it was constituted, and the present membership is 150. In the rear of the church building stands the monument of John H. Mills, the "Father of Orphanage Work in North Carolina."

Wallburg

Eleven miles north of Thomasville, in the country village of Wallburg, stands the church first called Piney Grove, afterwards changed to Wallburg. It was constituted on the fourth day of September, 1892. Rev. J. N. Stallings was the first pastor. It began with fourteen members and now has 156. In the year 1903 the Liberty-Piedmont Institute was established. The boys and girls in the institution have been provided through all the years since it was established with excellent religious advantages. Rev. E. F. Mumford, the principal of the school, is the present pastor of Wallburg Church.

Stoner's Grove

Stoner's Grove is located in the village of Southmont on the Southbound Railroad. It was constituted March 6, 1900. The church began its work with twenty members, and now the number on the church roll is

150. It has become an important church in the association, surpassing in activity and influence many of the older churches of the body.

Taylor's Grove

The church at Taylor's Grove was constituted September 9, 1901, with a membership of seventeen. That number has been increased gradually.

Gravel Hill

Gravel Hill church is located in Randolph County, near the Davidson line. The church was organized November 24, 1901. Its first pastor was Rev. L. G. Lewis. Its present membership is forty-three.

Center Hill

Center Hill Baptist Church was constituted October 18, 1907. It is located at South Lexington, the site of the Jr. O. U. A. M. National Orphanage and supplies religious privileges for a prosperous community. Beginning with a small number it has grown into a body of 140 members. It is a member of a group of churches known as the "Southmont Field."

Welcome

The village of Welcome sprang up on the line of the Southbound Railroad, and the Baptist Church was established shortly afterward. It is a small but active little band of sixty members, and is doing a fine service for its community.

Erlanger

The Baptist Church of Erlanger, in the beautiful village of that name on the edge of Lexington, was organized on the 29th of October, 1916. At first it worshiped in a building provided by the Erlanger Company, but now it occupies a home of its own. It is an active and progressive band of Christians with a membership of 158. The church has full time preaching service.

Rev. Henry Sheets

It would be improper to close this sketch of Baptist work and workers in Davidson County without making special mention of and laying special emphasis on the life and labors of Rev. Henry Sheets, who was for thirty years a consecrated pastor of churches in the Liberty Association, and a tireless worker for the development of the work of the Association. His crowning achievement was the *History of the Liberty Baptist Association,* from which most of the data in this chapter has been gathered. Mr. Sheets was a man of burning zeal, of superior intelligence and of unblemished life.

Thomasville Baptist Orphanage

[In its anniversary issue of July 28, 1921, *The Chairtown News* gave the following "Story of the Founding and Growth of the Thomasville Baptist Orphanage," written by Dr. Archibald Johnson]:

Dr. J. M. Fleming, of Warrenton, wrote the first article in the *Biblical Recorder,* advocating the establishment of an Orphanage for the Baptists of North Carolina. This splendid article attracted immediate and earnest attention. This was in the year 1884. A resolution was prepared to be introduced in the Baptist State Convention of that year, committing the convention to the establishment of the Orphanage, but the opposition was so strong that the gentleman who had the resolution in his pocket was advised not to introduce it, and he accepted the advice.

However, a few brave souls, feeling the vital importance of the matter without consulting flesh and blood, met in another church in the city (Raleigh was the city and the Tabernacle the place where the Orphanage advocates met) and organized what was known as the North Carolina Baptist Orphanage Association, under which the institution was operated for several years.

Thus the Orphanage was born outside the convention and it may not be amiss to say in spite of the convention, and began its work under its own charter and with a small, but determined band of Baptists behind it. John H. Mills, the father of the Orphanage work in North Carolina, was placed at the head of the institution, and began to form an organization that for efficiency and reliability has hardly been surpassed by any other in the history of the State. It was, however, the day of small things. With not a building on the grounds, the committee having the infant institution in charge, met in the first annual meeting in 1885, and Rev. Dr. Columbus Durham preached the sermon under a hickory tree, now marked by a memorial stone. Mr. Mills found the people wherever he went eager to help the work along. The first thousand dollars that came into the treasury for a building was given by Noah Biggs, a Napoleon of finance of Scotland Neck, who was destined to become one of the greatest benefactors

AUDITORIUM THOMASVILLE BAPTIST ORPHANAGE

RELIGIOUS FORCES OF DAVIDSON COUNTY   415

the orphanage ever had. The second large gift was from the sainted Dr. John Mitchell, who was never married, but who loved little children. Other buildings followed and in a short while there were a half dozen cottages with their kitchen in front of them across the road. All the houses were built on exactly the same plan. Like a Moravian cemetery, there was a dead level of democracy. If there had been enough of them they would have reminded a stranger of a high class cotton mill village.

Mr. Mills was a powerful personality. He could melt an audience to tears in his recital of the story of the Orphanage, and chase away the tears with laughter at a humorous incident, told in his inimitable way. His was a master mind and he was devoted to his work. It is related of him that on a visit to a conference in Washington city, President Cleveland heard him speak, and was so impressed with his power that he sent Senator Vance to him explaining that he wanted to see him to talk over a government appointment. Mr. Mills replied: "Senator, you tell Mr. Cleveland I am much obliged to him, but I have a better job now than he has." For ten years John H. Mills guided the Orphanage through the treacherous waves and out into the open sea. When he left the work in 1895 it was thoroughly established in the hearts of the Baptist people of North Carolina. Mills did foundation work upon which the present splendid structure rests.

Rev. J. B. Boone succeeded Mr. Mills, and began his work September 1, 1895. He was the Orphanage builder. He reconstructed every building on the hill. Mr. Mills had no patience with an architect, but did his own planning; Mr. Boone secured the best architect he could find and every house was erected by blue prints. Mr. Boone was not a magnetic speaker like Mr. Mills, but was a man of rugged strength. He could not sway an audience but he could build a house. Under his administration a great dining hall was erected, and the unsightly kitchens in front of the cottages were torn away. The central school building was also erected, and the whole school system was reorganized on the basis of the modern graded school. In Charlotte Mr. Boone had established and taught the first graded school in North Carolina and the Orphanage school work improved and modernized under his supervision was his joy and pride. His crowning work as General Manager was the reorganization of the school, making it one of the most efficient in the State.

Mr. Boone retired in 1905—a term of service exactly equal to that of Mr. Mills—and he was succeeded by Rev. M. L. Kesler, D.D., the present General Manager. Dr. Kesler was not a stranger to the work, as he had for years been a member of the board of trustees. Coming to the office in 1905, he has given twenty-one years of service to the institution. Within that time there has been immense development. The plant and the invested fund represent a half million dollars; a branch has been established in Lenoir County, and eighty-five children are there; the grounds have been beautified, and the social life of the institution has been uplifted. Dr. Kesler has waged fierce warfare upon the crude, both in the manners of the children and in their material surroundings. He has tried to eliminate the bleakness and dreariness of the old time Orphan Home, and make the Orphanage a beautiful and attractive place to live. He has had excellent success in his aim

REV. M. L. KESLER, D.D.
General Manager Thomasville Baptist Orphanage

to develop the esthetic and cultivate the finer things; at the same time his practical common sense has not allowed the refinements of life to submerge the practical and useful. The Orphanage is not only a beautiful, clean, wholesome, healthful place, but the children do as much work as they did in the old days when they had to do it by main strength and awkwardness. The children no longer bend over the wash tubs—they pull a lever and set in motion the modern machinery of a first-class laundry. And so all the way through. The denomination throughout the State has been mightily strengthened and enriched because of its devoted loyalty to the Orphanage, and the town of Thomasville is especially blessed by its hallowed influence.

In a personal letter to the author Dr. Johnson gives the following additional facts concerning the Thomasville Baptist Orphanage: It was organized in 1885. Its growth through the years has been substantial and steady. Today there are twenty buildings on the grounds, sixteen of these being cottages for the children with 450 inmates at Thomasville and 80 more at the branch institution in Lenoir County, making 530 in all. The current fund for the maintenance of the institution is $150,000, which is furnished by the Baptist churches and Sunday schools of North Carolina. The plant, including endowment fund, is estimated at $700,000. It is the second largest orphanage in the South. It is managed by a board of eighteen men who serve without pay. These men are nominated by the board subject to confirmation by the Baptist State Convention. More than 2,100 children have been inmates of the institution since its establishment. *Charity and Children,* the organ of the Orphanage, has a circulation of more than 22,000.

4. THE METHODIST PROTESTANT CHURCHES, METHODIST PROTESTANT CHILDREN'S HOME, YADKIN COLLEGE.

The first Methodist Protestant Church in Davidson County was organized at Friendship in 1834, during that period when the reform movement was taking definite shape in different sections of the country, and it was only four years after the organization of the Associate Methodist Churches into the Methodist Protestant Church. It is interesting to the reader to know that the first church of this denomination was organized in North Carolina at Whitaker's Chapel, Halifax County. Friendship organization first worshiped under a brush arbor near Yadkin College. This was followed by a log house, Peter Byerly donating the land. Improvements from time to time have been made and now they have a church with Sunday school rooms and a live organization. The first preacher was Rev. Mr. Snider, and the first members were Sandy Gobble and wife, and he was class leader for years. Others were Peter Byerly, Joe Perrill, Jacob Hedrick, Nick Miller, Jackson Davis, Sanford Phillips, Henry Walser, Isaiah Byerly; these with their wives compose the first church roll.

Mount Pleasant, north of Thomasville, is one of the older organizations of the denomination in the county and has owned jointly the building with an organization of the Methodist Episcopal Church, South. This latter, however, has been so diminished by removals and death that the Presiding Elder has proposed to sell out to the Methodist Protestants, and now the ground is being broken and material assembled for building an up-to-date church to be owned by the latter, as they have a live organization and a growing Sunday school. It is unfortunate that the facts concerning this splendid congregation have not been available, for doubtless there are many interesting incidents concerning the workings of the two denominations together for so long. But as history of most union churches goes, one or the other will eventually drop out. It seems that a record has not been kept.

Pleasant Grove in the southern part of the county is one of the oldest churches and was organized some time after Friendship, possibly in 1838 or 1840. Some of the older people of the community say that there was a log church there showing age seventy years ago, and that there were about thirty members at that time. It is to be regretted that the records were lost, for an organization of such age certainly has had a part in the spiritual development of its community. The first pastors there of which we have any record were: Revs. Josiah Snotherly, Alexander Robbins, William McCain, Joseph Causey and John Hinshaw. There is now a membership of ninety.

Pleasant Grove in the eastern part of the county was organized in 1847. This church is just off Highway No. 10, between Thomasville and High Point, and may be found by a large sign pointing to its location. It is a strong church and has outgrown its quarters three times and now has one of the best buildings to be found in the rural districts. As to the leaders in its organization no names have been furnished. It is well endowed, having property given by some of its members to the amount of $30,000. Present membership is 156.

Mount Carmel dates back to 1848. It was first organized as a Reformed Church by Rev. Thornton Butler. The first members were mainly of the Hedrick family. The present house of worship was built in the early eighties by Rev. M. L. Hedrick, who served the church for about fifteen years. The leaders of this church at that time were: A. S. Hedrick, John Hedrick, Robert Thomason, J. H. Hedrick, G. F. Hedrick and others. About 1905 the membership had become so reduced by removals and death that they ceased having regular services. August 2, 1907, representatives of the Reformed Church consisting of G. F. Hedrick and R. L. Hedrick, by official action of the Classis of North Carolina, made the title over to the Methodist Protestant Church, which was organized by Rev. J. H. Moton with thirteen members. The officers were as follows: Class leader, C. L. Hedrick; steward, C. A. Berrier; trustees, J. A. Young, J. H. Fritts, G. F. Hedrick and T. J. Fritts. There are at present eighty members, and the Sunday school runs all the year. Many improvements are being made, including a well kept cemetery, and there is some talk of a new church and an improved road by the church. The present pastor, Rev. M. I. Crutchfield, says at the regular services the house is well filled, and with the increasing interest there is no reason in such a prosperous community why they should not have one of the best country churches.

Shiloh Church was organized in 1856, the same year Yadkin College was chartered by the Legislature as a college. For a long time a prayer meeting was conducted by Daniel Potts, who was a licensed exhorter. This man worked for David Michael, who was the prime mover in having the first church built. Camp meetings were first held, but they were not continued for many years. The first enrollment of members consisted of the following: David Michael, Alexander Trantham, David Waitman, Colonel John Myers, Feltie and Riley Leonard. Revs. Allison Gray, A. W. Lineberry, J. H. Pegram, C. A. Pickens and J. N. Garrett were the first pastors. There have only been two churches erected at this place. The present splendid structure, the second on the grounds, was erected in 1909. Shiloh enjoys the distinction of being the largest Methodist Protestant Church in the county and possibly the largest rural church of any denomination. It is situated in a fine farming section and has a live Sunday school with other auxiliaries of the church.

Chapel Hill is known far and near on account of the great crowds that gather there for the annual camp meetings. There is a record of a quarterly conference that was held May 12, 1860, and the camp meetings had been abandoned, but in 1890 Rev. J. A. Laughlin revived these and they are still kept up. In the organization there were fifteen members. At present there are over one hundred. Many marks are here of those who in days gone by left home for a few days with necessary provisions to go and give the entire time to worship. This church is near the Randolph line seven miles southeast of Denton.

Bethesda, one of the best country churches, in one of the best communities, was organized in 1869 by Rev. T. H. Pegram, with eight charter members as follows: Mr. and Mrs. Alexander Evans, Mr. and Mrs. Joseph Clodfelter, D. C. Clodfelter, Mrs. Julia Waitman, Mrs. Hazel Wagner and Lorenzo Wagner. The second church was built in 1895, and this building was remodeled in 1924 by the addition of seven Sunday school rooms. It has a wide-awake organization with a membership of 152.

Pine Hill was organized in 1875 with twelve members by Rev. Henry Lewallen. They worshiped under an arbor and a few years later a church was built. The present membership is forty-six.

Alleghany Church is located eight miles south of Denton on the Salisbury-Troy road. The organization was effected by Rev. J. A. Laughlin in 1880, with a membership of twelve. The number of members is now seventy-five.

Yadkin College Church came into being in the year 1886 with about twenty members. Among the leaders were Gaither Walser and J. S. Phillips with a number of faithful women, and these were encouraged by the ministers living there. Dr. Lineberry was pastor at this time. Dr. Ferree, Revs. C. A. Pickens, R. R. Hanner, J. N. Garrett and other ministers of the church lived at Yadkin College for the benefits to be derived from having their children in their own church school, and these people meant much to the community. At the present time many improvements are being made, repairing and remodeling. There are many evidences of life and vigor in this organization.

Three and one-half miles southeast of Denton is a little church called Lineberry, named for one of the grand old men of the Methodist Protestant Church, Dr. A. W. Lineberry. This church was organized by Rev. C. A. Pickens in 1893 with fifteen members, and the present membership is eighty.

West Lexington Church was organized in 1897 by Rev. D. A. Braswell. This organization has passed through many ordeals, but has kept intact since its beginning. Those who took the most active part in its organization were as follows: G. G. Gibson, E. D. Turner, Alexander Leonard, Pinkney Earnhardt and R. H. Leonard. Though in the manufacturing district of the city, where the population shifts a great deal, yet some of the original members and members of their families still remain and are identified with all the activities of this organizaton. At the present time there is an active membership and a live Sunday school, and the pastor, Rev. M. Ivey Crutchfield, has the church going well and growing.

First Church, Thomasville, was permanently organized in 1907 by Rev. Edwin Suits. The people were gathered together some time before this by Rev. A. M. Hamilton, who was then a local preacher. Its present membership is 115. This church is the mother of two other churches, West Thomasville and Community Church. It is still enjoying prosperity, notwithstanding the loss in starting these other two organizations. They have a commodious building and an unusually large Sunday school and Christian Endeavor Society.

West Thomasville was organized in 1921 with twelve members. Since then the membership has more than doubled and they have a beautiful brick church completed and are doing their part in a spiritual work for the community in which they are located.

Canaan Church was organized by Rev. Edwin Suits in 1910, with a membership of twenty-one. The enrollment at present is sixty-six.

Facts concerning Spring Hill have not been available, only that the present number of members is 116. It is one of the oldest of the denomination in the county.

Jerusalem is a church that is owned jointly by Lutherans, Reformed and Methodist Protestants, the latter having in their organization about thirty members. They seem to work together harmoniously.

Cid Church was organized by Rev. J. W. Self, date not given. Enrollment about forty.

Community Church, Thomasville, is one of the new enterprises of the denomination. This church is doing a great work. It is the outgrowth of an idea of Mrs. C. F. Finch, who wished to build a church that would be a community center. She was one of the best workers in the denomination. Just in the midst of her activities, she was called from labor to reward. Her husband, C. F. Finch, set to work immediately to carry out her wishes and to build something in her memory that would even go far beyond her first plans. So a magnificent structure has been reared with all the equipment in operation and planned for doing every kind of church and community work. Rev. R. S. Troxler was pastor when this church was organized and the following men, mostly with their families, joined in the organization: J. W. Boyles, T. G. Perry, H. S. Hankins, J. W. Clodfelter, J. N. Myers, U. S. Myers, and Dr. R. V. Yokely. There were eighty-five members enrolled. The Sunday school has an enrollment at present of 329. A moving picture machine has been installed and each Sunday night after the sermon by the pastor, a picture is shown, usually illustrating the subject discussed. Most of them are Bible pictures or some subject teaching a moral. Large crowds gather each Sunday evening for this. There are rooms in the basement for every department, including Boy Scouts, and at present there is a kindergarten each school day.

Forty more Sunday school rooms are planned together with a playground to accommodate all the children, and swimming pools for both boys and girls. The present plant is valued at about one hundred thousand dollars.

The youngest church of the denomination in the county is State Street, Lexington. This was organized in the fall of 1923. The first members in this were: F. J. Cox and wife, J. W. Lindsay and family, J. A. Walser, Mrs. C. F. McCrary, J. B. Evans, Mary Noble Evans, Eva Walser, Mr. and Mrs. Curtis Koontz, Mrs. Albert H. Evans. These were the original organizers. Others came in later in the year. Rev. J. H. Abernethy was the first pastor and Rev. Dr. Whitaker the second. The first services were held in the Masonic Hall. Then the question of building came up. It was decided to build a parsonage with room enough to hold services and house a pastor also. By leaving out three partitions there is a seating capacity for about two hundred people, while there are five rooms for Sunday school work. This is a rather unique situation, for the pastor lives upstairs. The present pastor is Rev. N. G. Bethea. The outlook for this church is encouraging.

Other churches of which we have been unable to get a history are as follows: Denton, Pine Grove, Mount Ebal, Liberty, Canaan, Mount Pleasant in the lower part of the county, and Mount Zion.

The Methodist Protestant Children's Home at High Point had its origin in this county at Denton. In a little rented building on the campus of the Denton High School, which was then under the control of the Methodist Protestant Church, Miss Mabel Williams (now

Mrs. Robert Russell) and Miss Etta Auman (now Mrs. Dr. J. W. Austin) began work. This was in August, 1910, and they had less than fifty dollars in the treasury. Some of the business men of the church thought it was a foolish venture, but through the encouragement of Mrs. W. C. Hammer of Asheboro, President of the North Carolina Branch of the Woman's Home Missionary Society, and Prof. G. L. Reynolds, Principal of the Denton High School, the young ladies pushed their work. Soon the building was found to be inadequate to the needs, and men of means in High Point and other places made such attractive offers that it was removed to that place. Now there are two large buildings with a fine farm, and nearly one hundred children are being cared for, with property paid for valued at $350,000. The people of our county are proud that an institution of such worth had its birth among us.

Yadkin College

This institution has been a great influence in Davidson County. In 1851 the agitation began to establish a seminary under church control. It was then a question as to whether this institution should be established in Davie or Davidson. At the Annual Conference in Fayetteville in 1852, Mr. Henry Walser addressed the Conference on the subject, whereupon a committee was appointed to select a place for the school in one of the counties named. In 1853 the committee reported to Conference that they had agreed upon a location eight miles from Lexington and one mile east of the Yadkin River, where they had received an offer of ten acres of land and five hundred dollars for the building fund. This was the beginning of Yadkin College. In 1855

Mr. Walser reported that brick was being made and a contract had been let for the building.

ARTICLES OF INCORPORATION
An Act to Incorporate The Yadkin College Institute in the County of Davidson

Be it enacted by the General Assembly of North Carolina and it is hereby enacted by the authority of the same:
That Henry Walser, Thomas C. Crump, Alexander Robbins, J. J. Gamble, Allison Gray, David L. Michael, Jourdan Rominger, David Weasner and John A. Davis be, and they are hereby constituted a body corporate (and) politic, by the name and style of the Yadkin College Institute; and by that name may sue and be sued, plead and be impleaded, shall have succession and a common seal, and in general shall have, exercise and enjoy all such rights, powers, and privileges as are usually exercised and enjoyed by trustees of an incorporated academy within this State.

Sec. 2. *Be it further enacted,* That any five of the trustees (quorum) may constitute a quorum for the transaction of business and that on the refusal of the trustees to act or in case of death or removal out of the State of any of the trustees of the Institute aforesaid, the remaining trustees shall have power to fill such vacancy.

(Ratified the 3d day of February, 1855.)

The next year, 1856, report was made to the Annual Conference that Yadkin Institute was in operation. It was largely through the efforts of Henry Walser that the school was established. Professor G. W. Hege was the first principal.

In 1861 it was chartered as a college, and at that time there were eighty boarding students besides those living in the community. Out of the eighty students, sixty volunteered for service in the Confederate Army, and this broke up the school, for like most Southern colleges in this period it had to close. For six years there was no school. One man, Stanley Owen, still living, who was quite a small boy at that time, says, "I remember when there was not a man in that entire community."

During the war the building was used as a tobacco storage house. At the end of the six years Prof. H. T. Phillips opened a high school for the community. This necessitated quite a bit of cleaning up for the opening. By request of one of the industrious citizens, Mr. Wood, who believed that school work should be given as long hours as other work of the day, the school was run from sun-up to sun-down. H. T. Phillips was assisted by F. T. Walser. After this opening Conference placed Rev. J. C. Deans at the head of the Institute with Messrs. Phillips and Walser as assistants. In 1872 Rev. Shadrack Simpson was made President and the school opened again as a college. Ten successful years under his wise management followed and in 1881 the three-story building was erected. This structure was designed by Bentley Owen, now living in Gibsonville, N. C., and was built of brick made in the community, though funds came in from all over the State.

Prof. Simpson resigned for a professorship in Western Maryland College, a Methodist Protestant Institution, and it was then that Yadkin College dropped back into the high school class. Prof. Morgan was in charge until he left for Japan as a missionary. Prof. Holmes was then in charge from 1889 to 1898, after which he entered the pastorate. In 1898-1924 Yadkin College Institute was in charge of Prof. W. T. Totten, who did faithful work under adverse circumstances, for it was during this period that the State began the establishment of high schools in reach of almost every community, and loyally he battled against this until it was thought best to abandon it as an Institute.

The success of the school for the church was marked by numbers of ministers locating there. The first of these was Rev. C. A. Pickens, who was always a staunch advocate of Yadkin College. He was followed by Revs. Hanner, Lowe, R. H. Wills, Garrett and R. R. Michaux and possibly others.

Henry Walser remained chairman of the Board of Trustees until his death in 1875.

Had Yadkin College been better located possibly it would be in operation as a college today. Hon. Zeb Vance Walser, who graduated there in the class of 1879, says: "It was one of the great schools of the State; in fact it came very near at one time being the greatest school in the State." Numbers of cases could be cited of leaders in this county, as well as in other sections, of people who have become great leaders who were educated there. It has contributed more than any other institution to the pulpits of the Methodist Protestant Church in North Carolina. Some of its ablest leaders and those of other denominations and other states have felt the uplift given students who attended the Institute. By no means has Yadkin College been a failure. The splendid new Methodist Protestant College at High Point, worth in its beginning $565,000, with the first enrollment of 128 students, is a direct outgrowth of Yadkin Collge.

Davidson County is justly proud of her leaders who were educated there and of the sturdy numbers whose names are not so well known, but who help to form the backbone of the county, industrially, morally, intellectually and spiritually. Those who sacrificed as they thought for the time that the school might continue are still receiving compound interest for all they invested.

There are seven Methodist Protestant charges in the county, composed of twenty-eight churches, and these churches with their parsonages make a total of $200,000 property value. Thus from a brush arbor in 1834 has grown one of the powerful factors in character making, and when we look around us and see the stalwart characters that have been influenced by this church in intellectual development and see what they are worth in property and influence, surely we may again ask the question, "For who hath despised the day of small things?"

5. Moravian Churches

[For the following brief history we are indebted to Miss Adelaide Fries, Archivist of the Moravian Church, Winston-Salem, N. C.]

Friedberg (Hill of Peace) is the only Moravian Congregation in Davidson County; a branch of this congregation has a house of worship at Enterprise, four miles southeast from the Friedberg Church.

The beginning of the Moravian work in the county dates back to 1754 with Adam Spach (Spaugh) as the pioneer. His nearest Moravian neighbors were at Bethabara (Old Town) sixteen miles north from his home. He made several visits to these Moravians and asked that they would come and hold services at his house. From 1754 to 1770 other settlers came into this northern section of Davidson County, mostly from Pennsylvania, so quite a little colony was being formed and came to be called The South Fork Society. The first preaching service was held in the home of Adam Spach on December 2, 1759. The settlers were anxious for regular services and expressed their willingness to erect a building. This was a schoolhouse with a meeting hall and was consecrated March 12, 1769. The following year, 1770, February 4, the South Fork Society was formally organized. Soon thereafter fourteen married couples pledged themselves to the support of a resident minister, and on the 4th of April, 1773, the South Fork Society was accepted as a Moravian Congregation. February 19, 1786, the corner-stone was laid for the first church; and two years later the new church was consecrated. This first church was used for thirty-nine years, when it became necessary to have a larger building which was erected during the years 1823-1827, and is the main building in use at the present time, with considerable changes made in 1904, and a large addition for Sunday school uses completed in 1921. The present membership is 585 communicants.

The following family names of the early Moravian settlers are to be found at the present time: Spach (Spaugh), Frey, Hartman, Boeckel, Mueller (Miller), Voltz (Foltz), Graeter (Crater), Fishel, Tesh, Zimmerman, Rothrock, Weisner.

6. Presbyterian Churches

First Presbyterian Church of Lexington

Davidson County of which Lexington is the seat of justice, was originally a part of Rowan County. It was not, however, that part which was colonized by the Scotch-Irish Presbyterians except to a very limited extent. It was the region lying west of the Yadkin and north of the Deep River that was principally honored by them in their choice of lands and homes.

Some sixty-five or seventy years elapsed from the time of the first settling of this section of the State by Presbyterians before any serious effort was made to establish a church of the same faith and order anywhere in all the country now known as Davidson County. The people who chiefly settled this section were of German extraction, and consequently the first churches organized were of the Lutheran and Reformed denominations. At a later day the Baptists and Methodists began to establish churches, but the first Presbyterian church organized within the limits of the county was the church in Lexington. This event occurred on the 15th of July, 1827. Nine persons, two of them on profession of faith, united with the church in the organization; none of them, with three or four exceptions, were of Presbyterian descent or education.

As Lexington was situated on the main stage route north and east from Salisbury and the western part of the State, it not infrequently happened that Presbyterian ministers in their journeys to and from the Presbytery or Synod, or on other occasions, would stop to preach by invitation, or by appointment. The meeting house, the only one in town or immediate neighborhood, the property of no denomination in particular, a small log building, stood just outside the western limits on the road to Salisbury, and was for many years the only place of public worship.

The first Presbyterian minister who preached in Lexington for any length of time was the Rev. Davis C. Allen, ordained by the Presbytery of Orange. He was a native of Providence, R. I., and came to New Bern, N. C., in 1815 or 1816, where he stayed for some time with a relative in the capacity of bookkeeper. He afterwards studied at Brown University and Princeton and entered the ministry. Lexington was his first field of labor and the organization of the church was the first fruits thereof. He remained here about two years, after which he returned to New Bern where he had married, and eventually moved to Illinois and took charge of the church in Lewiston, where he died in 1839. His widow and five children returned to New Bern in 1840. Of them George Allen, ruling elder in the church at New Bern, still lives, widely known and esteemed as a zealous and efficient servant of the church.

Two ruling elders were elected and ordained and installed at the organization of the church—Joseph Conrad and Benjamin D. Rounsaville. Both of them were men of character and sterling worth. Mr. Rounsaville died early. Mr. Conrad lived to see his grandchildren gathered into the fold by the covenant-keeping God, and died full of years. He served in early youth an apprenticeship at the cabinet trade in Philadelphia, was converted there, and married to his first wife. Although not educated scholastically, he was for his opportunities intelligent, well informed, a reading and observing man, and made a valuable member of the session. He could conduct a prayer-meeting as well as handle a tool in the shop. His services were in requisition and not a little of his time and labor were given freely when the church edifice which still stands, though subsequently enlarged and improved by other hands, was first erected.

For the first five years until 1832 the little church appears to have made no progress in the way of increase. Indeed at one time it appears from the Presbyterial records the name of the church was erased from the roll. From 1827 when Mr. Allen left to 1832 the church was without the stated services of a minister, and only an occasional sermon was heard from some one passing or by some opportunities of the Presbytery.

In the latter years, however, Lexington and the surrounding country became the scene of an extensive and remarkable work of grace. Infidelity and unbelief, which had become alarming in the community, and the religious apathy of professed Christians were rebuked and many souls were added to the Lord. The preaching of the Word which was attended with this power of the Spirit was by the mouth of such men as Dr. Patrick J. Sparrow, then of the Presbytery of Concord; Dr. John Witherspoon, of Hillsboro, Rev. E. W. Caruthers and Rev. A. D. Montgomery, all of Orange Presbytery. Local traditions and the memory of older citizens point to the preaching and labor of Dr. Sparrow as perhaps the most signally blessed. At all events the immediate result was the resuscitation of the church, in the quickening of its life and a large increase of membership. Within a year sixty-seven persons were added to the church. In October of that year 1832 three new elders were elected and installed, namely: Dr. Charles L. Payne, Robert Foster and Henry R. Dusenberry. These have all long since passed from earth, but have left a fragrant memory behind and in their day served the church faithfully. The following year Rev. Philip Pearson came to the church and supplied it for about two years. He removed to South Carolina, and died in 1873 or 1874 while in charge of Midway Church, Harmony Presbytery. Rev. Jonathan T. Ely, native of New Jersey, student of Princeton Seminary, and ordained by Orange Presbytery, succeeded Mr. Pearson after an interval of more than a year. He remained in charge as stated supply only six or seven months, when his health failed, and he was obliged to give up the active work of the ministry.

Some time early in the year 1839 the Rev. Jesse Rankin began to labor in this field, teaching school and preaching for about the space of six years. Alfred Hargrave was elected and ordained Elder in May of the same year, and continued to serve until the day of his death which occurred in January, 1880. In September, 1843, the congregation made out a call for the first time for the services of a pastor, and Rev. Thomas R. Owen, laboring in the eastern part of the State, was chosen. The call was accepted, the time fixed and all arrangements made for the installation, and Mr. Owen and family had moved to Lexington, when for certain prudential reasons he was constrained to abandon a settlement as pastor, and shortly afterward left the place. Mr. Rankin still continued to supply the church. In 1845, March 31, a call was made for the pastoral services of Rev. Arch D. Montgomery, then a member of Orange Presbytery, preaching in Halifax County, Virginia. Rev. Dr. A. Wilson presided and charged the people. Rev. Mr. Sutten preached the sermon. Mr. Montgomery labored here for about eight years with success. From forty to fifty additions were made to the church during his ministry. In 1853, Mr. Montgomery resigned his charge and removed to Newberry, South Carolina, where he preached until shortly before the breaking out of the Civil War in 1861. He returned to this State eventually and spent his last days in the home of his daughter, wife of Hon. James M. Leach, of Lexington, where he died in 1870, full of years and full of peace. His remains were borne to Salisbury and interred in the English graveyard by the side of his wife who had preceded him to the better land a year or two before.

For two or three years after Mr. Montgomery's departure the church was without a minister. In 1856 Rev. John I. Boozer of South Carolina became stated supply and remained about two years. He married in Lexington and removed to Pine Bluff, Ark., where he died during the war. In June, 1856, the church elected its first Board of Deacons, namely: Andrew Hunt, Alex. C. Hege, and Robert L. Payne.

In January, 1859, Frontis H. Johnston, then a licentiate of the Presbytery of Concord, having been invited to this field with a view to settlement as pastor, began his first ministry here. In the month of May of that year he was called to the pastorate, and in the succeeding July was ordained and installed by the Presbytery of Orange. Rev. J. Henry Smith, pastor of the Greensboro Church, presided and preached the sermon. Rev. C. K. Caldwell, pastor of Buffalo and Bethel churches, delivered the charge to the pastor, and Rev. P. H. Dalton, Evangelist of the Presbytery, charged the people. The sacred tie thus formed remained unbroken for seventeen years, until July 1, 1876. It was formed too under the smile of Heaven, the preaching and other solemn services of the occasion having been attended with a gracious outpouring of the Spirit by which the church was greatly revived and strengthened. Between twenty and thirty souls were added to the church as the immediate result, and during this pastorate upward of 130 persons united with the church; and after all the several losses by death and removal and other causes, the varied trials incident to the war and its consequences throughout those seventeen years, it closed with more than double the membership with which it began. Some thirty or forty colored members after the war left the church to form a separate organization under the care of the Northern Assembly. In December, 1860, Dr. Robert L. Payne, Dr. Robert L. Beall and Prof. Charles W. Smythe were elected and ordained elders. The session now comprised seven Elders. At the same time Messrs. Isaac K. Perryman and John H. Mabry were ordained deacons, making four in all.

The first Sunday school in Lexington was organized at the Presbyterian Church and had its first meeting January 5, 1868. John H. Welborn was chosen by the Session to be the first Superintendent. The School began with fifteen teachers and forty-three pupils. The end of the year 1868 found the school with eighty-five pupils and twenty teachers.

In June, 1869, Thaddeus C. Ford was ordained elder, and at the same time Dr. Albert A. Hill and John H. Welborn were elected deacons. In August, 1871, Mr. Welborn was elected elder, together with William H. Hamner. These several elections were made to fill the vacancies by death which followed each other rapidly in the years just after the close of the war. Dr. Payne, Sr., Messrs. Smythe, Foster and Conrad among the elders and Messrs. Perryman and Hunt, deacons.

This church up to this time has given but two of her sons to the ministry. First, the Rev. John Milton Sherwood, a native of Guilford County, converted while attending school here under Rev. Jesse Rankin, and a communicant of this church until ordained by Orange Presbytery. Mr. Sherwood was for several years pastor of the church in Washington, N. C., whence he moved to Fayetteville and afterwards became editor of the *North Carolina Presbyterian* until his death. He was a good and useful man much beloved, and a church which he gathered in the neighborhood of Fayetteville, and to which he was ministering at the time of his death, was named "Sherwood" after him.

Second, Rev. Charles M. Payne, son of the ruling elder, Dr. Charles L. Payne, graduate of Union Seminary, Va.

In April of the year 1876, Mr. Johnston was called as pastor by the church in Winston, N. C., and in consequence, the relation to the Lexington church was dissolved, and his labors here ceased, on the first of July. Rev. Roger Martin of Virginia succeeded him as stated supply for two years when he was followed by Rev. Andrew M. Watson, formerly of the Presbytery of Memphis, Tenn.

Rev. A. L. Crawford was called as pastor, giving three-fourths of his time to the church, beginning April, 1883. This arrangement was changed in 1887 when he became supply for half of his time, until 1889 when he accepted the church of Taylorsville. During this pastorate there were added to the church thirty-six members, but the roll of the church showed a loss in membership because of the removal of more members than were received. The Sunday school had an enrollment of seventy-five pupils and ten teachers.

In July 1889, the Rev. W. P. McCorkle was serving the church as supply, having service two Sabbath evenings each month. The church seemed to have a period of spiritual life and growth. During two years there were added to the church fifty-two members and only

RELIGIOUS FORCES OF DAVIDSON COUNTY 441

four dismissed. Rev. Mr. McCorkle asked Presbytery to dissolve the relationship existing between himself and the church, much to the regret of the congregation.

Rev. Mr. Maxwell was called as pastor and began his services on Sunday, October 10, 1891. In September, 1893, he resigned to return to Scotland. Additions to church during pastorate, four.

Rev. Dr. McIver was called as stated supply, serving the church until May 3, 1896. During the two years there were added to the church membership nineteen. Mr. McIver accepted a call to Bolivar, Kentucky. On Sunday, May 3, 1896, W. B. Hamner resigned as Superintendent of the Sunday school which office he had acceptably filled for years. George W. Mountcastle was elected to the office of Superintendent.

Rev. E. W. Smith became stated supply of the church May 3, 1896. September 20, 1896, a Christian Endeavor Society was organized. Additions to the church, eight. Rev. W. Albert Gillon was called and began services as pastor in November, 1897, and served until October 7, 1900. August 11, 1899, W. Banks Dove and S. S. Hunter were elected elders of the church. Additions to church, twenty-five.

Rev. J. H. Grey began his ministry with the church June 2, 1901, acting as pastor until June, 1904. Additions to church, sixteen.

Rev. C. L. Leyburn, D.D., served as pastor from April, 1904, until November, 1908. O. E. Mendenhall was Superintendent of the Sunday school from 1906 until October, 1908, when Z. I. Walser was elected to succeed him, Mr. Mendenhall having resigned. Additions to the church, forty-seven.

February 21, 1909, Rev. T. R. Taggart of Norristown, Penn., was called as pastor, serving for one year. Additions to the church, nine.

Rev. W. T. Thompson, having been called as pastor, began his ministry here in May, 1910, serving until August, 1914.

Z. V. Walser was elected Superintendent of the Sunday school October, 1910, acting until the election of W. L. Crawford in 1914. Additions to church, fifty-five. Rev. W. A. Daniel became stated supply January, 1915, and continued as such until July, 1916. Additions to the church, seventy-five.

In June, 1917, Rev. L. T. Wilds became pastor, serving until February, 1923. From August, 1918, until January 12, 1919, Mr. Wilds was engaged in war work, Y. M. C. A. service. L. V. Phillips was duly elected and ordained and installed as Elder in June, 1919. George W. Mountcastle became Superintendent of the Sunday school in November, 1919. Mr. Wilds was granted another leave of absence for three months, which time was spent in finishing the research work for a D.D. degree, from Union Theological Seminary in Richmond, Va. April 10, 1921, Z. I. Walser, J. H. Thompson, and Z. V. Walser were elected elders of the church. Additions to the church, 153.

Rev. J. Rupert McGregor was called as pastor and began his ministry with the church in December, 1923. T. C. Hinkle served as Superintendent of the Sunday school from December, 1923, to December, 1924, being succeeded by Auburn Woods.

The church has in the ninety-seven years of its existence received into its membership more than one thousand names. It has had the services of twenty-two ministers, twenty elders and approximately twenty deacons. The present membership of the church is two hundred and sixty-seven, with a Sunday school enrollment of one hundred and ninety-five. The church has grown rapidly during the last few years. More members were added during the pastorate of Dr. L. T. Wilds than at any other period of its history. The hope for the future growth and service of the church is most encouraging. The past year has had the largest increase in the membership in its history.

Dacotah Presbyterian Church of Lexington

The Dacotah Presbyterian Church was organized on the 6th of April, 1919, when nine members were received as charter members. The beginning of the work which resulted in the organization of the Dacotah Church dates back to the pastorate of Rev. W. T. Thompson in the First Presbyterian Church of Lexington, 1910-14. Mr. Thompson and Captain F. C. Robbins began prayer meetings in the homes of the people in the Dacotah community very soon after Mr. Thompson came to Lexington. A Sunday school grew out of this work. Z. I. Walser of the First Church was the first Superintendent of the Sunday school. From the records it appears that he began his work during the year 1912. He held the position for five and one-half years. He was succeeded by R. C. Lyerly.

The present church building was erected in 1910. For a number of years the work was conducted as a mission of the First Church. In the early days of the mission the singing was organized and conducted by Lee Chrisman. Mrs. H. B. Turner was the organist. During this period Mrs. James Adderton and Mrs.

Richard Bragaw of the First Church were teachers in the Sunday school and conducted the Sunshine Club for the girls. The Session of the First Church agreed upon the organization of the Dacotah Church at a meeting held on September 22, 1918. The petition for organization was approved at the next meeting of Orange Presbytery. Prior to the organization and the election and the installation of the first pastor, Rev. J. H. Smith, several seminary students served as supply preachers during their summer vacations, one of these being Mr. Wolf. The first meeting of the Session over which Mr. Smith presided was held June 29, 1919. He began his ministry some time before that date. During his ministry the church progressed in many ways. The majority of the present membership were received into the church during his term of service. Mr. Smith ended his ministry in the Dacotah Church on February 24, 1924.

The church was without a pastor for several months after Mr. Smith left. During the summer of 1924 Ted Jones, a candidate for the ministry, supplied the church. During this period Miss Marian Moore assisted him in the work with the young people and in the Sunday school. They conducted Dacotah's first Daily Vacation Bible School with the help of several members of the First Church.

The next pastor, Rev. Wade H. Harrell, was licensed to preach by Winston-Salem Presbytery September 17, 1924, and began his ministry in the church September 21. He was ordained to the ministry and installed as pastor of the church Sunday, October 12, 1924. The officers of the Dacotah Church are: T. F. Harrison, H. A. Moody, and Raymond Shaw, deacons, and H. B.

Allen and L. B. Calloway, elders. The resident membership of the church is fifty-eight. The Sunday school enrollment is two hundred and sixteen. The Christian Endeavor Society has a membership of thirty-two. A Men's Club was organized recently.

First Presbyterian Church of Thomasville

The church was organized December 3, 1903, by a commission from Orange Presbytery composed of the following ministers: Rev. E. W. Smith, D.D.; Rev. E. L. Siler; Rev. J. H. Grey; Rev. I. N. Clegg and Elder W. C. Herndon.

Those who composed the membership of the organization were: Dr. James Bird, Mary C. Bird, Lew Bird, Mrs. Hattie Bird, J. T. Lowe, Edgar Sossaman, Mrs. E. C. Strayhorne, Miss Jessie Stone, Julius Morris, Charles M. Hoover, H. E. Ritche, Mrs. R. E. Ritche, A. E. Wharton and E. C. Strayhorne.

The first officers were: J. T. Lowe and Dr. James Bird, elders and H. E. Ritche, deacon.

Since that time the following men have served in the capacity of elders: Dr. P. S. Easley, Dr. C. E. McManus, C. T. Alexander, J. H. Donnell, J. A. Brown, D. F. Crinkley, L. E. Bird, J. C. Tiddy, C. R. Gray and F. C. Howard. Those who have served since then as deacons are: B. F. Martin, J. H. Donnell, W. G. Kirk, D. B. Barclay, L. C. Barclay, J. F. Harrison and G. R. Pierce.

The first minister was Rev. I. N. Clegg and he has been followed by the men here listed: Revs. D. M. Hawthorne, C. H. Phipps, W. B. McIlwaine, J. W. Clegg, H. A. French, J. H. Smith, J. R. Offield. Rev. A. N.

Moffett, a student for the ministry, supplied the church, and now Rev. J. K. Fleming is pastor.

During the history of the church there have been at one time or another as many as 147 communicants. By removal or through loss one way or another the church now has a membership of sixty-four. There have been during the history of the church twenty-six baptisms, both adult and infant.

Up until 1911 the organization had no church building in which to worship. But they now enjoy a handsome brick edifice which is completely furnished inside, and is paid for. With a poor start and laboring under many handicaps, the church has made no remarkable strides of progress, but the future is bright and all who have the best interests of the church at heart are prophesying for it a most prosperous future.

7. Reformed Churches

Pilgrim Reformed Church (Leonard's)

The German immigration into this section of North Carolina was at high tide from 1745 to 1755. These people came to North Carolina and took up great tracts of land in the most desirable sections of the State. The Germans were members either of the Reformed, or Lutheran, or Moravian Church. Being accustomed to regular services at home they naturally were zealous to enjoy the same privileges in this country. But there was one great difficulty in the way of this, viz., the lack of ministers. The best that could be done was to appoint the older men and others of marked piety to conduct services of prayer and read printed sermons. Sometimes the schoolmasters were appointed to conduct the meetings; but school-teachers were almost as scarce as ministers. The Abbott's Creek section attracted quite a number of settlers within the period above designated. Among these were Jacob Hege and his sons George and Henry; Peter Spengler, Valentine Leonard and his brother Peter; Henry Shoaf, Jacob Berrier, Philip Sauer (Sowers), Christopher and George Sprecher, Adam and Peter Hedrick, Peter Myer (Myers), Adam Conrad, Jacob Byerly and George Clodfelter. Most of these men were from the Palatinate in Germany and were members of the Reformed Church, as were their children after them.

The site of the church was selected by Jacob Berrier in 1753 or 1754. Jacob Berrier was the father of John Martin and David Berrier, some of whose descendants are still citizens of the same community. There was no house of worship built until several years later. A brush arbor was put up on the spot, under which services were conducted occasionally by some of the older men. In these meetings many prayers were made to God earnestly asking for a minister. The spot selected was on an unoccupied tract of land lying between the lands of Philip Sauer (Sowers) on the north and Valentine Leonard on the south. Philip Sauer came to North Carolina in 1753 and took up a tract of land north of the present location of the church. Soon afterwards he married. The first baptismal entry in the records of the Reformed congregation at this place is that of his first-born child, Anna Catharine Sauer, the date of whose birth was April 27, 1757, and whose baptism was evidently not long afterwards. The name of the officiating clergyman is not given. It is probable that Rev. Christian Theus, who lived in the forks of the Broad and Saluda rivers in South Carolina, baptized this child. He preached regularly in the upper part of South Carolina from 1739 to 1775 and also visited the German settlements in North Carolina and held services for the scattered Reformed people. He was the first Reformed preacher in this section of the country. Or it may be that the child was not baptized until 1759, when the Rev. Mr. Martin, a Swiss Reformed minister, preached regularly to the Reformed people on the waters of Abbott's Creek and the Yadkin River, as well as elsewhere in this section of the State. This baptismal record is an interesting book. There are thirty-six names of heads of families in the early records, though some of them had no children. The writing is in German and shows different hands. There are 179 baptisms from 1757 to 1798. Of these 179 baptisms, 145 are recorded prior to the year 1787, and 33 are recorded prior to 1772. The names of the god-parents (Taufzeugen in German), the persons who presented themselves with the parents at the altar in the baptism at the request of the parents, are given in nearly all the records.

The first records of Pilgrim Reformed Church are incomplete. The oldest book in the possession of the congregation is this record of infant baptisms dating from 1757. The names of the paternal heads of families as given in the list are as follows: Adam Hedrick, William Younts (Janss), Henry Happes, George Hege (Heeke), Jacob Leonard, Philip Leonard, Valentine Leonard, John Henry Darr, Michael Zink, Philip Sowers (Sauer), John Zink, Philip Zink, Michael Dag (Day), John Peter Spengler, Jacob Crotts (Kratz), Michael Leonard, John George Berrier, Peter Kiehn, Jr., Henry Hege, John Jacob Wagner, John

George Clodfelter, Peter Myer (Myers), Adam Conrad, John Henry Shoaf (Schaff), Henry Shoaf, Sr., Ludolph Younts, John Martin Berrier, David Berrier, Michael Myers, David Myers, Peter Myers, George Sprecher, Peter Everhart, Henry Conrad, Christian Grimes (Kreim), Peter Lopp (Lapp).

The first church, which was built within the period 1757-1764, was a substantial log structure. It was built after a common pattern of that day with a gallery at each end and on one side. The tall wineglass pulpit occupied the other side. The logs of which it was constructed were very large. The church stood on an elevated spot at the northeast corner of the graveyard. The trustees of the congregation still have in custody the peculiar S-shaped key to the inner bolt of that venerable structure, and also one of the staples that held the bolt in place. They also have one of the quaint collection devices, a ring made of wrought iron with an arrangement on one side for an inserted handle; to the ring was sewed a bag, and at the bottom of the bag was a small bell, presumably to attract the attention of the contributors. They also have the pewter baptismal bowl; its companions, a pitcher and goblet, were stolen some years ago.

This first house of worship was built on land claimed by Henry McCulloh, though a tract of fifty acres lying between the lands of Philip Sauer and Valentine Leonard was laid off as church property. After North Carolina was properly organized as a State and had confiscated the McCulloh lands, three elders of the congregation, Philip Sowers (Sauer), Peter Karn (Kiehn) and Martin Shiddles, legally entered the lands in the name of the congregation. The official grant was made October 8, 1783, to the above-named persons, "Elders in trust for the Dutch Congregation." The first recorded name of the church is the "Dutch Congregation" as given in this official paper; but the real name seems to have been "Pilgrim Church," or "The Church of the Pilgrims." It was called in the official records the "Dutch Congregation" because it was the church located in the community known as the "Dutch settlement on Abbott's Creek." It was the only church, when it was organized, in that part of Rowan County east of the Yadkin River. There was another Reformed Church across the Yadkin River four miles from the present site of Mocksville on "Dutchman Creek"; the name was "Heidelberg Reformed Church," but it was popularly called the "Dutch Meeting House," and the site is so called to this day.

December 17, 1792, a wedge-shaped piece of land containing eighty-six acres, covered neither by the Sowers, the Leonard nor the church tracts, was entered for the church. The grant was made to George Clodfelter, John Lopp, George Hege and Valentine Day, "Trustees for the Dutch Congregation." The congregation then held 136 acres of land. In the year 1787 the Lutherans came in as cotenants, and from that time on had the use of the church and the lands. There is no record as to the terms on which they were admitted. For thirty-four years the two denominations worshiped in the same church. In 1821 the Lutherans split, and the two congregations of that denomination were allowed by the Reformed to use the property along with themselves until the spring of the year 1903, when the Reformed congregation, to gain absolute title to the entire property, paid to the two parties of Lutherans the handsome sum of $3,100 and received from them a quitclaim.

The pastorate of the Rev. Mr. Martin covered the years from 1759 to 1764. He was a faithful minister and rode many miles on horseback in order to meet his appointments and visit his people. It is possible that the log church was built during his pastorate, though it may have been built between 1757 and 1759. The earliest marked grave is in 1761, though the present topography of the graveyard indicates that there were graves still earlier. It is altogether probable that persons were buried here even before the first church was built.

In 1764 the Rev. William Dupert succeeded the Rev. Mr. Martin, and his pastorate continued until 1768. Mr. Dupert was said to be a most earnest, hard-working man. His visits to the Dutch Congregation were made regularly four times a year unless hindered by sickness or high waters.

The next minister after Mr. Dupert was Rev. Samuel Suther. He is the "Dutch Minister" whom Governor Tryon says in his diary he heard preach. He began to preach for the "Dutch Congregation on Abbott's Creek" in 1768, and his pastorate continued until 1786. Most of the baptisms recorded in the Pilgrim Reformed Church register were administered by him. In fact but few baptisms in the original thirty-six families are recorded after 1786, the year that marks the close of his pastorate. From that time forward for several years the baptismal records are only fragmentary. Five years after the beginning of his pastorate, in the year 1773, the first Lutheran minister came to North Carolina in the person of the Rev. Adolph Nussman, who became pastor of churches in Cabarrus and Rowan counties west of the Yadkin River. In 1787 Rev. C. E. Bernhardt, another Lutheran minister, came to North

Carolina and labored, Dr. G. D. Bernheim says, "doubtless in that part of Rowan County east of the Yadkin River." He was the first Lutheran pastor east of the Yadkin River.

In 1786 the Rev. Mr. Suther went to South Carolina and took charge of the congregations in the "Forks," formerly served by the Rev. Mr. Theus. The Rev. Mr. Schneider was the next pastor at Pilgrim, and he served from 1787 to 1792. He was a very energetic man. He organized the congregations at Beck's, Fredericktown (Bethany), and Sowers (Arnold). Rev. Samuel Weyburg was pastor from 1793 to 1798. He was succeeded by the Rev. Jacob Christman, who served until 1803. In the latter year the Rev. Mr. Christman went to Ohio, and the congregation was then served until 1812 by Rev. Andrew Loretz and Rev. George Boger jointly. After the death of Rev. Andrew Loretz in 1812, Rev. George Boger continued to preach occasionally for the congregation at seasons of the year when the ministers sent down by the Synod could not hold the services. This arrangement was kept up through the long period of fifteen years. Had it not been for the faithful missionary pastors sent out annually by Synod the congregation would have suffered much more than it did. Within these fifteen years the congregation had the services of such consecrated men as Revs. James R. Reily, William Weinel, Henry Dieffenbach, Jacob Scholl, John S. Ebaugh, George Leidy, John Rudy and others. In 1828 Rev. William Hauck became the regular pastor of the church at Pilgrim and the other Reformed Churches in Davidson County. He remained until 1832.

The following is a list of the ministers who have served the congregation:

Rev. Christian Theus—occasional visits before	1759
Rev. Mr. Martin	1759-1764
Rev. Mr. Dupert	1764-1768
Rev. Samuel Suther	1768-1786
Rev. Mr. Schneider	1787-1792
Rev. Samuel Weyburg	1793-1798
Rev. Jacob Christman	1798-1803
Revs. G. Boger and A. Loretz	1803-1812
Revs. G. Boger, J. R. Reily, Wm. Weinel, H. B. Dieffenbach, J. Scholl, J. S. Ebaugh, G. Leidy and J. Rudy	1812-1827
Rev. Wm. Hauck	1828-1832
Rev. W. C. Bennet	1832-1838
Rev. David Crooks	1838-1846
Rev. F. Plassman	1846-1848
Rev. T. Butler	1848-1851
Rev. Wm. Sorber	1853-1856
Rev. T. Butler	1856-1857
Rev. P. A. Long	1858-1862
Rev. Thomas Long	1862-1887
Rev. G. D. Gurley (assistant)	1885-1886
Rev. J. H. Shuford	1887-1888
Rev. J. C. Leonard	1889-1897
Rev. H. A. M. Holshouser	1897-1903
Rev. W. H. Causey	1903-1907
Vacant	1907-1910
Rev. W. H. McNairy	1910-1911
Rev. J. A. Palmer	1912-1918
Rev. J. D. Andrew	1918-1924

In 1807 the Reformed and Lutheran congregations, having used the same house of worship jointly for twenty years, felt themselves able to build a larger and handsomer church. The old log church had been in use first by the Reformed alone thirty years, and then the Reformed and Lutherans jointly twenty years, in all fifty years. It had served an excellent purpose, but it was now to give place to a more stately temple to be erected a few feet away just outside of the graveyard enclosure. The logs of the sacred old edifice which had stood so long were sold to a gentleman who converted them into a residence. The second church, like the first, but a frame building, was two stories high with a gallery at each end and the south side; the pulpit was at the north side. In the northwest corner was a platform with banisters, where the elders and sometimes the deacons sat. This house of worship was occupied jointly by the Reformed and Lutherans until 1821, when there was an unfortunate rupture in the Lutheran congregation. One party of the Lutherans adhered to the North Carolina Synod; the other party organized themselves into a new congregation and connected themselves with the Tennessee Synod. But the Reformed congregation allowed both parties to occupy the property with themselves. The arrangement was continued as already stated until the year 1903. In 1882, sixty-one years after the Lutheran division, the erection of a still larger and more handsome church was undertaken. This new church, the third one on the grounds, was finished and ready for occupancy in the winter of 1882. The material for its construction was taken almost entirely from the church lands. This church was built by the Reformed and the two bodies of Lutherans and was used by the three congregations until 1903.

This third and last church built on these grounds is now the sole property of the Reformed congregation, which has a history at this place of one hundred and seventy years. Pilgrim is one of the oldest Reformed churches in North Carolina, and it has all along been active and influential. Its elders during this long period have been men of recognized standing in the community. Its present membership is 239, with a Sunday school of 220. This congregation has given to the Reformed Church four ministers, viz.: Revs. H. F. Long, D.D., W. A. Long, Ph.D., J. C. Leonard, D.D., and J. L. Bowers.

Beck's Reformed Church

Beck's is one of the old Reformed Churches in North Carolina. It has had a long and honorable history. Its first members were German settlers from the Palatinate and other sections of Europe. They brought with them their German Bibles, hymn-books and catechisms, some of which are still preserved as precious heirlooms in the homes of their descendants.

The name arose from the family of Becks (Pecks) in the community. This is still a common name in the membership of this historic congregation. The meagre records do not show that the church ever had any other name, though it is presumed that it had, just as the mother church of that section, Leonard's Church, was organized under the name of Pilgrim. But if there was such a name it has long since been lost sight of, and the church continues to be called "Beck's Church."

The deed of the Beck's Church land bears the date of November 5, 1787, and conveys fifty-three acres from

Dr. John Billings, L. Smith and others to Martin Frank and Frederick Billings of the "Profession of the Church of England," and David Smith and Henry Lookinbee of the "Profession of the Church of the Dutch Settlement on Abbott's Creek." Martin Frank and Frederick Billings were the trustees of the Lutheran Church, called in this deed "The Profession of the Church of England." David Smith and Henry Lookinbee were the trustees of the Reformed Church, called in the deed "The Profession of the Church of the Dutch Settlement on Abbott's Creek." These peculiar titles arose from the fact that the members of the Reformed and Lutheran churches could not speak English. The officials gathered from their broken explanations that the first-named trustees represented a denomination somewhat like the Church of England, and wrote the deed accordingly. The officials also understood that the latter trustees represented a denomination identical with the "Dutch Congregation on Abbott's Creek," already mentioned in the official records of 1783, and so wrote the title.

The pastor of the Reformed Congregation at Beck's Church in 1787 was the Rev. Mr. Schneider. He organized the congregation, though already when he came a log church had been built under the leadership of Rev. Mr. Suther. The citizens of the community suffered greatly during the Revolutionary War. The Reformed people, as at Leonard's Church, following the example of their pastor, Samuel Suther, were intense patriots. A notable example was Peter Hedrick, the great-grandfather of Rev. M. L. Hedrick. He was born

December 17, 1733. Later in life he came to America and settled in North Carolina on the Four-mile Branch near Beck's Church. The site of his home is well known. When the war broke out he enlisted in the American army. This excited the intense hatred of the Tories. In his absence one day a band of Tories came to his house and, holding a pistol in the face of his wife, cursed her and told her to give up all she had or die. She answered that she was helpless and begged them to spare her and her children and her property. They only abused her for her pitiful entreaties. They took all the provisions except a little salt, drove off the choice horses and cattle and shot the others, and then burned all the buildings. When Peter Hedrick returned a few weeks later and found his desolated home, he took his wife and children to Virginia until after the war, when he returned. He died January 24, 1789, and lies buried in the Beck's Church graveyard.

The log church was used by the congregation until the year 1878, when a large frame church was built which is still in use. The pastors have been those who served Pilgrim Church until the Lower Davidson Charge was formed in 1862; and from that date the pastors have been the following: Revs. M. L. Hedrick, A. R. Holshouser, W. H. McNairy, L. M. Kerschner, H. E. Sechler, W. H. Causey, Paul Barringer, P. M. Trexler, J. M. L. Lyerly, J. C. Peeler, A. S. Peeler.

Bethany Reformed Church

To write the history of Bethany Church is to give the history of the German people who settled in that community—a people simple in habits of life, industrious, of upright character, true devotion to the church, and strong in the faith of a Saviour's love.

The deed conveying the property was made August 1, 1789, and begins as follows: "This indenture made the first day of August in the year of our Lord one thousand seven hundred and eighty-nine between Frederick Miller of Rowan County in the State of North Carolina of the first part and the inhabitants of Brushy Fork belonging to the Societies of the Church and Presbyterian parties as the second part witnesseth, that said Frederick Miller for and in consideration of the sum of one pound and thirteen shillings current money of North Carolina to him in hand paid before the ensealing and delivering hereof by the aforesaid parties of the second part, the receipt whereof the said Frederick Miller doth hereby acknowledge . . . to be for the use of building a meeting-house and other religious purposes." Frederick Miller signed the deed by making his mark.

The first church was built about the time the deed was made. It was a log structure about 30 by 40 feet with galleries on three sides. The pulpit was in the usual goblet shape, supported by a poplar post, and was large enough for only one person. The first name by which the place was called was Fredericktown in honor of Frederick Miller. Later on it was called Possumtown. And thereby hangs a tale. It is said that while the good people were at church, some one without the spirit of worship in his bosom caught several opossums, stuck their tails through a stick and left them at Frederick Miller's house; and from that time the place was known as Possumtown, which clung to it until 1861, when the new church was dedicated. No one seemed to know what name would be given the church. The dedication sermon had been preached, Rev. P. A. Long read the service of dedication, and in that dedicated the church as Bethany. The name is beautiful, and it carries our minds to the place where Jesus so often rested just outside of Jerusalem.

This was a union church. "The Church Party" named in the deed was the Lutheran Church and the "Presbyterian Party" was the Reformed Church, names given by the county officials who knew nothing of our German people and their churches. It is not known when the first services were held, but certainly prior to the year 1789 when the site of the church was secured. The first church in this section of the State was the old Leonard's Church about twelve miles farther south on Abbott's Creek. The ministers who preached there held occasional service in distant communities where were found Reformed families. Prominent among those ministers who served Leonard's Church was Rev. Samuel Suther, who preached from 1768 to 1786. Following him was the Rev. Mr. Schneider. It is known that the latter organized Beck's Church in 1787, and it is likely that he also organized Bethany. The next ministers were Revs. Andrew Loretz and George Boger. From 1812 for a long period Bethany had no regular pastor, and the interest went down.

The fire was smothered; it was not extinguished. The harps were hanged upon the willows, but the love for Jerusalem still warmed the heart. A few remained faithful and upon the Lord's Day these with German hymn books and German Bibles in hand gathered and held service, singing the songs with the true fervor of the Fatherland. This condition of affairs remained until 1848, when Rev. Thornton Butler, a young North Carolinian who had just finished his education at Mercersburg, Pa., took charge of the churches in Davidson County. His charge consisted of five churches. The Rev. Mr. Butler held a conference with John Long, Samuel Yokeley and Henry Clodfelter as to the prospect of reorganizing Possumtown. Butler said that the only thing that would revive the church at that place was a camp-meeting. These German fathers were not given much to camp-meetings and were slow to move in that direction. They regarded the remedy severe although the case was a desperate one. Finally John Long said: "Anything to save the church." Accordingly arrangements were made and a camp-meeting was begun on Friday night before the third Sunday in August, 1851, and continued until Wednesday of the following week. This meeting was held by Reformed preachers, Butler, Welker and Ingold. The following year there were two camp-meetings: one on the first Sunday in August, held by the Lutherans, and one on the third Sunday of the same month, held by the Reformed. Subsequently camp-meetings were held each year on the third Sunday in August, the Lutheran and Reformed people uniting. The Reformed did not hold a meeting, however, after the year 1854; the last of the camp-meetings was held by the Lutherans in 1858.

It was during this period that the congregation was reorganized. Dr. G. William Welker says in the *Colonial Records* that under the ministry of Rev. Thornton Butler, 1848-51, it was revived and grew to become a prosperous church. In the spring of 1853 Rev. William Sorber was installed pastor over the Davidson churches. He was pastor at the time of the last camp-meeting held at Possumtown. The last meeting was known as the "Sorber Meeting."

The pastors succeeding Rev. William Sorber have been those mentioned in connection with Pilgrim Church, Bethany having formed a part of the original Davidson Charge, and later the Upper Davidson Charge. Bethany has given to the church several of her sons as ministers: Revs. Philip Allison Long, Thomas Long, John Albert Murphy, Joseph L. Murphy and William H. Causey. Prominent among the officers of the church in the later years have been John Long, Samuel Yokeley, Israel Long, Lewis Livengood, Henry Clodfelter, Hamilton Clodfelter and John P. Long.

The property was held in common by the Reformed and Lutherans until August, 1902, when a division was made. Three acres of land were reserved for the cemetery to be held in common; and the remaining land was divided into two parts, one part containing four acres and the other two acres. The Reformed received the two acres, and went to work at once to build a new church. The corner-stone was laid March 14, 1903. The work of building was steadily pushed to completion. November 15, a beautiful Sunday, the new house of worship was dedicated. The sermon was preached from Haggai 3:9, by Rev. J. L. Murphy, D.D., a son of the congregation. Rev. W. H. Causey, another son of the congregation, was also present and took part in the services. The act of dedication was performed by the pastor, Rev. H. A. M. Holshouser.

Beulah Reformed Church

Beulah Reformed Church is situated six miles northwest of Lexington. It is more frequently called "Sowers's Church." This congregation has had a long history. It was a preaching place before the congregation was organized. The tract of land on which the church was located was donated to the congregation by Elder Philip Sauer (Sowers) of the Pilgrim Church. Philip Sauer came from Germany to North Carolina in 1753 and took up large tracts of land on "Swearing Creek." He was the ancestor of all the people in this section of the State now called by the name Sowers. He was a member of the Reformed Church and an elder, and his interest in this church was large. It was largely through his influence that the first grant was made to the "Dutch Congregation on Abbott's Creek," Pilgrim Church, of which he was a member. When the country became more thickly settled and other churches were needed, he cheerfully donated eleven acres of ground for Beulah Reformed Church. That was about the year 1788. He showed his wisdom, too, in giving the land for the exclusive use of the "Reformirte Kirche." This was one of the few early churches that was never a union church.

The Rev. Mr. Schneider was the first pastor at Beulah. Under his ministry the old log church was built in 1788 or 1789 at the northeast corner of the present graveyard. This church was used until 1851, when a frame structure was built a few yards farther north. This latter church, after many remodelings, was used until the year 1923.

Among the family names prominent in the early history of this church are the following: Koontz, Everhart, Sowers, Livengood, Hege, Berrier, Grimes, Wehrle (Whirlow), Schaaf (Shoaf). Some of these names are still found on the roll of membership. Its pastors have been those mentioned elsewhere in connection with Pilgrim Church and for that reason are not repeated here. It was a part of the original "Davidson Charge," and has formed a part of the Upper Davidson Charge since the division of the Davidson Charge. Its present membership is about 325.

A handsome new house of worship was erected here within the last few years, with all modern accomodations for Sunday school and young people's work, an imposing structure which attracts the attention of all people passing by. Rev. J. D. Andrew was the pastor at that time.

Emanuel Reformed Church

This community was originally settled largely by German Palatines who came to America to escape persecution in the Fatherland. Many of them found a refuge and a home in the great colonies of North Carolina. The majority of Germans who came to this section of North Carolina came by way of the port of Philadelphia and many of them resided for a time in Pennsylvania, but others of these German Protestants came by way of the port of Charleston, and made their way up into North Carolina. These people were largely members of the Reformed and Lutheran churches and settled in the same neighborhoods. They brought with them their German Bibles, hymn books and catechisms. In all cases where it was possible they brought with them a minister and a school-teacher. When they could not secure the minister, they pressed the teacher into both places as far as possible. Always a rude church and schoolhouse were erected, and these were very generally owned jointly by Reformed and Lutherans. German emigration was at high tide from the year 1745 to 1755, and continued until as late as 1775 and even later in smaller numbers. Those people came to North Carolina to establish homes for themselves and their children. They were farmers as a rule but no matter what their trade in the Fatherland, they became farmers by necessity when they came here. This was a virgin country; no white men had ever lived here, and the Indians were the sole human inhabitants of the land. When those people located here, they were always careful to select land that gave promise of being fertile; hence most of them selected their farms on water courses. In nearly all church and private grants and deeds the lands were located by the stream upon which they were situated.

Emanuel Church was not established as early as several others in this section of North Carolina, but it has a history going back more than a century. A burying ground was laid out here as early as 1808, and perhaps earlier. The oldest tombstone bearing a date has upon it the year 1808, though some graves in those early years were not marked. The deed to the church lands bears the date of February 20, 1813. It was made to Philip Kanoy, Jacob Myers, Sr., and John Bowers by John Myers and his wife Elizabeth. The original tract contained three acres and the consideration named was five dollars. Philip Kanoy, Jacob Myers, Sr., and John Bowers are called in the deed "Elders of the Presbyterian and Lutherian German Churches." These names look peculiar to us in these days, but they are well understood now. The members of these denominations were Germans, and they could not write English, and could only speak it brokenly. All the county officials were English, and they made some ludicrous blunders in German names, especially the names of German churches. By the "Lutherian Church" was of course meant the Lutheran Church; and by the "German Presbyterian Church" was meant the Reformed Church. These same peculiar names and others just as remarkable occur in other church deeds and grants in this section of the State. In other cases the Reformed Church is called "The Calvinistic Party," "The German Calvinistic Church," "The Dutch Congregation"; but of course those English county officials knew nothing about the beautiful expressions of the German language and not a great deal about ecclesiastical denominations any way. Hence we must excuse their incorrect terms in naming churches and denominations.

The two above named elders, Jacob Myers, Sr., and John Bowers, were members of the Reformed Church. It is not known whether Philip Kanoy was Reformed or Lutheran. John Myers and his wife Elizabeth (the daughter of Jacob Bowers) who sold, or rather gave, the three acres of land for the church, were members of the Reformed Church. The deed says that Elizabeth Myers inherited the land from her father, Jacob Bowers, then deceased; and Jacob Bowers was also a member of the Reformed Church. Descendants of all the persons here mentioned are to this day living in this community and are members generally of Reformed and Lutheran congregations.

The first house built on the grounds here was a log structure, preceded by a brush arbor under which services were held whenever a visiting minister could be secured. Services were also held in the homes of the people whenever a minister or a school-teacher could be pressed into service. Prayer meetings and even preaching services were often held by the elders of the church in the long intervals when no minister could be had. The log house was used for both school and church purposes. In those days all the preaching and singing were in the German language, and both old and young people spoke German. The name by which the first church was known was "Bowers's Meeting House," after the original Jacob Bowers whose daughter Elizabeth Myers (wife of John Myers) donated the three acres of land. The proper name of the church has always been Emanuel.

The second house of worship was commenced in the year 1813 and finished in 1814. It was a frame structure, ceiled and weather-boarded, and painted white on the outside. It had two stories, with a gallery running around three sides. There were three doors by which to enter the building, and the pulpit was in the north side of the church. It is a great misfortune that no picture of this or the first one was ever made. Many would be delighted to be in possession of such photographs. This second house of worship stood on these hallowed grounds until December 12, 1901, when on a Sunday afternoon the sacred structure was destroyed by fire. It was a sad day for the whole community, sinners and Christians alike. This was a church made sacred to hundreds by the holy memories coming down from the past. Here fathers and mothers of generations past had met Sabbath after Sabbath, and lifted up their voices in prayer and praise to the great God, the Creator of all. Here they came to offer worship at the throne of grace. Here they came to hear the blessed Gospel preached, and to receive the rich comfort which the Heavenly Father has vouchsafed to all who love and trust Him. Time and again they had approached the Holy Communion table at this sacred chancel, and had feasted upon the food which nourishes unto eternal life. "Do this in remembrance of me"; "As often as ye eat this bread and drink this cup, ye do show the Lord's death till He come." Here they brought their children to be baptized, catechized and confirmed; at this altar many a sin-burdened soul had knelt and received pardon. What a blessed place! Here the minister spoke the last words of comfort over the coffins of scores of departed loved ones. No wonder hearts were sad when on that Sunday afternoon the smoke of the burning sacred old edifice was seen rising up toward the heavens. There was pain in many a heart and tears in many eyes.

But on the site of the burned church another much handsomer was erected the following year, surmounted by a graceful tower in which hangs a bell to summon worshipers to the house of God.

In the year 1925 the Lutheran congregation was disbanded, its few remaining members entering other organizations, and the Reformed congregation bought the Lutheran interest in the property. In the winter and summer following the house of worship was rebuilt and greatly enlarged by the addition of Sunday school classrooms connecting with the auditorium, the structure being both commodious and pleasing in appearance. Dedication services were held Sunday, August 29, 1926, the consecration sermon being preached by Rev. J. C. Leonard, D.D.

In the early history of this church the pastors were Christman, Boger, Loretz, Riley, Ebaugh, Rudy, Houck, Bennett, Crooks, Butler, Plassman, Sorber; in later years, Revs. P. A. Long, J. W. Cecil, M. L. Hedrick, A. R. Holshouser, C. Clapp, J. N. Faust, W. W.

Rowe, F. Cromer, L. W. Showers, I. S. Ditzler, W. H. McNairy, C. Woods, J. B. Swartz, D. C. Cox.

Emanuel Reformed Church has had on its roll of membership through these long years many great and good men and women. It would not be possible to give a complete list of these. This church has always stood for the old Reformed doctrines; its ministers have never been accused of being unorthodox. It has emphasized the importance of the means of grace, Holy Baptism, the Holy Supper, the catechism, the prayer meeting, the Sunday school. True evangelism is held up as of the greatest importance in saving souls and building Christian character. God has wonderfully blessed the use of these means, and as a result here is a prosperous and growing country church with a membership of 220. The history of any community or church is but the history of the individual men and women of said community or church.

Hebron Reformed Church

Hebron Reformed Church (Pleasant Retreat) is located in Davidson County about seven miles south of Winston, North Carolina. Previous to the establishment of this church this community had no convenient place of worship. But there were godly people living in the community who felt the need of a church within easy reach. Among these were Joseph Miller, a local Methodist minister, and Thomas Long, a member of the Reformed Church and a man of ability to lead. These two men met together and said: "There ought to be a church here," and took steps towards its establishment. Selection of a location for a church became necessary. There were two inviting spots: one on the land of

Michael Miller and the other on the land of Thomas Long. To vote in the civil election at that time it was necessary for a man to own fifty acres of land. Mr. Miller owned just fifty acres and to give a lot for the church would have disfranchised him. Thomas Long owned more than the required amount and he suggested that they select a lot on his land for the reason that he could give it and still be eligible to the right of voting. About this time a Mr. Jones who was a theological student came from a Seminary in Pennsylvania and passed through this community. He stopped with Thomas Long, who told him of the intention of the community to build a church in their midst. This gentleman encouraged the movement. He was shown the proposed locations. He favored the one proposed by Thomas Long and this became the building site.

The congregation was organized by Rev. Thornton Butler in 1856. He had charge of the Reformed congregations in Davidson County at this time. The members met August 13 to begin work for the erection of the church. The church was built and formally dedicated. It was a frame building filled in with brick and plastered.

In giving a historical sketch of this congregation it is befitting to dwell upon the life of Thomas Long, who was one of the charter members, an Elder when the first church was built, and afterwards became pastor of the congregation. He was born in Davidson County near Bethany Reformed Church. He was a son of John Long and a member of a large family. His brother Allison Long was a minister in the Reformed Church. Thomas Long received no education but that of the free schools of his day; but he was a man of great natural ability. He applied himself to a diligent study of the Bible, exercised a true and abiding faith in God, lived out the great truths of the Gospel, and thus by his own wise, persevering efforts he prepared himself to render the church in his day good service. He married Elizabeth Furguson and began life upon the farm. To them were born four children. After her death, he married Amanda Berrier and to them were born six children. During the Civil War there was a scarcity of Reformed ministers in North Carolina; so on the third day of May, A.D. 1863, he was licensed to preach the Gospel. When the Reformed churches in Davidson County were divided and made to constitute the Upper Davidson Charge and the Lower Davidson Charge, he became pastor of the Upper Davidson Charge. This was his first and only charge. Here he labored till 1887, when age and bodily affliction disqualified him for the duties of the ministry. Though he was without a college education, by purchasing good books and consulting Dr. G. William Welker he acquired a clear conception of the principal theological doctrines then held by the churches. A doctrinal sermon preached by him is remembered, in which he defended the Reformed view over against some other then being propagated, and his arguments were unanswerable. In some things he may not have held strictly to Reformed customs. He always knelt in prayer. He was a farmer and worked on his farm and raised fine crops. In the pulpit he was awkward, making few gestures and seldom changing his position. He preached without notes, but his sermons had power. It is not known that he ever received a stated salary. He served four congregations and often preached at schoolhouses and "stands" in different parts of the county. He later organized

Mount Tabor at the "Poor House," and when he resigned the charge he still retained this congregation for years; and when he became too feeble to stand and preach, these people so devoted to him made a high chair and he would sit and talk to them. He often traveled in a two-wheeled gig drawn by a little black mule, and with his long locks of hair flowing from beneath his broad-brimmed hat made a striking appearance. He advocated the neighborhood prayer-meeting in the community and great was the spiritual uplift received from these meetings. Father Long had a strong physical constitution, but by exposure and overexertion he became a great sufferer from rheumatism in his old age, and was practically helpless for many years before his death. He was in great demand in his community. He was sought by many for advice in the adjustment of difficulties and disputes.

As a scholar and preacher Father Long was not profound or eloquent, but very earnest and sincere. His message carried conviction because it came from the heart and his own experience. He did a good work and the churches of the Upper Davidson Charge—especially Pleasant Retreat—are greatly indebted to him for his long life of sacrifice and untiring efforts. His funeral was conducted by Rev. H. A. M. Holshouser, assisted by Rev. J. H. Shuford of the Reformed Church and Rev. Mr. Lutz of the Lutheran Church. His remains were placed in the little country graveyard, beside the church of which he was a member and pastor from its establishment till the end of his life.

Rev. G. Dickie Gurley supplied the congregation one year after Rev. Mr. Long's active pastorate but before he resigned. Rev. J. H. Shuford, a native of North Carolina, became pastor of this congregation in the spring of 1887 and preached until the summer of 1888. Rev. J. C. Leonard, a native of Davidson County, succeeded Rev. Mr. Shuford in 1889 and served until 1897. Rev. H. A. M. Holshouser, a native of Rowan County, became pastor in 1897 and remained until the end of the year 1903. Rev. W. H. Causey, a native of Davidson County, became pastor January 1, 1904, and remained until January 1, 1907. Successors have been the following: Revs. A. S. Peeler, D. E. Bowers, J. M. L. Lyerly, A. C. Peeler.

Classis met at this church in the spring of 1875. Dr. Jeremiah Ingold, of Hickory, a learned and pious man, was elected president. Rev. G. W. Welker of the Guilford Charge was present in his official capacity as stated clerk. Revs. J. C. Clapp, Thomas Long, J. W. Cecil, P. M. Trexler, J. H. Shuford, and John Ingle were also present. Sermons were preached during the meeting by Ingold, Clapp, Trexler and Shuford. This was Rev. Mr. Shuford's first attendance at Classis as an ordained minister.

The first building was used as a house of worship until 1902, when it was superseded by the present building. It had become very much dilapidated and did not meet the needs of the congregation nor the demands of the times. So the congregation under the pastoral supervision of Rev. H. A. M. Holshouser erected a new house of worship quite adequate to its needs. The church has been a religious center for the community ever since its organization. At this time it has a membership of over 100. It is active in the Sunday school and the benevolent work of the church, and is liberal towards the support of the pastor.

Mount Carmel Reformed Church

Mount Carmel Reformed Church is four miles west of Lexington in the County of Davidson. It is an offshoot of the Pilgrim and Beulah congregations. Rev. Thornton Butler, pastor of the Davidson Charge, began to preach at the schoolhouse of district number 26 in January, 1848, and he organized the congregation in August, 1849. Andrew Koontz and John Hedrick were the first elders and Samuel Koontz and John L. Hedrick were the first deacons. In 1855 an arbor was built near the schoolhouse, and this arbor and the schoolhouse served as the places of worship until the year 1880, when a neat and comfortable church was erected. The congregation was connected with the Lower Davidson Charge. This church suffered greatly from removals of its promising young people to other localities. The church was donated to the Methodist Protestant denomination in 1907.

Mount Tabor Reformed Church

Mount Tabor, a child of Pilgrim Church, is four miles east of Lexington in Davidson County. The house of worship was built and the congregation organized by Rev. Thomas Long in the year 1883. It was for several years incorporated with the Upper Davidson Charge. In 1888 it was detached from this charge and constituted an independent mission. It was in 1894 united with the Lower Davidson Charge. Its membership has grown from a handful to a large congregation. A new house of worship was built in 1910 during the pastorate of Rev. J. M. L. Lyerly.

Jerusalem Reformed Church

This church is in the southern part of Davidson County, distant some twelve or fourteen miles southeast of Lexington. The congregation was organized by Rev. Thornton Butler in 1858 for the convenience of the members of Beck's Church who were living too far from their place of worship. It is a union church and forms a part of the Lower Davidson Charge. It has never had a large membership, but has been active in good works. It has in the last several years suffered greatly from the exodus of its members to the towns. Its pastors have been Thornton Butler, P. A. Long, M. L. Hedrick, A. R. Holshouser, W. H. McNairy, L. M. Kerschner, H. E. Sechler, W. H. Causey, Paul Barringer, P. M. Trexler, J. M. L. Lyerly, J. C. Peeler, A. S. Peeler. The present church was built in 1909.

Hedrick's Grove Reformed Church

The original members of Hedrick's Grove were transferred mainly from Beck's. The congregation was organized the first Sunday in May, 1891, with forty-one members. Allen Hedrick, R. E. Hedrick and John Black were elected elders, and R. L. Beck, H. H. Hedrick and Franklin Hedrick, deacons. The pastor at the time was Rev. A. R. Holshouser.

The erection of the church was commenced in the fall of 1890. The corner-stone was laid on Thanksgiving Day, the address being delivered by Rev. J. C. Leonard, at that time pastor of the Upper Davidson Charge. This building was intended for both church and school purposes, with schoolrooms on the first floor and auditorium above. It was furnished during the winter.

The church was dedicated July 31, 1892. Rev. J. C. Leonard preached the sermon from Genesis 28:17. "This is none other but the house of God, and this is the gate of heaven."

An academic school was conducted here in 1892 and 1893 by R. E. Leonard and Crawford Clapp. Rev. W. H. McNairy also taught in the academy during several months of his pastorate in the church. The public school of the district was taught in this building every year until 1924.

Hedrick's Grove Reformed Church is located in a fine agricultural and lumbering district of Davidson County, and no other community in the county has made more rapid progress than this within the last few years. The members of this church come mostly from a long line of pious ancestors. It has had a substantial growth. In September, 1920, a meeting was held in the interest of a new church, when it was decided by unanimous vote to secure plans for a modern house of worship with proper Sunday school accommodations. The members of the church made the brick themselves and furnished the lumber. August 26, 1921, the first brick was laid by Rev. J. C. Peeler, the pastor. September 16 a large crowd assembled to witness the laying of the corner-stone. The sermon was preached by Rev. J. C. Leonard, D.D., who thirty-one years before had preached the sermon at the laying of the corner-stone of the old church, and had also preached the sermon at its dedication. This is a most beautiful and commodious church, and reflects the progressive and pious character of its builders.

Near this church on a beautiful lot of several acres of land the four churches of the charge built a handsome large residence for the pastor in the year 1923, this house taking the place of the one formerly occupied by the minister. The pastors have been: Revs. A. R. Holshouser, W. H. McNairy, L. M. Kerschner, H. E. Sechler, P. Barringer, P. M. Trexler, W. H. Causey, J. M. L. Lyerly, J. C. Peeler, A. S. Peeler. The Classis of North Carolina met in this church in 1892 and again in 1926.

Calvary Reformed Church

Moffitt's Grove schoolhouse, two miles west of Thomasville, was for many years a preaching point for all denominations. The Reformed Church had once organized a small congregation here, but it never amounted to much and was allowed to go down. In 1889 the Classis of North Carolina committed the interest here and in Thomasville to the care of Rev. P. M. Trexler, pastor at Concord. The intention was to get the members living in the town and in the country to unite their forces and build a church at the edge of Thomasville. The Rev. P. M. Trexler preached once a month during the classical year, but the plan proved impracticable. In 1891 the classis appointed Rev. J. C. Leonard, pastor of the Upper Davidson Charge, to look after the interest at Moffitt's Grove and instructed him to organize a congregation if deemed advisable. At the same time the Classis pledged two hundred dollars towards the building of a church. After several services were held the outlook seemed favorable, and accordingly Calvary Reformed Church was duly organized November 30, 1891, with the following charter members: D. A. Long, Mrs. D. A. Long, John A. Long, Mrs. Mary A. Clinard, R. C. Clinard, Margaret Kanoy, Cicero Kanoy, Minnie Belle Kanoy, Louella E. Kanoy, Martha Belle Kanoy, Lizzie Kanoy, Francis V. Kanoy, A. F. Kanoy,

Louisa V. Kanoy, F. W. Kanoy, Mary Ann Kanoy, John Shuler, Nathan Ward, Alice Ward, Lottie Kanoy, Eliza Kanoy, Sarah Kanoy. Immediately afterwards Bethlehem Black and Mrs. Bethlehem Black were received. The first officers were D. A. Long and F. W. Kanoy, elders, and A. F. Kanoy, deacon. All the services were held in the schoolhouse.

During the winter and spring the work of building a neat frame church was pushed forward. The lot was donated by Mr. and Mrs. D. C. Moffitt. The members of the church and friends in the community did a great deal of work. The new house of worship was dedicated May 29, 1892. The sermon was preached by Rev. P. M. Trexler, D.D., and the service was conducted by Rev. J. C. Leonard. In 1892 Calvary Church was attached to the Upper Davidson Charge. It remained in this connection until April, 1896, when it became a part of the newly constituted Thomasville Charge. Rev. J. C. Leonard was the pastor from the beginning of its history until April, 1896. His successors have been Revs. Clarence Clapp, J. N. Faust, W. W. Rowe, Fred Cromer, Lucian W. Showers, Irwin S. Ditzler, W. H. McNairy, C. Woods, J. B. Swartz, D. C. Cox.

Calvary Church is located in a prosperous farming community near the town of Thomasville. The congregation has grown and is at present in a flourishing condition. The future is hopeful. The church was rebuilt in 1923.

Heidelberg Reformed Church, Thomasville

In 1894 the Classis of North Carolina instructed Rev. J. C. Leonard, at the time pastor of the Upper Davidson Charge, to canvass the town of Thomasville, and if found advisable to organize a congregation. Accordingly Heidelberg Reformed Church was organized June 17, 1894. W. L. Myers and J. T. Long were elected elders, and T. A. Livengood and R. P. Murphy, deacons. The following became members at the organization: John A. Long, Mrs. John A. Long, Daisy L. Long, Joseph P. Long, Cora Long, W. L. Myers, Mrs. W. L. Myers, Randall P. Murphy, J. T. Long, Mrs. J. T. Long, T. A. Livengood, Mrs. T. A. Livengood, J. Lee Briles, Mrs. J. L. Briles, E. B. Clodfelter and R. T. Cecil. The congregation was organized in T. A. Livengood's house on Main Street, where all the services were held for several months. During the spring months of 1895 the services were held in a room over the store of W. L. Myers. The lot on Main Street was purchased in the summer of 1895 for four hundred dollars, and the erection of a house of worship was at once commenced. The work was pushed rapidly, and the lecture room was ready for occupancy in August, and the services were held in it until the auditorium was finished. The new church was dedicated December 15, 1895, Rev. J. L. Murphy preaching the sermon. The following Reformed ministers were present: Revs. J. W. Cecil, W. H. McNairy, J. L. Murphy, and the pastor, Rev. J. C. Leonard.

The pastors of this church have been: Dr. J. C. Leonard, Revs. C. Clapp, J. N. Faust, W. W. Rowe, F. Cromer, L. W. Showers, I. S. Ditzler, W. H. McNairy, C. Woods, G. E. Plott, J. A. Palmer. The church was rebuilt several years ago, and a parsonage erected on the adjacent lot. A new site has recently been purchased on a prominent street several blocks back from the Southern Railway, and a new church and parsonage are now under contemplation.

Religious Forces of Davidson County 479

The First Reformed Church of Lexington

January twentieth, nineteen hundred one, is a date full of meaning to the members and friends of the First Reformed Church, Lexington, North Carolina. On that date this church began its career as an organized body of Christian workers. At eleven o'clock a.m. those who had presented their names as charter members, together with many friends of the town and community, gathered in the new house of worship, already completed, for the first service of worship. It was a holy hour whose memory is fondly cherished by those who are still among us. The pastor, Rev. J. C. Leonard, D.D., preached the sermon from the text in Romans 12:2, "Be not conformed to this world, but be ye transformed by the renewing of your mind, that ye may prove what is that good and acceptable and perfect will of God." The letters of seventeen persons were already in the hands of the pastor, together with the names of five others who were ready to enter the organization. Immediately following the service the church was organized. Three elders and three deacons were chosen and inducted into office. All together at the end of the first day there were twenty-two members of the First Church. P. J. Leonard, E. A. Rothrock and C. C. Burkhart were the first elders. Mr. Leonard and Mr. Burkhart are still serving in this office. Mr. Rothrock is dead. J. T. Hedrick has also been an officer the whole period, first as deacon and later as elder. Besides these the following charter members are still among us: Mrs. P. J. Leonard, Mrs. E. A. Rothrock, Mrs. J. T. Hedrick, Mrs. Sallie Hinkle, Mrs. J. H. Sowers, Mrs. E. H. Holmes, C. H. Burkhart, Mrs. C. H. Burkhart, Mrs. Charles Rhodes, Mrs. J. F. L. Tussey, Mrs.

Amanda Sowers and Mrs. C. C. Burkhart have been called away by death, and the names of the other charter members have disappeared from the roll by dismission and otherwise.

Since that first memorable service twenty-five years have gone by. They have been great years in the history of this body. God has been with His people and has abundantly blessed their endeavors. The membership has grown from a handful to 525 people, and to over 200 in its mission, the Second Reformed Church. This church may well have implicit confidence in the words of Jesus: "Fear not, little flock for it is your Father's good pleasure to give you the kingdom."

The Sunday following the organization of the church the Sunday school was organized with fifty-five officers, teachers and scholars. C. C. Burkhart was the first Superintendent. He was later at the close of the year 1906 succeeded by J. T. Hedrick who continued in this office until the close of the year 1925, when I. L. Sink was elected. The school has now over 600 on its rolls and is one of the great religious forces of the town and community.

The work in Lexington was at first fostered by the Board of Home Missions. At the meeting of that body in July, 1900, Lexington and High Point were enrolled as missions from October first of the same year, and Dr. J. C. Leonard was commissioned as the first pastor. Seeing the urgent need at Lexington he entered upon the work there in July, though his commission did not go into effect until October. A lot was secured at the corner of Center and Salisbury streets at a cost of $900. This seemed a very high price twenty-five years ago, though today it appears insignificant. A loan of $1,000 was secured from the Board of Missions, and donations

RELIGIOUS FORCES OF DAVIDSON COUNTY 481

were secured from members and friends in the community and elsewhere. The first brick was laid by the missionary himself October 4, 1900. The work of building was pushed rapidly forward, and the house of worship was practically finished by January 20, 1901, before a single service had been conducted and before the congregation was organized, a course rather unique. The following invitation was sent out: "You are cordially invited to attend divine services in connection with the opening of the First Reformed Church, corner of Center and Salisbury streets, Lexington, North Carolina, at eleven o'clock a.m. and seven p.m. January twentieth, nineteen hundred and one." A note in the first church register says: "The church was filled with worshipers both morning and evening. The missionary preached in the morning from Romans 12:2, and in the evening from Psalms 68:12."

This was the house of worship as at first constructed, built of brick and covered with slate. The extreme dimensions were 40 x 51 feet, with auditorium, lecture room, pulpit-recess and tower, seating about 300. Another note in the church register says: "The interior walls are plastered, and the overhead ceiling is of paneled yellow pine under hard oil, and the wainscoting is finished in the same manner. The pews are pine and varnished. The pulpit floor, chancel and aisles are covered with a pretty shade of carpet. The entire cost of the church is a little more than $3,600. This temple was dedicated to the triune God Sunday, February 17, 1901. The consecration sermon was preached by Rev. J. L. Murphy, D.D., of Hickory, on the text: John 17:21. The subject was: 'The Glory of a United Church.' The sermon was a strong presentation of Gospel truth. Extra chairs were placed in all available space, and the church was crowded with over 400 people by actual count. The thank-offerings of the day amounted to $63. The day was ideal, and it was a happy congregation."

The parsonage was built on a part of the church lot in the autumn of 1901, and was occupied by the pastor and his bride (who was Miss Willie Bernice Cress), the marriage taking place January 29, 1902.

In the spring of the year 1907 the congregation of the First Church voted to rebuild and enlarge the house of worship. E. A. Rothrock, D. H. Hinkle and J. T. Hedrick were appointed a building committee. An architect was secured and the work was pushed rapidly forward through the summer. The first service was held in the rebuilt church the last Sunday in October. The sermon was preached by Rev. J. C. Clapp, D.D., amid the great rejoicing of a loyal people. The improvements consist of an enlargement to the rear adding about a third to the seating capacity, new pews, carpet on the entire floor, pulpit, chancel-rail, heating plant, complete electric light fixtures and other articles of furniture. The communion table and collection plates were later donated by the Junior and Senior Christian Endeavor Societies.

The interests in Lexington and High Point were served jointly by Dr. Leonard from the inauguration of the work until the first of the year 1903, when the Board of Missions constituted each church a separate mission, with Rev. D. E. Bowers as pastor of the High Point church. The Rev. Mr. Bowers had been associated with Dr. Leonard in the work for a year prior to this, giving his time to the High Point work. Beginning with 1903 the Lexington interest has had the entire time of Dr. Leonard.

July 1, 1910, the First Church notified the Board of Missions of the purpose of the Lexington church to go to self-support from that date. The church therefore had the assistance of the Board of Missions less than ten years. The congregation greatly appreciates the help extended by the Board of Missions during those years of its early growth, and has tried through the years to show appreciation by a liberal response to the missionary and benevolent calls from the Classis, Synod and General Synod.

When the consistory of the First Church met in annual session January 2, 1912, in the study of the pastor, Dr. J. C. Leonard, there was recorded in the minute book the story of the beginning of an enterprise which later became a magnificent reality. At the meeting J. T. Hedrick made a proposition to the consistory that if they would assume responsibility for the cost of the lot opposite the church and furnishings for the building, he would build and donate to the congregation a modern Sunday school house. The offer was received with enthusiastic gratitude and the proposition was accepted with hearty unanimity. The cost of the lot was $2,250, and the furnishings of the building amounted to about $1,500. The building itself involved an outlay of about $10,000. The several contracts were let early in the summer of 1912. Monday evening, July 1, a public service of ground-breaking was held, Dr. Leonard, throwing out the first shovelful of earth, and he was followed by J. T. Hedrick, Superintendent of the school, and many other grown people and children. The corner-stone was laid with appropriate ceremonies August 9, 1912. This beautiful building is located on the corner opposite the church at the intersection of Center and Salisbury streets. It is a modern structure planned for the best methods of Sunday school work in individual classrooms. In the center of the building is an auditorium, and opening into it on all sides are the classrooms, sixteen in number. Several of these are large and specially adapted to organized class work. Between the two main entrances at the front is the ladies' parlor. The basement is fitted up with toilet and cloak rooms and a large social room. The furnace room is also in the basement. The auditorium is seated with circular pews and the classrooms with portable chairs in sections and singles. A handsome large stained-glass window gives charm and beauty to the front of the building. The upper center panel has the figure of the Boy Christ, and the lower panel the Holy Bible, while the side panels contain lilies.

This beautiful building was solemnly dedicated Sunday, July 13, 1913, Dr. Leonard having charge of the service. The sermon was preached by Rev. W. W. Rowe. On the same day a bronze tablet on the inner south wall was unveiled, setting forth important facts connected with the erection and furnishing of this excellent Sunday school house.

In the year 1920 J. T. Hedrick fitted up splendid playgrounds on the lot back of the Sunday school building. He had in the preceding year proposed to the officers of the church to purchase the adjoining property at the corner of Salisbury and East First streets and donate same to the church to be fitted up for playground purposes. The proposition was most cheerfully accepted by the officers. The residence on the lot has been rolled back and made to face East First Street, and the entire lot between the Sunday school building and East First Street has been converted into recreation grounds for the children and young people. The grounds have been fitted up with modern approved apparatus.

Several years ago a large lot was bought at the corner of West Seventh Avenue and North Street, a block beyond the Robbins School. The funds were secured by Dr. Leonard, and the deed was made to the trustees of the First Reformed Church. At the time of the purchase it was thought that this neighborhood would grow rapidly and there might be need of a church in the community. Up to the present it has not seemed necessary to undertake such a work, but the lot is still held by the First Church.

The great Forward Movement was inaugurated in 1919 by the denomination with a financial budget calling for $10,847,425 for missions, educational institutions, Sunday school work, publication interests and ministerial sustentation. The quota of the Classis of North Carolina was $154,799.50. The quota assigned to the First Church was $14,521.65 and to the Second Church $1,100. The people of the two churches entered heartily into the spirit of the campaign, and this made success certain. Before the week set for the financial drive in April, 1920, both churches had gone over the top, the First Church with a subscription of $16,056, and the Second with the total of $1,725.

[In a beautiful brochure published recently by this church is the following paragraph on the pastor who organized the congregation twenty-five years ago and has ministered to the people down to the present time:]

Rev. Jacob Calvin Leonard, D.D., Pastor

"A mere outline of the biography of this beloved minister of the Gospel, devoted pastor in Lexington during the twenty-five years of the history of our work in this city, known and highly respected by all our citizens, can be given in our limited space.

"Born February 13, 1867, youngest son of Valentine and Rebekah Cox Leonard. Direct descendant in the fifth generation of the Revolutionary patriot, Valentine Leonard, who was born in 1718, came to America in 1746, soldier in the Revolutionary War and killed by Tories in 1781 near the close of the war. The mother Reformed Church of the community (Pilgrim) was from its origin about 1754 called 'Leonard's Church' in honor of this pioneer who was one of its first elders. Dr. Leonard's direct ancestors in America are: Valentine Leonard, 1824-1894; Jacob Leonard, 1789-1845; Jacob Leonard, 1758-1835; Valentine Leonard, 1718-1781. These men were descendants of Martin and Anna Spohn Leonard of the Palatinate, Europe. Received the rudiments of education in the public school at Pilgrim and in the Lexington Academy. In January, 1884, went to Newton to finish his preparation for college. In August, 1885, entered the Freshman class of Catawba College. Graduated in May, 1889, valedictorian of the class. Studied theology under Drs. J. A. Foil, P. M. Trexler and J. L. Murphy, and subsequently took post-graduate studies in Ursinus School of Theology, Pennsylvania. The following literary and theological degrees have been conferred upon him: A.B., B.D., A.M., D.D. Licensed to preach the Gospel May 4, 1889, and ordained to the Gospel ministry October 10, 1889. Pastor of the Upper Davidson

DR. J. C. LEONARD, Lexington
Author, Historian, Pastor First Reformed Church of Lexington

Charge, 1889-1897; Field Secretary of Catawba College 1897-1898; Professor of English and History in Catawba College 1899-1900; pastor in Lexington and High Point 1900-1903; pastor in Lexington 1900 to the present time. Taught school at Burkhart's the winter of 1883-1884, when sixteen years of age, holding a first-grade certificate. Taught a few months each of the two following winters at Brick schoolhouse, Lincoln County, while preparing for college. Fostered the building of Arnold and Pilgrim Academies in 1890 and 1891. Taught the Pilgrim public school two terms in 1889-1890 and 1890-1891. Principal Pilgrim Academy 1893-1894. Remodeled Pilgrim Church 1891. Remodeled Beulah Church 1893. Organized the following congregations and built churches for them: Calvary, Moffitt's Grove, November 30, 1891; Heidelberg, Thomasville, June 17, 1894; First Lexington, January 20, 1901; First, High Point, March 24, 1901; Second, Lexington, June 5, 1904. Member of the committee that organized the First Church, Salisbury, June 28, 1896. Also on the committee that organized the First Church, Greensboro, March 1, 1903. Has attended every annual meeting of the Classis of North Carolina in his ministerial life of thirty-seven years. Stated Clerk of Classis since 1892, thirty-four years. Many times delegate to Potomac and General Synods, which bodies he has frequently addressed. Several times representative of Catawba College and the Reformed Church in the South before Eastern, Pittsburgh and Ohio Synods. In 1920 elected a member of the General Synod's Board of Missions for a term of six years and reëlected in 1926. Twenty-five years a trustee of Catawba College. Six years a trustee of Claremont College. Twelve years a member of Lexington School Board. President of the

General Synod of the Reformed Church in the United States, 1923-1926. Chairman of the committee that purchased the site of the new Lexington High School at the corner of State and West Second streets, and also the site of the new Colored Graded School. Member of the building committee of the new High School. Has delivered numerous educational, religious, philanthropic and fraternal addresses in a wide section of the country. For ten consecutive years delivered a lecture each Thanksgiving evening in Lexington. January 29, 1902, was married to Miss Willie Bernice Cress, of Concord, North Carolina. In this family is one son, Jacob C., Jr., now a student in medical college. Has preached 4,512 sermons and delivered many catechetical, Sunday school, prayer-meeting and other religious addresses. Baptized 466 infants and 687 adults. Received into the church 997 by confirmation; 416 by certificate; 194 by renewal of profession—total 1,607. Married 320 couples. Conducted 678 funerals. In Volume V, *History of North Carolina,* The Lewis Publishing Company, is a biographical sketch of Dr. Leonard in which is the following statement: 'A man of earnest convictions, strong in character and personality, and of a deeply religious nature, Rev. Jacob C. Leonard, D.D., pastor of the First Reformed Church of Lexington, North Carolina, has led a busy life filled with usefulness, and his life has been abundantly blessed to the advancement of the Master's kingdom. . . . A man of earnest purpose, laboring willingly at all times, Doctor Leonard has been the moving spirit in the upbuilding of the church with which he is associated, its present prosperous condition being largely due to his wise efforts. And in the multiplicity of the heavy duties of his local pastorate, he has always found time to help in many other general enterprises of the church and state'."

The Second Reformed Church of Lexington

The Second Reformed Church of Lexington, though a separate organization, is in reality a part of the First Church. In the fall of 1903 the Nokomis Cotton Mills donated a lot to the trustees of the First Church near the Raleigh road bridge. The members of the First Church felt the need of religious work in this section of the town. It was felt that the most effective way of reaching the community was through a church right in the midst of the people. A pretty little church was built during the fall and winter, and was ready for occupancy March 13, 1904. At 3 o'clock in the afternoon Dr. J. C. Leonard preached the first sermon in this church. The church was dedicated May 22, 1904. Rev. J. C. Clapp, D.D., preached the sermon from Psalms 26:8. The congregation was organized June 5, 1904, with twenty-one charter members. The last annual report to Classis showed 214 members, and several have been added since.

The Second Church has done a truly great work in the community in which it is located. It ministers to a population of over five hundred souls. The Sunday school, of which Elder T. A. Swing is the efficient Superintendent, is well organized, and has an enrollment of over 400.

During the summer of 1917 the Second Church was rebuilt at a cost of over one thousand dollars. Eight classrooms were added, and a furnace was installed in the basement. The church was rededicated July 8,

1917. The sermon was preached by Rev. A. D. Wolfinger, D.D. The house of worship was again rebuilt and greatly enlarged in 1921. Then in 1922 a handsome residence for the minister was erected on the lot adjoining the church. Plans are now under consideration for further improvements. The work of the Second Church was under the care of Dr. Leonard from the first. He had the assistance at different times of the following students: A. S. Peeler, J. L. Yearick, L. A. Peeler, C. C. Wagoner, J. A. Palmer, C. Woods, W. C. Lyerly, F. L. Fesperman, J. W. Huffman, A. O. Leonard. Revs. S. W. Beck, M. A. Huffman, J. A. Palmer and J. C. Peeler have also assisted in the work at this place. Rev. A. O. Leonard has had charge of this church since May, 1922. A fact worthy of special note is that the Nokomis Cotton Mills and the Lexington Chair Company have taken deep interest in this work and have contributed liberally to its support. A handsome new house of worship was built in 1926.

Bethlehem Reformed Church

The first service was held by the late Rev. David E. Bowers, under a brush arbor erected for the purpose, September 9, 1913, with an audience of about three hundred people. The location is on the Winston-Lexington highway in the upper part of the county, out in the open country. An acre of land was donated to the trustees of the church by Mrs. Katherine Stewart and her children. The house of worship was completed during the winter, and Bethlehem Reformed Church was dedicated May 31, 1914, by the pastor, Rev. D. E. Bowers, in the presence of a very large assembly of worshipers. The sermon was preached by Rev. J. C.

Leonard, D.D., of Lexington. Rev. J. A. Palmer, of Thomasville, also delivered an address. The Rev. Mr. Bowers continued as pastor until his death, October 28, 1921. His successors have been Revs. J. M. L. Lyerly, Ph.D., and A. C. Peeler.

8. METHODIST EPISCOPAL CHURCHES

It is but to repeat a well-known fact to say that Methodism is the youngest of the Nation's religious denominations in what is known now as Davidson County. Perhaps the facts would not be badly distorted in making the same statement with reference to the entire American continent. Prior to the Revolutionary War the five other major denominations now represented in Davidson County, then a part of Rowan County, had already established themselves along both sides of the Yadkin River.

Naturally, the oldest of these was the Protestant Episcopal Church, or what was known then as the Established Church of England, and was recognized by the early settlers as the Established Church of the Province of North Carolina. Between 1735 and 1755 the Lutheran, the Reformed, the Presbyterian and the Baptist denominations were represented by church organizations. Every shipload of incoming settlers brought adherents to these churches who, fired by the urge of an open door to worship God with freedom of conscience, came filtering through the forest with axe and saw and Bible to make their home and future in a new land. The settlements thus established were naturally characterized by racial and nationalistic cleavages brought over from the old-world civilization. The settlers on the east bank of the Yadkin were predominantly German, while those on the west bank were mostly Scotch-Irish. Along with these were, of course, a great number who drifted in from various sources, holding to no particular religious or national creed, and who interpreted the freedom of the new world in terms of unrestrained license rather than disciplined religious liberty. This gave Methodism a natural setting for its revivalistic type of Gospel propagation, and in the year 1780 the first Methodist circuit rider, Rev. Andrew Yeargan, halted his horse before the cabin of some pioneer on the banks of the Yadkin. The Methodists had been in Eastern Carolina for four years previous to this time. The West had not yet heard of Methodism. In the year 1780 a circuit was organized which included all of Western North Carolina. It was known as the Yadkin Circuit and Andrew Yeargan was appointed as preacher in charge. There were only eleven members, two of whom were John and Mary Spainhour Doub, the parents of Peter Doub. The part of this circuit which he was able to reach included the present counties of Rowan, Stanly, Montgomery, Davidson, Randolph, Davie and Iredell, besides all the territory north to the Virginia line. We do not know where Andrew Yeargan came from nor where he went after one year of service on this circuit. The conference minutes do not indicate that he was ever received on trial, but he was the first circuit rider to penetrate the wilds of Western Carolina, the first pioneer Methodist preacher who braved the perils of the wilderness to bring the gospel to the fathers.

Since Davidson County was at that time a part of Rowan County it is fitting to give here a few extracts from a paper written by Prof. W. M. Pickens on "History of Methodism in Rowan County": "Yeargan evidently confined his activities to the Yadkin Valley. In 1781 and 1782 there are no records of the Yadkin Circuit in the general minutes. The next year, 1783, the Yadkin Circuit took its place in the minutes again with a membership of three hundred and forty-eight. In 1784 the Salisbury Circuit was listed in the minutes as a separate pastoral charge with Jesse Lee as its pastor. He says that he found a number of truly affectionate Christians along the banks of the Yadkin. Lee kept a journal of his activities. There is but one church building mentioned by him as existing in the boundaries of his work, it being the Jersey Meeting House which was located near the Trading Ford crossing of the Yadkin River." This church, a Baptist Church, is still in existence.

Hudson says: "The church in which the old pioneers preached mostly was the Temple of Nature; the roof was the blue firmament; its floor, the green earth swept by the winds; its lamp, the radiant sun; its seats, the rocks, stumps, and logs. The voice of the preacher mingled with the free songs of the birds, the splash of the rippling streams, the neighing of the horses, and the cries of penitent souls."

Of the men who were assigned to the work in Rowan in the early years the one who became the most prominent was Jesse Lee. Lee was born on March 12, 1758, and was converted under the preaching of Robert Williams in 1774. Four years later he was drafted into the Continental Army much against his will. While he was very friendly to the movement for the liberty of the colonies, he had very decided prejudices against bearing arms. He was put in charge of the baggage of that part of the army in which he was enlisted and, therefore, served his country without doing violence to his scruples. While there he lost no chance to preach the gospel of Methodism and his influence in the Continental Army probably assisted the rising tide of Methodism as nothing else could have done.

In 1784 Jesse Lee had as his helper on the Salisbury Circuit, which now replaced the Yadkin Circuit and included what is now Davidson County, a man by the name of Isaac Smith. The membership of the churches at that time was three hundred and seventy-five. In 1785 Joshua Hartley and Hope Hull were assigned to this circuit. There are some references in various records to the work of Hope Hull in Davidson County while serving the Salisbury Circuit. He was in the first year of the itineracy while here and went from here to Georgia and became president of the University of Georgia at Athens, and died there in 1818.

Hull was a fine example of the old fashioned Methodist preacher. Lorenzo Dow, who describes a service held by Hull, says that towards the close of the sermon Hull pointed his finger towards him and said: "Sinner, there is a frowning Providence above your head and a burning hell beneath your feet, and nothing but the brittle thread of life keeps you from falling into endless perdition. 'But,' says the sinner, 'what must I do?' 'You must pray.' 'But I can't pray.' 'If you don't pray you will be damned.' And as he brought out the last expression, he either stamped with his foot on the box on which he stood or smote his hand upon his Bible, which both came home like a dagger to my heart. I had liked to have fallen backward from my seat, but saved myself by catching hold of my cousin, who sat by my side, and I durst not stand for some time lest I should tumble into hell."

Bishop Asbury held a conference in Salisbury in February, 1786. The bishop had traveled all day in the rain and reached Salisbury late in the evening of the day conference was to open. There were twenty-four preachers present and the session lasted three days. The reports show that Methodism was growing in the Yadkin Valley and an invitation was given for the conference to meet there again the next year. The societies continued to grow for the next fifteen years, and in 1802 the Yadkin and Salisbury circuits were put in the Virginia Conference where they remained until the formation of the North Carolina Conference.

In the same year that Davidson County was severed from Rowan County and made a separate county, 1822, a piece of ground was bought and deeded to the Methodist Church for the purpose of erecting a house of worship in the present county. This is the oldest of such deeds now appearing on the books in the office of the Register of Deeds at Lexington. It is not certain just where this piece of land lies because the description and markers indicated in the deed are not very specific. It is dated August 2, 1822, was signed by Ephraim Spoolman, and for a consideration of two dollars was conveyed to Elisha Mendenhall, Thomas Cooper, Meshack Plumer, John Welborn, Obed Aydellett and William Thomas, as trustees. The nearest that the deed comes to identifying this parcel of land is indicated in the opening sentence of the description, "beginning at a stone and stake on the west side of the burnt meeting-house ground."

The oldest recorded deed to property that is still being used as a place of worship by the Methodist Church is that of Siloam Church in the southern part of the county. This deed is dated December 16, 1833, and is signed by Thomas Hutin and John Loftin.

Another deed signed by Martin Everet, December 26, 1826, and conveyed to Frederick Clayton, John Alspaugh, John Alfred and Thomas Blake, as trustees, contains the following: "Beginning at a sourwood on Martin Everet line."

Still another, dated July 25, 1828, signed by John Myers and conveyed to John Welborn, James Needham, A. Gray, Isham Nance, William Carroll, J. Loftin, A. Lambeth, John W. Thomas and David Mock, as trustees, describes the location as "beginning at a post oak in a hollow on the northwest side of the Raleigh road on David Mock's line."

Wesley's Chapel, now a part of the Linwood Circuit, is said to have been organized over a hundred years ago, but no record has been found of the deed nor of the facts concerning the organization. This church is noted for the large number of Methodist preachers that it has produced from its membership. Many of the names of the older ones have been lost, but in recent times the following preachers have come from this church: John H. Fitzgerald, J. B. Fitzgerald, J. W. Fitzgerald, O. P. Fitzgerald, E. W. Downum, J. H. Lanning, J. T. Lanning, D. G. Wilson and C. O. Kennerly. This church is now in the process of being abandoned and a new building is to be erected at Tyro.

Macedonia Church at Southmont had its beginning long before a building was erected. A brush arbor had been used by the Methodists for several years before a church was built in 1862 under the leadership of Rev. John W. Lewis. Among the notables who frequently preached at this arbor were Peter Doub, Alfred Norman, N. H. D. Wilson. R. L. Holmes, a devoted

REV. WILLIAM ARNOLD LAMBETH, D.D.
NATIVE OF THOMASVILLE

Son of Colonel and Mrs. Frank S. Lambeth. Now Pastor of Mount Vernon Place Methodist Episcopal Church, South, Washington, D. C.

layman, together with his good wife conducted a Sunday school in the log schoolhouse for several years before the church was built at the beginning of the war. The present church was erected about twenty years ago under the leadership of Rev. D. P. Tate.

No definite facts can be learned concerning the beginnings of the thriving churches, Mount Olivet and Good Hope, on the Davidson Circuit; but from information derived from the oldest inhabitants it is certain that organizations existed long before the Civil War and there have been at least three church buildings on or near the Mount Olivet site. Midway is also a very old organization and this thriving congregation has just completed a handsome new brick church which is the third building used by this congregation. A new church has just been completed at Welcome under the leadership of Rev. J. W. Fitzgerald, who also built the Midway church. A new church has been constructed at Reeds Cross Roads under the leadership of Rev. R. F. Hunneycutt. It is expected that this church and the new one at Tyro will absorb the membership of Bethel Church. The Bethel Church deed was recorded May 8, 1834, and signed by Joseph Farrabee. There are a number of churches in the southern part of the county that were built in comparatively recent times, among them Jackson Hill, Denton, Clarksbury, Pleasant Grove and Newsome. A church at Poplar Springs was abandoned recently to make way for the new church at Newsome. Some of the churches on the Thomasville Circuit date back to the days of the Civil War.

As late as 1854 there was not a church or Sunday school in Thomasville. However, services were sometimes held at a little arbor near the residence of Mrs.

Mock. A Sunday school was organized at the brush arbor in September, 1855, under the leadership of Uncle John Carmalt, a full blooded Scotchman and a staunch Methodist of the old type, who had recently moved to this section. Later the Sunday school was held in a depot, then in a shoe shop, then in the chapel at Glen Anna Seminary, and finally in a Methodist Church built in 1863. Since that time the church has had only six Sunday school superintendents, Charles F. Lambeth being the present Superintendent. G. P. Dodson was Superintendent for thirty-two years. There have been thirty-four pastors, beginning with Rev. R. P. Bibb, of the Davidson Circuit, who made Thomasville one of his preaching points as early as 1855. Rev. Dr. Braxton Craven was pastor in 1868. Four preachers have gone out from this church; C. C. Dodson, Junius Harris, W. A. Lambeth and Leach Hoover, the latter being an Episcopal rector. This was also the home church of Miss Ellen Morphis, later the wife of Rev. Marcus A. Wood, with whom she went to China as a missionary. She died in China, leaving a son, Rev. C. A. Wood, who is now superintendent of the Children's Home. The church has flourished steadily and was made a station about forty years ago, and a handsome modern building now adorns the old site.

Like many other churches in this section of North Carolina the beginning of the First Methodist Church of Lexington dates back to the days just following the Revolutionary War when Jesse Lee, Lorenzo Dow, Hope Hull, Peter Doub and others traveled from place to place preaching in the open where no covering was available. Several years prior to the Civil War the Methodists of Lexington organized a church and it was made a part of the Davidson Circuit. It con-

RELIGIOUS FORCES OF DAVIDSON COUNTY 503

tinued as a part of the Davidson Circuit until the year 1878 when it was made a station under the pastorate of Rev. T. S. Campbell. A church was built on the site now occupied by the colored Methodist Church on the corner of North Salisbury and First streets. Before this church was built, probably 1855, Mrs. J. H. Hargrave and Major J. P. Stimpson conducted a Sunday school in the grand jury room at the courthouse. This building was used until 1873 when a church was built on the site now occupied by the First Methodist Church on South Main Street. This site was deeded by R. T. Earnhardt, Esq., to a Board of Trustees composed of Bennett Nooe, J. H. Hargrave, Sr., H. H. Caudle, R. T. Earnhardt, J. P. Stimpson, S. W. Rice, F. C. Robbins and L. C. Hanes. This church was burned on the night of August 2, 1902, and in the following year the present building was erected at a cost of $13,500. Since that time some additions have been made to the church building. The church has been served by some of the most prominent figures in North Carolina Methodism. Among them were, as far back as 1848, Alfred Norman, father of Dr. W. C. Norman, John Tillett, father of Attorney C. W. Tillett, of Charlotte, and of Dr. Wilbur F. Tillett, of Vanderbilt University. Also Lemon Shell, William Harris, Caswell King, John W. Lewis and T. B. Reeks. Later came W. D. Meacham and R. G. Barrett, who built the church that was burned; then Charles H. Phillips, J. C. Thomas, L. E. Thompson, T. A. Stone, M. V. Sherrill, J. E. Gay, T. A. Boone, J. E. Thompson, R. H. Parker, C. G. Little, J. D. Arnold and J. N. Huggins. The church has been served in recent years by A. L. Stanford, A. W. Plyler, W. H. Willis, J. P. Hipps, W. L.

Hutchins and W. R. Shelton. George L. Hackney, a prominent layman, has been superintendent of the Sunday school for about fifteen years.

Davidson County has contributed a fair share to the ranks of the Methodist Ministry. Information is not available for giving a complete list of its ministerial sons, but in addition to those already given it is a noteworthy fact that the well-known Marcus L. Wood was born near Handy, in the lower part of the county. John Frank, now a missionary in Japan, was born in Jackson Hill, as was the late Earnest Newsome, a former Army and Navy Chaplain, G. F. Smith, of the North Carolina Conference, and A. R. Surratt of the Western North Carolina Conference. J. E. Woosley and A. S. Raper of the same conference were born and reared in the Arcadia section. L. S. Burkhead, for whom Burkhead Methodist Episcopal Church in Winston-Salem was named, was born in the southern part of the county.

Most of the charges in Davidson County were included in the Salisbury District up until the year 1910 when they were all placed in the Winston District. There are now nine pastoral charges in the county composed of a total of thirty-one churches. These churches have a combined membership of 5,941. The names of these charges, the names of the churches in each charge, and the pastor of each charge as appointed recently by Bishop Edwin B. Mouzon, at the conference session held at Gastonia, North Carolina, October 20-26, 1926, are as follows:

Davidson Circuit is composed of the following churches: Arcadia, Bethel, Centenary, Good Hope, Mount Olivet, Reeds. Pastor is R. C. Goforth.

Denton Circuit is composed of the following churches: Clarksbury, Denton, Jackson Hill, Newsome, Pleasant Grove, Siloam. Pastor is C. P. Goode.

Lexington—W. R. Shelton, pastor First Methodist Church; A. S. Raper, pastor Erlanger Methodist Church.

Linwood Circuit is composed of the following churches: Cotton Grove, Linwood, Macedonia, Wesley's Chapel. Pastor is G. W. Fink.

G. D. Herman, pastor Thomasville Main Street Methodist Church.

T. J. Houck, pastor Thomasville Bethel and Trinity churches.

Thomasville circuit is composed of the following churches: Fairview, Fairgrove, Pinewoods, Pleasant Hill, Prospect, Unity. Pastor is D. R. Proffitt.

Welcome Circuit is composed of the following churches: Center, Ebenezer, Midway, Vernon. Pastor is W. G. Pilcher.

9. Grace Episcopal Church of Lexington

In the early days of Lexington a few families of the Episcopal faith were represented in the community. Occasional services were held in the time of Bishop Ravenscroft, the first Bishop of North Carolina, 1823-30. During the episcopate of Bishop Ives, 1831-1853, there was erected one of the first, if not the first, buildings, for religious worship in the community. It stood near the present location of Wennonah Mill. This building was blown down some years after by a severe storm that visited this section, and was never rebuilt. For many years the congregation, small in numbers, took no steps to replace this building. It was composed of such families as the Caldcleughs, Longs, Lindsays, and Holts. The Caldcleughs deeded the site of the present cemetery for a church lot, but for some reason no church was ever built upon it. Later still Dr. Lindsay gave a lot on what is now the corner of First Avenue and State Street. There a wooden structure was erected in 1857. This property was sold, and the present brick building was erected in 1901 on South Main Street between Fourth and Fifth avenues. It is a beautifully appointed church, in keeping with its purpose for the worship of Almighty God. There are hardwood floors, a beautiful pipe organ, a memorial to Mrs. Frances Holt Hunt, one of the most devoted members during her lifetime; also a Tiffany window exquisite in design and execution, as a memorial to one of the strong supporters of the church, the late Colonel W. E. Holt. This building was consecrated October 13, 1903.

For many years the church did not have a resident minister, but was supplied by ministers from neighboring missions or parishes occasionally or at stated intervals. Among those who served in the past were Revs. George B. Wetmore, Charles Ferris, Frederick Fetter, Finner Stickney, Richard W. Barber, Judson Carmon Davis, D.D. Dr. Davis was a man of rare charm and of versatile gifts. His ministry was most acceptable to those to whom he ministered and of great benefit to those who had the privilege of knowing him. Dr. Davis retired from the active ministry in 1910 on account of advancing years. After an interval Rev. R. Percy Eubanks was appointed to take charge of the mission, and ministered for something over a year. In 1913 Rev. Theodore Andrews came to Lexington as full time minister, the first resident minister in the history of the mission. At the Convention of the Diocese of North Carolina held in May, 1914, Grace Church was admitted as a self-supporting parish. The wardens were Charles A. Hunt, who served to the end of his life in that capacity, and Dr. David J. Hill, who only retired when incapacitated by ill health. Mr. Andrews resigned the parish, and left October 1, 1918. He was succeeded by Rev. D. R. Ottman January 1, 1919. Mr. Ottman remained only a short time, and was succeeded by Rev. A. Whitfield Cheatham. He resigned in 1919. The Rev. Wilmot S. Holmes accepted the rectorship, and came to the parish April 1, 1922. At the present writing he is in the fifth year of his rectorship.

During the rectorship of Rev. Mr. Andrews a rectory was built adjoining the church, which added greatly to the parish equipment.

There are between fifty and sixty communicants of the parish with a strong Woman's Auxiliary Chapter, and a chapter of the Brotherhood of St. Andrew active in its assistance of the rector.

CHAPTER XVIII

A UNIQUE COUNTY IN THE HEART OF A GREAT STATE

1. A COUNTY OF EXTENSIVE AREA

This large county of Davidson contains 569 square miles, covering 364,160 acres. The 1920 government census shows a population of 2,559,123 in the whole State of North Carolina. All these thousands of people could be given homes in Davidson County and nobody be crowded, since there would be only seven people to the acre. This county is a great empire itself.

Davidson County is divided into seventeen townships: Arcadia, Alleghany, Abbott's Creek, Boone, Cotton Grove, Conrad Hill, Emmons, Hampton, Healing Springs, Jackson Hill, Lexington, Midway, Reedy Creek, Silver Hill, Thomasville, Tyro, Yadkin College.

There are in the county two cities and numerous towns and hamlets. The following names are familiar: Thomasville, Lexington, Denton, Linwood, Holtsburg, Lake, Welcome, Charity, Eller, Midway, Enterprise, Arcadia, Yadkin College, Reeds, Tyro, Churchland, Cotton Grove, Southmont, Feezor, High Rock, Newsome, Bain, Handy, Jackson Hill, Hannersville, Cid, Gordontown, Light, Silver Hill, Snider, Jubilee, South Lexington.

2. A FREE YADKIN RIVER BRIDGE

Early in 1912 the *Evening Post* of Salisbury began to discuss the advisability of a free bridge across the Yadkin River between Rowan and Davidson counties. In that day there was a considerable interest in the project and many voices joined in the agitation. It was in the early days of February, 1916, that the thing began to take on definite form. One of the early advocates of a bridge was J. B. Snider, of Davidson County, now a citizen of the town of Yadkin on the Rowan side of the river. In February of 1916 he paid a visit to the *Evening Post* and in advocacy of the bridge offered to agitate for interest on the Davidson side of the river, and the *Evening Post*, prompted by interest manifested and openly expressed, called for a mass meeting to be held in the Rowan County courthouse the evening of February 22.

In the *Evening Post* of February 23, 1916, is to be found a news story which gives an account of the mass meeting attended by citizens of each of the two counties. J. F. Hurley was made chairman of the meeting and W. C. Maupin was made secretary, and a committee to push for a free bridge was named. That committee was made up of the following citizens: From Rowan, W. F. Snider, H. A. Rouzer, J. H. Ramsay, W. H. Woodson, W. D. Hartman, D. A. Beaver, N. W. Collett, A. H. Price, M. C. Quinn and W. H. Burton; and from Davidson County, A. A. Young, D. V. Griffith, M. A. Lomax, J. B. Snider, W. B. Mears, Dr. F. L. Mock, C. H. B. Leonard, C. C. Shaw, H. B. Varner and J. B. Bailey. This committee met and named A. A. Young as chairman and H. A. Rouzer, secretary.

The meeting voted to endorse a free bridge and heard talks from W. H. Woodson, A. H. Price, D. V. Griffith, J. B. Snider, Mayor Burton, of Spencer, J. H. Ramsay, N. W. Collett and A. A. Young. The article in the *Evening Post* referred to declared that the opinion was unanimous that the toll bridge ought to be bought. The sentiment was to deal with the owners of the bridge and buy it. It was also generally agreed that the owners of the toll bridge are deserving of every consideration and that they will do the right thing at the right time.

Those familiar with the running story of the agitation for a bridge know that all was not smooth sailing. There was a road building campaign on in Davidson County and there was division of opinion as to the county's joining in to build the bridge. There were many who from the outset were openly favorable to the project and worked to that end; there were others who were hostile to the project and some who were indifferent, many believing that it was a project for Rowan and Salisbury rather than for the two counties. But as the big highway building program came along it was also very clearly established that the bridge would come and after several efforts to buy the old bridge from the owners the two counties awaited the development of the State program which took charge of the bridge as a unit in the big highway project. Effort was finally made to buy the toll bridge, but the two sides could not agree on a price, and things went along until the State entered into a big road building campaign and then we all knew that the larger and open bridge would come.

3. Hydro-electrical Development

The Yadkin River borders Davidson County on the west and south many miles, from the Forsyth to the Montgomery County line. Within the last quarter century developments hitherto undreamed of have been successfully carried out. First the Whitney dam was built below Newsome in the days of the late Captain E. B. C. Hambley. This was considered a mammoth project. This development was entered upon in the first years of the twentieth century. After the lapse of about fifteen years the Badin dam was built at the Narrows of the Yadkin. The Southern Aluminum Company, the concern fostering this great enterprise, was taken over by the Tallassee Power Company. The Badin dam was 187 feet high, likely the highest in the whole South, and the back-water completely covered the Whitney dam. But on the first of September, 1926, this latter company began operations on a much larger scale in the building of an immense dam at High Rock. Forces of men and machinery were unleashed at three points, as outlined in the *Lexington Dispatch*.

Only sixteen months will be taken to complete the entire project, a record time for such an operation in this country, it was announced by S. A. Copp, of Badin, general superintendent of the Tallassee Power Company. The work will be complete by January 1, 1928. Approximately two thousand men will be thrown into the three divisions of the operations already under way. One division will build the dam, another division will clear the 19,000-acre basin and the third will rebuild five miles of the trackage of the Southbound Railroad. The dam will be fifty-nine feet high and will join the sections of Stafford's Mountain together. It will have a crest line 1,000 to 1,200 feet long. The power house will be located on the Davidson County side of the river and will have 40,000 installed horsepower. W. S. Lee, president of the Southern Power

Company, will supervise the building of the dam, which will be done with Southern Power Company equipment. The Southern Power Company will distribute all the power generated at the High Rock dam, and all will be for public use. None of the current from this place will be used at Badin, Mr. Copp stated. The Southern Power Company is now building a big steel tower transmission line from Badin to High Rock and this line will be extended on to High Point. The line is almost complete to High Rock and the dam site. The line to High Point will be built later. This will probably go through or near both Denton and Thomasville, though Mr. Copp was not in position to state the exact location of this line. It appears likely, however, that Denton will get its long desired supply of hydro-electric power and will be in position to go ahead with its development of high speed.

The plant of the Ball Mountain Quarries, Inc., is being trebled and all of the crushed stone used in concrete for the power dam will be quarried there. This tremendous consumption, however, will still leave the quarries ample stone to supply the regular trade. The enlarged equipment of the quarries, now being rapidly installed, will be ready for operation by the first of October when the contractor will begin taking stone at the dam site. This will mean the enlarging of the already considerable colony at Ball Mountain through the addition of a greatly increased number of workers.

The lake to be created in Davidson and Rowan counties will cover approximately 19,000 acres of land. This is about two and a half times the acreage covered by Lake James, in McDowell County, although the head of Lake James dam is higher than the one here will be. The water in this lake would twice completely fill the basin of the Badin Lake, despite the fact that the Badin dam is 187 feet high and the lake consequently of much greater depth in the river basin proper than will be the case here. The new lake will have a shore line of three hundred and sixty miles. It will be twenty-three miles long on the Yadkin River and the main body will be two miles wide at its widest point. It will extend up the Yadkin to about the Upper Sowers's Ferry place, near Boone's Cave, and eddy water will touch the shore of Davie County for a short distance. Up Abbott's Creek the lake will extend twenty miles to a point northeast of Lexington and within about a half mile of the corporate limits. The water will back up to practically the height of the old Finch mill dam. On Second Dutch Creek in Rowan the water will back for twenty miles to a point south of Salisbury. For lesser distances arms of the lake will extend up numerous creeks and branches in both counties. Other creeks in Davidson that will be affected are Flat Swamp Creek, Four-Mile Branch, Puddle Creek, which is a branch of Abbott's Creek, Swearing Creek, North Potts Creek and South Potts Creek.

Southmont will not be affected as the nearest approach of the water is some distance below that community, which is located on a ridge. One arm of the lake will come within sight of Linwood, but will not affect this community itself. No church or school house in the entire basin will be cut off by the waters, although a number of residences and other buildings will have to be moved. A number of graveyards will be moved to other locations. None of these are large, some being as small as two-grave family burial plots. Above all, the builders will avail themselves of every possible scientific means of making the lake the most healthful and sanitary body of water of its kind in the entire country. Every foot of the basin will be carefully cleared. Five big camps of workmen are to be installed at once, each of these to house from one hundred to two hundred men. From seven hundred and fifty to one thousand men will be at work soon on the clearing operations. Each of these camps will be model camps and the best living conditions possible will be provided. The first clearing operation is at the dam site to make way for the builders of that gigantic structure. It is estimated that from twelve thousand to fourteen thousand acres will have to be cleared, although complete survey of the area in this respect has not been made. Approximately three million feet of lumber will be cut in the clearing operation, along with several hundred thousand crossties and immense quantities of cordwood. All of this will be for sale.

The dam will be of a type similar to the Falls development, or the lower Badin dam. Concrete piers and steel gates will form the structure. These gates will be thirty feet high and forty feet wide. The dimensions of the power-house have not been received yet, but it will be located in Davidson County. So rapidly have plans been maturing in the past few weeks and months that complete estimates of the cost of the work have not been compiled. Several million dollars will be required to bring the project to completion.

The Walton Construction Company, of Roanoke, Va., has the contract for the rebuilding of the five miles of railroad track between Southmont and High Rock. This concern will throw three large forces of workers on the job simultaneously, attacking the task at both ends and the middle. Instead of crossing the Stafford Mountain in a gap some distance from the river, the road will hug the side of the mountain and pass around the river end of this eminence not far from the end of the dam and the power house. Fills will be built of rock so that the waters of the lake cannot at any time affect the solidity of the track foundations. Despite the considerable change in location, engineers have found a way to take the road around the side and end of the mountain and actually improve the grade and eliminate a portion of the present curvature.

While nearly half the actual basin of the lake will be in Rowan County, the line being the middle of the river, the major portion of the men working on the various construction jobs will be located in Davidson County. All of the railroad contracting force will have their camps in this county. The five hundred to six hundred men who will be employed on the dam itself when the work there hits high speed will be mainly located on this side of the river. Part of the camps for the basin clearing operations will also be in Davidson.

At the site of the dam work is beginning at once on the erection of seven permanent houses of very attractive type to be used by the operating force of the hydro-electric plant. Until the plant is ready for operation these homes will be used in connection with the building operations.

The Tallassee Power Company will have about twenty-five thousand acres in all in the basin area.

Land that is not covered by water will be for sale. The power company has no desire to hold large boundaries of land not in actual use. All industries that may desire to locate on any of this land near to the source of a great new supply of electric power will receive the cordial coöperation of the company. The fact that the Southern Power Company is now rushing to completion a one hundred thousand horsepower steam-power plant on the Rowan side of the lake basin makes this section more inviting for the location of large industries.

4. Superb North Carolina

[The following article recently appeared in *The Earth Mover*, a magazine published at Aurora, Illinois, and is given herewith as a sample of outside appreciation:]

One must deal in superlatives to do justice to North Carolina, she is first in so many things. In beauty and variety of landscape, historical associations, perfect highways, educational facilities, in the progressiveness, enthusiasm and lovable qualities of her people, North Carolina stands unexcelled.

In scenery there can be nothing more beautiful than her Blue Ridge Mountains in June, when rhododendron and laurel and flaming azalea bloom on the mountain sides in wild profusion. These are the highest mountains east of the Rockies.

In North Carolina, on Roanoke Island, Sir Walter Raleigh made his three ill-fated attempts to establish an English colony, thirty-five years before the Pilgrim Fathers landed in Massachusetts. The first child born in America of English-speaking parents was Virginia Dare, of North Carolina. The Mecklenburg Declaration of Independence, adopted by the citizens of Mecklenburg County, North Carolina, antedated by more than a year the ringing of Liberty Bell at Philadelphia. The Battle of Guilford Court House, which made that liberty possible through the subsequent surrender of Cornwallis at Yorktown, was fought in North Carolina, near the beautiful city of Greensboro. The first successful flight of a heavier-than-air machine was made by the Wright Brothers in 1903, among the sand dunes of Kitty Hawk, North Carolina.

A single State highway, No. 10, 550 miles long, crossing the State of North Carolina from Morehead on the east, to Murphy on the west, passes seventeen colleges and universities and seventy-six modern high-class schools. One of these universities, recently endowed with the Duke millions, is to be made the largest and best university in the world. North Carolina's College of Agriculture, on the same Route 10, includes the largest textile training school in the world.

The smokers of the world revere the name of Durham. Winston-Salem is the largest tobacco manufacturing city in the world. Greensboro makes three-fourths of the denim used in the United States; Thomasville, near High Point, the greatest number of chairs of any place in the world.

Astounding are the figures given by the United States Department of Commerce in valuing North Carolina's manufactured products during 1923—$951,911,000. A conservative estimate of the value of those products during 1925 is: textiles, $400,000,000; tobacco products, $300,000,000; furniture, $50,000,000; forest products, $118,000,000; minerals, $10,000,000; miscellaneous, $75,000,000. To these should be added the value of crops in 1925, $318,661,000, and of livestock, $73,688,000. North Carolina paid in Federal taxes last year the astounding sum of $166,962,875, exceeded by only three states in the Union.

Why should not such a state have spent in a single year, 1925, $4,910,224 for State institutions and buildings; $160,000,000 for private buildings, and $27,827,000 for roads?

This issue of the *Earth Mover* tells something about the methods and progress of road construction in this great State—great in beauty, in tradition, in achievement, in hospitality of her people. When one considers the unutterable devastation, despair, and heartache wrought by the Civil War, the rise of North Carolina to her present pinnacle of glory is one of the miracles of history.

The figures on payment of Federal taxes were for the year ending June 30, 1925. The figures for the fiscal year ending June 30, 1926, show a little over $192,000,000 paid to the Federal treasury from this State.

5. Interesting Records in Two Old Books

Among the books which I have examined in my researches during the last several years for material to be given place in the proposed *Centennial History of Davidson County* is one with the title: *Geography; or, Description of the World,* by Daniel Adams, A.M. This interesting though quaint work was published by Lincoln & Edwards, of Boston, in 1816. The author of this book also produced another under the title: *The Scholar's Arithmetic.*

In this first named book, in a description of North Carolina, occurs the following remarkable paragraph: "Curiosities. Near Salisbury, there is a remarkable subterranean wall of stone, laid in cement, plaistered on both sides, from 12 to 14 feet in height, and 22 inches thick. The length yet discovered is about 300 feet. The top of this wall approaches within about one foot of the surface of the ground. When built, by whom and for what purpose, is left wholly to conjecture. A similar wall has lately been discovered about 6 miles from the first, from 4 to 5 feet high, and 7 inches thick."

In 1820 a treatise in two volumes was published by the printing house of Benjamin Warner, of Philadelphia, under the title, *A Universal Geography, or A View of the Present State of the Known World*, the author being William Guthrie, Esq., the astronomical part of the work being contributed by James Ferguson, F.R.S. This work was issued two years before the formation of Davidson County. Volume I contains an outline description of the State of North Carolina. Many of the conclusions would not stand in the light of present-day known facts in the history of our great State. But they were accepted as facts a century ago. They served to give the readers a fair understanding of our resources as understood in those far-away times. The State itself has made great progress since these large volumes were published.

It is stated in one place that apples and peaches are sometimes destroyed by late frosts in the spring, and occasionally even by severe winter frosts. A plentiful fruit harvest may be counted upon, the author says, only about every other year. He further declares that when there is a good fruit year, the crop of peaches and apples is so great that notwithstanding the "cider and brandy made and the quantities preserved and dried, yet thousands of bushels are lost, perish, or are eaten up by hogs turned into the orchards."

Mention is made of numerous beautiful horses, sheep and cattle. "Hogs roam at large in the woods, where in a good year they find support enough from acorns, roots and the like. Towards winter they are penned up and fattened with Indian corn, or a pen is made in the woods, to which the husbandman resorts daily with his bag of corn, blows the horn, or otherwise calls his hogs together, feeds them there, and dismisses them again into the woods."

In another paragraph the author tells us that the exports are "tar, pitch, turpentine, rosin, boards, scantling, shingles, Indian corn, flour, rice, tobacco, cotton, pork, peach brandy, bees' wax, flax seed." We are also informed that domestic manufacture is carried on extensively. In every country house there is at least one loom on which is woven cloth from flax, cotton, wool and their mixtures beyond a sufficient quantity for home consumption. Other articles of domestic manufacture are hats, guns, rifles, clocks, earthen ware, leather and wooden products. Mention is made of paper mills, flour mills, oil mills. This wise observation is made: "The manufacture of whiskey and brandy from grain and fruit is too extensively carried on for the morals of the people." In 1820 there were three banks in the whole State: the State Bank, the Cape Fear Bank, and the Bank of Newbern, each of these having branches elsewhere. At Fayetteville there was a branch of the Bank of the United States. Prevailing diseases were said to be fevers and agues. There was one college or university in the State in 1820, that at Chapel Hill. But there were many male and female academies in various sections of the commonwealth. The people are described as being "inquisitive, social, hospitable, civil, and even polite, especially to strangers. In the lower parts they may be divided into the rich and the poor. The rich are the large planters, owning the rich lands on the rivers and margins of water; they have frequently very large plantations, and a number of negro slaves, more or less. The poor inhabit the poorer land on the ridges between the streams. They own no slaves, or a very few."

Marketing advantages in 1820 were quite different from what they are now. This author tells us: "In winter, but especially in the fall of the year until Christmas, the produce is carried to market by wagons, the roads and weather then being generally good. On the great market roads it is not uncommon to a traveler in such season in one day to count a hundred wagons going to or coming from market. A wagon and team with five horses generally carries 4,000 lb. weight, sometimes more; with less the wagoner thinking it not worth his while to start. He carries his provisions with him, and as much of provender for his horses as he can. There are no inns, as in the northern states, on purpose for the wagoner, where he stays all night, nor does he choose to do so, should he meet with such a one. He camps out all night in the woods, choosing a place where wood and water are to be had. Coming to such a place in the evening or in the night, he unharnesses his horses, waters them, and ties them to his wagon; he then gathers fire wood and kindles a fire, over which he cooks his coffee and his victuals which he carries with him. Meanwhile he feeds his horses. After having supped, or more properly dined, he lies down either before the fire or in his wagon, but rises from time to time in the night to keep his horses in feed. In the morning after he has prepared his breakfast, he partakes of it, and drives his team merrily again along the road. Everywhere the wagoner is permitted to take fire wood in the woods, and even to cut down small trees for fire wood; no one is jealous of it, as fire wood, is plenty everywhere. Wagoners, used to this mode of traveling, prefer it to being confined in houses and stables. Travelers moving from one part to another, with their families, sometimes consisting of many children, make use of the same method of traveling."

An interesting observation is made as to the character of home construction: "There are some good brick houses in the State, many more are of frame work, but the greater part are log houses, some convenient, but with the neglectful you find them merely cabins, often without glass windows, at one end having a wooden chimney to a large fireplace. In this large fireplace large log fires are made, and the housedoor kept open, to admit light. Stoves of iron, or of potters' ware, are used chiefly by the Germans."

All these observations sound quite familiar to men and women of advanced years still living, who heard their parents or grandparents relate most interesting incidents of manners and customs of bygone days. The young people who live in Davidson County today can scarcely get a just conception of those primitive days. The descendants of those pioneers enjoy the rich and abundant blessings of all modern conveniences. Communiciation and travel are so easy and convenient now, with the telephone, telegraph, railroad and air transport, automobile, hard-surfaced roads. But we must ever be grateful to our pioneer ancestors for the sacrifices they made in those days of primitive living. Their lives and labors made possible the good conditions under which we live and labor today. They laid the foundations of civilization, good government and religious institutions. They blazed the trail through the unbroken forests and mountain fastnesses where later we built our fine highways. They built log schoolhouses and churches for the worship of the true God, and in consequence of their action and determination we have a fine system of public school education, and a great civilization founded upon the Christian religion. There may be a tendency to smile when we read about the cramped conditions under which they lived; but on second thought our meditations assume a trend of reverence and veneration for the heroes and the heroines of those early years. We count it a high honor to have descended from men and women of such rugged Christian character.

www.ingramcontent.com/pod-product-compliance
Lightning Source LLC
Chambersburg PA
CBHW060908300426
44112CB00011B/1388